This Indenture MADE the _Thirteenth_ Day of _May_ in the Year of our Lord one thousand, seven hundred and _eighty-four_ BETWEEN _Alex.r Bryson of Brougham in the County of Antrim Taylor_ of the one Part, and _John Duchy of Cushyachey_ of the other Part, WITNESSETH, that the said _Alex.r Bryson_ doth hereby covenant, promise and grant, to and with the said _John Duchy — his_ ——— Executors, Administrators, and Assigns, from the Day of the Date hereof until the first and next Arrival at _Philadelphia_ — in America, and after for and during the Term of _two_ ——— Years to serve in such Service and Employment as the said _John Duchy_ or _his_ Assigns shall there employ _him_ according to the Custom of the Country in the like Kind. In Consideration whereof the said _John Duchy_ ——— doth hereby covenant and grant to and with the said, _Alex.r Bryson_ ——— to pay for _his_ Passage, and to find allow _him_ Meat, Drink, Apparel and Lodging, with other Necessaries, during the said Term; and at the End of the said Term to pay unto _him_ the usual Allowance, according to the Custom of the Country in the like Kind. IN WITNESS whereof the Parties above-mentioned to these Indentures have interchangeably put their Hands and Seals, the Day and Year first above written.

Signed, Sealed, and Delivered, in the Presence of

Esther Gibbons
Wm. Weir

Alex.r Beard

John Duchy

WHITE SERVITUDE IN PENNSYLVANIA

Indentured and Redemption Labor in Colony and Commonwealth

By

CHEESMAN A. HERRICK, Ph.D. LL.D.

Life Member American Historical Association,
Member Historical Society of Pennsylvania, and
Presbyterian Historical Society

NEGRO UNIVERSITIES PRESS
NEW YORK

In Memoriam

RAYMOND MACDONALD ALDEN

Classmate and Friend

"None knew thee but to love thee,
Nor named thee but to praise."

PREFACE

The subject matter of this book was presented in its original form as a thesis at the University of Pennsylvania in 1899. Several of those who read the manuscript at that time advised publication at once, but the writer felt that there was available much additional material which should be incorporated, and he delayed publication for further investigation.

In 1900, Frank Reid Diffenderffer of Lancaster, Pennsylvania, published a useful study on the same subject. The following year, a scholarly essay on *The Redemptioners,* by Karl Frederick Geiser, was brought out at New Haven, Connecticut. On the appearance of these two works the writer's first impulse was to give up all thought of publishing this study. As the years passed, however, he found much new material; particularly, Postlethwayt's book on the African trade in the John Carter Brown Library, Providence; the manuscript papers of Benjamin Peter Hunt in the Boston Public Library; the records of indentures before the mayors in Philadelphia; manuscripts in the Public Record Office, London; and various other manuscript sources in Philadelphia, West Chester, Doylestown, and other places. Also, Dr. Geiser urged the continuance of the study with a view to its later publication and Mr. Diffenderffer, in his preface, expressed the hope that ultimately some one with "love and leisure for the work" would "write a story of the redemptioners with the philosophical spirit and the amplitude it deserves."

While the author does not claim that his qualifications meet the standards set by Mr. Diffenderffer, or that his essay is of such merit as to supersede that of Dr. Geiser, he feels that the importance of the subject warrants all that has been written on it, and much more. Pennsylvania was the typical proprietary colony; colonial administration and the relations between an English settlement in North America and the mother country were clearly shown in Pennsylvania's history. Knowledge of the social development of Pennsylvania—how the colony was planted and grew—is well-nigh indispensable to one who would understand the earlier period in the evolution of American democracy. Pennsylvania's labor system was at the center of her economic and political life, it was vitally related to her immigration; Pennsylvania's attitude towards slavery and her industrial future were profoundly affected by her labor system.

The list of those to whom the writer is indebted is quite too long to be given in full. John Bach McMaster originally suggested the study, and Henry Rogers Seager supervised the first writing and gave valuable help in the arrangement of the material. Charles M. Andrews, of Yale University, has given aid and encouragement at every stage of the work. He arranged for the making of transcripts and photographs in the Public Record Office in London, and has offered numerous suggestions for additional material; most important of all, he has read the proof in full and has made several corrections. The manuscript was read by A. T. Volwiler, of Wittenburg College, and the proof was read by Morris Wolf and D. Montfort Melchior, of Girard College. To scores of librarians the writer acknowledges his lasting indebtedness, but most of all to the librarians of the Historical Society of Pennsylvania.

Edward Gibbon, in the preface of his *Decline and Fall,* said that diligence and accuracy are the only merits which the writer of history may claim. These merits may be coveted by the humblest writer in the historical field. For twenty-eight years this study has been a constant companion and friend. It has been twice rewritten in its entirety. Some parts of it have been rewritten four times. It has become an intimate, almost sacred, part of the writer's life. Here a little, there a little, it has slowly taken form. For so long a time, in fact, has the work been under the writer's hand that he yields reluctantly to the suggestion of finality implied, in its publication. But to this end the task was begun, and is now concluded. The work is published in the hope that it may prove not altogether uninteresting, and possibly also of some value.

Girard College,   C. A. H.
January 1, 1926.

CONTENTS

ILLUSTRATIONS

WHITE SERVITUDE IN PENNSYLVANIA

PART I. INTRODUCTORY

CHAPTER I

THE INFLUENCE OF LABOR ON COLONIAL DEVELOPMENT

For its continued success a colonizing power should supply a labor force, constant and efficient. Labor is a necessity for the development of a new community; of the factors in production it is the scarcest, the most difficult of transportation and adjustment, and the slowest to respond by increase. Land in English North America was in abundance, and could be easily secured; capital was quite readily transferred from the home country, or it supplied any deficiency by the rapid multiplication of itself. Land in plenty is a requisite for successful colonization, but, even with plentiful land, colonial ventures have more often failed than they have succeeded, because of lack of suitable labor; "lands without hands will not enrich any kingdom." [1]

According to economic theory, industry is limited by capital; but, through lack of labor, its limit is not always reached in older communities and seldom if ever in newer countries. Capital is an accumulation of labor and, like land, yields most when quickened by human toil. So dependent is capital upon labor that what is taken to new settlements often wastes away through lack of a labor supply. In the production of necessities and luxuries alike, land and capital are useless except as they command labor's aid.[2]

---

[1] Child, *New Discourse of Trade,* 191, 192. Cf. Ireland, *Tropical Colonization* (Chs. IV, V, and VI), for the application of this principle to colonies in the tropics. According to Ireland, one of the three essentials for tropical colonies is "to obtain the reliable labor absolutely necessary for the successful development of a tropical colony." Preface, vii. This subject is further treated by Ireland in *Far Eastern Tropics.*

[2] Merivale, *Colonization and Colonies,* 256.

The disparity between the plentiful supply of natural resources and the scarcity of labor in a colony may well be one ground for limiting the principle of *laissez faire*. Such limitation, it is said, is not to overrule the judgment of individuals as to their interests, so much as it is to give effect to that judgment. The principle of such regulation found expression in what came to be known as "systematic colonization," or "the Wakefield system of colonization," set forth by Edward Gibbon Wakefield, first in *A Letter from Sydney* (1829), and finally in *A View of the Art of Colonization* (1849). Natural desire for possession, and traditional ideas of land ownership which colonists carry with them from older countries, lead them to become land owners, and those needed as laborers set themselves up as proprietors. Wakefield urged that land be held in colonies at such prices as would necessitate settlers' remaining hired laborers for a time. Thus, he theorized, land would be made artificially scarce, a supply of laborers would be furnished, town industry would be begun, markets would be assured, and general prosperity would result.[3] The Wakefield system cannot fairly be dismissed as impractical;[4] personal differences of Wakefield with the Colonization Society and the South Australian Association, prevented his theories from ever having had a fair trial.[5]

Three forms of labor were employed in the English colonies of North America, evidencing in different sections, and at different periods, marked variations of interest and influence. These three forms were free labor, indentured (often called redemption) labor, and the labor of slaves. Free laborers bargained for wages in the open market, and were hired for a definite time, generally of considerable extent; they were privileged to withdraw from their service if they so wished, though this might mean the for-

---

[3] The fifth suggestion in the *Art of Colonization* was: "That the supply of laborers be as nearly as possible proportional to the demand for labor at each settlement; so that capitalists shall never suffer from an urgent want of laborers and laborers shall never want well-paid employment." Gannett, *Edward Gibbon Wakefield*, 62, 63.

[4] Professor Cunningham termed Wakefield "a judicious and farseeing man." *Growth of English Industry and Commerce in Modern Times,* 605.

[5] Gannett, *Edward Gibbon Wakefield* ("Builders of Greater Britain" Series. New York: 1898), 50-84; Mill, *Political Economy,* II, 585-587; Egerton, *Short History of the British Colonial Policy,* 282-284.

feiture, wholly or in part, of the wages earned.[6] Indentured laborers were those remanded to a state of servitude by law, or those who by legal process, or custom, had voluntarily disposed of their time for a term of years.[7] However secured, such servants must be regarded as servile laborers. No matter how kindly they may have been treated in particular cases, or how voluntarily they may have entered into the relation, as a class and when once bound, indentured servants were temporarily chattels. They were recognized as property; they sold themselves or were sold for given terms, and had no protection as to the place or nature of their service except such as was extended by quite general legislation. Indentured servants often got scant justice under the laws of the time.[8] Into the nineteenth century this form of labor was often termed slavery (*weisse Sklaverei*).[9]

Indentured servants were in the later period, and especially among the Germans, also known as redemptioners. Various explanations account for these terms. "Indentured" was derived from the legal contract by which the servant was bound; "redemptioners," it has usually been held, came from the terms of agreement by which emigrants took passage, engaging to pay for their passage on arrival or within a specified time thereafter; if they had not the means to do this and no friends advanced the money, they were required to sell themselves to become free from the cap-

---

[6] Watson, *Annals,* III, 469; Kalm, *Travels,* I, 387.

[7] For custom as regulating such sales, cf. Bruce, *Economic History of Virginia in the Seventeenth Century,* II, 5, 6. The Pennsylvania Supreme Court, in a decision rendered 1793 ("Respublica vs. Keppele"), reviewed at length the institution of indentured labor. It was found to have originated with the early settlement in Virginia, and was thought necessary "from the circumstances of the country." If there were no indenture stipulating for the service, then such laborers were sold, it was said, "according to custom"; some of the early laws spoke of them as "servants according to custom," "servants bound to serve the accustomary five years," etc. *Dallas Reports,* II, 198.

[8] "These servants were in a very degraded situation. They were a species of property holding a middle rank between slaves and freemen; they might be sold from hand to hand; and they were under the correction of laws exceedingly severe." Justice Blanchard, *Dallas Reports,* II, 198.

[9] Seidensticker, *Geschichte der deutschen Gesellschaft von Pennsylvanien,* 21; Isaac Weld, *Travels,* I, 122; Fearon, *Sketches of America,* 149; Mittelberger, *Journey to Pennsylvania, passim.*

tain.[10] If such emigrants did not pay within the customary time, usually thirty days, or the time agreed upon, they were subject to legal procedure under the laws of debt. The term "indentured" was applied most largely to servants from Great Britain. The British regulations for the trade required that a legal agreement, or contract, must be executed for each emigrant before he was taken on shipboard. This contract described in some detail the obligations and rights of the respective parties. (Illustration, frontispiece.) German emigrants, on the other hand, were bound by vague, general agreements or by custom alone. The whole passenger list often signed the same paper, each agreeing to pay a given sum after reaching a stated destination. (Illustrations opposite.) With the British passengers the chief thought was of the agreement or indenture; with the Germans it was of being freed from the debt for passage. The idea of "redemptioners" seems, however, to have been more than merely being freed from the ship's captain, especially as the larger number of these passengers were so freed by taking on other and similar obligations. At times the word "redemptioners" was applied to British servants and followed them until they had canceled their indebtedness, and often long afterwards.[11] Narrowly, redemptioners meant those whose price of passage was paid on arrival, sometimes by friends, but more often by sale; in a wider sense, it was applied to those who by servitude redeemed themselves from a debt for their passage; the service freed the immigrant from the one who had purchased the credit of the ship's captain or owner. Indentured servants were those who by service canceled obligations that existed in the form of a legal agreement.[12]

In the manuscript record, preserved in the Public Record

---

[10] Jefferson, *Writings* (Ford Edition), IV, 159. This is the view taken by Geiser, *Redemptioners*, 6.

[11] Fiske included under indentured servants convicts, kidnaped waifs, and redemptioners. *Dutch and Quaker Colonies*, II, 325.

[12] Walterhausen, *Arbeits-Verfassung der englischen Kolonien in Nordamerika*, 36.

It is impossible to make an entirely satisfactory distinction in the use of these terms. When a redemptioner had been sold, he had the legal status of an indentured servant; on the other hand, one under indenture was frequently termed a redemptioner. The terms seem to have been used loosely and sometimes interchangeably.

Wir Endes Unterzeichnete ich _Sullean_ Kapitain vom Schiff _Favorite_ zu einer / und wir Passagieren zur anderer Seite / nehmen an / und verpflichten uns hiemit wie Leute von Ehr

Fürs ersten wir Passagieren um mit obengemeltem Kapitain ——————
unsere Reise von hier anzunehmen nach _Philadelphia_ in Nordamerika / uns während der Reise still / und als gute Passagiers verpflichtet sind zu betragen / und mit der hier unten gemelte / zwischen den Kapitain und uns übereingekomme Speise vollkommen zufrieden zu seyn / und in Anschung des Wassers und weitere Prevision / wenn es die Nothwendigkeit durch conträren Wind oder lange Reise erfordert / zu schicken nach den Maaßregelen / so der Kapitain nothwendig finden wird.

Zum anderen nehmen wir an unsere Fracht auf folgende Condition zu bezahlen:
Die / so imstande sind selbige in Amsterdam zu bezahlen / geben ein Person / es sey Mann oder Weib

Kinder unter 4 Jahr alt / sind frey.

Von 4 bis unter 14 Jahren zahlen ▓▓▓▓▓ _dritthalb und eine halbe Guinea_

Von 14 Jahren / und älter zahlen ▓▓▓▓▓ _fünfzehn Guineen_

Die / so hier nicht bezahlen können / und in Amerika —————— bezahlen wollen / geben

Kinder unter 4 Jahren sind frey.

Von 4 bis unter 14 Jahren zahlen ▓▓▓▓▓▓▓▓▓ _vierlein und eine halbe Guinea_

Von 14 Jahren / und älter zahlen ▓▓▓▓▓ _dreyzehn Guineen_

Die / so ihre Fracht in Amerika zahlen / sollen gehalten seyn / selbige in 10 Tagen nach Ankunft beyzubringen. Keinem Passagier soll erlaubt seyn ohne Fürwissen des Kapitains in Amerika vom Schiff zu gehen / und insonderheit Solche / so ihre Fracht noch nicht bezahlt haben. Soll einer der Passagiers auf der Reise mit dem Tod abgehen / so soll die Familie eines solchen / wenn er von hier aus über die Halbscheid des Weges stirbt / verpflichtet seyn / seine Fracht zu bezahlen; stirbe er aber an diese Seite des Halbweges / soll der Verlust für Rechnung des Kapitains seyn.

Dahingegen verpflichte ich Kapitain _Sullean_ mich / die hierunter gezeichnete Passagier von hier getreulich (wenn Gott mir eine glückliche Reise gibt) überzuführen nach _Philadelphia_ in Nordamerika / ihnen die nöthige Bequemlichkeit im Schiff zu machen / und ferner zu versehn mit den am Fuß dieses gemeldten Speisen / für welche Ueberfahrt mir die obengemeldte Fracht muß bezahlet werden / und welst täglich unter denen Passagiers soll ausgetheilet werden / nemlich einer ganzen Fracht / eine halbe aber in Proportion / und Kinders nichts /

Sonntag. Ein Pfund Rindfleisch mit Gersten.
Montag. Ein Pfund Mehl, und ein Pfund Butter für die ganze Woch.
Dienstag. Ein halb Pfund Speck mit Erbsen gekocht.
Mittwoch. Ein Pfund Mehl.
Donnerstag. Ein Pfund Rindfleisch mit Ardäppfell.
Freytag. ▓▓▓▓▓▓ _ein halb Pfund Reis._
Samstag Erbsen, ein Pfund Käs / und 6 Pfund Brod für die ganze Woche. _und zu Zeit_
Ein Maß Bier / und ein Maß Wasser per Tag; auch soll Essig eben als auf dem Schiff mitgeschickt

Die hier der und der und der die ihre reise und die
Sie unternommen und wenn Tiere und so sogleich sofort und sogleich
die gestellet das kontrakt muß zum besten beygegeben werden

geſchickt werden/ nicht allein daſſelbige reinlich zu halten, um allezeit gute und friſche Luſt zu schöpfen/ sondern auch insonderheit zur Erquickung der Leute.

Wir versprechen Obengemeldtes Alles nachzukommen/ und verbinden zu dem Ende unsere ver=
sohnen, und Güter wie nach Rechten.

Actum in Amsterdam den 29 August 1803.

1 Jacobus de Haas Crikes
2 Cranius Wakuinga und frau
3 Josef Libl
4 Johannes Schöne
5 Alexander Schlösser
6 ~~Franuska van der Schor~~
7 D. Hämel und frau
8 Joseph Hamel
9 maria magdalena hamel
10 FRANS SES WESSELS
11 ☓ Maria Landman
12 Carl Friedrich Erdmann
13 ☓ Peter Boekhout
14 Gerret Terlinden
15 Johannes Beuerurgel
16 Jacob Hönig
17 Jan Plankman
18 ☓ Dirk Pimpies
19 ☓ Johannes Megnes
20 bram Thimon
21 MANSKOLEN

AGREEMENT
Society of Pennsylvania]

Office at London, of those who had taken passage from England during the week from June 12 to June 19, 1775, are included ninety-nine persons listed as "redemptioners." This was more than half of the total number of passengers recorded as leaving England during that week. Following the entry as to the reasons for leaving England was this explanation: "These People, on their arrival at Maryland, are to be disposed of for a Number of Years, provided they are not found capable to pay the Captn for their passage as P Agreement." [13]   These passengers bore English names and were registered as having resided in London, Kent, Bristol, and many other parts of England, and a few as having come from Scotland. They embarked on the ship "Nancy" from London and were bound for Baltimore. The probability is that these redemptioners made up the complement of passengers for this particular voyage, and no doubt the same arrangement existed as was practiced by the German redemption ships from Rotterdam, in which all signed one agreement. These papers establish conclusively that "redemptioners" as a title was not limited in its application to German passengers. In the *Registry of Servants bound before the Mayor of Philadelphia (1771-1773)*, the language was, "German and other redemptioners."

The collection of papers under "Emigration" in the Public Record Office contains also many names against which was entered the explanation as to why they left the country: "indented servants." Some of these records contained the specific mention of four years as the term which the passengers were to serve, employing a definite agreement as to term of service. "Number of Years" in the redemption record mentioned above indicated that these passengers were to be sold for a long enough term to pay for the price of their voyage, if the price was not forthcoming in some other way.

The distinction between indentures as above used and indentures of apprentices was recognized by judicial decision. In 1793 a minor was bound, with his guardian's consent, to serve until he was 15 years old; he ran away, but was seized and lodged in jail, whereupon a writ of habeas corpus was issued and the question came before the Supreme Court of Pennsylvania. The court held that the point to be decided was whether a minor could be

---

[13] P.R.O., Treasury Registers, *Emigration Records,* Bundle 2, No. 25.

bound as an indentured servant in Pennsylvania, and it was unanimous in the opinion that he could not. The court ruled that the claims of right to bind a child as servant within the state were without foundation in either common or statute law. The custom as it applied to immigrants included children as well as adults, and was thought a necessity; as practiced, it was affirmed to be mutually beneficial to the state and the immigrants. It was held that as no necessity existed for the binding of children within the state, the custom should not apply to them. Though a father was entitled to the service of his child, he could not bind him to serve another unless it were for the child's good in the learning of a trade. "Trade" must have been given a liberal interpretation, for poor children were often bound to what was termed some "art, trade, occupation or labor." What were in effect indentured contracts were sometimes converted into what appeared as apprentice agreements by inserting the words "art or trade," as, "teaching the art or trade of housewifery."[14]

Indentures for misdemeanor were sometimes assigned within the colonies, but the number of servants so secured was small. England sent out larger numbers as transported felons. The most numerous class, however, were the poor and unfortunate who voluntarily signed indentures that they might get passage to the New World. A suggestion of colonizing with the poor of England was made a century before the founding of Pennsylvania. Sir George Peckham, in his work on "The Advantages of Colonization" (1582), showed that in addition to a profit to the savages, the English sovereign, and the trade of the realm, those who were living in "penurie and want" would be advantaged by being sent out as servants. The seventh chapter of Peckham's work was written to prove that colonizing in the New World was "not a matter of such charge or difficulty, as many would make it seem."

---

[14] *Dallas Reports,* II, 198, 199.

The following record indicates the converting of an indentured contract into an apprenticeship:

"Henry Snyder, with his own consent, assigned by DR. ELIJAH GRIFFITH to ERHART SNYDER of LANCASTER COUNTY, Coverlet Weaver, to serve the remainder of his Term of his Indenture. Recorded in Book B, page 267. This assignment being made for the express purpose that the said HENRY may learn a trade."

MS. *Registry of Redemptioners,* October 1, 1824. Book C., p. 127.

Great numbers of people, the writer said, were ready to go out ("hazard their lives") to serve for one year for food and clothing only, in the hope that they could "thereby amend their estates." [15] This suggestion was repeated in many of the schemes of colonization, and was quite generally acted upon in founding the British North American settlements.

The third class of laborers consisted of slaves, chiefly Negroes, bound to service for life, with less protection than was offered to indentured servants and with little chance of rising above their station. Moreover, their status descended to their offspring.

A classification slightly different from the above has sometimes been made. The English customs official at Annapolis wrote just before the Revolution, "Persons in a state of servitude are under four distinct denominations: Negroes, who are the entire property of their respective owners; convicts, who are transported from the mother country for a limited term; indentured servants, who are engaged for five years, previous to their leaving England, and free-willers, who are supposed, from their situation, to possess superior advantages." [16]

In addition to the foregoing hired or servile labor, there was the important factor of the labor of the family household. In the colonial era subsistence was cheap, and the demand for helpers great; early marriages were common and large families the rule. In New England and the Middle Colonies, at least, women as

---

[15] Peckham, *"Advantages of Colonization"* in Hart, *American History Told by Contemporaries.* I, 152-157. Cited from Richard Hakluyt, *Voyages, Navigations, Traffiques, and Discoveries.*

[16] Eddis, *Letters from America,* 63. A colonial writer has the following: "We have four Sorts of People. 1. *Masters* that is Planters and Merchants. 2. *White Servants.* 3. *Indian Servants.* 4. *Slaves* for Life, mostly *Negroes.* White Servants are of two Sorts, viz. Poor people from *Great Britain,* and *Ireland* mostly, these are bound or sold, as some express it, for a certain Number of years, to reimburse the transporting Charges, with some additional Profit; the others are Criminals judicially transported, and their time of Exile and Servitude sold by certain Undertakers and their Agents." Douglass, *British Settlements in North America,* I, 206, 207.

French emigrants to the New World in the seventeenth century were mostly poor tradesmen who were bound to service for three years to pay for their passage. (*Cambridge Modern History,* VII, 77.) These French

well as children labored in the fields, and supplemented to no inconsiderable degree the work of slave, servant, and hired freeman.

Free hired labor occupied a subordinate place in all the American colonies. The attractions to an unencumbered freeman to become on his own account a producer, the independent proprietor of an estate, were too great for him long to remain a laborer for hire. Land was abundant and could be easily secured, and freemen early chose to be "lords of their own domain." [17] For a time at least the furnishing of free laborers to a new settlement, instead of satisfying the labor demand, only increased it and made more servile workers necessary.[18] Georgia, the last of the original thirteen colonies to be settled, had in the beginning restricted land ownership. Each family was to have twenty-five acres and, according to the original plan of settlement, no one could come into possession of more than five hundred acres.[19] A Swedish naturalist who visited Pennsylvania at the middle of the eighteenth century affirmed that free labor was too scarce for the needs of the colony and too expensive for employment.[20]

---

laborers under indenture were termed *engagés*. Baird, *Huguenot Emigration*, I, 217, 218.

Walterhausen (*Arbeits-Verfassung*, 33) classifies laborers in the English colonies as follows:

I. Indentured
II. Free
III. Criminals or Felons
IV. Slaves,
    1. Negroes
    2. Indians.

[17] The same principle operated to delay the establishment and retard the development of manufactures in the colonies and in the early history of the states. Fearon, *Sketches of America*, 300, 301.

[18] Wakefield, *England and America,* Chapters on "Slavery" and "Art of Colonization." "Good wages and plentiful lands make freemen into landlords who in turn reward with similar liberality other freemen who in turn become other landlords." Adam Smith, *Wealth of Nations,* Edition of 1791, III, 108.

[19] Burke, *European Settlements,* Edition of 1770, II, 265.

[20] Kalm, *Travels,* I, 389. See also Smith, *History of Delaware County,* 260. The high price of labor and its consequence are well illustrated in the following incident: A master who had to sell a pair of oxen to pay his servant said that he could not afford to keep the servant longer. The latter

The same condition continued to the close of the eighteenth century, at which time an English observer said of Pennsylvania: "The difficulty of hiring a tolerable servant induces many to deal in this way," i. e., to secure redemption servants.[21] "Nothing would be wanting to make life perfectly happy (humanly speaking), had we good servants," wrote Samuel Breck of Pennsylvania. Furthermore, the "vast quantity of uncultivated lands," and "prosperity and unexampled increase of our cities" united to scatter the "menial citizens" and made it "extremely difficult to be suited with decent servants." [22]   So easily was a livelihood obtained, said Breck, that fickleness, drunkenness, and insolence frequently marked the behavior of servants. He declared that one left because of too much to do, another had not enough, a third would quarrel with a fourth, a fifth would get drunk and be absent for a week—"in short," they were said to be "the most provoking compounds of folly, turpitude, ingratitude, and idleness" that could "possibly be conceived by one that has not lived in America." In the same connection Breck said, "They can, if prudent and constant, lay up money enough in two or three years to buy a handsome tract of new land." [23]

The labor problem in the English North American settlements was not unlike that of other colonies. The need was for cheap labor, and for labor which could not rise above the status of hired laborers, or which rose above this status with difficulty. Persons of a different race could be utilized, as could those who did not understand the language and customs of the new country.

The industry and life of a given district are closely bound up with its form of labor. It follows, then, that the history of labor in a new society is a fairly accurate index to the progress of that society, and, further, that conditions and changes in the labor supply indicate other social conditions and changes; labor has a determining effect in the growth of a new country. An

---

said that he would serve another year for more cattle. "But," said the master, "how shall I do when all my cattle are gone?" The servant answered, "You shall then serve me, and so you may have your cattle again." Winthrop, *History of New England*, II, 219, 220.

[21] Priest, *Travels*, 145, 146.

[22] Breck, *Recollections*, 296, 299.

[23] *Ibid.*, 299, 300.

understanding of the labor history of Pennsylvania is therefore necessary for one who would understand the complex history of this commonwealth. But the experience of Pennsylvania in dealing with her labor problem is of broader interest.

We search in vain for the origin of master and servant of the same race. The law of God given to the Israelites through Moses was: "If thou buy a Hebrew servant, six years he shall serve: and in the seventh he shall go out free for nothing." [24] This no doubt only approved an earlier custom. The colonial system of production, in which there was often the promiscuous mixing of the proprietor's family, bought servants, and slaves, was not inaptly compared to the old patriarchal organization.[25] Servile labor of indentured servants and slaves existed side by side in the early history of all the American colonies. Indentured servants have been long regarded as the chief support of the American industrial system in the seventeenth century.

New England practiced the holding of white servants who came under voluntary indentures; she also received some of the transported felons from England; in both cases the indentures were recognized as property. The Mayflower numbered in her limited passenger list twelve servants. In 1633 the ancestor of Josiah Quincy arrived in Boston with six servants.[26] Indentured servants in New England were spoken of as a "steady stream of laborers, forced to sell their services to pay the expense of their transfer to the better conditions of the New World." [27] Massachusetts also furnished bond servants to other settlements, for Quakers who could not pay their fines in Boston were ordered sold out of the colony. A considerable number of these are thought to have been sold, and no doubt other white men were similarly disposed of.[28] In the period 1637-1640, emigration to New England was checked and the development of industry impeded.[29] Furthermore, this region did not have conditions of

---

[24] *Exodus,* 21 : 2.

[25] Raynal, *British Settlements,* II, 181; Walterhausen, *Arbeits-Verfassung,* 49.

[26] Edmund Quincy, *Life of Josiah Quincy,* Vol. I, Ch. I.

[27] Weeden, *Economic and Social History of New England,* II, 520.

[28] Butler, *American Historical Review,* II, 15, 21; Besse, *Sufferings of Quakers,* II, 197.

[29] Weeden, II, 165, 205; Palfrey, *History of New England,* I, 370 sqq.

soil and climate favorable for extensive agricultural production, and agriculture was the chief dependence of the American colonies; New England had a larger proportion of free laborers.

Different environment and trend to industry gave a markedly different history to the middle and southern colonies. Servile labor seemed necessary and it was greatly in demand. This problem, which has "always been one of the chief causes of slavery," found the old solution. For New World colonization laborers had to be secured who could produce under the New World conditions. The aborigines, with low stamina and slight power of resistance, were early tried in English, Dutch, and Spanish colonies, but in every case they failed. To furnish white servile laborers was the earliest successful policy of the English home government, and it was half a century after the first permanent settlement before Negroes became an important substitute, chiefly because the supply of indentured servants was insufficient. In 1664 the Committee of the Council of Foreign Plantations made a report at length on the subject, in which there was an account of supplying the colonies with servants, and recommendations for a better supply in the future.[30] Of the previous practice the report said that servants sent to the colonies were blacks and whites. Blacks were bought by way of trade, and sold at about twenty pounds per head. They were considered "the most useful appurtenances of a plantation," as they were servants for life. Up to this time (1664) the white servants were secured from different parts of Great Britain. They were transported to the colonies, at about six pounds per head, and were exchanged for commodities at different rates, depending upon their fitness for work and their trade. One of the ways of getting servants for transportation was by commuting sentences of felons condemned to death. What were termed "sturdy beggars, gypsies, and other incorrigible rogues, poor, idle, and debauched persons" were also sent.[31]

Early in the Hanoverian period, Parliament legislated on the transportation of and trade in servants. A statute recited that

---

[30] For an account of appointment of this Committee, see *Cal. of State Papers,* "Colonial Series," 1661-1668, p. xxvii.

[31] *Ibid.,* p. 229.

there were many idle persons in London, and elsewhere in the realm, who were so desirous of employment that they would enter into service in some of the American settlements, but that these persons were without the right of contract for themselves, and it was not safe for merchants or captains to enter into a contract to take them; therefore, it was enacted that whenever a person between the ages of fifteen and twenty-one desired service in America, it should be lawful for such a person to enter into a contract to be transported thither, but all such contracts were to be witnessed in London before the lord mayor and outside of London before two justices of the peace.[32]

In the founding of the English commercial system, of which colonies were an element, the question of furnishing indentured laborers or slaves became part of larger questions: what should be the industries of the colonies and how could the interests of the mother country be best furthered in dealing with them ? These questions were reduced to another, viz., were the colonies to be agricultural alone or were they to have a diversified industry? If white servants were supplied, it could hardly be otherwise than that economic activity would be varied; if the colonists were limited to the manual toil of blacks, it was clear that they would remain exporters of raw products and importers of manufactured goods. As early as the reign of Charles II, English merchants made representations to the king on the importance of the slave trade. The slave trade was favorably commented on in a report of the Board of Trade and Plantations, January 14, 1734-1735. In 1745, Postlethwayt, a British merchant with unusual insight into colonial affairs, wrote a pamphlet to prove that the African trade was the great "pillar and support" of the British plantation trade; he argued against furnishing white laborers on the ground that this would make the colonies rivals of the mother country in manufacturing; on the other hand, he held that supplying them with blacks would keep them agricultural, which would be to the advantage of the mother country. He opposed supplying laborers from Great Britain, as this would drain the country of husbandmen, mechanics, and manufacturers; he also looked with disfavor upon colonizing with foreigners, as had been done in Pennsylvania, and said that the Palatines in this colony had interfered

---

[32] *4 George I*, ch. 11, sec. 5.

with British manufactures.[33]   By this method of reasoning, colonies were regarded as desirable only when they did not compete in production with the capital and labor of the home country. Many Englishmen of the eighteenth century regarded the sugar colonies with peculiar favor because these colonies would never become rivals of England.

This question assumed a new aspect about the middle of the seventeenth century due to the activity of the Royal African

---

[33] Postlethwayt, *The African Trade the Great Pillar and Support of the British Plantation Trade in America.*   This was anonymously published in 1745 in the form of a letter signed "A British Merchant."   On the title-page there is the statement that the trade in Negroes was of the greatest consequence, and that the African Company should be the most flourishing of any in the kingdom; and further that the African Company was of greater benefit to England than was any other company ever formed by British merchants.

The plantation trade of England, it was affirmed, was founded upon and upheld by the slave trade.   France had derived much advantage from a stimulation of the slave trade.   The same advantage was pointed out for Holland's African trade.   England was held to be in danger from depending on outside countries for commodities which she might produce in her own colonies by the use of slave labor.   The African and American trades were considered more valuable than was the East India trade.   The great population of Africa was made a premise in this line of reasoning. The first gain would be had in the selling of England's manufactures in Africa, to be followed by gains in the trade from Africa to the plantations and back to England.   If no Negroes, said Postlethwayt, then no rum, sugar, rice, indigo, or further improvement in the commodities produced in the plantations.   Continuing, he said, that the decline of the slave trade would mean the loss of revenue and the turning of great quantities of British manufactures "a begging."   The neglect and loss of the forts on the African coast would be regarded as calamitous and it was suggested that this would lead to the ruin of the plantations.

Throughout this tract there was implied the effect of furnishing slaves to the plantations upon the plantations themselves.   In the following passage, which is the heart of the matter, Pennsylvania is referred to as illustrating a form of colonization particularly objectionable: "As *Negroe Labour* hitherto has, so that only can support our *British* Colonies, as it has done those of other Nations.   It is that also that will keep them in due Subserviency to the Interests of the *Mother-Country:* for while our Plantations depend only on Planting by Negroes, and that of such Produce as interferes only with the Interests of our Rivals, not of their *Mother-Coun-*

Slave Company.[34]   The company asked for the support of the home government in taking the slave trade from the Dutch, and for a monopoly of the colonial market as a means of disposing of the slaves.   In 1663, it addressed a petition to the king in which the attempt was made to show that the trade of Africa was necessary for the existence of the plantations, the plantations depending, it was said, on the supply of Negroes.   This petition recited what the Royal Company had accomplished since the king's

---

try, our Colonies can never prove injurious to British Manufactures, never become independent of these Kingdoms, but remain a perpetual support to our *European* interests, by preserving to us a Superiority of Trade and Naval Power.

"But if the whole *Negroe Trade* be thrown into the Hands of our Rivals, and our Colonies are to depend upon the labour of *White Men* to supply their Place, they will either soon be undone, or shake off their Dependency on the Crown of *England.* For the *White Men* cannot be obtained near so cheap or the Labour of a sufficient number be had for the Expense of their Maintenance only, as we have of the Africans.   Has not long experience also shown that *White* Men are not constitutionally qualified to sustain the toil of planting in the Climates of our *Island Colonies* like the Blacks?

"Were it possible, however, for the *White Men* to answer the end of *Negroes* in planting, must we not drain our own Country of *Husbandmen, Mechanicks and Manufacturers* too?   Might not the latter be the Cause of the Colonies interfering with the Manufactures of these Kingdoms, as the Palatines attempted in Pennsylvania.   In such Case, indeed, we might have just Reason to dread the Prosperity of our Colonies; but while they can be well supplied with *Negroes,* we need be under no such Apprehensions: their Labour will confine the Plantations to *Planting* only; which will render our Colonies more beneficial to these Kingdoms than the *Mines* of *Peru* and *Mexico* are to the *Spaniards.*"

Postlethwayt, *The African Trade,* etc., 3-38.

The interference of the labor of the Palatinates with the industry of the mother country had been noted in a report of the Board of Trade and Plantations to Parliament in 1732.

Postlethwayt recommended that the African trade remain open to the subjects of Great Britain, that the African Company be reimbursed for its expenditures subsequent to 1713, and that provisions be made for the protection of British interests on the coasts of Africa through the building of forts and the establishment of settlements.

[34] A Fourth African Company was organized in 1662 to send three thousand slaves a year to the American settlements.   The Royal African Company was organized in 1672 and bought out the rights of the Fourth African Company.

restoration and complained that the Dutch were attempting to drive them from the coast of Africa.[35]

English theorists and the tradesmen of the realm alike desired to further the traffic in Negro slaves. Members of successive royal families were directors of, or held stock in, slave-trading companies. The operation of these companies was considered honorable, and representative men of the time were in their management. Merchants demanded that the slave trade be kept a monopoly, and secured a decision that as Negroes were merchandise the acts of navigation governed their purchase, transportation and sale. The African trade was generally thought of as inseparably connected with the plantation trade, and manufacturers as well as merchants clamored to have it fostered. Petitions of merchants were repeatedly before the Board of Trade and Plantations for the abolition of colonial acts restricting slave importation through fixing a duty on all brought in. It was urged that if these acts could not be abolished, they should be so amended that the purchaser and not the importer would pay the duty.[36]

Instructions of His Majesty's government to deputy-governor Gordon in Pennsylvania in 1731 were in accord with the well-established policy of the British sovereigns. Notice was taken of the duty levied on the importation of Negroes, "to the great Discouragement of Merchants trading thither from the coast of Africa," and it was expressed as the will and pleasure of the king that the governor should not give his assent to any law imposing duties on Negroes imported into Pennsylvania.[37]   Just

---

[35] Mellick, *Story of an Old Farm,* 220. See also Egerton, *Origin and Growth of English Colonies,* 126, for a statement of the British Board of Trade in 1775 that the colonies should not be permitted to check the slave trade on the ground that this trade was profitable to the nation.

[36] Contrast this with the brilliant statement of Lord Macaulay that the Stamp Act found two million Americans as loyal as the inhabitants of Kent and Sussex and left them rebels. Franklin said in his examination before the House of Commons (1766) that earlier than 1763 the sentiment of the colonies was favorable to Great Britain. Franklin, *Works.* (Bigelow), III, 416, but Franklin's later writings hardly confirmed this statement, e. g., *Causes of American Discontent Before 1769.*

[37] *Cal. State Papers,* "Colonial Series," 1661-1668, pp. 175, 176.

In 1664, the company addressed another petition to the same general effect. In this it was more definitely stated that the American plantations would fail through want of Negro servants. The prayer was here made

before the outbreak of the Revolution, the Earl of Dartmouth declared anew Great Britain's policy: "We cannot allow the colonies to check or discourage, in any degree, a traffic so beneficial to the nation." [38]

The issue growing out of the labor supply had no small part in hastening the separation from Great Britain. "To me," says Sabine, "the state papers teach nothing more clearly than that almost every matter brought into the discussion was practical and in some form or other related to labor"; he continued with the statement that one who examines the acts of Parliament which were obnoxious will find that nearly all of them restricted labor. No less than twenty-nine laws restricted colonial industry. These, it was held, were aimed at the North, and England was said to have lost the affection of the mercantile and maritime classes of the northern colonies a generation before she alienated the South. These laws forbade the use of water power, the erection of machinery, the introduction of looms and spindles, and the working in wood and iron; the same laws set the mark of the king's arrow upon trees which rotted in the forest; they forbade the markets for boards and fish; they also seized sugar and molasses, and the vessels in which they were carried. "To me, then," says this writer, "the great object of the Revolution was to release labor from these restrictions." [39]

The British government attempted to preserve a proper balance between blacks and whites in those colonies that were essen-

---

for royal protection and a convoy of ships to guard the company against the Dutch on the west coast of Africa. *Ibid.*, 215.

Queen Anne gave instructions to the governor of New York and New Jersey, 1702, to afford encouragement to merchants, in particular to those of the Royal African Company. Mellick, *Story of an Old Farm*, 220.

Burke, *Speech on Conciliation with America*, thus analyzed the colonial trade: "The export trade to the colonies consists of three great branches: the African, which, terminating almost wholly in the colonies, must be put to the account of their commerce; the West Indian, and the North American trade. All these are so interwoven, that the attempt to separate them would tear to pieces the contexture of the whole, and, if not entirely destroy, would very much depreciate the value of all the parts."

[38] See Board of Trade, *Journals*, Vol. 40, p. 72 (1730), for such a petition against an act passed by South Carolina.

[39] Sabine, *The American Loyalists*, 1, 2. (Boston : 1847.)

tially slave. It was recognized by most colonial writers that the West Indies were settlements in which there were proportionally too many blacks.[40]   South Carolina, because of the number of slaves, was endangered both from internal uprisings and from invasions of the Spaniards. After an Indian outbreak, the South Carolina legislature referred to the small number of whites in that colony and the danger from the increasing number of the slaves (1716) ; the success of the colony, it was thought, would be jeopardized unless care was taken to encourage the importation of white servants. At this time a bounty of twenty-five pounds was offered for each indentured white person brought in if he had not less than four years to serve, and for those who should be brought inside of two years five pounds additional was promised. But the securing of white servants in this colony was not to be left wholly to the pleasure of the planters. Every owner of a plantation who had ten slaves, young or old, was directed to take from the recorder a white servant, when it came his turn to do so, and to pay the amount that had been advanced to the importer; under this act, however, one was not compelled to take as his servant a Catholic or one convicted of a capital offense.[41]

The efficiency of Georgia as an outpost or "buffer" against the Spanish settlements to the south would, it was thought, be increased by restricting altogether the introduction of Negroes; the economic demands for slave labor, however, compelled an

---

[40] Cf. Burke, *European Settlements*, II, 117. In 1691 merchants and others trading to foreign plantations submitted a petition to the House of Commons in which it was said "that the plantations cannot be maintained without a considerable number of white servants, as well to keep the blacks in subjection as to bear arms in case of invasion." Cited in Geiser, *Redemptioners*, 25.

The policy of keeping down the number of slaves by taxing their importation and the unstable conditions in colonies with a relatively large number of slaves were frequently discussed in the Board of Trade. Jamaica was the scene of disorders due to slave insurrections about 1730, and the Board had many communications from the governor and other residents of the island, merchants trading thither, and others. For a somewhat detailed account of the conditions in Jamaica because of the large numbers of Negroes there, see *Board of Trade Journals,* Vol. 33, p. 29 sqq.

[41] McCrady, "Slavery in South Carolina," *American Historical Association Report, 1895,* 637.

abandonment of this policy, or the failure of the colony.[42] Insur-. rections occurred in the southern colonies and the whites, often far outnumbered by Negroes, felt that their safety depended upon limiting the slave importation, which was done again and again. Five to one was the ratio suggested by Burke, who urged that at least this relation be preserved, and that the whites be used as overseers and drivers.[43] Burke also noted with favor the French custom of compelling all vessels from France to America to carry white servants indentured as laborers—for a vessel of sixty tons or less, three servants; sixty to one hundred tons, four servants; and one hundred tons and upwards, six servants. These were to be under contract to labor for at least three years, and were to be between the ages of eighteen and forty and to be physically sound and strong. To ascertain that the provisions were complied with, officers of the French admiralty were to pass on the servants before their shipment, and a similar examination was made by the commissary on their arrival in America.[44]

The policy of limiting slave importation by the colonies is unmistakable, and it is shown alike in public declarations and legislation. Certain industries were so dependent on slave labor that those who used their product felt that they were sanctioning and supporting slavery; cane sugar was one of these, and there was an early anti-slavery movement in the attempt to find a substitute for this. A company of Dutch gentlemen [45] secured the services of a practical sugar refiner, and sent him out to try the making of sugar from maple trees by free labor. Some twenty-three thousand acres of maple forests were secured in the Middle Colonies, but the whole plan was pronounced abortive and visionary, though "based on the best of philanthropic intentions." [46]

---

[42] Burke, *European Settlements,* II, 270.

[43] *Ibid.,* II, 132.

[44] *Ibid.,* II, 44, 45.

[45] In the main, those who later formed the Holland Land Company.

[46] Alfred Huidekoper, *Life of Henry J. Huidekoper,* Agent of the Holland Land Company, cited in *Journals of John Lincklaen,* 11. John Lincklaen was also an agent of the Holland Land Company. His journals mention repeated attempts to produce maple sugar, the attempts resulting unfavorably because of deep snows, poor transportation, and lack of markets.

The indentured labor system was fairly established in Virginia before slaves were introduced. Earlier than 1630 considerable numbers of servants were being brought, and they continued more numerous than slaves throughout the greater part of the seventeenth century.[47]   The Plymouth settlers had as sojourners for some months in 1627 a company of men who had set out for Virginia, but had been turned from their course at sea and had had their ships disabled.   Bradford records that the two chief men of this Virginia company had "many servants," most of whom were Irish.   Others of the company had one or two servants apiece, but most of them were under contract to the two adventurers mentioned above, who were owners also of the larger part of the goods of the expedition.   Land was secured upon which to employ the servants temporarily, as the company could not proceed at once.   During the winter the ground was cleared and in the spring it was planted; the growing crop seems to have been sold when the company took its departure in the summer.   One of the proprietors scandalized the Puritan community and had to run away in a small boat.   As he could get no passage and was in danger of being lost, he came back and gave himself up.   The Puritan chronicler adds: "But they pact him away and those that belonged unto him by the first opportunitie, and dismiste all the rest as soone as could, being many untoward people amongst them." [48]

There was little early demand for Negroes in Virginia; instead there was an evident desire for white servants.   One of the early tracts directed to this end was termed *Leah and Rachel, or The Two Fruitfull Sisters, Virginia and Mary-land*. The title-page to this tract was a direct appeal to such as had to beg, steal, or go to prison, or who were in danger of suffering "shamefull deaths."   All such were assured that by going to the colonies named they would better their condition, as in these colonies there was plenty for human need.   The writer said that servants who were characterized by affability and industry could secure an estate, as the masters would allow them to clear land for some

<hr>

[47] Ballagh, *White Servitude in Virginia,* 41; Bruce, *Economic History of Virginia,* II, 62.

[48] Bradford, *History of Plymouth Plantation* (Massachusetts State Department Edition), 263-265.

tobacco of their own at idle times, and they could easily get a pig and a calf and raise them for the increase. But prospective servants were cautioned against the "mercinary spirits" who might defraud them, and they were advised to make all contracts in writing.[49]

In 1625, there were reported to be in Virginia four hundred and sixty-four white servants and only twenty-two Negroes; in five years preceding the Negroes had increased but two.[50] Slavery was of slow growth for over fifty years; in 1661, there were said to be two thousand Negroes and over eight thousand white servants.[51] Governor William Berkeley, in an account of the colony for 1671, estimated Virginia's population at forty thousand—two thousand black slaves and "six thousand Christian servants for a short time." He said that about fifteen hundred of these servants were introduced each year; the greater number of them were English, a few were Scotch, and fewer yet were Irish. Of the slave trade the governor wrote that not more than two or three ships of Negroes arrived in seven years.[52] Around'

---

[40] Reprinted in Force's *Tracts*, Vol. III, No. XIV, pp. 10, 11 and 14. See transcript of title-page in bibliography under "Hammond." Compare *Leah and Rachel* with Alsop's *Character of Mary-land* noted below in Chapter III.

[50] Bruce, *Economic History of Virginia*, I, 572. In an enumeration of 1625, William Tucker, of Elizabeth City, was said to have fourteen white servants, and was credited with three of the twenty Negroes then owned in the colony. Brown, *Genesis of the United States*, 1034.

Hotten's *Original List* of those who came to Virginia shows the following division of a total of 1315 early arrivals : Masters, freemen, and their families, 806; (bond) servants, 481; Negroes, 24; hired servants, 3; Indian servant boy, 1. Summary in *Hunt MSS.*, IV, 258.

[51] Bruce gives the following table which shows how slowly Negro, slavery increased in Virginia:

Imported into the colony, 1635, 26 Negroes
1637,	28	"
1638,	30	"
1639,	46	"
1642,	7	"
1643,	18	"
1649,	17	"

The average of the numbers last given continues about the same until' 1659. *Economic History of Virginia*, II, 75.

[52] Cited, Merivale, *Colonization and Colonies*, 270; Bruce, *Economic History of Virginia*, I. 610.

1683 it was practically impossible to buy a large tobacco crop in Virginia unless one had servants to offer in exchange. Immediately following 1680, the Royal African Company began a larger exportation of Negroes to Virginia and these slaves soon took the place of whites as laborers. It must needs be remembered, however, that tobacco culture was fairly established, and that tobacco became a staple of Virginia, under the system of white indentured labor.

Slavery and servitude had the same relations in North Carolina as in Virginia. The attempt to supply North Carolina with indentured white servants instead of Negro slaves is well compared to the relations earlier existing between Negro and Indian slavery in the West Indies. "Both Indian slavery and white servitude were to go down before the black man's superior endurance, docility, and labor capacity." [53]

The other colonies in the South had few distinguishing features. Maryland is of interest in the present study because of its geographical position, its more temperate climate, and its mixed system of agriculture. The first mention of slaves in Maryland was in an act of 1664, though it is probable that they were introduced earlier from Virginia.[54] An act to encourage the importation of slaves was passed in 1671, and slavery was fixed upon the colony, though it was long before slaves took the place of indentured servants, and the latter formed a considerable element in the population down to the Revolution. The practice of sending convicts and felons to Maryland was resisted to little purpose, for England continued to send them for almost one hundred years after the first act to prevent their importation was passed. These convicts were held for seven or fourteen years, according to the crimes for which they were transported. The provision to check their importation was by fixing penalties on the masters of ships that brought them, but the Maryland charter was suspended and the objection was withdrawn.[55] At first indentured laborers were brought into Maryland by the

---

[53] Bassett, *Slavery and Servitude in North Carolina*, J. H. U. Studies, XIV, 77.

[54] Walterhausen, *Arbeits-Verfassung*, 50, gives 1663 as the date for the introduction of slaves.

[55] Browne, *Maryland,* in "American Commonwealth Series," 181.

planters themselves, but later masters of ships brought servants to sell for their unexpired terms.[56] About the middle of the eighteenth century the so-called Palatines began to be introduced as servants into Maryland and from this time to the disappearance of the system (circa 1820) it had a different character.[57]

After slavery became common in the South, labor was degraded and indentured servants lost caste. Many of them, when their indentures were discharged, moved into the upland regions; some of the "poor whites" of the South, as well as those of the middle class, are no doubt descended from these servants. Slave labor tended to caste, to aristocracy; indentured labor, to the breaking down of social and political barriers, to democracy. In the Virginia convention of 1830 a delegate from the western part of the state spoke for free labor against the slave aristocracy: "The Old Dominion has long been celebrated for producing great orators; . . . but at home or when they return from Congress they have Negroes to fan them asleep. But a New York, a Pennsylvania, an Ohio, or a western Virginia statesman, though far inferior in logic, metaphysics, and rhetoric, has this advantage, that when he returns home he takes off his coat and takes hold of the plow. This gives him bone and muscle, and preserves his republican principles pure and uncontaminated." [58]

In the South, indentured servants were utilized on plantations as overseers, drivers, and superintendents, and during the eighteenth century, after they had ceased to labor in the fields, they were in demand for such service. In some sections they were employed as herdsmen, in which capacity they received part

---

[56] Brantly, "English in Maryland," in Winsor's *Narrative and Critical History,* III, 545. The claims for the number of indentured servants in Maryland in this article seem extravagant. The writer says, "Owing to its equable climate Maryland had more of these servants than any other colony."

[57] Studies of this subject are by Hennighausen, *Redemptioners and the German Society of Maryland,* and McCormac, *White Servitude in Maryland.* Further reference at some length under Maryland will be found in the chapters dealing with transportation of convicts and felons, and runaway servants.

[58] Cited in Turner, "Frontier in American History," *Report of American Historical Association, 1893,* 201, 222, and 223.

of the increase of the stock; again, they had a share of the corn or tobacco crop.[59]

Under such climatic conditions as prevailed in Pennsylvania, the black man had neither superior endurance nor greater labor capacity. Those who here imported slaves did so at a risk, for many slaves became diseased, and frequently they died, as a result of the climatic changes. The difficulty of acclimating Negroes was so great that it was a common practice to take them first to the West Indies, and later to import them from those islands. Thus, the changes in climate were more gradual, and the results were less likely to be fatal. In cases of disease and unfitness for labor, Pennsylvania masters could not manumit their slaves without becoming legally responsible for their future support. This deterred men from becoming masters.[60] Again, the amount which was necessary to be paid as a lump sum for a slave was considerably more than was required for a servant, and, besides being paid at one time, it was wholly lost if the slave died. The better adjustment of white men to the climatic conditions of the northern colonies gave servants an advantage in the operation of the two systems.

The "docility" of the Negro might make him more useful as a servile laborer under certain conditions and while performing certain sorts of labor, but as climatic conditions in Pennsylvania were not favorable to him, so the form of labor demanded was not such as his docility could satisfy. The diversified production and industry which prevailed in Pennsylvania required a higher order of labor than that of slaves. Governor Thomas, in a communication to the Board of Trade and Plantations, said that the servants in Pennsylvania were not mere manual laborers, they were tradesmen engaged in industry in the colony, carrying on manufactures of several sorts and directly interfering with the industries of Great Britain. Governor Thomas cited advertisements which appeared from week to week in the newspapers. An examination of these newspapers confirms the governor's statement; many of the servants were offered as tradesmen, and it

---

[59] Walterhausen, *Arbeits-Verfassung,* 64

[60] Kalm, *Travels,* I, 390.

was not expected that they would be employed for raising hemp and flax or in the production of potash.[61]

The opposition of Pennsylvania to Negro slavery is well known. The first public declaration in America against the evils of that institution was by the Germantown Friends in 1688. Similar declarations were made in 1697 and at least a dozen other times during the first half of the eighteenth century; in the early days of the Revolution all Friends were ordered to free their slaves or suffer loss of standing in their society. It was in Pennsylvania that the first act for the gradual emancipation of slaves was passed and, again, it was here that the first abolition society was recognized by law. No subject was more often before the Pennsylvania Colonial Assembly than the exclusion of slave importation by a prohibitive duty.[62] Instances might be multiplied showing the hostility of Pennsylvania to slavery, and its dependence upon indentured and redemption servants. The opposition to the enlistment of servants in the Spanish war (1740), and in the French war, evidenced further that the colony depended largely upon white servants for carrying on its industry.

New York in her industry and labor history had some similarity to Pennsylvania, but there are several differences between these colonies. New York was founded nearly three-quarters of a century earlier, and yet, fifty years after Pennsylvania's settlement, she rivaled New York in industry and production; and before the outbreak of the Revolution New York was surpassed. It is difficult for one of this generation to consider New York as other than the Empire State, or her seaport as other than the metropolis of the North American continent. But as late as 1787 the state of New York was regarded as "one of the smaller states." This difference in development is readily explained. Pennsylvania was largely an agricultural colony, and her agricultural district lay open to settlement. Pennsylvania did not have the hostility of the Indians to deter settlers as did most of the

---

[61] Governor Thomas to Board of Trade, October 20, 1740. Pamphlet in Library of Historical Society of Pennsylvania, 6.

[62] Summary of acts to this end, DuBois, *Suppression of the Slave Trade,* 204-231.

other colonies. Pennsylvania early developed a somewhat varied industry; she began shipbuilding, and gave considerable attention to commerce. Pennsylvania, besides, made efforts to secure, and welcomed, a class of immigrants which New York either purposely or thoughtlessly turned away. When, in 1709, England distributed the Palatines who had been invited to London to serve as colonists, a colony estimated at 3,200 was sent to New York.[63] But this colony was neither well received nor well treated, and its members so reported to deter others from coming; at the same time, Pennsylvania was holding out inducements and, as a result, the large German migration was to Pennsylvania.[64]

More than this, many Germans who had settled in New York, after they had been dispossessed of their holdings, transferred their residence to Pennsylvania. New York's governor wrote in 1693: "More families are daily removing to Pennsylvania and Connecticut to be eased of taxes and detachments." Later, Rev. John Miller confirmed this, with a declaration that the burdens imposed in New York had led two or three hundred families to forsake that colony and remove chiefly to Pennsylvania and Maryland. Some of the immigrants of 1709 passed on from the Hunter tract, on which they were first located, to the interior in the Mohawk region, and some, on an alleged invitation, came to Pennsylvania and became pioneers in parts of Dauphin, Lebanon, and Berks Counties.[65] The great migration which

---

[63] Diffenderffer, *German Exodus to England*, 341.

[64] Cobb, *Story of the Palatines*, 267; Kalm, *Travels*, I, 271, 272. An account of the attempt to utilize the Germans for producing naval stores and the failure of this is given in Lord, *Industrial Experiments in North America*, 44-51. Says Jacobs, one explanation of the failure of the German settlement in New York was the attempt to force the Germans to produce tar. *German Emigration to America*, 114-116. To the foregoing Dr. Jacobs adds an account of insufficient food, and danger from Indian attack. *Ibid.*, 121. The German migration from New York into Pennsylvania has been made the subject of a separate monograph by the Pennsylvania German Society. Richards, in Vol. IX, Pennsylvania German Society Publications.

[65] "The people got news of the land on the Swatara and Tulpehocken in Pennsylvania; many of them united and cut a road from Schochary to the Susquehanna river, carrying their goods there and made canoes and floated them down the river and drove their cattle overland. This happened in the spring of the year 1723 . . . and this was the beginning of the

threatened to convert an English colony into a German colony was received in Pennsylvania, not in New York; the colony first to feel the influence of German thrift and industry was Pennsylvania; it was this German immigration that served to give Pennsylvania, in part, its labor supply, and that served to make the history of the colony peculiar. Environment and public sentiment both favored the system of indentured labor in Pennsylvania, and this colony occupies a unique place in her labor history. Indentured servants were held within its territory when the Quaker settlement began; the system was recognized by the laws framed in England before the settlers left, and it was practiced from the first. This system of labor was more important to Pennsylvania than it was to any other colony or state; it continued longer in Pennsylvania than elsewhere. Indentured and redemption labor profoundly affected Pennsylvania's political, industrial, and social life.

Tulpehocken settlement." Weiser, *Autobiography.* Cited in Sachse, *Sectarians* (1742-1800), 276. See also Jacobs, *German Emigration,* 135.

For distribution of Germans see: Cobb, Chapter on, in *Story of the Palatines,* 258-303. Cobb says that after 1710 all German emigrant ships except one, and that a ship driven from its course, were landed at Philadelphia. *Story of the Palatines,* 267; Mann, *Life of Mühlenberg,* 166-167; Kalm, *Travels.*

For account of ill treatment which the Germans had in New York, see Cobb, *Story of the Palatines,* 148-200.

CHAPTER II

INDENTURED LABOR IN PENNSYLVANIA
BEFORE 1700

No evidence is conclusive to show how early servile labor was introduced into Pennsylvania. A white servant was early brought to the Delaware, and was retained by Governor Printz on his Tinicum Island estate. Men described as the lowest class of the Swedes "were to remain in slavery and were employed in digging earth, throwing up trenches, and erecting walls and other fortifications." The Swedes held Negro slaves on the Delaware in 1638.[1] The Dutch company agreed to supply the colonists with as many slaves as it conveniently could, and its traders were anxious to keep the market in their own hands. In 1655, a trader was given permission to take some Negroes on a sloop from New Amsterdam to Virginia, but he was put under oath with a bond of five thousand pounds not to run in at South (Delaware) Bay or River.[2] The Dutch representative on the Delaware wished to have a part in the trade with Maryland, and to that end recommended the construction of a "tobacco magazine and balance" at New Amstel (New Castle). In the same connection, he said: "I solicit most seriously that it may please your honor to accommodate me with a company of *negroes,* as I am very much in want of them in many respects." [3]

.The servant system was practiced on the Delaware during the period of Dutch control. In 1663, Governor Stuyvesant answered a petition of Beckman, who feared being driven out of the colony, and granted that he might remain at Fort Christiana, cultivate land, and keep five or six servants. Fifty laborers were landed in 1663, and these were to serve both as farmers and soldiers; at the same time, six or seven girls came to keep house for them. These servants had been secured in Holland, with the understanding that they were to labor in the colony for a term

---

[1] Smith, *History of Delaware County,* 33.

[2] Hazard, *Annals,* 181.

[3] *Ibid.,* 331.

of years to defray the expense of bringing them over. Some of them were hired out for a yearly wage of sixty, seventy, or eighty guilders.[4]

The *Laws of the Duke of York,* introduced on the Delaware in 1676, probably made little change in the status of servants already held, or in the future practice within the territory. The legislation presented in this body of laws legalized by more formal statement a practice already common. The introduction to the Laws stated that they were compiled out of those already in force in the colonies and plantations.[5]   In accordance with the usual practice of the time, whites only were called Christians, and it was provided that whites should not be held in bond slavery, captivity, or villenage, except in the following cases: those adjudged to such a state by authority (criminals) and such as willingly had or should sell themselves into servitude. In either case it was ordered that a record of the bond should be entered at the court of sessions having jurisdiction in the region.[6]

Having recognized the servant system, acts were necessary for its regulation. One was for instruction of servants, and the punishment of those who were not amenable to their masters;[7] another provided a penalty for runaways, forbade harboring such, and regulated the manner of their return;[8] again, runaways were to be pursued with "hue and cry" and brought back at public charge.[9]

---

[4] Acrelius, *History of New Sweden,* 100.

[5] *Duke of York's Book of Laws,* 3; Armstrong, *Introduction to Upland Court Record,* 26.

[6] *Duke's Laws,* 12. In 1678 there is a record to the effect that "a man-servant is sold, with his consent, to Israel Helm, for twelve hundred guilders, for four years." Hazard, *Annals,* 450. Israel Helm was a member of the council of Captain Carre on the Delaware in 1668. *Hazard,* 371.

[7] *Duke's Laws,* 20.

[8] *Ibid.,* 28.

[9] *Ibid.,* 38. A summary of this legislation is furnished in Appendix I. Among the orders made and confirmed at a court of assizes in New York, in 1672, was one declaring that in the future "hues and cryes" for the return of servants should be at the expense of the master, while those for the pursuit of criminals should still remain at the charge of the government. The reason given was that the profit of the pursuit of servants by masters "redounds only to themselves." *Ibid.,* 72.

Runaway servants early became troublesome members of
colonial society. In 1662, William Clayborne of Maryland
wrote to the Dutch authorities giving notice of runaway servants
who had escaped into the territory on the South River, and asked
to have them seized.[10]   A later record is to the effect that certain
Englishmen had been in the settlement to secure runaway servants.[11]   Further information of a similar character was given in
November, 1662, that an English runaway servant was hanged.[12]
To guard against the escape of runaways and their shipping on
departing vessels, Governor Lovelace issued a proclamation in
1672, making a pass necessary for carrying either a debtor or a
servant out of the colony.[13]   A later act made it necessary for
strangers to carry passes in traveling; if they were not provided
with passes, they were subject to arrest.[14]

Servants were not allowed to trade;[15] the time of their labor,
with food and rest, was regulated;[16] they could not be abused
without their masters' becoming amenable to the law, and in
cases of serious abuse they would be freed by the court of sessions;[17] but in all cases of causeless complaint a servant was
subject to three months' extra service 'for each complaint.[18]   No
bond servant could be assigned under the law for a longer term
than one year, except with the consent of the court of sessions;[19]
faithful service for five or seven years was to be rewarded, provision being made that the servant could not be sent "empty
away";[20] the master, too, was protected, for in case a servant

---

[10] Hazard, *Annals,* 337.

[11] *Ibid.,* 339.

[12] *Ibid.,* 340.

[13] *Ibid.,* 395.

[14] *Duke's Laws,* 72.

[15] *Ibid.,* 37.

[16] *Ibid., in loc. cit.*

[17] The Mosaic law was: "If a man smite the eye of his servant, or the
eye of his maid, and destroy it; he shall let him go free for his eye's sake.
And if he smite out his manservant's tooth, or his maidservant's tooth; he
shall let him go free for his tooth's sake." *Exodus,* 21:26, 27.

[18] *Duke's Laws,* 38.

[19] *Ibid.,* 38.

[20] *Ibid.,* 38.

had been negligent, he might be compelled to make satisfaction by additional service, according to the judgment of the constables and the overseers of the parish.[21] The above laws are significant not only because they embodied a custom that existed before they were declared, but because in addition they served as a foundation for later legislation.

The servant system was recognized in the administration and interpretation of laws. At a meeting of the justices of the Upland Court on April 3, 1678, at the house of Justice Peter Cock, passes for traveling were considered. At the same time, there came up the case of a servant who wished to be freed from his indenture.[22] In the record of Upland Court there was a minute on the levying of a poll tax for public expense to which was appended a list of "Tydable" persons. In all there were one hundred and thirty-seven assessed as taxable in the Upland jurisdiction. Seven servants were named, of whom six were counted.[23]

---

[21] *Ibid.*, 38.

[22] *Upland Court Record*, 99. The following is the record: "Benjamin Goodman, servant to oele Swensen desiering to bee freed from his mastr, alleging that his tyme is out . . . Ordered that oele Swensen bring at the next Court ye Indenture or his witnessess that can Testify about ye businesse." *Upland Court Record*, 102. Oele Swensen is given as one of the justices of the Court. *Ibid.*, 94.

At the November session of the justices in 1678, the case of Benjamin Goodman came up again, and he was set at liberty.

Upland Court Record, November 12, 1678:

"Benjamin Goodman p'ferring in Court a Peticon, showeing that hee was assigned and set ouer from mr. Charles Ballard of ye province of maryland unto oele Swensen of this River to serve him or his assignes the terme of three years, wch was expiered the 19 day of april Laest past, and yt ye sd oele Swensen doth still deny the Peticonr his freedom and therefore desires that his sd master Either may make itt appeare that hee hath longer to serve or bee ordered to give him his free dome, with sattisfaction for ye overplus:

"The Court Haueing heard what by Lasse Cock was sayed touching the premisses, and oele Swensen producing noe Indentures alledgeing that the same were Lost, Doe therefore Judge that the Peticionr ought to be free." *Upland Court Record*, 114.

[23] In listing "oele Swensen" and servant (probably Benjamin Goodman above noted), the servant was not counted; if this were not a case in which the authority of master were in dispute, it would indicate a difference be-

William Penn's settlers found Pennsylvania occupied by Swedes, Dutch, and English, and, from the first, regard was had for practices that had previously obtained. The laws agreed upon in England and the first laws enacted after the arrival of Penn's colonists in America showed that the Quakers recognized and also wished to encourage the indentured servant system. One of the laws made in England provided servitude as a possible punishment for crime; another guaranteed to servants just and kindly treatment, and, further, that they be put in "fitting equipage" at the expiration of their indentures, "according to custom." [24] From 1682 to 1700, there were reënactments in various forms of the principal laws passed before 1681. Trade with servants was prohibited; a penalty was prescribed for servants who ran away; the time of any servants who came into the colony without a definite term of service was fixed at five years for those who were seventeen years of age or above, while for those who were not seventeen, the term was until they reached the age of twenty-two years. [25] Freedom dues were fixed, so that the master or mistress gave at the expiration of a servant's term one new suit of clothing, ten bushels of wheat, or fourteen bushels of Indian corn, one ax, two hoes (one broad and the other narrow), and a discharge from the service. [26] Servants bound to serve within the province were protected against being sold elsewhere, without their consent, and on pain of ten pounds' forfeiture no servant could be sold or turned over, except with the knowledge of two justices of the peace. On the other hand, masters were protected against their servants' running away by the requirement that all travelers should carry passes, and in addition, for each day's absence without leave, servants were subject to an extension of their terms for five days, with additional time for costs and damages. [27]

---

tween a servant and an indentured servant. *Upland Court Record,* 76-80.

In the list noted there is mentioned one slave, the entry being, "James Sanderling and slaue." *Ibid.,* 79.

[24] Numbers 24 and 29, *Duke's Book of Laws,* 101, 102.

[25] *Duke's Laws,* 152, 153.

[26] *Ibid.,* 153.

[27] *Ibid.,* 177, 213.

William Penn proposed the law for five days' extra service for each day's absence without leave, also additional service for costs and damages, September 8, 1683. *Colonial Records,* I, 80.

When William Penn secured possession of his territory and planned for its settlement, he offered favorable terms to induce settlers to take servants with them. In his first published account, "made public for the information of such as now are, or may be disposed to transport themselves or servants to those parts," Penn appealed to three sorts of people: First, those who would buy land outright; second, those who would take rent land; and third, servants. For the latter it was said that fifty acres of land would be allowed to the master for "every head," and fifty acres to each servant when the time of his service had expired.[28] The *Conditions and Concessions* of William Penn, published as his agreement with the first purchasers, and serving also as rules of settlement, took the system of "head land" for granted, and provided for quitrents as follows: "For every fifty acres that shall be allotted to a servant, at the end of his service, his quitrent shall be two shillings per annum, and the master or owner of the servant, when he shall take up the other fifty acres, his quitrent shall be four shillings by the year, or if the master of the servant (by reason in the indentures he is so obliged to do) allot to the servant fifty acres in his own division, the said master shall have on demand allotted him from the governor the one hundred acres, at the chief rent of six shillings per annum." [29]

The system of assigning "head land" which was practiced earlier in other colonies [30] was also used in Pennsylvania. During

---

The acts named were passed at assemblies held in Chester, December, 1682, and in Philadelphia, 1683. After such laws as these were passed, they were made public in a proclamation; e.g., at a council in Philadelphia, March 23, 1683, it was passed in the affirmative that "there should be a Proclamation issued out to this effect, that no person should deal with any servant for goods or money, either for themselves or for others." *Ibid.*, I, 74.

Also, "at a Councill in Philadelphia, ye 29th of the 6th Mo., 1683," William Penn presiding, "the Governor put ye Question whther a Proclamation was not Convenient to be put forth to Impower Masters to Chastise their Servants and to punish any yt shall inveyle any servant to goe from his Master." They unanimously agreed and "Orded" it accordingly. *Ibid.*, 79.

[28] Account of 1681, Hazard, *Annals,* 510.

[29] *Ibid.,* 518.

[30] For this system in Virginia see Coman, *Industrial History of the United States,* 33. Early settlers in Maryland could increase their hold-

the early period, "servant" was applied to any person who labored at any calling or trade for hire. The inference seems warranted that relatives and friends of the early settlers were brought in under the denomination of servants to secure the land bounties. Over four and a half thousand acres of land are recorded as surveyed for "head land"; sometimes deeds were recorded as "in the townships allotted to servants." [31] No record has been found showing that the practice here noted was approved by statute; it was a regulation by the proprietor, and was withheld or withdrawn by him or his successors at pleasure. It probably was withdrawn about 1700 and for these reasons: the abuse to which the practice had been subjected; increased importation of so-called servants; and growing scarcity of land.[32] In addition, trading in servants became a business in the years immediately following 1700, and such trade did not fall within the scope of the original *Conditions and Concessions,* where "servant" is used as applying to those who accompanied settlers.[33]

---

ings with every servant (Browne, *Maryland,* "American Commonwealth Series," 158), and a servant had fifty acres of land and a year's necessaries on expiration of time of service. Brantly, "English in Maryland," in Winsor, *Narrative and Critical History,* III, 545.

[31] Futhey and Cope, *History of Chester County,* 146-154; Stone, in Winsor, *Narrative and Critical History,* III, 478.

[32] Futhey and Cope give record of survey of "head land" in 1702, *History of Chester County,* 154.

[33] Diffenderfer seems at error in inferring that the gift of "head land" continued during the eighteenth century. *The Redemptioners,* 269-275. A more probable statement is that by Shepherd, "Conditions and Concessions related exclusively to the first purchasers." ("Land System of Provincial Pennsylvania," *Report of American Historical Association, 1898,* 118.) A similar change was made in Maryland in 1683 when by the abolition of the Conditions of Plantation "all connection between the distribution of land and the importation of servants came to an end." McCormac, *White Servitude in Maryland,* 26.

One can hardly share Mr. Diffenderfer's opinion of the *Conditions and Concessions* as "scarce." He speaks of all his researches to trace the origin of head land custom as unavailing, and records the discovery in *Conditions and Concessions* as notable. Since 1850, at least, the conditions of settlement in Pennsylvania have been easily accessible and the supposed origin of the head land custom quite evident. See Hazard, *Annals,* 510. Fenwick's *Proposals for Settlement in New Jersey* (1675) might have given the suggestion for the *Conditions and Concessions* of Penn. In the third

Penn on his first visit brought servants.[34] Sixty or seventy others were sent out while the "Welcome" was still upon the sea.[35] The manuscript record of arrivals shows the bringing in of a goodly number of servants in the period for which it was kept. Passengers on those early ships were classed as "free persons" and "servants." [36] The reward to the early servants varied; sometimes it was entered as "wages and lands," but more often it was specified definitely.   An early contract promised in return for four years of service ten bushels of corn, one cow, one calf, and fifty acres of land.[37] A later record gives meat, drink, washing, lodging, and six pounds per year for a term of four years. Other contracts were for two pounds ten shillings; six pounds; and four pounds under the same conditions.[38]

Penn sought to encourage the bringing in of servants by allowing fifty acres of land for each servant brought to the colony. Browning is of the opinion that Penn intended to allow fifty acres to the master when he brought the servant into the colony, also fifty acres additional to the servant when his term of service was completed.[39]   In 1702, one John Roberts received title by deed to seven hundred and fifty acres of land due as "head rights" for a parcel of "servants and others" whom he had brought in about 1683-1684." [40]

Records of early arrivals in Bucks County, as in Philadelphia, classified incomers as masters and mistresses, with children and

---

proposal of Fenwick we read: "Who are minded to go as servants, who must be carried . . . ; they are to serve 4 years and then be made Free of the Country; their Masters are to give them a suit of Cloaths, and other things suitable; a cow, a hog, and so much wheat as the Law there in that Case allows; with Working Tools to begin with: and then he is to have of me, or his Master a hundred acres, paying the yearly rent of a penny for every acre," etc. Fenwick, *Proposals,* original leaflet in Library of Historical Society of Pennsylvania, p. 1.

[34] Cox, *MS. Transcript of Record of Arrivals in Bucks County,* 35.

[35] Hazard, *Annals,* 595.

[36] See record of arrival of "Rebecca" from Liverpool, August 31, 1685. MS. Record, Library of Historical Society of Pennsylvania.

[37] Cox, MS. *Transcript of Record of Arrivals,* 43.

[38] *Ibid.,* 52, 53.

[39] Browning, *Welsh Settlement of Pennsylvania,* 259.

[40] *Ibid.,* 128. This indicated dilatory payment of the head land.

EARLY RECORD OF ARRIVAL OF SERVANTS

[Original Historical Society of Pennsylvania]

servants. Though sometimes five, six, and seven years are given, the usual term of service was four years, and it was often stated that servants were to have fifty acres of land apiece when their terms had expired. A case occurs of one who was to work out his passage money "by the day" and "then be free," and of another who should get three pounds fifteen shillings per year for four years and the customary fifty acres of land.[41] A single Bristol ship of 1685 brought in the widow, with the married son and family, of Jasper Farmer, and "their servants," nineteen in number, all named and all set down as having come from Ireland. The same ship brought two other settlers, one with seventeen servants and another with seven.[42] The record of arrivals at Philadelphia from 1682 to 1686 shows a total of 530, of whom 193 were termed servants. Of the total of 253 of those listed as arriving in Bucks County, eighty-two were classed as servants.

As these servants were brought to Pennsylvania, others were being received into New Jersey and Maryland. Interrelation of the colonies led to what was perhaps the most interesting enactment of the whole body of early laws in the form of a provision passed at New Castle, May, 1684. This recognized the need for intercolonial comity between Pennsylvania and New Jersey and agreed that in the "hues and cryes" and warrants, also legal processes issued in New Jersey (for runaway servants in the enumeration) should be of like force in Pennsylvania, as though issued here, provided that, in less than two months, New Jersey should pass an act granting to the warrants and legal processes of Pennsylvania the same validity in New Jersey.[43] This act had

---

[41] Cox, MS. *Transcript*, 31, 40. A count of the names classed as servants in Bucks County, in the early arrivals (1677-1681) gives sixty-seven.

[42] For these there is no mention of time of service or land bounty. Original MS. *Record of Arrivals* for September 10, 1685. William Penn is credited by Geiser (*Redemptioners*, 26) with a statement that two servants to a family of five was the proper relation of freemen and servants. Geiser thinks that the proportion of servants was larger than this. Of the early immigrants into Maryland the probable ratio of servants to freemen is given as six to one. McCormac, *White Servitude in Maryland*, 28.

[43] *Duke's Book of Laws*, 168, 169; *Votes of Assembly*, I, 26. A similar arrangement had been made in the New England Confederation of

disappeared in 1693, and there was no reënactment of it for a long period, though the same general principle was involved in a law permitting slaves to come from New Jersey duty free, in the eighteenth century, and in suspending the duty on certain articles from West New Jersey and the lower counties.[44]

The provisions above noted are illustrations of Penn's advanced notions of government; the same principles were expressed in his "Plan for Union." The sixth section of the plan provided for the adjustment of differences between colonies on account of offenders who had fled from justice or those who had sought by going to other colonies to escape obligation, and was clearly meant to apply to runaway servants.[45] Property in white servants was recognized by early legislation (December, 1682), as was property in slaves. An act was passed that neither slaves nor white servants were attachable for debts, "to the end that the means of livelihood" should not be taken away.[46]

A law making registry necessary for servants as well as freemen was passed in 1684;[47] a further law concerning rewards for apprehending a runaway servant was passed in May, 1685.[48] The system seems to have been disturbed very little by the complications attending the suspension of William Penn's government and the establishment of Benjamin Fletcher's authority as lieutenant-governor in 1693. In a petition for laws, made by the

---

1643. Following is the eighth article of the Plan of Union which the Confederation adopted:

"It is also agreed that if any servant run away from his master into any other of these confederated Jurisdiccons, That in such Case, vpon the Certyficate of one Majistrate in the Jurisdiccon out of which the said servant fled, or upon other due proofe, the said servant shall be deliuered either to his Master or any other that pursues and brings such Certificate or proofe." Preston, *Documents Illustrative of American History*, 92.

[44] *Votes*, II, 302.

[45] *Plan for Union*, "Memoirs of the Historical Society of Pennsylvania," VI, 264, 265. For William Penn's ideas on the theory and practice of government, see Bettle, *Notices of Negro Slavery*, 354.

[46] *Duke's Laws*, 152; reenacted 1693, ibid., 212.

[47] *Ibid.*, 170.

[48] *Ibid.*, 177.

freemen, the laws governing the servant system were enumerated. Among the laws passed under Fletcher's administration, one is of interest which provided that in case of debt, if no estate were found and if the creditor so desired, the debtor should satisfy the debt by such servitude as the county court might order.[49]

Occasional controversies which reached the colonial council and the courts show that servants were sold within the province. In 1683, one who had parted with a servant petitioned the council for aid in securing payment. The council, after taking the matter into consideration, appointed a committee to aid in making collection.[50] Free labor was scarce for fifteen years after the settlement of Penn and commanded good return. Unskilled workmen had fourteen to fifteen pounds a year with their living. Women had from six to ten pounds a year with what was termed a good living. Workmen by the day could command from eighteen pence to half a crown and their keep, though in harvest they had three to four shillings a day and food.[51]

Indentured servants brought less than one-half as much per year as could be commanded by free laborers. Explanations of this difference are suggested in the "freedom dues" which the master furnished when the service was completed, in the possibility of the servant's running away, and in the fact that he could shirk more than would be permitted to a free laborer. A craftsman, either as free laborer or servant, would command considerably more in the colonial market than could be secured for an ordinary toiler. The time still to serve, physical condition, nationality, and employment for which servants were suited, all affected the price for which they could be sold.[52]

---

[49] *Ibid.*, 200.

[50] "Councill held at Philadelphia ye 20th 1st Mo. 1683." "The petieon of Nathaniell Allen was read, shewing that he had sould a serv^t to Henry Bowman, for six hundred weight of beefe, wth ye hide & Tallow & six pounds sterl., which ye said Bowman delayed to pay ye said Peticoner." The Council quaintly ordered that three of its members "should speak to Henry Bowman concerning this matter." *Colonial Records,* I, 63.

[51] Thomas, *History of Pennsylvania,* 32, 33.

[52] See *post,* Chapter X, for prices of servants.

Pennypacker's account of the colonial cases tried before 1700, and the Pennsylvania *Colonial Records,* show that the courts and the provincial council, which served as a form of higher court, had repeatedly to do with litigation growing out of dealings with servants.   Robert Terrill was early brought before the council on the double charge of selling rum to the Indians and of entertaining other people's servants unlawfully.   The accused was reprimanded and a proclamation was ordered to suppress such practices.[53]   In 1685, the county court of Philadelphia petitioned the council for a decision in a case where the rights of selling servants out of the province were involved.   After securing evidence from the court, the master of the ship against whom the charge was made was summoned and presented his indentures.   It was found that these passengers could not claim protection under the law to prevent servants, under indenture to be brought to Pennsylvania, from being sold to any other place without their consent.[54]

The following table of values of servants in Virginia based upon the county records is offered as an approximation for that colony:

MALE SERVANTS

1 year to serve, 2 to 4 pounds sterling
2   "   "   "   6 " 8   "   "
3   "   "   "   8 " 14   "   "
4   "   "   "   11 " 15   "   "
5   "   "   "   12 " 16   "   "
6   "   "   "   13 " 17   "   "

FEMALE SERVANTS

1 year to serve, 1 to 3 pounds sterling
2   "   "   "   3 " 5   "   "
3   "   "   "   4 " 8   "   "
4   "   "   "   8 " 12   "   "
5   "   "   "   12 " 14   "   "
6   "   "   "   not to exceed fifteen pounds.

Bruce, *Economic History of Virginia,* II, 51, 52.

[53] *Colonial Records,* I, 117.

[54] Act, below, Appendix I. The record of this case is as follows: "Petition from ye County court of Philadelphia was read, sitting forth that severall servants brought from England in ye Last Ship that came hether, that are to serve in this province, and yt ye Master Intends to Carry them to Virginia, wch is Contrary to ye Laws of the Province, Requesting ye Councills Consideration of the same.

"Ordered yt ye Messenger given notice to ye Mr. of ye Ship to appear

The law last noted was also involved with different results in a case that came to the Philadelphia court from New Castle. The record of the petition was: "Hee is an indented servant to ffrancis Scot & is willing to serve him or any other in this province, but yt his said Mr. intends to sell him out of the province into foreign parts agt the petitioners will, & to that end hath got yee petitioner on board a ship & threatens to put him in Irons to carie him away, and yrfor craving release that hee may stay in this province and serve his time." An examination of both parties in the open court showed that the master did intend to send the servant out of the province, and to that end had gotten him on board a ship, but the servant escaped in the ship's boat. Scott was directed, first, not to sell his servant, except according to law; and second, he was bound under the sum of thirteen pounds to take his servant to New Castle, and there present him before magistrates, "and by them be ordered as they should see cause." [55]

A case involving an attempt to recover damages for harboring a runaway came before the court thus early.[56] The plaintiff claimed that the defendant had harbored his servant contrary to the statute, and sued for fourteen pounds ten shillings damages (at the rate of five shillings per day). Defense was entered that the servant had been illtreated by the plaintiff, and that he had not been able to find a justice in New Castle, where he lived, before whom to bring the case; hence he had fled to the defendant for protection. The finding in the case was for the defendant. "Even in that early day," added Pennypacker, "a jury in the Quaker province declined to punish a man for giving succor to an abused runaway." A further examination of the legal procedure shows that the same courts which remanded offenders to servitude for unpaid fines or debts, that bound out poor children until they were

---

before ye Councill tomorrow morning." The record for the following day shows that the master of the ship appeared before the Council and presented the indentures of the servants, which being read, "they Rann to serve James Skinner from ye Day of ye Date untill their first arrivall in Virginia, or any other part of America, and after, for and duringe the terme of four years." *Colonial Records*, I, 161, 162.

[55] Pennypacker, *Colonial Cases from MS. Docket*, 77, 78.

[56] "William Guest vs. Philip England," Pennypacker, *Colonial Cases*, 96-98.

twenty-one, and that lengthened the terms of servants for running away or other damages, also protected all of these persons against illtreatment from their masters.

Another dispute over the term of service found its way to court where the master was ordered to free the servant from the indentures, to pay freedom dues according to the custom of the country, and to assume all costs.[57]   In early cases, involving a conflict of the rights of master and servant, the decision was generally in favor of the servant.

From 1694 to 1700, laws were passed in Pennsylvania affecting such matters as general administration, regulation of trade, and rates of interest, but no record has been found of any new act governing the servant system.   By the close of the seventeenth century Pennsylvania's period of beginnings was at an end.   The tide of English, Scotch, Irish, and German immigration had set in; foundations of future industrial development were laid; proprietor and people had gained wisdom by experience; ships had brought from overseas the seeds of a prosperous future; and well might the benevolent founder say, "I have led the greatest colony into the New World that ever any man did on private credit," and that "the most prosperous beginnings" which ever were made in America were made in his settlement.   In the eighteenth century, Pennsylvania entered on a period of unprecedented prosperity.   The servant system had to do with inaugurating the new epoch, and for more than a hundred years continued an essential part of it.

---

[57] Pennypacker, *Colonial Cases,* 110.

PART II. DEMAND FOR INDENTURED AND REDEMPTION SERVANTS IN PENNSYLVANIA

CHAPTER III

DEMAND FOR SETTLERS CREATED A DEMAND FOR INDENTURED SERVANTS

Under the conditions of her economic life, western Europe had a lack of employment contemporaneous with the opening of the New World to settlement. It was because men had but a slight chance in the old home that they were willing to stake so much on the uncertainties of life in a new and untried land. Conditions in the colonies as compared with Europe were, it may be said, in the nature of repulsion and attraction, complementary to each other.[1]

Attractions were sent forth in various forms from all the colonies. White laborers were requested by the governor of Barbadoes in letters to the home government in the seventeenth century. One of these to Secretary Lord Arlington was significant: Europe was termed a "magazine of people," and it was requested that His Majesty should send a constant supply of these to the colonies. Loss of whites as well as Negroes in colonization was considerable, and was deplored by those who regarded the welfare of the colonies directly, as well as by those who felt that the population of the mother country was being swallowed up in colonial ventures. In the letter mentioned, the governor of Barbadoes lamented what he termed the "woeful loss" of those who came from old settlements.[2] When the first chapter in British colonization in America was closed, it was felt that not more than one-fifth of those sent out had adjusted themselves, and gained a permanent settlement. James Anderson, in writing on England's relations with her colonies in 1782, contrasted the possible advantages to England had additional manufactures been introduced at home instead of founding colonies. It was thought that not only could England have kept her population by such

---

[1] Bruce, *Economic History of Virginia*, I, 575, 576.
[2] *Cal. State Papers*, "Colonial Series," 1661-1668, p. 217.

policy, but that she would also have gained by immigration; and, besides, she would have been spared the expenditure for colonial defense. It was urged that emigration be forbidden, and that a counter-attraction be offered at home and the statement was added that "the interest of Great Britain has been hurt by the establishment of her North American colonies." Anderson found a crumb of comfort, however, in the possibilities of future trade advantages as a return for the loss.[3] The position here taken was in no sense exceptional, rather, it was the exception to find such advanced thinkers as Burke and Franklin occupying another position. Burke said that it was not well understood how a country could grow more populous by sending a part of its population away, but he found the truth of this seeming paradox in that people sent out led to prosperity, and that with this there was no danger of depopulating, for other people would come to take the places of those who had gone.[4] Franklin, earlier (1751), in his *"Observations on the Increase of Mankind and the Peopling of Countries"* (in which he used the unfortunate word "boors" as applied to Palatines), urged that Englishmen and not Germans should be utilized for colonies; he argued that the Englishmen who thus settled would increase rapidly, and that their places at home would soon be supplied because of the prosperity that would result from a healthy settlement.[5]

Pennsylvania was founded at the beginning of a new era in English colonization. William Penn was the first among the promoters of colonial enterprise in England to practice "systematic colonization," and in adopting this policy, he was only putting into practice the lessons of the Dutch.[6] In systematic colonization

---

[3] Anderson, *The Interest of Great Britain with Regard to her American Colonies Considered,* 87, 109, 116, and Appendix, 35. Anderson further speaks of the rapid increase of population that had firmly settled in North America, holding that in a healthy country with a plentiful food supply, the population would increase by about two-thirds of the original number in thirty years. He, however, contradicts his main contention in a passage in which he says that while England had lost some of her population, it was more than made up in the gain to commerce and industry. *The Interest of Great Britain,* 70, 71.

[4] *European Settlements,* II, 292-294.

[5] Franklin, *Works* (Bigelow), II, 233, 234.

[6] Payne, *European Colonies,* 106, 107.

settlers were a first requisite. Increased population in a colony made a demand for additional immigration. Pennsylvania's population increased rapidly from the first; until the outbreak of the Revolution, Pennsylvania's supply of European settlers never received any serious check. In the period immediately preceding the Puritan Revolution emigrant ships which were to sail from the mother country to New England were detained. To guard against any such policy being practiced to retard the growth of his colony, Penn secured the grant that emigrants should have "license and liberty" to go to the colony and to transport "convenient shipping." [7]

Two other conditions bore directly on Pennsylvania's prosperity and increase of population, viz., the granting of political and religious privileges and the maintaining of harmonious relations with the Indians. Penn's frame of government and early laws were all in strict accord with the principle that a government should be administered for the good of the governed.[8] Though Penn, by his charter, was constituted true and absolute proprietor, subject only to the king of England, he made most wise and moderate use of his power. His first letter to the people of the territory was, "You are now fixed at the mercy of no governor who comes to make his fortune great; you shall be governed by laws of your own making, and live a free, and if you will, a sober and industrious people." Few countries or settlements illustrate better Sir Walter Raleigh's saying, "No nation can want people that has good laws." Privileges granted to them made the people of Pennsylvania jealous of their rights, and Penn's successors were compelled to acknowledge the political freedom and continue the grants begun by him. Whatever the factional struggles, however we may regard the contests of proprietary party and popular party, it was the spirit of William Penn, wise lawgiver and magnanimous governor, that dominated in the rule of Pennsylvania until 1776. Just before the Revolution, Crève-cœur, writing for European readers, thus estimated Penn as the organizer of a colony: "The wisdom of Lycurgus and Solon never conferred upon man one-half of the blessings and uninterrupted prosperity which the Pennsylvanians now possess; the name of

---

[7] Charter, *Duke's Book of Laws,* 85.
[8] *Duke's Laws,* 91-103.

Penn, that simple but illustrious citizen, does more honor to the English nation than those of many of their kings." [9] Repeatedly explanation of prosperity in Pennsylvania was coupled with liberal government; in 1739 this was put forth as the sole explanation of the good times then being enjoyed: "It is not to the fertility of our soil or the commodiousness of our rivers that we ought chiefly to attribute the great progress this province has made, within so small a compass of years, in improvements, wealth, trade and navigation, and the extraordinary increase of people who have been drawn from every country in Europe; it is all due to the excellency of our Constitution. Our foreign trade and shipping are free from all imposts, except those small duties payable to his Majesty by the statute laws of Great Britain. The taxes are inconsiderable." [10]

Freedom of religious worship was well known and made Pennsylvania a haven of refuge for the persecuted, as well as a place of choice for those of peculiar religious beliefs. As a result the colony had a population of mixed denominations and sects. "The colony possesses great liberties," said an eighteenth century traveler, "above all other English colonies, inasmuch as all religious sects are tolerated. We find there Lutherans, Reformed, Catholics, Quakers, Mennonists or Anabaptists, Herrnhuters or Moravian Brethren, Pietists, Seventh Day Baptists, Dunkers, Presbyterians, Newborn, Freemasons, Separatists, Freethinkers, Jews, Mohammedans, Pagans, Negroes and Indians." [11]

Reasonable security against Indian attack was not without influence in attracting Europeans as settlers in Pennsylvania. Indian outbreaks were frequent in most other colonies, and accounts of them no doubt were much exaggerated to keep would-

---

[9] Crèvecœur, *Letters from an American Farmer,* 247.

[10] Andrew Hamilton on retiring as speaker of the Assembly, 1739. Cited in Sharpless, *Quaker Experiment in Government,* 55, 56.

[11] Mittelberger, *Journey to Pennsylvania* (Translation), 54. "Pennsylvania, therefore, and its appendage Delaware, profited by the late date at which they were founded; they represented a more advanced stage of opinion than the colonies which started in the time of James I. Their proprietary government remained undisturbed until the Declaration of Independence, and in 1776 these two states were the only ones in which all Christians, whether Protestants or Catholic, stood socially and politically on an equal footing." Fiske, *A Century of Science,* 138.

be emigrants at home, but the success of the Quaker peace policy was well known. Voltaire uttered a current thought of the time when he stated that the Shackamaxon treaty was the only one never sworn to and the only one never broken. Freedom from Indian outbreak removed from Pennsylvania a barrier to immigration which was raised against other colonies. Life and property alike were here secure, and industry rested on the foundations of plentiful population and liberal supplies of capital.

Political and religious privilege and economic security were inseparable from the industrial development of the Quaker colony, but the wise proprietor was not content to let these privileges and the prosperity that followed in their track do unaided the work of securing settlers. He carried on a well-planned and active campaign of solicitation in which were set forth the natural advantages of the colony, the opportunities offered to settlers, and the ways by which these opportunities might be realized. These efforts to secure settlers were directed mainly to Great Britain and Germany, to a less degree to Holland and France, and they were not without influence in Switzerland and other European countries. In some cases the appeal was directly for servants; generally it was not, but the influence upon the servant system could not but have been considerable.

Immediately following his grant, Penn had published in London *Some Account of the Province of Pennsilvania* (1681), which, in addition to an argument in favor of colonies, furnished a description of Pennsylvania, recited the conditions on which it was to be settled, and gave information to those who wished to emigrate. The following year saw Penn's *Brief Account,* also Loddington's *Plantation Work the Work of this Generation,* which has sometimes been credited to George Fox. In 1682, Penn's *Frame of Government* with the accompanying *Laws Agreed upon in England,* appeared as a pamphlet.

Soon after the securing of the charter the Free Society of Traders in London was organized, a society which purchased twenty thousand acres of land in the colony and stimulated emigration.[12] It was to this society that Penn sent the letter said by Frederick D. Stone to have been the most important of all

---

[12] Proud, *History of Pennsylvania,* I, 191, 192.

the early pamphlets. This letter, written after a residence of some months in the colony, "may be considered a report from personal observation of what he found his colony to be." [13]   In the same period a pamphlet was published in London entitled *Information and Direction to such Persons as are inclined to America, more especially those related to the Province of Pennsylvania.* The authorship of this is not certain, but if it was not written by Penn himself, it was, without doubt, written at his suggestion. The heading of the pamphlet is followed on the title-page by an enumeration of the advantages in the colony.[14]   *A Planter's Speech to his Friends in London* was issued in 1684,[15] as was Thomas Budd's *Good Order Established in Pennsylvania,* in 1685; and in the same year the second most important description, William Penn's *Further Account.* These are but part of the early propaganda for settlers, distributed in England, and several of these pamphlets had successive editions.

A more elaborate work than any of the preceding was the interesting and attractive early account of Pennsylvania given by Gabriel Thomas. Thomas came in the first ship with settlers in 1681,[16] and thirteen years later he undertook to give an account of what he termed "The Richness of the Soil, the sweetness of the situation, the wholesomeness of the Air, the Navigable Rivers, and thus the prodigious Increase of Corn, the flourishing Condition of the City of Philadelphia." [17]   This history was dedicated to William Penn, and the work was spoken of as "a true and genuine Description of that (once) obscure, tho' (now) glorious

---

[13] Letter in full, Proud, I, 246-264.   See Stone, in Winsor, *Narrative and Critical History,* III, 498.

[14] The following summary precedes the body of the pamphlet:

"I.   The Advance that is upon Money and Goods.

"II.   The Advance that is upon Labour be it of Handicraft or others.

"III.   The Advance that is upon Land.

"IV.   The Charge of Transporting a Family, and Fitting a Plantation.

"V.   The way the Poorer Sort may be Transported, and Seated with Advantage to the Rich that help them."

(Sachse, *Fatherland.* Appendix, Plate 13, photographic reproduction of page.)

[15] Proud, *History of Pennsylvania,* I, 226.

[16] Thomas, *History of Pennsylvania,* 45.

[17] Dedication and title-page of *History of Pennsylvania.*

Place." Gabriel Thomas described the climate of the country, the harvest, and the method of clearing land,[18] and went on to speak of the general high wages that could be obtained. Under the latter head he said, "Poor People, both Men and Women, can here get three times the Wages for their Labor they can in ENGLAND or WALES." [19] Certain occupations were spoken of with their remunerations: A blacksmith, with one Negro helper, made fifty shillings in one day's labor; carpenters (both house and ship), bricklayers, and masons would receive from five to six shillings per day; shoemakers, tailors, weavers, tanners, curriers, sawyers, bricklayers, feltmakers, glaziers, coopers, butchers, bakers, wheelwrights, millwrights, binders, ropemakers, gunsmiths, printers, and bookbinders were enumerated, and it was said that they were all in demand, and that their services would be well rewarded.[20] It is obvious that the purpose of Thomas was to get settlers. He was, however, so eager to make Pennsylvania attractive that he seems to have overreached himself. In one place he claimed that farmers would get a good price for their grain in the trade to Barbadoes,[21] but in speaking of the food of the laborers, he says, "Corn and flesh and what ever else serves Man for Drink, Food and Rayment, is much cheaper here than in England or ELSEWHERE." [22]

If there were uncertainty as to the purpose of Gabriel Thomas, the appeal in his conclusion would remove it: "Reader, what I have here written is not a *Fiction, Flam, Whim* or any sinister *Design*, either to impose upon the Ignorant or Credulous, or to curry Favour with the Rich and Mighty, but in meer Pity and Pure Compassion to the Numbers of Poor Labouring Men, Women and Children in ENGLAND, half starv'd, visible in their meagre looks, that are continually wandering up and down, looking for Employment without finding any, who here need not lie idle a moment, nor want due Encouragement or Reward for their work. . . . Here are no beggars to be seen. . . . nor,

---

[18] Thomas, *History of Pennsylvania*, 7.
[19] *Ibid.*, 9, 28.
[20] *Ibid.*, 28, 32.
[21] *Ibid.*, 34, 35.
[22] *Ibid.*, 33.

indeed, have any here the least Occasion or Temptation to take up that Scandalous, Lazy Life." [23]

Such a work as that interesting account of the servant system of Maryland in the seventeenth century, given by George Alsop in his *Character of the Province of Mary-land,* must have been effective in emphasizing the demand for laborers in all the colonies. Alsop had come over as a servant in 1658, and so continued for four years; then he returned to England and published his account. It was dedicated to Lord Baltimore, and the merchant adventurers, and "we may infer that it was paid for by them." [24] There were four parts to the tract, of which the third was "the worst and best Usage of a Mary-land Servant, opened in view." Alsop was a rollicking, ignorant and adventuresome fellow, who might have gone to Maryland from choice, or he might have been transported by the commonwealth.[25] His address was coarse and careless, and from the style of his book one might safely infer that it was intended to reach the lower classes; but the appeal was to these classes more direct. He recommended the well-to-do to stay in London, but the "low" were advised to remove to Maryland.[26]

Alsop was engaged on a plantation near Baltimore. "The four years I served there," he says of his life, "were not to me so slavish as a two years' Servitude of a Handicraft Apprenticeship was here in London." His life is described as five and one-half days of service a week in summer, with three hours in the middle of the day for rest, and little or no work in winter. Later, he claims that "the servitude was regarded as but an apprenticeship to set up on one's own account when this apprenticeship ended." Women servants were said to be especially fortunate

---

[23] *Ibid.,* 43, 44. Mittleberger also says that in 1750 there were in Pennsylvania no beggars, for each locality looked after its *own* poor. *Journey to Pennsylvania,* 67.

Just at the outbreak of the Revolution we have another "pleasing view of this abundance . . . never disturbed by the melancholy sight of poverty," for, we are told, there was "no want in Pennsylvania," instead there was "a spirit of benevolence" and a "most engaging hospitality." Raynal, *British Settlements,* I, 164, 165.

[24] Maryland Historical Society Edition, Introduction, 10.

[25] *Ibid.,* 9.

[26] *Ibid.,* 55.

in the arrangements they could make on arrival, because women were so largely in demand.[27]   Alsop concluded his account of servant life with this appeal: "That which I have to say more in this business, is a hearty and desirous wish, that the several poor Tradesmen here in *London* that I know, and have borne an ocular testimony of their want, might live so free from care as I did when I dwelt in the bonds of a four years' Servitude in Maryland." [28]   One may be disposed to question the honesty of George Alsop, and the accuracy of his description, but it is beyond question that he described a system largely practiced, and that his description stimulated emigration under indentures.

The second most important demand of Pennsylvania for laborers was upon Germany.   Until about 1800, Philadelphia was at once the objective of German emigration and the distributing point for German settlers.   There was between the Quaker and the German a good deal of sympathy, a fact to be kept in mind in accounting for the large numbers of Germans who came, as well as in explaining the alliances of Germans and Quakers for the control of the Pennsylvania Colonial Assembly.[29]

The founder of Pennsylvania was half Dutch, his mother being the daughter of an Amsterdam merchant.[30]   Penn by travel and acquaintance prepared the way for the coming of Dutch and German settlers, but these in the main were without means or had but limited means.   They availed themselves of the aid that was offered, at first by some society or church, later largely by ship's companies.   Penn made several journeys, apostolic or missionary, through Holland and Germany, teaching and preaching.   The most important of these was in 1677 and this has been described at length.   Penn was accompanied by George Fox and other Friends, and throughout the journey he kept a diary which fortunately was preserved.   It is worthy of note that this mission was not

---

[27] *Ibid.*, 54, 57-59.

[28] *Ibid.*, 63.

[29] Gerhard Croese, *History of Quakers,* Cited in Pennypacker, *Settlement of Germantown,* 212.

[30] Seidensticker, "Penn's Travels," *Pennsylvania Magazine History and Biography,* II, 277 sqq.

fruitless.[31]   The journey extended over a period of three months, during which time Penn visited the sections of Germany that were rendered the most desolate by religious persecutions and wars. One result of this journey was to bring Penn into personal contact with many of the German mystics and religious leaders of the period.   One charge brought against German pietism is that it "paved the way for Quakerism and other heresies."[32]   Whether this be true or not is not important to the present discussion; it is true that there was much similarity of thought between the German mystics and the Quakers.

The journeys of Penn, and his acquaintance with Germans were important in turning the tide of German migration to his colony.   Large numbers did not come at once, nor even during Penn's life, yet the way had been opened for the future inflow. Both Penn and his agent in Holland, Benjamin Furly, looked to Germany for colonists.   For a number of years after Penn's grant, Furly was at Amsterdam publishing descriptions of the colony and furthering emigration.   Most of the publications were German and Dutch translations of the descriptions earlier circulated in England, though some of them were new.   The propaganda not formerly published was chiefly letters and descriptions.   One of these was from *Cornelius Bom,* printed in Rotterdam in 1685.   Bom, whose description was written the preceding year, said of Pennsylvania that nowhere in history could be found another instance of such remarkable growth of a new country, and that immigrants were coming from many parts of the world. Further, the favorable situation of Philadelphia for trade would, it was thought, bring the entire country "into a good condition." [33] Other letters similar in character were received about this time. One written from Germantown by Joris Wertmuller referred directly to the servant system: "If anyone can come here in this land at his own expense, and reaches here in good health, he will be rich enough, especially if he can bring his family or some

---

[31] Judge Pennypacker records the conversion of Germans to Quakerism and the migration of whole families from Kriegsheim to Germantown. *Settlement of Germantown,* 14-16.

[32] Seidensticker, "Penn's Travels," 251, 252.

[33] Translated from the Dutch by S. W. Pennypacker and printed in his *Hendrick Pannebecker,* 32-37.

man-servants, because servants are here very dear. People bind themselves for three or four years' service for a great price, and for women they give more than for men, because they are scarce. A good servant can place himself with a master for a hundred guldens a year and board." [34]

A letter from Jacob Telner termed the country "an exceptionally excellent land," and declared that those who attempted to belittle it were unworthy of attention.[35] At the time these favorable reports from Pennsylvania were being circulated there was issued a *Collection of Various Pieces Concerning Pennsylvania,* gathered and published by Benjamin Furly.[36] In this it was stated that the country was inhabited by Swedes, Hollanders, and English, and that these settlers would furnish necessities for newcomers until they should be able to provide for themselves. There was embodied a statement that servants, at the expiration of their service, would gain land and become citizens, and then follows: "He [Penn] gives notice that those who have not wherewith to pay, will find good masters who, for four years' service, according to the custom of the colonies, will have them taken over, that period being finished they will be free and will have fifty acres of land forever, at the same price as other servants."[37]

Immediately following the grant to Penn, two companies were formed in Germany, looking to settlements in Pennsylvania. One was the Frankfort Land Company, in which Pastorius was interested; the other was the Crefeld Company. The Frankfort Company was formed in 1682, as a result of Penn's visit to Germany in 1677. This company was instrumental in the settlement of Germantown in 1683. As it chanced, the parts of Germany visited by Penn were soon to be invaded and ruthlessly ravaged by the armies of Louis XIV, and soon Germans were seeking some escape from the devastation of that invasion.[38] Pennsylvania

---

[34] Wertmuller, March 16, 1684. Pennypacker, *Settlement of Germantown,* 102, and *Hendrick Pannebecker,* 30.

[35] *Hendrick Pannebecker,* 38, 39.

[36] Reprinted in *Pa. Mag. of Hist. and Biog.,* VI., 312 sqq.

[37] *Ibid.,* 312, 316, 318.

[38] Seidensticker, "Penn's Travels," *Pa. Mag. of Hist. and Biog.,* II, 263; Sachse, *Fatherland,* 143, 144; Pennypacker, *Historical and Biographical Sketches,* 21.

was a way opened. "It was thus William Penn himself who opened
the gate through which Germany poured a continuous and widen-
ing stream of emigration into the new province." [39]   One of the
ablest of Pennsylvania's Quaker historians was of the opinion that
Penn returned in person to Holland and Germany about 1686.
At the same time when Penn's invitations and the favorable reports of his early settlers were being widely circulated in Germany, the Germans who had settled in New York "spread the
story of their wrongs far and wide among their kinsmen," thus
turning the tide from New York.[40]

The early German settlers of Pennsylvania, on the other hand,
invited their countrymen from over the seas.   Pastorius found
in the colony in 1684 people from Brandenburg, Schleswig, Hol-
stein, Switzerland, and other districts,[41] and reports from these
supplemented the work of Penn and Furly in securing settlers.
The Frankfort Land Company, too, was active.   Daniel Falcker's
efforts were added to those of Pastorius, and descriptions were
published simultaneously at Frankfort and Leipzig.   An agent
of the Frankfort Company was in Pennsylvania in 1694 and 1700,
and in 1702 there was issued at Frankfort a history of the colony
said to be for the information of those interested.   The work was
in the form of questions and answers, and there were one hundred
and three of these in all.   Among the special points considered
were descriptions of the country, an account of the inhabitants,
including the Indians, and directions for reaching America.[42]
One result of the Mennonite settlement was the establishment
of harmonious relations and close communication between the
branches of this Society in Germany and in the colony.[43]

References to people's bringing servants with them, and the
record of arrivals, indicate that in the main these early Germans
came, as did early Englishmen, either as proprietors or in the

---

[39] Proud, *Hist. of Pa.,* I, 302, 303.

[40] Jacobs, *German Emigration,* 135.

[41] Pennypacker, *Settlement of Germantown,* 89.

[42] Stone, in Winsor, *Narrative and Critical History,* III, 502.

[43] Scheffer, *Pa. Mag. Hist. and Biog.,* II, 117.   Money was sent out
from the Ephrata community in Pennsylvania to pay passage of poor
laborers who wished to come to the New World but had not means to do so.

service of proprietors.[44] As the whole German migration was not large in the early period, it may safely be inferred that the number of German servants during the corresponding time was not considerable. The account here given is rather as a preliminary to the later German migration than for its importance because of its own proportions.[45]

Results of the various demands for settlers were quickly seen in the increase of Pennsylvania's population. In the history of American colonies Pennsylvania's growth was unprecedented. Twenty-three ships of immigrants came during the fall of 1682 and the winter following. In 1685, the population was 7200, including English, Scotch, Irish, Dutch, Swedes, Finns, and French. Penn thought that the English at this time were not more than one-half of the total population.[46] The cosmopolitan population attracted attention. An early act of naturalization for the Swedes added political enfranchisement to religious liberty.[47] The minister of the Swedes said in 1697, "The English have received us extremely well, and some of them even came to our meetings. . . . Our language is preserved as pure as anywhere in Sweden. There are about twelve hundred persons that speak it. There are Welshmen who speak their own mother tongue, besides Englishmen, Dutchmen and some Frenchmen."[48] In the appli-

---

[44] Record of arrival of "American," June 20, 1683. Had on board "Jacob Shoemaker, born in ye Palatinate, in Germany, servant to Danl Pastorius & Compa." MS. in Library of Hist. Soc. Pa.

[45] The writer chooses to follow Rupp, *Introduction to Thirty Thousand German Names,* Pennypacker, *Settlement of Germantown,* and Seidensticker, rather than Diffenderffer, *German Immigration into Pennsylvania.*

[46] Stone, in Winsor, *Narrative and Critical History,* III, 491, 492.

[47] *Ibid.,* 485.

[48] Rev. Andrew Rudman, cited in Holm, *Short Description of New Sweden.* "Memoirs of the Historical Society of Pennsylvania," III, 102.

Gabriel Thomas, with an almost contemporaneous account of the colony, says that its population was above twenty thousand on a modest computation. *History of Pennsylvania,* 37, 38.

The following estimate is made of the population in the colonies in 1700, by Abiel Holmes (*American Annals,* II, 54): 262,000 in all; 120,000 in New England; 142,000 in the middle and southern colonies; and 20,000 in Pennsylvania.

cation of the Quaker principle of brotherly love, adherents of all faiths, or of no faith, were equally welcome.

Penn, as soon as he secured his grant, made known the liberal character of the constitution he proposed; his aim was to promote human happiness, and the Pennsylvania settlement was the practical means to realize this end.[49] Within half a century after Penn's death, one of the greatest political writers of the eighteenth century could say that while Penn was not held in high estimation as a theologian, at least not outside of the Society of Friends, he was regarded by the world at large as a political writer of force and the founder of a successful commonwealth.[50] When the privileges offered in Pennsylvania were made known, "humanity went through Europe gathering the children of misfortune. From England and Wales, from Scotland, Ireland and the Low Countries . . .   on the banks of the Rhine and from the highlands above Worms, the humble people renounced their German homes." [51] The policy of Penn was the policy of proprietors who succeeded him, and ultimately of the commonwealth that succeeded them.

When the Colonial Assembly was charged by Governor George Thomas (1741-1742) with looking with disfavor upon the "yearly increase of Germans," it was disavowed in the following positive terms: "Who they are that look with jealous eyes on the Germans the Governor has not been pleased to inform us, nor do we know; Nothing of the kind can be justly attributed to Us or any preceding Assembly to our knowledge; On the Contrary, the Legislature of this Province, before the late Provision made in the Parliament of Great Britain, have generally . . . admitted the Germans to partake of the Privileges enjoyed by the King's natural born Subjects here." Later the same body declared, "it is evident that the greater the number of people which come into the Province the more the Proprietor's Interest is advanced." [52]

The number of servants received was not sufficient to supply the demand. A petition of Philadelphia merchants in 1761 called

---

[49] Proud, *History of Pennsylvania,* I, 167-169.
[50] Burke, *European Settlements,* II, 195-198.
[51] Bancroft, *History of the United States,* I, 568, 569.
[52] *Colonial Records,* IV, 508, 509.

attention to the inconvenience that resulted from lack of "laborers and artificers," and said that the importation of German and other white servants had nearly ceased. Tench Coxe could well say of Pennsylvania that it had been the policy, both preceding and following the Revolution, to "receive all sober immigrants with open arms" and to give them the free exercise of their trades, their occupations, and their religion.[53]

Pennsylvania's demand for white servants was in part a demand for foreigners, and as such it was disapproved by some who had to do with colonial affairs. One result of this demand was a population which was cosmopolitan, and somewhat alien. This had its immediate effect in the diverse character of Pennsylvania's industry. But in general the immigration of aliens was looked upon with favor by colonial writers; Burke mentioned it with approval. In 1774, Washington also wrote on German immigration to James Tilghman, of Philadelphia, saying that personal and political motives made it necessary that he settle his lands on the Ohio River "in the cheapest, most expeditious and most effective manner." Many expedients, he said, had been offered, but he thought most favorably of securing Palatines. He said that he wrote therefore to Philadelphia to learn how these could be secured on the most favorable terms. Further, he could not understand why so few Germans came to Virginia.[54]

The answer to Washington's question is clear in the light of what is now known of Pennsylvania's pressing demand for settlers. Phineas Bond, the British consul at Philadelphia in 1791, who had spent most of his life in America, significantly commented on a Pennsylvania law favorable to aliens: "This regulation is con-

---

[53] *View of the United States,* 74.

[54] *Washington's Writings* (Sparks Edition), II, 382, 383.

Washington, with his businesslike directness, suggested the following questions to be answered by the traders engaged in the business: Was there difficulty in obtaining these people in Holland, and if so why? Were they engaged at any time or were particular seasons more favorable? Were they engaged previously or on arrival of ship? Upon what terms was engagement made, and what did these people stand the importer on their arrival in Philadelphia? Was it customary to send an intelligent German? Did the ships carry an outgoing cargo and if so what? And, finally, what was the best plan for importing two hundred or more Palatines to Alexandria?

formable to that policy which has uniformly prevailed in Pennsylvania to influence migrations hither from foreign countries as the most decided mode of increasing the consequence of this State; but . . . it is fit it should be understood that regulations of this sort *only* prevail in *this* state—no general plan of naturalization, whereby aliens are rendered competent to hold and to transmit their possessions to their representatives, exists *out* of this State." [55]

For more than a century following the founding of Pennsylvania an unmistakable demand for settlers was a demand for indentured and redemption servants. From the foundation of the colony through the eighteenth century, Pennsylvania's demand for servants was made effective through being registered where it would attract a goodly supply of these settlers.

---

[55] Bond, "Letters." *Annual Report of the American Historical Association for 1897*, 482. The italics are in the report.

CHAPTER IV

DEMAND FOR WHITE SERVANTS DUE TO DIVERSIFIED INDUSTRY

The English, Irish, Scotch, and German immigrants who settled in Pennsylvania early began manufactures. Pennsylvania was settled after the initial difficulties in New World colonization had been overcome. The early explorers could get settlers only by appealing to gold as a lodestar, and settlers came out expecting to amass wealth and return. This phase of colonization had passed when Pennsylvania was founded. In general it may be said that the working classes emigrate only after the ground has been broken by the adventurers.[1]

Manufacture was fostered by Pennsylvania's colonial government, and eighteenth century writers regarded Pennsylvania's commerce and industry as exceptional, both in extent and variety. In 1710, the city of Philadelphia was termed "noble, large and populous."[2] In general, after 1730 Pennsylvania was regarded as one of the leading industrial and commercial settlements of America. It was in part to satisfy the labor demand of an industrial community with diversified production that the indentured labor system assumed such proportions.

Pennsylvania's geographical position, with her rich material resources, gave a basis for manufactures. Here was ore waiting to be worked. Iron was early discovered and quite extensively smelted in the colonial era. Flax and hemp were grown. The splendid trees which grew on the river banks were utilized for shipbuilding, and the rich limestone valleys early produced wheat extensively. Then again, Pennsylvania's settlers were from countries where they had been schooled in industry. The founders of Germantown were from Crefeld, Germany, a place long noted as the "city of weavers." Pennypacker said of the early German

---

[1] Egerton, *Origin and Growth of English Colonies,* 70.

[2] Anderson, *Origin of Commerce,* III, 75. The same view is expressed in Douglass, *British Settlements;* Burke, *European Settlements;* and Holmes, *American Annals.*

colonists, "Most of them were linen weavers." [3]   Irish and French
settlers were also familiar with textile industries. William Penn
encouraged industry. Pastorius, in a letter of 1684, gave notice
of Penn's intention to establish weaving,[4] and, in 1686, Abraham
op den Graef claimed Penn's prize for the first piece of cloth
woven in the colony. Gabriel Thomas said of the Germantown
linen that it was of a quality that the "genteel" need not be
ashamed to wear. Pastorius devised a town seal for Germantown, representing on three leaves of clover a vine, a stalk of
flax, and a weaver's spool, with the motto, *Vinum, Linum, et
Textrinum.*[5]

Richard Morris, writing of Philadelphia in 1690, said that a
large flock of sheep was kept in the "town liberties" and that a
woolen manufactory was already at work which kept several
carders and spinners employed, and make good "Stuffs and
Sarges." [6] Near Germantown was built in 1690 the first paper
mill in all North America. William Bradford wrote in 1691,
saying that he hoped to make paper in less than four months.[7]

---

[3] Cited in Winsor, *Narrative and Critical History,* III, 490.

[4] Pennypacker, *Settlement of Germantown,* 97.

A characteristic agreement was entered into between Jan Streyphers and
Jan Lensen, of Crefeld, providing for settlement in Pennsylvania, land and
service. Lensen was bound to transport himself and his wife, and the
agreement continued, "I further promise to lend him a Linnen weaving
stool with 3 combs, and he shall have said weaving stool for two years
. . . and for this Jan Lensen shall teach my son Leonard in one year
the art of weaving, and Leonard shall be bound to weave faithfully during
said year." *Ibid.,* 5.

[5] Townsend Ward, "Germantown Road," *Pa. Mag. of Hist. and Biog.,*
V, 368.

[6] *Ibid.,* IV, 200.

[7] This early development was sufficient to invoke the muse of a verse-
maker whose measures halted somewhat in the following strains:

> "The German-Town of which I spoke before,
> Which is, at least in length one mile or more,
> Where lives High German People and Low Dutch,
> Whose Trade in weaving linen Cloth is much,
> There grows the flax, as also you may know,
> That from the same they do divide the Tow ·

Shortly following the Quaker settlement in Pennsylvania there came an attempt on the part of the home Government to exercise a closer supervision over the industries and trade of the colonies. In 1696, the Board of Trade and Plantations began its work. Governors were directed to correspond with it and to submit journals of the councils and assemblies in the colonies as well as other official intelligence. Admiralty courts were also provided and it was evident that a new effort was to be made for the enforcement of the navigation acts. A law of 1699 recognized the textile industry in the colonies, and provided that no wool or woolen manufacture should be loaded in any plantation for shipment to any other plantation.[8] Of this act, William Penn wrote from London to his agent, James Logan, then in Pennsylvania, in July, 1705: "[As] for the *wool act* here, in England, I will lay the mischief of it to America before the Council of Trade, and use my utmost endeavours to have it amended this next Parliament; though they are jealous here of encouraging manufactures there."[9] England's interest in her

---

Their trade fits well within this habitation,
We find convenience for their Occasion,
One trade brings imployment for another,
So that we may suppose each trade a brother;
From linen rags good paper doth derive,
The first trade keeps the second trade alive;
Without the first the second cannot be,
Therefore, since these two can so well agree,
Convenience doth appear to place them nigh,
One in Germantown, t'other hard by.
A paper mill near German-Town doth stand,
So that the flax which first springs from the land,
First flax, then yarn, and then they must begin,
To weave the same which they took pains to spin.
Also when on our backs it is well worn,
Some of the same remains ragged and Torn;
Then of the rags our paper it is made;
Which in process of time doth waste and fade:
So what comes from the earth, appeareth plain,
The same in Time, returneth to earth again."

Richard Frame. Printed by William Bradford, 1692. Cited in Penny-packer, *Settlement of Germantown*, 164.

[8] Holmes, *American Annals*, 48.

[9] Janney, *Life of William Penn*, 499. (Sixth edition, Philadelphia: 1882.)

North American colonies did not cease with the passing of restrictive measures; the Parliament passed an act for the encouragement of trade to America in 1707, and from this time there was a close following of colonial affairs.

The textile industries in Pennsylvania grew steadily in the eighteenth century, though the manufactures were chiefly in the homes of the people, and in consequence difficult to trace. In 1727, Charles Brockden and his associates sent a petition to the Pennsylvania Assembly asking for aid in the manufacture of sailcloth and saying in support of their petition that they had been engaged in this industry for some time and that they had produced a good merchantable product.[10] James Logan spoke hopefully of the culture of silk before 1730, as did Patrick Gordon a little later.

Cheap materials and established trade united to produce in Pennsylvania a demand for white laborers which demand had a profound influence on the importation of servants; the servant trade began in real earnest in the decade from 1720 to 1730, and the introduction of white servants under indenture went hand in hand with the industrial progress of the colony.

The year 1730 has been termed a turning point in the expansion of England, in the strengthening of her colonial system and in the promotion of commerce. The peace policy of Walpole brought prosperity; 1730 was termed the "promising year."[11] The time was important also because of the information then made available concerning colonial conditions. In 1731 F. Hall published an illuminating tract on the *Importance of the British Plantations in America,* with an account of their trade, suggestive methods of improving the trade, and a description of several colonies. Anderson commented on the intelligent information in this pamphlet, and made it the basis of his account of conditions in the colonies and of England's trade with them.[12]

Pennsylvania's products for export about 1730 were: wheat, flour, and biscuit; meats, including barrel beef, pork, hams, and bacon; cheese and butter; leather, apples, cider, "strong beer,"

---

[10] *Votes of Assembly,* III, 14.

[11] Anderson, *Origin of Commerce,* III, 419.

[12] *Ibid.,* 420 sqq. The pamphlet mentioned is in the Colwell collection at the Library of the University of Pennsylvania and is credited to F. Hall.

beeswax, linseed oil, skins of various sorts, and some tobacco. The production of hemp at this time was referred to as extensive, a bounty in the province of one and one-half pence per pound being added to that allowed by Great Britain.[13]   Three hundred and ninety-one pounds, six shillings, nine pence were paid from May 3, 1726, to August 5, 1730, as Pennsylvania bounties on hemp, yet Hall felt that this did not include all of the trade in hemp.[14]

England's colonial interest was reflected in 1732 in a report from the Board of Trade and Plantations to the House of Commons, considering manufactures and trade in the American settlements.   Of Pennsylvania it was said that her people had fallen into the manufacture of woolen and linen cloth, but this was qualified with the addition that it was for the use of their own families only, and the manufacture was excused as necessary for the employment of the agricultural servants during the winter. The report added of Pennsylvania: "The deputy-governor writes that he does not know of any trade carried on in that province that can be injurious to this Kingdom, and that they do not export any woolen or linen manufactures; all that they make, which are of the coarse sort, being for their own use."[15]

The report above mentioned no doubt refers to a communication sent by lieutenant-governor Patrick Gordon under date of November 10 of the preceding year.   Gordon acknowledged a letter of June 10, preceding, which required him to send "the best and most particular account of any Laws made, Manufactures set up or Trade carried on in the Province of Pennsylvania, which may in any wise affect the Trade, Navigation and Manufactures of Great Britain."   In answer, Gordon said: "I know not of one Law in force in this Province that can in any wise affect the trade Navigation, or Manufactures of Great Britain, nor do I know of any Trade carried on here that can be injurious to that Kingdom.   For as the merchants and trading People of this Colony principally depend on the British Trade, it is their

---

[13] *Statutes at Large,* IV, 185.

[14] *British Plantations in America,* 91, 92.

[15] Anderson, *Origin of Commerce,* III, 454.

manifest interest to carry that to the greatest height they are capable."[16]

Patrick Gordon denied that Pennsylvania produced either woolen or linen cloth for export, but held that it was necessary for the inhabitants to manufacture cloth for domestic use. He said that the people were generally in debt and did not have the means to buy imported cloth, and that if they did not produce cloth at home their families would go naked. He added that inhabitants from the North of Ireland and Germany "sometimes sold a Piece or two of Linen of their own making to their Neighbours, or others for the buyer's own use."

Concerning restrictions on colonial production, and the economic relations of the colonies with the mother country, Patrick Gordon made interesting observations which can best be presented in his own quaint language: "The Merchants & Traders of this Province use their utmost Industry in contriving methods to make Returns for the British Goods imported, and if more of such Returns could possibly be made, more of such Goods would be purchased therefore all Restraints on the People to prevent their furnishing themselves with necessaries by their own Industry as Cloathing, Iron work for building Ships, Houses and the Utensils of Husbandry, as some have inconsiderately proposed, would have no other effect than to render so many of His Majesty's subjects much more miserable & altogether useless, without bringing any manner of benefit to Britain, for as no man sells Goods but in Expectation of being paid, and as the Country, as the Case now Stands, purchases as much of British Goods as it can possibly pay for, 'tis in vain to oblige the People to buy more, that is, what they cannot pay for." Gordon then reviewed the various products of Pennsylvania, as wheat, flour and bread, pelts and tobacco, iron products, hemp and silk, and characterized the developments of Pennsylvania's industry as slow.

Gordon's predecessor as lieutenant-governor in Pennsylvania had urged the encouragement of the manufacture of potash and pearl ash in the northern colonies on the ground that it would furnish employment for laborers during the winter, and thus

---

[16] Board of Trade, *Proprieties,* Vol. 13, S.15. This letter was repeated under date of Nov. 12, 1731, and appears again in the same volume of the Board of Trade papers as S.50.

prevent the introduction of woolen and linen manufactures.[17] The
London merchants also saw in this trade the saving of money
otherwise paid to Russia. In 1729, a bounty was allowed by the
British government for masts, spars, bowsprits, pitch tar, and
turpentine. The same act permitted pig iron to come in from
the plantations duty free.[18] All this was made subject to the
general regulations, and to the several acts for governing plantation trade in such commodities as sugar, tobacco, and wool.

The iron industry is more easily traced in Pennsylvania than
are the textile industries. Iron ore was discovered in the region
during the Swedish occupation. Penn early (1685) called attention to the presence of iron ore in his description of the province.
The first iron seems to have been smelted in Pennsylvania in
1692, or before, probably in the forge of a blacksmith. A furnace
was set up in Berks County in 1716, one in Chester County in
1727, and one in Bucks County in 1727. James Logan wrote
in 1728 that four furnaces were in full blast, and by 1730 the
iron industry was fairly well established. Writing of conditions
in the colony in 1731, Patrick Gordon said: "It has been thought
that Iron would be a more certain Return, but those concerned
in these expensive Works have from the lowness of the Price in
Britain been disappointed in their Expectation." [19]

Patrick Gordon wrote again on conditions in Pennsylvania
under date of October 2, 1735: "As to Iron, it is generally
allowed, that what is produced here is as fine and good as any
whatsoever, but the great Expense that attends Works of that
kind in a Country where Labour is so dear has given no small
Damp to these Undertakings. On a suitable Encouragement
given, I am persuaded that this Province and some of the adjacent Colonies may be able to import [export] such Quantities of
Pig Metal and Bar Iron as may very greatly abate the necessity
Britain has hitherto lain under of supplying itself therewith on
disadvantageous terms, from foreign Nations." [20]

Improvements in machinery and the means of transportation
increased the quantity of iron until it came to be an article of

---

[17] Board of Trade, *Plantations General,* Vol. XI, June 27, 1729.

[18] *Ibid.,* pp. 7, 8.

[19] Board of Trade, *Proprieties,* Vol. 13, S.15.

[20] *Ibid.,* S.44.

export. Robert Grace at the Warwick furnace found the making of stoves after Franklin's model a profitable venture. Colonial furnaces were described as baronial and patriarchal, resembling a feudal holding or a southern plantation. They were located where forests were within easy reach, and generally had a farm adjacent; with the slaves, white servants, and free laborers, one of these furnaces formed a little settlement.[21] Proprietors of furnaces clamored for Negro slaves, and complained against the enlistment of redemption servants.[22] Both of these forms of servile labor were utilized, the former usually as manual laborers and the latter as skilled workmen.

Colonial iron furnaces were dependent upon the forests for fuel; their location was therefore changed with the cutting away of the forests. Most of the furnaces were located on creeks so that the water power might be used for the blast, and later for operating slitting machines and trip hammers, or tilting hammers, for the making of plate steel. The region of Lancaster developed a variety of manufactures in iron and steel, especially in stove plates, and later in rifled gun barrels.[23] The iron industry of Pennsylvania contributed guns and munitions for the American army during the Revolution.[24]

As was stated above, on October 2, 1735, Patrick Gordon wrote to the Board of Trade, in answer to an inquiry of June 17 preceding, in which he had been asked whether any laws laying restrictions on the trade and shipping of Great Britain were in force on March 25, 1731, or whether any had been passed since that time. To both of these questions Gordon replied emphatically and unqualifiedly in the negative.[25] But the Board of Trade was not satisfied, and in 1737 issued elaborate instructions to the governors for enforcing the laws, particularly the Sixth of George II, for the encouragement of the trade of the sugar colonies. The governors were directed to inform themselves on the various laws affecting trade then in force, which were reviewed

---

[21] Swank, *Iron in All Ages*. The *Potts Manuscripts* at the Historical Society of Pennsylvania are a rich mine of information on the iron industry of Pennsylvania.

[22] See Chapter XII on "Enlistment of Servants."

[23] Weld, *Travels*, I, 117.

[24] *Potts Manuscripts*, Library of Historical Society of Pennsylvania.

[25] Board of Trade, *Proprieties*, Vol. 13, S.58.

from that passed in the twelfth year of Charles II's reign. There was also included a list of collectors of customs and of ships.[26]

The Delaware River has often been termed "the Clyde of America." Shipbuilding was closely related to Pennsylvania's early prosperity. Penn brought a shipbuilder on his first voyage, and a shipyard was soon established. Penn said, in 1683, "Some vessels have been built here and several boats." Gabriel Thomas gave a detailed account of the wharves and drawbridges, the "stately oaks," and the occupations connected with the building and fitting out of ships. Jonathan Dickinson, a Philadelphia merchant, wrote in 1718: "Here is a great employ of ship-work, it increases and will increase." Before 1730, as many as twenty ships, several of them three-masters, could be seen on the ways at one time in Philadelphia. Nearly one-half the tonnage trading to the port at this time was owned in Philadelphia, and this with the sale of ships and other manufactures gave to the Quaker colony a material prosperity hitherto unknown in the New World.[27]

---

[26] Board of Trade, *Plantations General,* Vol. 12, N.22.

[27] Hall, who claimed intimate knowledge of Philadelphia's commerce, reported further that there were exported timber, sawed boards, staves, masts, and spars; likewise, that some two thousand tons of shipping were sold annually, after having been loaded with the produce of the country. *Plantations in America, 73.*

Joshua Gee gave the following account of the industry and trade of Pennsylvania in 1729: "Pensilvania, within forty years, has made wonderful Improvements; they have built a large and regular City; they have cleared great Tracts of Land, and raised very great Quantities of Wheat and other Provisions; and they have, by Way of Jamaica, beat out a very great Trade for their Corn and Provisions to the Spanish West-Indies; and if this trade be properly nursed up, it may draw the Spanish Coast very much to depend upon us for a Supply of Flower, bisket, etc., which may be of great advantage to us.

"It is already attended with that good Consequence, that it hath supplied them with Gold and Silver, which is frequently brought home by our trading Ships from thence, and has very much enlarged their Demands upon us for Broad-cloth, Kersies, Druggets, Serges, Stuffs, and Manufactures of all sorts.

"They supply the Sugar Plantations with Pipe and Barrel-Staves, and other Lumber, with Flower, Bisket, Pork, etc. But this is not sufficient for their Clothing, and therefore are forced to make something by their own Labour and Industry to answer that End." *Trade and Navigation,* 23, 24.

The Board of Trade reported in 1732 that Pennsylvania built many brigantines and small ships for sale to the West Indies.[28] Shipbuilding had by the year named become an important industry, affecting directly the internal condition of the colony as well as influencing it indirectly through an increase in external trade. Penn had provided for the commercial welfare of his city in granting two markets a week and two fairs a year.[29] But the city became more largely commercial and industrial than Penn anticipated. He planned for a large, roomy town to reach from river to river; instead, the city grew along the banks of the Delaware, a manufacturing and trading settlement, fringing the river front for several miles. Penn regretted, in his later years, the predominance of the commercial over the picturesque in the city he had founded.[30] It was a full century before the city reached back from the Delaware; the improved navigation of the Schuylkill, and the development of the oil, coal, and iron trades later made the Schuylkill important as a shipping point.

The iron industry of the colonies came under renewed and special regulation of the British government. From repeated accounts of travelers who were in Pennsylvania about the middle of the eighteenth century, it must have been well known that iron and steel were being manufactured in the colony. In 1750, an act was passed by Parliament to encourage the production of pig iron in the colonies and to prevent the manufacture of steel, or the continuance of the operation of rolling, plating, or slitting

---

[28] Anderson, *Origin of Commerce,* III, 454.

[29] Philadelphia charter of 1701.

[30] The extensive nature of Philadelphia's trade was commented on by Kalm in his *Travels,* Vol. I; by Douglass, *British Settlements,* II, 333; and Holmes, *American Annals.* According to Holmes the trade of Philadelphia was:

$$1736 \begin{cases} 211 \text{ entrances} \\ 215 \text{ clearances} \end{cases}$$

$$1742 \begin{cases} 230 \text{ entrances} \\ 281 \text{ clearances} \end{cases}$$

$$1749 \begin{cases} 303 \text{ entrances} \\ 291 \text{ clearances} \end{cases}$$

American Annals, II, 144, 159, 182.

Boston had, in 1749, 489 entrances and 504 clearances. *Ibid.,* 182.

mills.[31] In May, 1750, the Board of Trade considered this, and other acts, when it was ordered that the secretary transmit the act mentioned, with the other acts, to the governors of the several North American colonies, and that the governors be required to "transmit to their Lordships Certificates containing an Account of every Mill or Engine for slitting and rolling of Iron; and every plateing Forge to work with a Tilt Hammer; and every Furnace for making Steel, at the Time of the Commencement of this Act erected in his Colony." [32]

Under date of October 18, 1758, lieutenant-governor James Hamilton reported at length on the iron and steel industry in Pennsylvania. He said that one mill for the slitting or rolling of iron, one for the plating of iron, and two furnaces had been erected; this report was supplemented with a statement of the locations and proprietors of these various enterprises.[33] Lieutenant-governor William Denny a few years later made a similar report, in which he gave the names of eight furnaces and summarized their production from Christmas, 1749, to January 5, 1756. In addition to the eight named, Denny said that information of two furnaces had not been received, and that report on them would be submitted later. The summary of this report showed 3,378 tons of iron manufactured in Pennsylvania in the years mentioned.[34]

Following the French War there was in Great Britain a new interest in the colonies, especially in anything having to do with their trade and industries. The colonies were considered useful for the direct contribution of their products to the mother country, and, further, for supplying a balance of trade and furnishing commodities to export to other countries. American books were already received in England, despite the later contemptuous sneer of Sydney Smith, and European travelers' accounts of the New World were eagerly sought, sometimes going through successive editions.

Reports on the industry and trade of Pennsylvania could not but arouse the suspicion and distrust of the home government,

---

[31] Bishop, *History of American Manufacturers,* I, 625.

[32] Board of Trade, *Journals,* Vol. 58, 201-203.

[33] Board of Trade, *Proprieties,* Vol. 18, V.73.

[34] *Ibid.,* Vol. 20, W.24, W.25.

and in 1766 the Board of Trade wrote to Governor John Penn directing him to prepare and forward a report for the next session of the House of Commons, furnishing "particular and exact accounts" of the manufactories that had been set up and carried on in Pennsylvania since 1734, and also to state what public encouragement had been given to these.[35]   In his answer Governor Penn said that he had tried to ascertain the facts and that he could not find that the least public encouragement had been given to manufacture.   He reported two manufactories at that time, but these, it was claimed, were not successful, as the high price of labor made their products more expensive than was the same quality of goods imported from England.   The first of these establishments was in Philadelphia for the manufacturing of coarse cloth, and the report said that it was soon to discontinue. The other was at Lancaster for the manufacture of glass to supply a local demand.   According to the report, neither of these was thought to be important and Governor Penn promised additional information if there should be changed conditions.[36]

Governor Penn's answers seemed evasive and in 1773 questions were again submitted by the Earl of Dartmouth.   It was stated that His Majesty had not as full information as was desired concerning the "State and Progress of the Commerce, Cultivation and Inhabitancy" of Pennsylvania and other colonies.   The request was made for as full and accurate answers as possible to the questions submitted.[37]   Samuel Hazard examined the papers in the office of the secretary of the commonwealth, after which he felt that the Earl of Dartmouth's questions, twenty-one in all, were submitted to persons competent to answer them, and that a report which was made on the thirtieth of January, 1775, embodied the several replies.   Four of the questions were directly on the trade, manufactures, and the probable future production of the province.   These were answered by submitting a report from the books of the deputy collector of the customs at Philadelphia.[38]

---

[35] *Colonial Records,* IX, 343.

[36] *Colonial Records,* IX, 353, 354.

[37] *Pennsylvania Archives* (First Series), IV, 464.

[38] *Ibid.,* 597, 598.   The report from the books of the deputy could not be found.

Beginning about 1730 there was a conflict of economic interest between the colonies and the mother country, and between the continental colonies and those of the West Indies. These differences grew steadily with the passing of the years; finally they assumed political aspects, and ultimately widened into the breach which resulted in the American Revolution. At first Pennsylvanians were credited with being amenable to the recommendations of Great Britain in their production and trade.[39] Imports in 1730 were most largely from Great Britain and in part the British goods were paid for by the gold and silver received through a favorable trade balance with the West Indian colonies. Hall said that with certain Philadelphia traders he had computed that a cash balance of not less than £60,000 was sent annually from Philadelphia to England.[40] Lieutenant-governor Patrick Gordon, writing of the conditions in Pennsylvania in 1731, and relations with Great Britain and the West Indies, made the following recital: "Of Manufactures, we have neither Woollens nor Linens that are exported; But as this Country chiefly depends on, and subsists by, raising of Wheat with some Tobacco in the lower Countries, all that the Husband-men can spare from the Sustenance of their Families is commonly sold by them to pay for the British and West India Goods they want, and they are so far from laying up anything in Store out of their crops that they are too generally in Debt." [41]

The conditions above described continued and probably became more acute as trade increased. When Dr. Franklin was examined before the House of Commons in 1765, he said that the value of the probable annual imports into Pennsylvania from Great Britain was in excess of £500,000, while the estimated value of Pennsylvania produce sent to Great Britain was not above £40,000 annually. The balance was made up in money, or bills of exchange, or in goods imported into the colony for

[39] Hall, *Plantations in America*, 93.

[40] *Ibid.*, 97.

[41] Board of Trade, *Proprieties*, Vol. 13, S.15. Lord Cornbury, Governor of New York (1702-1708), wrote on the scarcity of commodities for trade with England, saying it "sets men's wits to work, and has put them on a trade [woolen manufacture] which I am sure will hurt England in a little time." Egerton, *Origin and Growth of English Colonies*, 118, 119.

reëxport. The colony, it was said, was drained of specie and had not the means to pay the stamp tax levied by Great Britain.[42] Just at the outbreak of the Revolution, Abbé Raynal termed England "a gulph" into which were sunk the metals which the colonies had received from various parts of the world.[43]

Pennsylvania's industrial development became involved in the controversy which gradually developed between the northern colonies and the tropical colonies in North America. The former came to be called the "bread colonies" and the latter the "sugar colonies." The issue was clearly drawn, and the greater strength of the continental colonies was mentioned in the applications of the sugar colonies to the Board of Trade. The sugar colonies were shown to have but limited areas, and to be deficient in people when compared with the bread colonies.[44] Barbadoes, Antigua, and St. Christopher petitioned the Board of Trade for a monopoly of the market for sugar in the northern colonies, and also for some restriction on the trade of the northern colonies with the rival sugar colonies of the French, Spanish, and Dutch.[45]

A counter petition to the above was submitted by Pennsylvania in December, 1731. In this it was set forth that Pennsylvania was one of the bread colonies, her productions being chiefly wheat and wheat flour, other grains, beef, pork, butter, horses, and timber. It was claimed that the population was "very numerous," and that there was a demand in Pennsylvania annually for woolen manufactures exceeding the combined demand of all three of the sugar islands. It was also claimed that Pennsylvanians took from Great Britain large quantities of linens, silks, haberdashery, and ironware, for husbandry and for the building and furnishing of their homes. It was stated that Pennsylvania traded her products as above enumerated for sugar, rum, and molasses. She also traded the manufactures imported from England with the Indians for furs. The colony, it was further said, bought from England all that she needed except her food, and it was urged that freedom of trade was imperative to get the money

[42] Franklin, *Works* (Bigelow), III, 411.

[43] Raynal, *British Settlements,* 168, 169.

[44] Board of Trade, *Plantations General,* Vol. 11, B.; also Vol. 12, N.24.

[45] Board of Trade, *Journals,* Vol. 42, p. 50.

with which to make these purchases from the mother country.[46]

But Parliament gave heed rather to the appeals from her tropical islands and in 1733 passed the sugar or molasses act termed, "An act for the better securing and encouraging of the trade of His Majesty's Sugar Colonies in America." For importations from other than the British Islands five shillings per hundredweight was to be paid on sugar, six pence per gallon on molasses, and nine pence per gallon on rum. The duty was to be paid in advance of landing the goods, and in case of a violation of the act the goods were to be confiscated.

This act was regarded by the northern colonies as doubly unfair. It denied to the bread colonies a market for their goods, and prevented them from purchasing sugar, molasses, and rum in markets where these could be secured at the greatest advantage. The act was not strictly enforced, but its passage disaffected the colonists and tended to widen the breach between them and the mother country.

In the account of his travels through the middle colonies (1759-1760), Andrew Burnaby made observations on the state of industry in Pennsylvania, and offered comparisons between Pennsylvania and other colonies.[47] Speaking of Virginia, he said: "Not one-tenth of the land is yet cultivated, and that which is cultivated is far from being so in the most advantageous manner." Burnaby characterized the climate of Virginia as tending to make the inhabitants indolent, easy-going, and good-natured, and said that they seldom showed any spirit of enterprise. Of Maryland, he said that the character of the inhabitants was much like that of the Virginians, and that the state of the two colonies was similar. In Pennsylvania, however, he found cultivation carried to a high degree of perfection, a great plenty and variety of grain being produced.[48]

Manufactories were found in operation in Pennsylvania, and

---

[46] Board of Trade, *Proprieties,* Vol. 13, S.13.

[47] Hazard said of this book that it gave an account which was on the whole very fair of both persons and things. Cited in Winsor, *Narrative and Critical History,* VIII, 489. Professor A. B. Hart says of Burnaby, "His well-written book is one of the best sources of our knowledge of colonial society." *American History Told by Contemporaries,* II, 87.

[48] Burnaby, *Travels,* 19, 31, 70, 80.

Burnaby said that the Germantown thread stockings were in high favor. He was, he said, informed ("creditably") that during the preceding year about sixty thousand pairs of stockings had been manufactured in Germantown.[49]   When undergoing his examination before the House of Commons (1765), Franklin was asked whether there were any fulling mills in America, to which he unqualifiedly replied, "A great many." Again Franklin was asked, "Did you never hear that a great quantity of stockings were contracted for, for the army, during the war, and manufactured in Philadelphia?" Franklin replied, curtly, "I have heard so." [50]

Of Philadelphia's shipbuilding and trade about the middle of the eighteenth century, Mittelberger wrote: "Many large and small merchant-vessels are built there near the water.   The trade of the city and country to other countries and colonies increases perceptibly from year to year; it consists in fruit, flour, corn, tobacco, honey, skins, various kinds of costly furs, flax, and particularly a great deal of flaxseed or linseed, also fine cut lumber, horses, and all kinds of tame and wild animals.   In return the incoming vessels bring all sorts of goods, such as Spanish, Portuguese, and German wines, the best of which cost a rix-dollar, the most inferior a florin per quart.   Also spices, sugar, tea, coffee, rice, rum, which is a brandy distilled from sugar, molasses, fine china vessels, Dutch and English cloths, leather, linen, stuffs, silks, damask, velvet, etc.   There is actually everything to be had in Pennsylvania that may be obtained in Europe, because so many merchantmen land here every year.   Ships are coming from Holland, Old and New England, Scotland, Ireland, Spain, Portugal, Maryland, New York, Carolina, and from the West and East Indies.   By 'West Indies' the people of Pennsylvania mean the Spanish and Portuguese America, and also the American Islands, whether they belong to the English or to other nations." [51]   A little later Burnaby described Pennsylvania's trade as surprisingly extensive, reaching, among other places, to Great Britain, the West Indies, and every other part of North America, the Madeira Islands, Lisbon, Cadiz, Africa, and the Spanish Main.[52]

---

[49] *Ibid.*, 81.
[50] *Works* (Bigelow), III, 434.
[51] *Journey to Pennsylvania* (Translation), 49, 50.
[52] *Travels*, 81.

The pertinence of the facts presented in this chapter and the probability of the correctness of the conclusion deduced from them appear when attention is directed to advertisements for the sale of white servants and for the recovery of those who had run away. Advertisements of servants for sale almost invariably made the claim that they either were all mechanics or tradesmen or that tradesmen were included in those to be sold. For example, in the *American Weekly Mercury* for June 19, 1729, appeared the announcement: "Several very likely servants, tradesmen and husbandmen, lately arrived from Bristol; to be sold very reasonable by Captain *Samuel Bromage* or Mr. Thomas Sharpe"; in the *Mercury* for September 10, 1730: "In Philadelphia on board Mary Pink, servants of both sexes. One smith, a barber, a tailor and the rest for plantation work"; in the *Pennsylvania Gazette* for November 27, 1740: "Just imported from Bristol in Brigantine Seneca, Men and Women Servants. Men mostly husbandmen and tradesmen." The *American Weekly Mercury* for January 3, 1740, contained the following advertisement: "TO BE SOLD. Two Servant men's time by trade shoemakers, Enquire of the Printer." [53] In 1817, when an English traveler was in Philadelphia, a cargo of redemptioners was advertised as follows: "13 farmers, 2 bakers, 2 butchers, 8 weavers, 3 taylors, 3 masons, 2 shoemakers, 3 cabinet-makers, besides men of several other occupations as cooper, barber, and wheel-wright." [54]

Quite likely masters of vessels, and servants, took liberties in claiming trades with which those to be sold were not thoroughly familiar. The trade to which a servant made claim was important in securing for him a ready sale. A case in point was reported from Maryland. A servant was bought as a gardener; later it was found that he knew nothing at all of this occupation. Upon being questioned, he made known that the captain had explained to him on shipboard that when he arrived in the colony he would need to have the name of some trade in order to be assured of finding a place quickly, and as he was informed that

---

[53] This advertisement was reinserted on January 8, 15, and 22, and on February 5, 12, and 19, indicating that for these men there was not a ready sale. It is probable that those just imported were preferred to those being re-sold in the colony.

[54] Fearon, *Sketches of America,* 148, 149.

the trade of gardening was easy to learn and not exacting, and that gardeners were in demand in Maryland, he had adopted that trade. This servant was supposed to have been a gentleman who had been enticed on shipboard and sent to the colony against his will. His bearing was so unusual that the term of his service was ended by his master's giving him his liberty. He returned to Europe, after which he forwarded to the master a liberal reward for the kindness rendered him, yet his identity could not be discovered.[55]

An examination of the advertisements for runaway servants for each ten years from 1720 to 1770 indicates in some measure the occupations in which white servants were engaged. In the year 1720, there were advertised 43 runaways, of whom 3 were ironworkers and blacksmiths, 3 were carpenters and joiners, 2 were plasterers and bricklayers, 3 were gardeners and farmers, 1 was a sailor, 1 a shoemaker, and 1 a butcher. For 23 of the total no occupations were given. In 1730 there were advertised as having run away 2 ironworkers and blacksmiths, 6 carpenters and joiners, 1 ditcher, 3 tailors, 1 shipwright, 1 shoemaker, 1 hatter, 2 weavers, 1 tanner and skinner; 36 were advertised in all, of whom 17 were given without occupations.[56]

In 1740, there were advertised, in the *Pennsylvania Gazette*, 64 runaways, of whom 3 were listed as carpenters and joiners, 3 as masons and bricklayers, 3 tailors, 1 gardener and farmer, 1 shipwright, 1 sailor, 1 barber, 2 shoemakers, 1 binder, 1 butcher, and 3 weavers; 37 had no occupations given. For the year 1750, there were inserted in the *Gazette* advertisements for 144 runaways, of whom 2 were termed clock makers, 1 a mason, 1 a "corker" (caulker), 4 ironworkers and blacksmiths, 1 a house servant, 2 carpenters and joiners, 2 plasterers and bricklayers, 2 coopers, 4 tailors, 3 sailors, 1 barber, 4 binders, 1 hatter, 5 weavers, 2 tanners and skinners, and 1 miller; no occupations were given for 95 runaways for this year. Seventy-nine runaways were advertised for in 1760 (*Pennsylvania Gazette*), in which were numbered 1 schoolmaster, 3 carpenters and joiners, 2 tailors, 1

---

[55] Eddis, *Letters from America*, 78-89.

[56] The newspaper examined for the years 1720 and 1730 was the *American Weekly Mercury*. Andrew Bradford, who published the *Mercury*, repeatedly advertised for runaway servant printers and bookbinders.

gardener, 1 dyer, 6 blacksmiths, 1 "nailor" (a maker of nails), 3 weavers, 1 cooper, 1 brickmaker, 1 pump borer, 1 baker, 1 sawyer, and 1 skin dresser, and 39 were described without occupations being given. In 1770, there appeared, in the *Gazette,* 201 advertisements for runaway servants, of whom 6 were said to be carpenters, 3 bakers, 10 weavers, 3 tanners, 3 coopers, 5 tailors, 3 blacksmiths, 2 shoemakers, and 2 farmers. In this year, 135 runaways were advertised without occupations being given. Though the trade previously followed could not have proved conclusive in fixing the identity of a runaway, it was given in approximately one-half of the advertisements, and as given shows a large proportion of skilled laborers.[57]

We are not limited to information from within the colony to determine the occupations of servants. A ship from London arrived at Upland near the end of August, 1682, with "Richard Townsend, Carpenter, Servant for five years, to have fifty acres of land and salary."[58] In June of 1683, a ship arrived with one listed as a glassmaker, who was "servant to the Society" for a period of four years.[59] The papers on emigration preserved in the Public Record Office in London mentioned the former occupation of those who were leaving England. Four different weeks were summarized in the years 1773, 1774, and 1775. In these four weeks a total of 699 is recorded as having left England, of which number 474 were designated as "indented servants" or "redemptioners." Of the 474, 430 were male and 44 were female. Ninety-nine persons were listed as weavers, hatters, tailors, or rope-

---

[57] The figures above given seem small as compared with an examination of any single number of the papers to which they refer, or in contrast with the statements of several writers who have asserted that the colonial papers were filled with advertisements for runaway servants. The writer spent no little time in the examination of these advertisements, and feels that the above facts are trustworthy. The seemingly large number based on a cursory examination results from the reinsertion of the same advertisement in successive issues. Thus, for 1730, 3 advertisements only were not reinserted; 6 appeared twice; 19, three times; 5, four times; and 3, five times. In 1750, one runaway servant was readvertised 16 times. This phase of the subject will be further considered in Chapter XI, on "Runaway Servants."

[58] Arrivals, MS. in Library of Historical Society of Pennsylvania.

[59] *Ibid.*

makers; 81 were said to be farmers and gardeners; 52 were designated as carpenters, bricklayers, painters, and shipbuilders; 21 were bookkeepers, clerks, or of related callings; and 4 were printers and millers.[60]

Free laborers were not available for the early industrial development of Pennsylvania; on the other hand, slaves were unsuited for the colony's labor requirements. Thus, white servitude had a large influence in establishing industry in Pennsylvania.

Conditions in Africa were unfavorable to the industrial development of Negroes. Industry was primitive, there was the use of only simple tools, the number of craftsmen was small, and the division of labor was slight. These economic characteristics of the inhabitants of Africa persisted with the Negro slaves in North America, and the absence of skill in industry was one of the weaknesses of slave labor.[61]

A further significance in this aspect of the subject is found in the transfer of industry to the New World by the bringing in of skilled artisans. This is the most effective and in some cases the sole way in which an industry established in one country can be introduced into another.[62] The relations between the manufactures of Great Britain and those of the North American colonies and of the states which sprang from them have shown again and again that the bringing of workmen has meant the bringing of industry.

The system of white servitude planted in the fertile soil of Pennsylvania the seeds of a great industrial future. Pennsylvania's industrial beginnings in colonial times were a foundation

---

[60] Emigration record, transcripts from MSS. in Public Record Office, reproduced in part in Appendix II.

[61] Tillinghast, *The Negro in Africa and America*, 28-45, 137-139. "The Negro slave can only fulfill one of two functions. He may be the appendage of a luxurious establishment, or he may be the instrument of a monotonous and unintelligent form of tillage where labour can be organized in large gangs." *Cambridge Modern History*, VII., 55.

[62] "The history of particular industries," says Cunningham, "abounds with illustration of the manner in which the enterprise and intelligence of some one immigrant, or group of immigrants, have been directly instrumental in planting a craft in places where, though it had not previously existed, it could be advantageously carried on." *Western Civilization in Its Economic Aspects*, II, 277.

for the later greatness of the commonwealth in manufactures. The momentum of an early start, which came in part from the labor supply of the colonial period, is ncessary to explain the present industrial greatness of both Pennsylvania and Philadelphia. Free laborers were not forthcoming to satisfy the labor need of the colony; even if there had been no compunction against Negro slavery, slave labor could not have satisfied this need; and, as will be shown in the succeeding chapter, there was in Pennsylvania a pronounced sentiment against Negro slavery.

CHAPTER V

DEMAND FOR WHITE SERVANTS INCREASED BY SENTIMENT AGAINST NEGRO SLAVERY

Throughout the colonial period, even before the Quaker settlement, some slaves were held in Pennsylvania, but the prevailing sentiment was against slavery. This made necessary the finding of a substitute form of labor. The redemption system as a milder sort of servitude supplied in part the demand for laborers. The feelings of both Quaker and German, representing nearly or quite two-thirds of the population, must be kept in mind in studying indentured and redemption labor in Pennsylvania. In other words, the slave history of this colony is a background from which white servitude cannot well be separated and on which it stands out in strong relief.

It is clear that slaves were early introduced into Pennsylvania, and that they were held as laborers even by the Quakers. Scarcity of laborers was held to account for, but not to justify, the practice of slavery.[1] The question of the relation of Friends to slavery was older than Pennsylvania, having been raised concerning slaves in Barbadoes as early as 1671.[2] George Fox visited these islands, it is said, in the interests of blacks; he advised his sect to treat them well, to teach them religion, and after a term of years to free them.[3] Quakers in Barbadoes were prosecuted in 1675 for violation of an act forbidding them to bring their slaves to meetings. Benjamin Furly early wrote of Pennsylvania: "Let no blacks be brought in directly. And if any come out of Virginia or Maryland in families that have formerly bought them elsewhere, let them be declared (as in ye west jersey constitution) free at 8 years' end."[4] Though the firm

---

[1] Michener, *Retrospect of Early Quakerism,* 328.

[2] Bettle, *Notices of Negro Slavery,* "Memoirs of the Historical Society of Pennsylvania," I, 363; see Michener, 329, 330, for citations from George Fox.

[3] Besse, *Sufferings of the Quakers,* II, 308.

[4] Walton and Brumbaugh, *Stories of Pennsylvania,* 15. The meaning here is not clear, see *Pa. Mag. of Hist. and Biog.,* XIX, 303. Photographic reproduction of the Statement of Furly in Sachse, *Pietists,* 444.

friend of mankind, William Penn held slaves. Watson quotes from a letter of Penn to his steward at Pennsbury (1685) in which he contrasted slavery and white servitude. Speaking of servants he said: "It were better that they were blacks, for then we might have them for life." [5] The fact that Penn owned Negroes has been urged unduly by some writers, to his discredit. We are told that "Penn employed blacks without scruple" and that his direction for emancipating his slaves was not regarded by his heirs.[6] Though Penn died a slaveholder it was without doubt through neglect or inability on the part of his representatives to carry out his directions. A clause of his will (executed in 1701) was, "I give to my blacks freedom as is under my hand already."[7]

It is certain that Friends used slaves well, a fact in which there is some palliation, though one can scarcely account

---

[5] *Annals,* II, 262.

[6] Bancroft, I, 572, 573.

In opposition to the above statement of Bancroft, see an address of Job R. Tyson, *The Social and Intellectual State of the Colony of Pennsylvania Prior to the Year 1743.* In this it is set forth that the assertion of Bancroft is due to a confusion of William Penn and Thomas Penn, that William Penn was not in the colony for the last seventeen years of his life, and that the man of whom it was claimed that he was Penn's slave was but five years old at the time of William Penn's death. (Tyson, p. 11 and Appendix.) But a letter of James Logan to Hannah Penn, May 11, 1721, refers to Penn's provision in his will and clearly establishes the fact that he died a slaveholder: "The Propriet. in a will left with me at his departure hence gave all his Negroes their freedom but that is intirely private, however, there are very few left. Sam died soon after your departure hence & his bror James very lately. Chevalier by a written Ordr from his Master had his Liberty several years agoe, so that there are none left but Sue whom Letitia claims or did claim as given to her when she went to England but how rightfully I know not, these things you can best discuss. She has several children, there are besides 2 old Negroes quite worn out, the remaindr of those wch I recovered near 18 years agoe of E. Gibbs estate." James Logan to Hannah Penn, *Penn Manuscripts,* Official Correspondence, Vol. I, p. 97, Library of Historical Society of Pennsylvania. The unwillingness of Hannah Penn to have a Negro go to Barbadoes in 1701 is shown by the *Penn-Logan Correspondence,* I, 42.

[7] Michener, *Retrospect,* 336, 337; Janney, *Life of Penn,* 438.

for slavery among the Quakers from motives of kindness to the Negroes as has been suggested by one writer.[8]

Although there were individual cases of slaveholding in Pennsylvania, the fact remains that slavery as an institution was not in favor. Few slaves were bought and these were well treated and early emancipated. The Free Society of Traders looked to the possible freeing of Negroes.[9] It should be noted that Penn furthered measures for bettering the condition of both Negroes and Indians. Soon after his second arrival in Philadelphia, he issued an address to the Monthly Meeting, "exhorting and pressing them to the full discharge of their duty, every one, in reference to this people." He particularly recommended that provision be made for the education and spiritual welfare of Negroes, and as a consequence a Monthly Meeting was appointed for them.[10]

Agreement between Quaker and German on questions of colonial policy was common. On the holding of slaves the Germans took probably as advanced ground as was that held by the Quakers. The German Quakers made what is generally recognized as the first public declaration against the iniquity of human slavery at Germantown in 1688, but an earlier worthy, saved from oblivion by Samuel W. Pennypacker, had marked out the path for them. Cornelius Plockhoy, in 1662, announced the principle of human brotherhood: "No lordship or servile slavery shall burden our company."[11] Henry Melchior Mühlenberg, the great German Lutheran leader in Pennsylvania, was outright in his

---

[8] Michener, *Retrospect*, 329.

[9] "That if the Society should receive Blacks for Servants, they shall make them free at fourteen years end, upon Consideration that they shall give into the Society's Ware-house two-thirds of what they are Capable of producing on such a Parcel of Land as shall be alloted them by the Society, with a stock and necessary Tools, as shall be Adjudged by the Society's Surveyor. And if they will not accept of these terms, they shall be servants till they will accept it." *Pa. Mag. of Hist. and Biog.*, V, 45.

[10] Proud, *History of Pennsylvania*, I, 423.

Minute of the Monthly Meeting of Philadelphia in 1700. "Our dear friend, the Governor, having laid before this meeting a concern that hath lain upon his mind for some time, concerning the negroes and Indians . . . this meeting concludes to appoint a meeting for negroes to be kept once a month." Bettle, *Notices*, 367.

[11] Pennypacker, *Settlement of Germantown*, 211.

opposition to Negro slavery.[12]   It was a rare thing, says Dr. Mann, to find a German slaveholder in colonial Pennsylvania.[13] In Berks, a county made up largely of Germans, there were in 1790 four hundred and sixty-four whites to one slave; in Cumberland County, with its large intermixture of Scotch-Irish, whites to blacks were but forty-four to one.[14]

Antislavery discussion in America began with the memorial of the German Friends in 1688, a memorial that spoke with no uncertain tone, but it is worthy of note that this from a German Quaker Meeting was considered "too weighty a matter" for the Society at large, and the Yearly Meeting postponed action to give time for "mature considerations."[15]   The Society quickly responded, however, for from the Annual Meeting of 1693 there was issued an "exhortation and caution" against buying or keep-

---

[12] Mann, *Life of Mühlenberg*, 62, 63.

[13] Notes to *Halle Reports*, 167.

[14] Rupp, Note to Rush's *Manners*, 24.

[15] The following extract is from the minutes: "A paper being here presented from some German Friends, concerning the lawfulness and unlawfulness of buying and keeping negroes; it being adjudged not to be so proper for this meeting to give a positive judgment in the case, it having so general a relation to other parts and therefore at present they forbear it." (Bettle, *Notices*, "Memoirs of the Historical Society of Pennsylvania," I, 365.)   Pennypacker says that the handwriting seems to be that of Pastorius, and he credits the authorship to him. (*Settlement of Germantown*, 61, 148, 151.)   Pastorius was the author of the following:

> "If in Christ's doctrine we abide,
> Then God is surely on our side,
> But if we Christ's precepts transgress
> Negroes by slavery oppress
> And white ones grieve by usury,
> Two evils which to Heaven cry,
> We've neither God nor Christ His Son,
> But straightway travel hellwards on."

Pastorius to his children. Pennypacker, *Settlement of Germantown*, 62.

It has sometimes been denied that the Quakers who made the protest were German; again, the effort has been made to take the credit of this important document from the Quakers. Unquestionably they were German Friends. Says Pennypacker, "The evidence that those who sent and those who received it [the protest] regarded each other as being members of the same religious society, seems to me conclusive"; Watson, *Annals*, II, 261, 262; Bancroft, I, 573; *Settlement of Germantown*, 148.

ing Negroes. This was summed up in the declaration that Friends might buy Negroes only to set them free.[16] In 1696, several papers were presented to the Yearly Meeting from subordinate meetings and the following proclamation was issued by the former: "That Friends be careful not to encourage the bringing in of any Negroes," and that due attention should be given to the welfare of those already in the colony.[17] Isaac Norris early in the eighteenth century opposed a declaration of Friends against the purchase of slaves, and in 1705 bought two Negroes himself.[18]

Again in 1711, the Quarterly Meeting of Chester addressed to the Yearly Meeting held at Philadelphia a memorial against buying, and encouraging the importation of, Negroes, and said that the buying still continued. At this time the Yearly Meeting reaffirmed its recommendation of 1696 and directed that all merchants and factors write to their correspondents to discourage sending any more Negroes into the colony.[19] That this declaration was not without effect appears from the instruction of Jonathan Dickinson, a Quaker merchant of Philadelphia, to his correspondent in Jamaica: "I must intreat you to send me no more Negroes for sale, for our people do not care to buy. They are generally against any coming into the country. Few people care to buy them except for those who live in other provinces." [20]

The Yearly Meeting of Philadelphia in 1712 addressed to the Yearly Meeting in London a letter asking that Meeting to communicate with Friends in other colonies, and to discourage the importation of Negroes; this request was acceded to, as is shown by the reply of the London Yearly Meeting in 1714.[21] In 1714, the Yearly Meeting at Chester recommended unanimously that Friends should not thereafter be concerned in the importation of any slaves, nor purchase any that had been imported. In 1715, a minute was adopted by the Chester Monthly Meeting to the effect that the Quarterly Meeting should take into further

---

[16] Watson, *Annals,* II, 262; printed in full in *Pa. Mag. of Hist., and Biog.,* XIII, 265-270.

[17] Bettle, *Notices,* 366; Michener, *Retrospect,* 335.

[18] *Penn-Logan Correspondence,* II, 82.

[19] Bettle, *Notices,* 369.

[20] Watson, *Annals,* II, 264.

[21] Bettle, *Notices,* 372, 373.

consideration the buying and selling of Negroes, which was giving encouragement to bringing them into the province, and the desire was expressed that no Friend should buy Negroes who should be imported after that time.[22] From 1715 to 1717, the Yearly Meetings further directed that Friends should not only stop importing, but must also decline to buy any slaves that had been imported into the province.[23] This injunction was not obeyed by all Quakers, for in 1730, 1735, 1736, and 1737 the Yearly Meetings in Philadelphia were informed that though importation of slaves by Friends had practically ceased, some of them continued to buy Negroes imported by others. It was then recommended that Monthly Meetings enforce the former directions of the Yearly Meeting. Questions for information were later sent to the several Monthly Meetings, and replies were received in the years from 1738 to 1743. From these replies it appeared that the number of Friends who continued to purchase slaves was decreasing.[24] With the progress of the eighteenth century, declarations of the Monthly, Quarterly, and Yearly Meetings were more pronounced, and they finally culminated in a resolution that all Friends who refused to manumit their slaves would be disowned by the Society.[25] The various Monthly Meetings in Philadelphia, Chester, and Bucks Counties had committees on the number of slaves held, manumission, etc. Records have been found of the disowning of Friends by their Meetings, and, in 1783, reports were current that Friends had freed their slaves. A manumission by one Joseph Pratt in the Goshen (Chester County) Monthly Meeting was in the wording: "All mankind have an equal, natural and just right to liberty." [26]

A Quaker historian says that his sect was not content merely with freeing their Negroes; in 1779, the Yearly Meeting took up the question and decided that something was due to former slaves for their past services. It was agreed that a return should

---

[22] Smith, *History of Delaware County*, 226.

[23] Bettle, *Notices*, 371-373.

[24] *Ibid.*, 375.

[25] For these declarations see Michener, *Retrospect*, 339 sqq.; Bettle, *Notices*, 378.

[26] *Cope Manuscripts*. The Gilbert Cope collection has an original manumission of 1784 to take effect in 1798.

be made to former slaves as a matter of justice and not of charity. "The state of the oppressed people," they said, "who have been held by any of us in captivity and slavery calls for a deep inquiry and close examination how far we are clear in withholding from them what under such an exercise may open to view as their just right." Many former owners were reported to have paid for the hitherto unrequited labor of their former slaves.[27] In the diary of Richard Barnard for 1780 is the interesting note: "Gustin Passmore said he would be willing to leave to the judgment of indifferent men what was due to the Negro woman that had lived with him until she was between thirty and forty years old."[28] Augustin Passmore in 1777 made a provision which bore on this same case. The slave woman to whom he had extended manumission bore a child before she became free, but he filed a paper binding himself and his heirs to release all claims to this child.[29] Among the court papers of Chester County is a petition expressing a desire to free some five or six Negroes at the age of thirty. These had been the slaves to Deborah Parke, and the petition was said to be in accordance with an agreement between herself and her children.[30]

Individual action supplemented and strengthened the work of the Quaker Society as a whole. Benjamin Lay, a planter in Barbadoes, who was raised to the slave trade, later became convinced of the evils of slavery; he then abandoned his plantation, came to Philadelphia, joined the Quakers, and issued a treatise against slavery. Anthony Benezet, with his Philadelphia school for blacks, attracted much attention.[31] Granville Sharp attacked the theory of the necessity for slaves, and urged that the climate in North America was wholesome and that the colonists could get on without the use of slave labor if they wished to do so. John Woolman gave himself to preaching against the evils of slavery, and earned the title, "Quaker abolitionist."[32] Indi-

---

[27] Sharpless, *Quakers in the Revolution*, 230.

[28] *Cope Manuscripts.*

[29] Original in Cope Collection.

[30] *Cope Manuscripts.*

[31] Bettle, *Notices*, 374; Brissot, *New Travels in the United States*, I, 220; Wakefield, *Excursion in North America*, 19, 20.

[32] See selection from his *Journal* in Hart, *Contemporaries*, II, 302-308.

vidual cases of manumission were common for nearly half a century. Ralph Sandiford, who at his own expense circulated a work (*The Mystery of Iniquity*) on the evil of slavery, was among those who early freed their Negroes.[33]

Prohibitive duties on Negro importation were levied again and again, either to prevent Negroes being brought in altogether or to limit the number. Acts were passed by the Colonial Assembly in 1705, 1710, 1711, and 1712, but these were promptly disallowed by the home government.[34] England, after the Peace of Utrecht, fostered the slave trade and wished the colonial market for slaves. It is not surprising, therefore, that from 1713 to 1729 several restrictive measures against Negro importation were disallowed by the home government. The earlier duties were fixed generally at five pounds, but in 1729 a compromise measure levying a tax of but two pounds was passed, and though never considered by the home Government, it was permitted to become a law according to the terms of Pennsylvania's charter.[35] This

---

[33] Watson, *Annals,* II, 265; Bettle, 374.

[34] Michener, *Retrospect,* 337, 338; *Pennsylvania Statutes at Large;* DuBois, *Suppression of the Slave Trade.*

[35] *Statutes at Large,* IV, 123-128. Instructions to deputy-governor Patrick Gordon in 1731 forbade him to give assent to any law imposing a duty upon Negroes imported into Pennsylvania if such duty were to be paid by the importer: "Additional Instructions to Our Trusty and Welbeloved Patrick Gordon Esqr., Deputy Governor of our Province of Pensylvania in America, and in his Absence to the Commander in Chief of Our said Province for the time being. Given at Our Court at St. James's the Tenth Day of December 1731, in the Fifth Year of Our Reign.

"GEORGE R.

(L.S.)

"Whereas Acts have been pass'd in some of Our Plantations in America for laying Duties on the Importation and Exportation of Negroes, to the great Discouragement of the Merchants trading thither from the Coast of Africa; And Whereas Acts have likewise been passed for laying of Duties on Felons imported, in Direct Opposition to an Act of Parliament pass'd in the 4th Year of Our late Royal Father's Reign, *for the further preventing Robbery, Burglary and other Felonies, and for the more effectual Transportation of Felons;* It is Our Will and Pleasure, that you do not give your Assent to or pass any Law imposing Duties upon Negroes imported into Our Province of Pennsylvania payable by the importer, or upon any Slaves exported, that have not been sold in Our said Province and continued there for the Space of twelve Months. It is our further Will and

continued in effect until 1761, when after a good deal of discussion the amount of duty was made ten pounds,[36] and this in turn continued until 1773, when the amount was raised to twenty pounds.[37]

It was the Quaker majorities of the early Colonial Assemblies which passed these restrictive measures; the record of the Assembly for the entire period shows that it was Quaker agitation and Quaker initiative that had kept this question before the legislature. In brief, it was Quaker opposition to slavery that restricted Negro importation and gave a market for white laborers under indenture.[38]

When the attempt was being made to secure the increased duty on Negroes in 1773, Dr. Benjamin Rush prepared on request a statement which was to accompany a petition to the Assembly. This attacked the general doctrine that slavery is necessary even to produce rice, sugar, indigo, or other tropical products. No production, the statement urged, was of sufficient consequence to warrant the violation of the laws of justice and humanity. The first edition of this tract was published in Philadelphia in 1773, and called forth an answer by a West Indian. This resulted in a second edition of Rush's statement reviewing the answer. The second edition took more positive ground than the first. Rush set forth the situation in the West Indies, showed the loss of slaves in the passage, and the loss in the islands, and

---

Pleasure, that you do not give your Assent to or pass any Act whatsoever for imposing Duties on the Importation of any Felons from this Kingdom into Our said Province of Pennsylvania."   G. R.

Pennsylvania Archives, First Series, I, 306.

[36] *Statutes at Large,* VI, 104-110.

[37] Sharpless, *Quakers in the Revolution,* 232. The notes to *Statutes at Large* (VI, 110) are to the effect that the act of 1761 was repealed in 1780.

[38] Spears, in his *History of the Slave Trade,* accounts for Quaker opposition as he accounts for attempts to limit the importation of Negroes into South Carolina, i.e., from fear of slave insurrections. He says that "sheer cowardice" animated the Pennsylvania legislators (p. 94), and generalizes as follows: "Not one act passed by a colonial legislature showed any appreciation of the intrinsic evil of the slave trade" (p. 97). But Mr. Spears could not write the history of the slave trade without acknowledging Quaker antipathy to it, and later in his work he shows a more just appreciation of Quaker sentiment in this country and England. See Chapter IX of *The Slave Trade.*

concluded that not only was the slave trade repugnant to religion, but that it was against the true interests of both the mother country and the colonies. He declared that the economy of nature, the air, the heaven, and the earth, all conspired together against the slave trade.

Colonial newspapers indicate that Negroes did not find a ready sale in Pennsylvania. If such notices as the following could run for five successive issues of a paper, the commodity advertised was not in great demand: "To be sold cheap for ready money or for the Country Produce, a fine young Negro Wench fit for all manner of House Business, as also a season'd Young Negro Man." [39] Also in the same year occurs three times over: "Two very likely Negro Men to be sold by Edward Rogers in Water Street. Very Reasonable." [40] Negroes were offered with "sold on credit" inducements, or "cash or credit," and "cheap for ready money." [41]

Free Negroes in Philadelphia were objects of interest to travelers. Peter Kalm commented on the scruples of Quakers, adding that they were "no longer so nice" and that they had "as many Negroes as other people"; but immediately following he remarked on the free Negroes who were lucky enough to have as master some zealous Quaker.[42]

In Pennsylvania as elsewhere manumission was subject to abuse, masters attempting by this legal process to relieve themselves of caring for old or broken-down slaves. As early as 1722, the Assembly received a petition against setting Negroes free when they were old and incapable of working for a living. Two days later a report was made on the petition saying that such practices were wrong and ought to be prevented by law, and the petitioners were therefore granted the privilege of bringing in a bill to this end.[43] However, the bill did not become a law at this time, but in 1725 the matter was again taken up and

---

[39] *American Weekly Mercury,* February 19 and 24, and March 5, 12, and 19, 1730.

[40] *Ibid.,* May 7, 21, and 28.

[41] See for example *American Weekly Mercury,* August 13, 20, and 27, and September 3, 10, 17, 1730, also *Pennsylvania Gazette,* January 11, 1770.

[42] Kalm, *Travels,* I, 390, 391.

[43] *Votes of Assembly,* III, 336, 337, 339, and 345.

after a preamble saying that free Negroes were an idle, shiftless, and slothful people, often a burden to their neighborhood and a bad example to other Negroes, an act was passed prohibiting manumission unless the master would become bound in the sum of thirty pounds, to indemnify the public against charges incurred in caring for the person freed. Neither could slaves be freed by will without similar security.[44] Such regulations influenced men against becoming responsible for slaves. The relation of master and slave in Pennsylvania was not to be easily set aside. Slaves that were freed became in many cases idle and troublesome and an expense to their former masters.[45]

Masters frequently gave their slaves partial freedom, either hiring them out or permitting them to hire themselves out to labor for others, the slaves dividing their wages with their masters. Sometimes slaves by this means were enabled to earn a sum sufficient to purchase their freedom. The Colonial Assembly was made aware of this practice in the session of 1722-1723, when was presented "The Petition of Several Persons in this Province, setting forth, that the keeping of *Negroes,* to be hired out to do all or most of the servile work in and about the City of Philadelphia, debars the Petitioners from being employed, to the utter Ruin of themselves and Families," and praying that the practice of hiring out Negroes might be discouraged or wholly prevented. The petitioners represented themselves as poor and honest men who had emigrated from Europe in the hope of finding work.[46]   In 1751,

---

[44] *Statutes at Large,* IV, 61; Smith, *History of Delaware County,* 261.

[45] Kalm, *Travels,* I, 394.

[46] Read and ordered to lie on the table, November 22. *Votes of Assembly,* II, 243; Watson, *Annals,* I, 98.

Concerning the choice of members of Assembly a letter was dated in New York, September 12, 1738, as follows: "To my Friends in Pennsylvania." This was a three page pamphlet in which was the following: "Another Instance of candid Treatment of the Public, is that of the State House, about which some Thousands, above what was enacted and proposed for that End, are already expended, and instead of imploying the Common People or Poor Laborers in the Service of the Country, and Circulating Money for their Support, as all good Common Wealths in erecting Public Edifices have required, the Stewards own Negroes are the Workers and he generously pays himself out of the Country's Cash in his own keeping, as may be supposed from a Vote lately passed in Favour of the late Trustees." From the *Du Simitiere Papers,* Ridgway Branch, Library Co. of Philada.

the magistrates of Philadelphia complained against practices reported to them, which were, in brief, that Negro slaves, claiming to be free, went about and sought employment for themselves, having promised to pay their masters a certain sum for the privilege. Such Negroes, it was stated, had disturbed the public peace, and the demand was made that laws be passed to regulate these persons.[47]

Such advertisements as follows were not uncommon: "To be hired by the Year or Month, a very likely Negro Man named Scipio, fit for some sorts of Labouring Business in the House or out of Doors, he is also a good Cook. There is likewise to be Hired or Sold a very likely Negro Boy about 16 years of Age (this town born), he understands something of the taylors trade." [48] Slaves were sometimes offered for service at a distance, and for a considerable time; for example, in 1770, two or three young Negro men and as many young women were advertised to go into the country for a few years.[49] A Philadelphia master also wanted a place for a slave with such good qualities as understanding all kinds of housework, fond of children, and well-recommended for good temper and integrity.[50] In 1771, a Negro named Sarah was sold before the mayor of Philadelphia for ten years, no indication being given of the consideration, freedom dues, or other facts. On December 12 of the same year, a free Negro named Pompey was indentured before the mayor for a term of fifteen years and two months, the amount of the consideration being fifteen pounds.[51]

Negroes to be hired were usually advertised over the names of their owners, not so those offered for sale. In the latter case directions were generally appended to inquire at the printing office, at a store, or at some other well-known place. Most often the direction was, "Inquire of the printer hereof." From the frequency of the occurrence of this in the *Pennsylvania Gazette*, Ford reasons that Franklin, in addition to keeping a stationer's

---

[47] *Pennsylvania Gazette,* March 5, 1751.

[48] *American Weekly Mercury,* June 18, 1730.

[49] *Pennsylvania Gazette,* April 5, 1770. Similarly, November 29, 1770.

[50] *Ibid.,* May 24, 1770. Thomas Jefferson favored the hiring out of his Negroes with his estates. *Writings* (Ford Edition), IV, 342, 416, 418.

[51] *Record of Indentures,* Pa. German Soc. Pubs., 40-43.

store, did business as a slave broker.[52]   That Franklin was a
broker in slaves to any extent seems improbable; he had his profit
from the advertising, and also furnished information of the seller
to any would-be purchaser.   This custom of having the advertiser
identified through the publisher of the newspaper is still common.

Not only did sellers avoid having their names appended to
advertisements, but purchasers likewise did not wish the publicity
that newspaper advertisements would give.   The following request of a purchaser found a place in the *Pennsylvania Gazette:*
"WANTED, A few Negroes, Men, Women, Boys, and Girls.
Those Persons who have any for Sale, may apply to the Printers
of this Paper, and be informed of a Purchaser." [53]

The same feeling that opposed the large importation of
Negroes made those that were here objects of special kindness.
Slaves lived in close proximity to their masters, and Pennsylvania saw slavery at its best; slaves were mostly house servants,
and they lived chiefly in towns.   As compared with redemption
servants, they probably had as good food and perhaps as good
or better treatment.   The only noticeable difference was that
they were held for life.   May it not have been that a master would
give slaves better care than he gave white servants because the
slaves were his for life ? [54]   An account of slavery could hardly be
more favorable than was that of J. Hector Saint-John Crèvecœur
in his *Letters from an American Farmer,* written to Abbé Raynal
from the vicinity of Carlisle, Pennsylvania.   Crèvecœur, although
he held slaves,[55] spoke of his correspondent as one who had
pleaded the cause of humanity in championing the rights of the
poor African.   In the dedication he said, "You view these provinces in their true light, as the asylum of freedom."   Writing of
"Charlestown" [Charleston], he compared the unhappy lot of the
slaves in the South with that of those in Pennsylvania.   "We
have slaves likewise in our northern provinces," said he, adding:

[52] *Many-Sided Franklin,* 318, 321.   Also Heston, *Slavery and Servitude in New Jersey,* 25.

[53] Issues of June 21, July 5 and 19, August 2, and December 6, 1770.
Requests for slaves were unusual, as the supply seems to have been in
excess of the demand.

[54] Kalm, *Travels,* I, 394.

[55] *Letters,* 24.

"I hope the time draws near when they will be all emancipated: but how different their lot, how different their situation, in every possible respect! They enjoy as much liberty as their masters, they are as well clad, and as well fed; in health and sickness they are tenderly taken care of; they live under the same roof, and are, truly speaking, a part of our families. Many of them are taught to read and write, and are well instructed in the principles of religion; they enjoy many perquisites, many established holidays, and are not obliged to work more than white people. They marry where inclination leads them; visit their wives every week; are as decently clad as the common people; they are indulged in educating and cherishing, and chastising their children, who are taught subordination to them as to their lawful parents; in short, they participate in many of the benefits of our society, without being obliged to bear any of its burthens. They are fat, healthy, and hearty, and far from repining at their fate; they think themselves happier than many of the lower class of whites: they share with their masters the wheat and meat provision they help to raise; many of those whom the good Quakers have emancipated have received that great benefit with tears of regret, and have never quitted, though free, their former masters and benefactors." [56]

It sometimes happened in Pennsylvania that free Negroes passed into a condition of servitude. Children of those who were free might be put to service by the overseers of the poor with the assistance of a magistrate.[57] Two magistrates were empowered by law to bind out able-bodied Negroes who were idling their time and wandering from place to place.[58] Free Negroes who entertained or harbored a slave without the knowledge of the master were to pay five shillings fine for the first hour and one shilling additional for each succeeding hour. If they were unable to pay this fine, or refused to pay it, they were then subject to servitude.[59] Negroes not known might be seized and subjected

---

[56] Crèvecœur, *Letters*, 221, 222. Raynal, writing later, said that while slaves were not so badly treated in Pennsylvania as in other colonies, they were still "exceedingly unhappy." *British Settlements*, I, 163.

[57] *Votes of Assembly*, II, 469.

[58] *Statutes at Large*, IV, 61, 62.

[59] *Ibid.*, 62.

to imprisonment and servitude. In 1730 there appeared a "Notice of a strange negro man in the custody of the sheriff of New Castle; he was said to have been taken up as a runaway in the preceding October, but no one had appeared to claim him or give any account of him. After a description of the man it was declared, over the name of the sheriff, that if a master or owner did not appear before the twentieth of August, the man would be sold for the payment of his prison charges.[60]

Sex relations between whites and Negroes were annoying and early came to the attention of the Colonial Assembly. Persons were remanded to conditions of slavery and servitude in the attempts to regulate in this matter. In 1722-1723 a petition was presented to the Assembly against "the scandalous and wicked Practice of Negroes cohabiting with and marrying white People." Two days after this petition a committee report said that "intermarriage was an Indecency, and ought to be prevented by Law." The petitioners were granted the privilege of bringing in a bill; the bill was presented; and it was enacted that Negroes and whites were not to be joined in marriage, and for such marriages a fine of one hundred pounds was fixed.[61] A white man or woman cohabitating with a Negro man or woman under pretense of marriage could be fined thirty pounds, and if unable to pay the fine was subject to sale into servitude not to exceed seven years.[62] Children who were born from the above relations were to be put out to service until they reached the age of thirty-one years. A free Negro who married a white person was to be sold as a slave, and a free Negro man or woman who committed adultery or fornication with a white man or woman was to be sold as a servant for a period not to exceed seven years.[63]

Instances are numerous of the unequal standing of Negroes and whites before the law. The death penalty for the burning of a house was visited upon a Negro in 1737. The behavior of Negroes in and about the city of Philadelphia was then char-

---

[60] *American Weekly Mercury*, July 3, 1730.

[61] *Votes of Assembly*, I, 336, 337, 339, 343.

[62] *Statutes at Large*, IV, 62, 63.

[63] *Ibid.*, 63. Enacted 1725-1726, repealed temporarily in 1761 but not finally repealed until 1780.

acterized as insolent.[64]   Negroes were sentenced to death for
burglary in November, 1762.[65]   Slaves occupied an anomalous
position, as they were regarded both as property and human
beings, and the problem which presented itself in cases of misdemeanor was how the human part could be punished without
robbing the master of his property.   To aid in this, special courts
were established for the trial and punishment of Negroes.[66]   The
punishment of Negroes was unusually sure and swift, though
sometimes they escaped, as in the case of one sentenced to death
for burglary in 1770; a petition for pardon was sent in by the
master and others, and the governor's council recommended that
the pardon be granted on the condition that the master transport
the Negro out of the province at once, and give security that he
would never return.[67]   A death penalty was fixed for the murder
of a Negro by a white man, but no record was found in the present
investigation of the execution of a white man for that crime.
When a master did kill his slave, he was advised to leave the
country and thus avoid being an object of prosecution.[68]

Side by side stand the evidences of Pennsylvania's opposition to slavery and the scarcity of labor consequent thereon.   In
August, 1727, when the prohibitive duty was being considered,
a petition from ironworkers was presented to the Assembly, complaining of labor scarcity and high wages.   It was urged that
the excessive cost of labor was a great discouragement and
hindrance to the development of the iron industry, and the petitioners prayed that Negroes for the ironworks be admitted, free
of duty.   The petition was considered for two days, when a
motion to grant it was carried in the affirmative.   Then a motion
was made that similar liberty of importing Negroes, duty free,
be general.   After a long debate, the Assembly divided equally,
at which the speaker decided the question in the negative.[69]   Again

---

[64] *Colonial Records,* IV, 243, 244.

[65] *Ibid.,* IX, 6. A special court tried a Negro for housebreaking in 1721,
adjudged him deserving of death, and he was executed within five days.
American Weekly Mercury, July 17, 1721.

[66] Accounts of such courts occur in *Colonial Records,* IX, 704, 705; and
X, 73 and 276.

[67] *Ibid.,* IX, 699.

[68] Kalm, *Travels,* I, 391, 392.

[69] *Votes of Assembly,* III, 31.

in February, 1761, when the bill laying a duty of ten pounds on Negroes and mulatto servants imported into the province was before the council, a petition against it was presented from twenty-four Philadelphia merchants and firms. Philadelphia, it was said, was suffering from lack of laborers; some had been taken by enlistment into the king's service (See Chapter XII), nearly a total stop had been put to the importation of German and other white servants, and industry was crippled because of the high price of labor.[70] The merchants requested that at least the bill might not go into immediate effect, saying that they would lose thereby as they had already given orders for slaves to their agents at a distance.[71]

The Pennsylvania council in 1778 addressed to the Assembly a statement that the former Assembly had been furnished with heads of a bill to emancipate infant Negroes, so that the gradual abolition of slavery might be brought about in an easy manner. The address spoke of slaves then held as "not competent of freedom" and said that they ought not to be meddled with. It was further said that if this measure were attempted all importation must stop, and that this would abolish slavery which was regarded by the council as the "opprobrium of America." [72] The act for gradual emancipation followed and went into effect in 1780, but before this was put into operation many slaves were manumitted. The American Abolition Society was recognized by law in 1781, with its objects to further manumissions, to buy the freedom of deserving Negroes, and to secure rights to slaves unjustly held in

---

[70] An examination of advertisements in the *Pennsylvania Gazette* for 1760 does not show a single cargo of servants offered for sale in that year. The record of arrivals of foreigners gives no ship for 1760. The enlistment of servants by the king's officers during the French War made ownership of them uncertain and led to fewer purchases of them and a decline in the trade.

[71] *Colonial Records,* VIII, 575, 576. (Also *Votes of Assembly.*) The bill, however, passed into a law, March 14, 1761. Chapter 467, reported by title in Bioren, *Laws,* I, xxix. A supplement to the above act is given in Law 468, passed April 22. This was in force until 1780. *Statutes at Large,* VI, 104-113.

[72] *Pennsylvania Archives,* First Series, VII, 79. Futhey and Cope (*History of Chester County,* 423) believe that the act for gradual emancipation at this time was due to the agitation of the Quakers.

bondage. Supplementary acts to carry out the intent of the law for gradual emancipation were passed from time to time; thus, in 1788, one was made forfeiting all vessels engaged in the slave trade, and imposing a fine of one thousand pounds for the building and equipping of vessels for that trade.

The total abolition of slavery in Pennsylvania was accomplished with little difficulty; self-interest impelled to such action. The economic law holds that whenever a higher order of labor can be secured, a lower order is more expensive. Slavery has disappeared whenever free laborers could be secured to do better and more economical work. Turner is right in his conclusion: "Nothing can then preserve slavery but paramount economic needs. In Pennsylvania, since such needs were not paramount, slavery was doomed." [73]

The gradual abolition of slavery substituted an apprentice system; that is, servitude for a term of years, for servitude for life. Under the act of abolition, masters were required to bring all slaves for registry by a day appointed. After that day all children born of slave parents were to become free on becoming twenty-eight years of age. Slavery in Pennsylvania is thus closely related to labor under indenture. Turner in his study, *The Negro in Pennsylvania,* says that in its legal origin slavery was probably a divergence from servitude. The same study notes the gradual movement of Negroes as a class from a status of slavery through that of limited servitude, to that of apprenticeship, and finally to a status of freemen. [74]

Misunderstandings and irregularities in the enforcement of emancipation were not avoided. A test case was twice argued before the supreme court of Pennsylvania in 1789. Samuel Moore, of Chester County, had failed to register his slaves according to the act of 1780, in consequence of which a suit was brought for their liberty in the name of Negro Betsey. Thomas McKean sat as chief justice, and in giving his opinion stated that Betsey was no worse off for having been born before the passage of the act; he thought that she was better off with a good master than with poor parents, and said that her master had not yet realized any return for the expense to which he had been put for her. On the ground of

---

[73] *The Negro in Pennsylvania,* 53.
[74] *Ibid.,* 89, 90.

expediency and justice, McKean ruled that the slave should continue with her master, but the three associates dissented from
their chief's opinion on the ground that Moore had been careless, and it was ordered by the court that the Negroes be discharged. Thus, judicial interpretation gave effect to laws that
embodied Quaker and German opposition to the ownership of
human beings.[75]

The number of Negroes in Pennsylvania in the colonial period
was never large, and though not definitely known, several estimates are of interest.[76] In 1721 it was thought that there were
from 2,500 to 5,000 slaves.[77] In 1754, the number of Negroes was
estimated at 11,000.[78] Writing in 1757, Burke said that Pennsylvania had few blacks, and that they constituted not more than
one-fortieth of the total population.[79] Franklin estimated that there
were 30,000 Negroes in the province in 1766,[80] but in 1775, Governor Penn felt that there were not more than 2,000 Negroes in
Pennsylvania.[81] In Phoenixville and the region about there were
few slaves and no free blacks at the time of the Revolution.[82]

When the slaves were registered in Chester County a total
of 495 were listed, though there must have been a considerable
number not registered. Of the total, 472 were slaves for life and
23 until they should be thirty-one years old. More than four-
fifths of these Chester County slaves were Negroes, two only
were Indians, and the balance were mulattoes.[83] In 1785, there
were in Montgomery County 108 slaves; at the same time 80
bound servants were listed.[84] Tench Coxe reported the number

[75] "Respublica vs. Negro Betsey," et al., Dallas Reports, I, 469 sqq.

[76] All colonial population figures are estimates. The rapid growth of
Pennsylvania made estimates of doubtful value. See Dexter, Estimates of
Population in American Colonies, 5 sqq.

[77] Documents Relating to Colonial History of New York, V, 604.

[78] Bancroft, II, 391; Burnaby, Travels, 81.

[79] European Settlements, II, 206.

[80] Raynal, British Settlements, I, 163.

[81] Pennsylvania Archives, First Series, IV, 597.

[82] Pennypacker, Phoenixville and Vicinity, 86.

[83] Futhey and Cope, History of Chester County, 424.

[84] Buck, "History of Montgomery County," in Scott, Atlas of Montgomery County, 8. The redemption trade had fallen off during the Revolution.

of slaves as greatly decreased in 1793. At this time, he thought, there were not in the city of Philadelphia more than 273 slaves of both sexes and all ages, while for the whole state the number given was less than 3,000.[85]

Coxe's explanation for the "limited number of slaves" was the "migration hither of free yeomanry." Redemptioners were regarded as freemen, and it was expected that in time they would become good citizens. Among the first of the arguments against slavery in all North America was that blacks being brought to be owned by some one would take the place of and keep away whites who might otherwise come "owning themselves."[86] In 1773, a New Jersey tax of ten pounds per head on slaves had as its explanation the encouragement of the importation of white servants for the better peopling of the country. There, too, the slave was regarded as a chattel while the white servant was expected to become a citizen.[87] Thomas Jefferson, as late as 1805, spoke of the securing of German immigrants to take the place of blacks, as if he took for granted the desirability of so doing, and further said that he had often considered the matter of how to bring in the Germans. He felt that if anything were done as a government measure, it must be by the states, as the Federal government had only enumerated powers and the obtaining of immigrants at general expense was not one of these; but he doubted and despaired of the state governments taking up any general measure, at least not until some strong circumstance should force it upon them.[88]

As one studies, even in outline, the history of slavery in Pennsylvania, he is impressed with the need for and the extent of white servitude as a substitute for slave labor. Had not white laborers under indenture been ready to hand, it would be more difficult to say how Pennsylvania would have stood on the question of slavery; but it is not hard to see that these laborers made possible both a response to the Quaker and German sentiment against slavery and the preservation of unusual economic prosperity. Indentured labor had as its redeeming feature

---

[85] Coxe, *View of the United States,* 488.
[86] Weeden, *Economic and Social History of New England,* II, 520.
[87] Spears, *History of the Slave Trade,* 93.
[88] Jefferson to J. P. Reibelt. *Writings,* VIII (Ford Edition), 402, 403.

that it was temporary servitude. Slavery was hopeless, for it was without end; it not only rested on the individual throughout life, but it was likewise the slave's solè endowment to his off-spring.[89] By the end of the eighteenth century, slavery as a factor in the labor history of Pennsylvania had practically dis-appeared.[90] For more than a hundred years there had been

[89] The indentured system has been thus contrasted with slavery: "Finally, though the puritans and the followers of Penn, who founded the colonies of New-England, flourished with superabundance of land and without negro slaves, they did not flourish without slavery. Though their religious sentiments prompted them to abstain from the purchase of negroes, so severely did they, on that very account feel the want of constant and combined labour, that they were led to carry on an extensive traffic in white men and children, who, kidnapped in Europe, were virtually sold to those fastidious colonists, and treated by them as slaves. But the number of Europeans kidnapped for the purpose of sale in those parts of America where negroes could not be sold, though considerable in proportion to the number of settlers then wanting combined labour, was small when compared with the number of Europeans, who, first decoyed to America by the offer of a passage cost free, and the promise of high wages, were then transferred for terms of years to colonists who paid for their passages. These under the name of *redemptioners,* were, for a long period, the principal servants of those colonies in which slavery was forbidden by law. Even so lately as within the last twenty years, and especially during the last wars between England and America which put a stop to Irish emigration, vast numbers of poor Germans were decoyed to those states which forbid slavery, and there sold for long terms of years to the highest bidder by public auction. Though white and free in name, they were really not free to become inde-pendent land-owners, and therefore it was possible to employ their labor constantly and in combination." Wakefield, *England and America,* 212, 213.

"The members of the society for the abolition of slavery have not the least objection to buying an Irishman or Dutchman, and will chaffer with himself or the captain to get him indented at about the eighth part of the wages they would have to pay a *country born.* But to tell the truth, they who are thus purchased generally do themselves justice and run away before half their term is up. This, then, like every other abuse, falls hard only on the best subjects." In another letter Mr. Rowan wrote, "Swarms of Irish are expected here by the spring vessels, and the brisk trade for *Irish slaves* here is to make up for the low price of flax seed." Cited from Rowan's Letter of 1797 from Wilmington, Del. McLaughlin, *Matthew Lyon,* 43.

[90] The history of slavery in New Jersey offers interesting comparisons with an account of it in Pennsylvania. The growth of the slave system in New Jersey was to a great extent modified by the presence of the Quakers. In the eighteenth century the use of slave labor was general in East Jersey

opposition to the practice of slavery. This opposition was in the nature of a demand for indentured and redemption servants that the labor needs of the colony might be supplied.

---

though not so in West Jersey, and the growth of the antislavery sentiment was in certain sections only. The three great Quaker counties, Burlington, Gloucester, and Salem, at the beginning of the nineteenth century, contained twenty-three per cent of the total population of New Jersey, but only three per cent of the slave population. Cooley, *History of Slavery in New Jersey*, 3, 35.

The subject of slavery was not prominent with the Quakers of Maryland, and for a hundred years after the settlement of the colony, wills, etc., showed that slaves were held. In 1759-1760 there was objection on the part of the Yearly Meeting in Maryland to the importation of Negroes, but not to the holding or buying of those already in the province. In 1777 the Quaker Society in Maryland decided against slaveholding, and the members promptly emancipated their slaves. Scharf, *History of Maryland*, I, 271.

PART III. SUPPLY OF SERVANTS UNDER INDENTURE

CHAPTER VI

HOME SUPPLY OF SERVANTS

While the supply of indentured laborers for Pennsylvania was largely from abroad, some were remanded to a state of servitude from within the colony. Colonial administration and justice sought to dispose of offenders, dependents, and unfortunates, and adopted a plan to which the modern convict labor systems of certain American states may be likened. It was the old yet new question of how to deal with the criminal, the pauper, the debtor, the dependent. As England transported felons, beggars, and the like, to labor in the colonies, so Pennsylvania judged that certain classes of her offenders and delinquents should serve for a term of years under indentures. Servants secured at home included criminals, debtors, persons arrested on suspicion and unable to pay jail fees, orphans and those otherwise helpless. The system of peonage in recent years in several American states is only a modern survival of this old-time practice of selling the labor of a criminal during the period when he is under sentence.

Servitude for misdemeanor is very old. The Levitical law required restitution in case of theft, but when a thief had nothing with which to make restitution, he was subject to sale.[1] Sir Thomas More not only criticized the death penalty for theft, pointing out that it increased rather than decreased the amount of stealing, but he also recommended the substitution of labor as

---

[1] *Exodus* 22:3.

Aristotle thought slavery a natural institution: "It is also from natural causes that some beings command and others obey, that each may obtain their mutual safety; for a being who is endowed with a mind capable of reflection and forethought is by nature the superior and governor, whereas he whose excellence is merely corporeal is formed to be a slave; whence it follows, that the different state of master and slave is equally advantageous to both." *On Government*, Bk. I, Ch. 2.

To the Honourable Gentlemen Justices of the County of
Chester now sitting at Chester at the Court of Common Pleas
there held for the said County The humble Petition of John
Watson prisoner in the County Goall

Humbly Sheweth

That your honours petitioner having Last Court been tryed for an
Action of felony before your Honours And Received According to
your honours Judgments Received Corporial punishment, And now
Lying a perishing Confined for my fine And Charges with some
Small Debts And having nothing to Support me nor to pay the
above fine Charges And debts But by servitude therfore your honours
Petitioner humbly begs your honours may Consider my Case
(being a perishing And nuther friends nor money to Support me)
And Judge me out a Servt what time your honours Shall think
proper for the above articles And your honours petitioner as
in Duty bound Shall ever pray

John Watson

PETITION TO BE SOLD AS A SERVANT

[Original in *Cope Manuscripts*, Historical Society of Pennsylvania]

a punishment.[2] An inhuman law of Edward VI's reign said that as idleness and vagabondry were the mother of all thefts and other mischief, and that as the number given to these was very large, it should be possible for one who had been idle three days to be brought before two justices and branded with a letter "V," when such vagabond became a slave to the one who took him up and could be forced to work by beating, chaining, and otherwise. Be it said to England's credit that this law seems not to have been enforced. (1 Edw. VI, ch. 3.)

Servitude for crime within the territory occupied by Pennsylvania was older than the colony. In the period of Dutch control one who had wounded a soldier at Fort Amsterdam was condemned to serve the company, "along with the blacks," and was ordered sent to the Delaware River by the first ship.[3]

Two or three things led to the sale of criminals in early Pennsylvania. The first was the mild character of Penn's laws. He reduced materially the number of crimes for which capital punishment was inflicted. This left the criminal to be punished and reformed, and society to be protected. It was believed that one means of accomplishing these ends was to place the one convicted under a bond to labor, or to sell him, which sale was usually into the country, away from the greater temptations of the towns. Other treatment was hardly possible. Sufficient jails were not available for offenders, jails were unfit for use, and they did not offer adequate protection. Prisoners might well prefer to be sold into temporary servitude, as authorities might wish them to be sold.[4] Sentencing to servitude was often practiced by early courts as the only means of punishing those who came under their jurisdiction. A Chester county court of two hundred years ago imposed servitude for eight years upon one who had stolen deerskins to the value of forty shillings. From the proceeds of the sale of the indenture the former owner of the skins was to have three

---

[2] *Utopia*, "Camelot Edition," 94, 95, 157.

[3] Hazard, *Annals*, 49.

[4] See below for petitioning of debtors to be sold. An account of the inadequacy and offensiveness of early prisons is given in McMaster, *History of the United States*, I, 99.

times their value, and the costs of the trial were ordered paid.[5]
Sentencing to servitude was made mandatory for housebreaking,
and for the willful firing of houses, woods, ricks, stacks, etc.,
unless the offender could make good four times the amount stolen,
or the damage suffered.[6]

Forgers and counterfeiters, in addition to other punishment,
were required to return double the amount defrauded and to pay
a fine of one hundred pounds. If unable to pay, they were ordered
to be sold by the court trying the offense, but the term for which
they could be sold was limited to seven years.[7] Servitude for
counterfeiters was visited as an alternative punishment as late
as 1760, when an act further to continue this practice was disallowed by the king of England.[8]

The operations of justice on a frontier are shown by the
proceedings of the first court of Lancaster county in 1729. An
accused man was brought to trial charged with the theft of fourteen pounds seven shillings. Though the amount said to have
been stolen had been returned, and the prisoner plead not guilty,
the jury found a true bill against him, and the court judged that
in addition to being publicly whipped with twenty-one lashes "well
laid on the bare back," he should pay fourteen pounds seven
shillings with the costs to the government and the costs to the
plaintiff. The prisoner was then committed to the sheriff until
his fine and costs were paid; he set forth to the court that he had
neither estate nor effects with which to pay, whereupon the
sheriff was ordered to sell him to the highest bidder for a term
not to exceed six years, and to make a report. The report made
in the year following said that the sheriff had sold the prisoner
for six years for sixteen pounds, and that he was not able to
collect one pound and seven shillings of this amount; after hearing this report, the court accepted the amount received as satisfy-

---

[5] Cope, MS. Transcript, *Chester County Court Record*, 143-145; Cheyney, *Philadelphia Manufacturer*, March 16, 1891.

[6] *Statutes at Large*, II, 11, 12. Passed 1701, disallowed by the queen in
Council, 1705-1706.

[7] *Ibid.*, III, 331, 332. Passed 1721 and 1722-1723; reënacted 1723, 1729,
and 1739. *Ibid.*, IV, 113, 359.

[8] *Ibid.*, V, 248, 300, 307, 443.

ing the charges, and the sheriff was relieved.[9]   A person who had stolen one hundred and fourteen dollars in Philadelphia in 1748 was similarly sold into servitude.[10]

In early Pennsylvania, as elsewhere at the same time, debt was regarded as crime.   Benjamin Franklin was not representing a fiction when he said that the debtor came into the power of the creditor: "What would you think of that prince or the government, who should issue an edict forbidding you to dress like gentlemen or gentlewomen on pain of imprisonment or servitude? Your creditor has authority, at his pleasure, to deprive you of your liberty by confining you in jail for life, or to sell you for a servant if you should not be able to pay him." [11]   Imprisonment for debt was common and at times debtors were sold as servants to satisfy the accounts against them.   The county court at its option, and if desired by a creditor, could order the sale of a debtor to satisfy his obligation.   The act making this possible was passed in 1700, and though disallowed in England, it was soon repassed with special reference to those who were suspected of being able to pay but who concealed their property.   At the solicitation of creditors, the county court was empowered to sell as servants those debtors who were unmarried and under fifty-three years of age, but for a term not to exceed seven years; those who were married and not more than forty-six years of age were subject similarly to sale for a term of not more than five years. The only persons exempt from the action of this law were masters of vessels trading to the province.[12]

Prisoners for debt were sometimes held, subject to their finding a purchaser, as appears from a petition to the governor in 1706 from forty-four poor debtors.   The practice of selling debtors, says the annalist Watson, had a wholesome effect on those who would be prodigal, and few got into jail.   It was no

---

[9] Mombert, *History of Lancaster County*, 119-121; Cheyney, *Philadelphia Manufacturer*, March 16, 1891.

[10] *Pennsylvania Gazette*, April 16, 1748.

[11] Franklin, *Works* (Bigelow), I, 450.

[12] Passed 1705 and 1706, and allowed to become a law by lapse of time. Legislation on this subject again in 1723 and 1724.   Repealed 1729.   Revived in part in 1730, and finally repealed in 1810.   *Statutes at Large*, II, 250, 251.

doubt more common, as Watson infers, to sell single men, and the small number of sales by order of the court is probably accounted for through single men escaping the law by seeking a friendly purchaser when they found their debts growing too large.[13]   In the Assembly of 1729-1730 an earlier act, thought to be too harsh, was repealed, and it was provided that a debtor, by surrendering his goods and accounts and taking oath, could go into insolvency, and that he could not thereafter be held for obligations due before.   But this law worked badly, as is shown by the proceedings of the Assembly in the following year.   On January 11, the Assembly had a petition from "diverse inhabitants," in which it was set forth that inconveniences and abuses had arisen under the late act; its repeal was therefore desired, and a reënactment, with suitable amendments, of the earlier law fixing servitude for debt.[14]   A bill was introduced which was passed into a law, and continued in force for upwards of seventy-five years.   According to the preamble of this bill, ill-disposed persons, especially single men and those indebted for small sums which they could have paid by their labor, had wronged their creditors and defeated the intention of the legislature as embodied in an earlier law.   It was therefore ordered that persons under forty, unmarried, and with no children dependent upon them, and indebted for not more than twenty pounds, should be subject to arrest, as before the act of 1729, and that persons imprisoned for less than forty shillings, willing to make satisfaction by servitude, might be adjudged to that state by two magistrates.[15]

---

[13] Watson, *Annals*, I, 358, 359.

[14] *Votes of Assembly*, III, 132, 147.   *Court Papers* (1732-1744).   Historical Society of Pennsylvania.   In 1751, there were thirty-seven debtors in the jail in Philadelphia.   *Record of Indictments*.

[15] *Statutes at Large*, IV, 211-213.   This continued as Pennsylvania's law on debt until repealed in 1810.   *Ibid.*, II, 251.   Gottlieb Mittelberger, at the middle of the eighteenth century, has the following to say to the operation of the law of debt: "If any one contracts debts, and does not or cannot pay them at the appointed time, the best that he has, is taken away from him; but if he has nothing, or not enough, he must go immediately to prison and remain there till some one vouches for him, or till he is sold.   This is done whether he has children or not.   But if he wishes to be released and has children, such a one is frequently compelled to sell a child.   If such a debtor owes only five pounds, or thirty florins, he must serve for

To his Majestys Justices of the Peace at their Court of Common
pleas held at Chester for the Said County the Twenty Ninth Day of
November Anno Domini 1737

The Petition of David Robinson —

Humbly Sheweth   That Whereas Your Petitioner being a
Prisoner in the Common Goal of the Said County at the Suit of Evan
Ellis for four pounds thirteen Shillings & Nine pence And being
also Indebted to Divers persons in Severall Sums of money as
mentioned in the Schedule hereunto Annexed And having Nothin
to Satisfie the Said Debts Prays that Your honors will be pleased
to Admitt me to pay by Servitude

And Your Petitioner as in Duty bound will pray
David Robinson

To his Majestys Justices at their Court of Common pleas held
at Chester for the Said County the First Day of March Anno Dom
1737/8

The Petition of Charles Kennison —

Humbly Sheweth   That Your Petitioner being Confined in the
Common Goal of the Said County at the Suit of Richard Lloyd for
five Pounds Sixteen Shillings Debt & Costs Also a debt of Two
pounds Twelve Shillings to Wm Jones besides Cost Your Petition
humbly prays that Your honors will be pleased to Admitt me
to pay by Servitude & Your Petitioner as in Duty bound will pray
Charles Kennison

PETITIONS TO BE SOLD FOR DEBT

[Originals in *Cope Manuscripts*, Historical Society of Pennsylvania]

The practice of voluntary servitude for debt was common. In 1724, one Henry Hawkins, of Philadelphia, bound himself as a servant for three years to John Harris, of Conestoga, the latter paying Hawkins' lawful debt of £12. Harris was in the courts for bad treatment of Hawkins, and when at a later time the master wished a license to trade with the Indians, his neighbors vouched for him as being a man of good character, having, as it was said, never been in trouble except with his servant Hawkins.[16] Edward Wall, a debtor of Chester county, was in 1832 duly adjudged as owing £5, which he could not pay; he was thrown into jail and petitioned to be sold as a servant.[17] On June 15, 1737, debtors in the Philadelphia jail petitioned to be sold for their debts.[18] The same year James Ferguson petitioned the court of Chester county, saying that he owed a debt of £20, for which he had been six months in jail, and that he had suffered great hardship from cold and hunger. The petitioner acknowledged the debt and expressed a willingness to serve his creditor four years in satisfaction of the debt and costs. The court adjudged that the debtor should serve four years and three months.[19] (Petitions to be sold to satisfy debts are shown opposite.)

But not all debtors were sold, as appears from a list of thirty-seven in the Philadelphia jail in 1751[20] It may have been that slowness of sale led debtors to advertise for purchasers. A single issue of the *Pennsylvania Gazette* in 1759 had two such requests. One debtor said that he had served a regular apprenticeship at sea, but he offered himself to any purchaser who would satisfy an obligation of about £17. Another prisoner for debt asked that negotiations for his sale be made through the printer of the *Gazette*.[21] A debtor in Lancaster County jail was released to

---

it a year or longer, and so in proportion to his debt; but if a child of 8, 10, or 12 years of age is given for it, said child must serve until he or she is 21 years old." *Journey to Pennsylvania*, Translation, 91.

[16] *Cope Manuscripts.*

[17] *Ibid.*

[18] *MS. Court Papers* (1732-1744), Historical Society of Pennsylvania.

[19] *Cope Manuscripts.*

[20] *Records of Indictments*, Historical Society of Pennsylvania.

[21] *Pennsylvania Gazette*, October 10, 1759.

serve one who paid his obligation, but he promptly ran away,[22] as did another in Chester County who was released on bail with an indenture as security.[23]

Notice of a runaway servant in 1739 recited the facts that the fellow had come as a freeman, but that he had later fallen into bad company, which brought trouble upon him and reduced him to servitude.[24] (The petition on the opposite page shows how a freeman might become a servant.)

Other aspects of servitude are to be observed in the Record of Indentures before the mayor of Philadelphia. In 1772, John Miller, a freeman twenty-five years of age, appeared and bound himself as servant for one year for a consideration of £20. The agreement specified that Miller was to be found in meat, drink, washing, and lodging only.[25] Differences in indentures from including or not including "freedom dues" are shown in comparison of the foregoing with an agreement of Alexander Miller, who bound himself for two years for a consideration of £12 6s. 6d., the difference in terms being that the latter was to have in addition to all "necessaries" the customary two complete suits of apparel, one of which was to be new.[26]

In 1782, the overseers of the poor in Philadelphia, in accordance with a late act of the Assembly, offered to sell two women on the ground that they were public charges.[27] Seven years later the same officers advertised that there were in the workhouse at Philadelphia a number of men and women whom they were authorized to bind out for terms not exceeding three years. Those who desired to purchase these were directed to call on the steward of the workhouse who would show those to be sold and make known the terms.[28]

In 1787, the keeper of the workhouse at Philadelphia advertised for sale one described as a strong German servant girl with

[22] *Ibid.*, January 27, 1774.

[23] *Ibid.*, July 10, 1776.

[24] *Ibid.*, July 20, 1739.

[25] *Record of Indentures before Mayor*, p. 180, American Philosophical Society.

[26] *Ibid.*, p. 640.

[27] *Pennsylvania Gazette*, May 8, 1782.

[28] *Ibid.*, February 3, 1789.

To the Worshipful the Mayor Recorder and Aldermen
of the City of Philadelphia

⁘ The Petition of James Gaynor

Humbly sheweth

That your Petitioner came lately into this
Province and lodged at one Simon Wyer's where by his
Persuasion he spent a considerable Sum of Money ——
But perceiving his Money wasted and that he was
in no Employment he bought a Flat which cost him
twenty nine Pounds.

Your Petitioner afterward finding flatting of little
Advantage was discouraged and thereupon the ——
said Simon Wyer one morning artfully persuaded him being
in drink, to bind himself for a Servant to him for
four Years and to convey him the said Flat in ——
Consideration of forty Pounds to be paid him at the ——
Expiration of the Time. And further told your ——
Petitioner that whenever he repented of the Bargain
it should be broke,

Your Petitioner perceiving the unjustice done ——
him has since frequently desired his Master to
discharge him from his Service according to his
Promise and likewise offered to release him from
all Demands on Account of the said Contract. But his
Master in Pursuance of his first unjust Design
has refused so to do contrary to Equity and Justice.

Wherefore your Petitioner prays on consideration of the Premises that your Worships would
be pleased to relieve your Petitioner in such ——
manner as you shall think proper and he will
ever pray &c;

HOW A FREEMAN BECAME A SERVANT (1740)
[Original Court Papers, Historical Society of Pennsylvania]

the attending explanation: "For no other fault but impertinence to her mistress.".[29] A few years later the Philadelphia workhouse advertised for sale an Irish servant girl with three years to serve. In this instance no explanation was given as to why she was in the workhouse.[30]

Persons wandering about who could not give satisfactory accounts of themselves were not infrequently seized on suspicion and lodged in jail. Notices with descriptions of these were then inserted in the colonial newspapers, and if a master came to claim them, the court would lengthen the term of service to make return for rewards, costs, etc.; but if no owner appeared, in due time the persons confined would be advertised for sale to pay prison charges. In 1770, there were advertised in the *Pennsylvania Gazette* upwards of forty persons seized on suspicion, generally with the notice, "thought to be runaway servants." [31] A limited number of servants was thus furnished by those sold to satisfy the jail fees.

Children were often bound to service under indenture, sometimes by parents and guardians, but more often as orphans, by order of the courts. Thirty-three were put out at one time by the court of Chester County, the court fixing their terms of service.[32] The value of giving schooling or of teaching a trade was early recognized.[33] Children whose parents were not able

---

[29] *Pennsylvania Packet,* August 10, 1787.

[30] *Pennsylvania Gazette,* January 28, 1801.

[31] See Chapter XI on runaways. There seems to have been no means by which the master could be compelled to take a servant if he did not want him.

"Philadelphia, March 20, 1760.

"To be sold out of the goal of this City, by Issachar Davids, by order of the magistracy, to satisfy costs and expences, a runaway servant boy, named William Aberdeen, his master John Walker, of Chester County, having refused to take him out. He is a lively healthy boy about thirteen years old.

"N.B. If the said master does not take him out, and pay the fees, in three weeks from this date, he will be sold to pay the charges, by Issachar Davids, Goaler." *Pennsylvania Gazette,* April 3, 1760.

An advertisement of persons seized and held on suspicion of being runaways (1742-1743), in Hart, *History Told by Contemporaries,* II, 299.

[32] Futhey and Cope, *History of Chester County,* 430.

[33] Martin (*History of Chester and Vicinity,* 75) gives an account of an

to support them might be bound by overseers of the poor.[34]   The
act of 1713, establishing orphans' courts, gave the judges the power
to authorize executors and administrators under certain conditions to apprentice orphans.[35]   A boy sixteen years old was
offered for sale from the Philadelphia workhouse in 1755.   The
lad was described as having been born in the province, and as
being able to read, write, and cipher.[36]

What ordinarily passes as the apprentice system differs from
that now under discussion in that there was the agreement to
teach a trade, and it was later ruled by the superior court that a
father could not legally bind his child unless he were apprenticed
to learn a trade.[37]   But "trade" was given a very liberal interpretation; thus "The art or trade of house-wifery" was not uncommon.   The indentures indicated the operation of the system
as it applied to people within the colony.[38]

The history of indentured labor throws an interesting sidelight on the sad fate of a people whose sufferings, as depicted

indenture in which the boy was to serve five and one-half years if taught
to read and write, and but five years if not.

[34] *Statutes at Large*, II, 253.

[35] *Ibid.*, III, 18; *Votes of Assembly*, II, 135, 136.

[36] *Pennsylvania Gazette*, January 28, 1755.

[37] "Respublica vs. Keppele" *Dallas Reports*, II, 197, 198.

[38] An indenture of 1743 was as follows: "This Indenture Witnesseth
that Elizabeth Hastings, Daughter of Henry Hastings of West Bradford in
the County of Chester and Province of Pensilvania, Yeoman, hath put herself and by these presents doth voluntarily and of her own free will and
with the consent of her Parents put herself Apprentice to Phebe Buffington
of West Bradford afforesaid, and after the manner of an apprentice to serve
her from the day of the Date hereof for and During the Term of Five
Years Eight Months next ensuing the date hereof, During all of which
Term the said Apprentice her said Mistress faithfully shall serve, her
secrets keep, her Lawful Commands gladly every where obey.   She shall
do no damage to her said Mistress nor see it to be done by others without
Letting or giving notice thereof to her said Mistress.   She shall not waste
her said Mistress's goods nor lend them unlawfully to any.   She shall not
commit fornication nor Contract matrimony within the said Term.   At
Cards, Dice, or any other unlawful Game she shall not play whereby her
Mistress may have Damage.   With her own goods nor the goods of others,
without Licence from her said Mistress she shall neither buy nor sell.   She
shall not absent herself Day nor Night from her Mistress's Service without her leave, nor haunt Ale-Houses, Taverns, or Play Houses, but in all

in Longfellow's "Evangeline," have touched the hearts of two generations of English readers. The inhabitants of Nova Scotia, to a considerable number, were by a council of war ordered distributed among the English colonies. "French neutrals" they were called at the time, but they are now best known as Acadian peasants. Nine hundred of these are said to have been received into Maryland, and as a resident of the colony reported, they soon became such a burden that it was not known what could be done with them. Indentures for a short term were offered to them, but these were refused, and the Acadians insisted on being treated as prisoners of war. They were dependents and as no provision had been made for their support, and as they would not accept servitude, they became objects of private charity.[39]

Bancroft well says that relentless misfortune pursued these exiles.[40] Upwards of four hundred were assigned to Pennsyl-

---

things behave herself as a faithful Apprentice ought to do, During the said Term. And in Consideration of the said Term the said Mistress shall procure and provide for her said Apprentice sufficient Meat, Drink, Apparel, Lodging and Washing fitting for an Apprentice both in health and sickness During the sd Term, Together with Two Cows and Two Calves, Each Cow and Calf to be worth Four pounds of Current money of Pensilvania in the following manner—One Cow and Calf to be delivered unto above named Henry Hastings for the use of said apprentice in the spring in the year 1746 and the other Cow and Calf in the spring in the year of Our Lord 1748. And the said Mistress shall learn her said Apprentice to Sew and Knitt so as to know how to make a man's shirt and knitt Stocking and to give her one month's schooling in Reading and Writing within the said Term and at the Expiration of said Term said Mistress shall procure for her said Apprentice One full Suit of new Apparel besides her working Apparel. And for the true performance of all and every the said Covenants and agreements either of said parties bind themselves unto the Order by these presents. In witness whereof they have Interchangeably put their hands and seals this ninth day of April One Thousand Seven hundred and forty and three. 1743.

Signed, Seald and Delivered   "Phebe Buffington (Seal)
in the presence of
"John Buffington
"Amy Bate
"Jno. McCarty."

Furthey and Cope, *History of Chester County,* 431.

[39] Daniel Dulany, "Letter from Maryland," *Pa. Mag. of Hist. and Biog.,* III, 147.

[40] Bancroft, *History of the United States,* II, 434.

vania, and soon there arose the question of how to care for them. It is both reported and denied that the Pennsylvania authorities proposed to sell them with their own consent. No record has been found to show that the whole party was offered for sale at one time, but there is much to warrant the opinion that many of them were offered indentures. The redemption system was at its height; helpless and unfortunate people were offered indentures to relieve their distresses; and as the Acadians were of this class, they were beyond question solicited to accept indentures until they could learn the English language, and adjust themselves to the situation in which a strange fate had placed them. It scarcely appears that such a policy was altogether iniquitous, as seems to have been inferred by some who have undertaken Pennsylvania's defense by claiming that indentures were not offered. These people had been thrust upon the province and they were unable to help themselves; it surely was not a heinous offense to offer them an opportunity to accept what seemed the only means of self-help.[41]

An address of Governor Morris conveyed to the Assembly the information that some of the Acadians arrived in November, 1755.[42] At various times the Assembly was in receipt of petitions from Acadians; one of these, from John Baptiste Galerm, charged the wrongs for which they were all suffering upon a few of the French neutrals who lived at the lower end of the Bay of Fundy.[43] In February following, commissioners were appointed to prepare a bill distributing the neutrals among the several counties of Pennsylvania. The bill, which was reported from the commission and passed in March of 1756, is significant. It recognized that these people were in the colony because it was most advantageous to the British interest for them to be; they were without means, and were kept at public charge; it was thought that

---

[41] Entick (*History of Seven Years' War*) charges Pennsylvania with wishing to sell the Acadians with their own consent. Walsh attempted to free the colony from the charge. See Walsh. *Appeal*, 89 and 437 sqq. See also on this controversy William B. Reed, "The French Neutrals in Pennsylvania," in *Contributions to American History*, Pubs. of Hist. Soc. of Pa., 1858.

[42] *Votes of Assembly*, IV, 519.

[43] *Ibid.*, 537-539.

the several townships and parts of the province might give them an opportunity to secure their subsistence by their own labor. Commissioners were appointed with authority to dispose of the poor Acadians by distributing them through Philadelphia, Chester, Bucks, and Lancaster counties. Moreover, the commissioners were enjoined to exercise their authority and to provide for the distribution within twenty days from the passage of the act. To supplement the work of the commissioners it was further ordered that the overseers of the poor in the several townships of the counties named should receive and provide for the persons assigned to them.[44] The duty imposed by this act seems to have been neither pleasant nor easy, for in October a remonstrance appeared from one of the commissioners, reciting the difficulties of his task: some of the neutrals refused to work, others could not find work, and the inhabitants disliked to employ them.[45] Governor Denny, in a proclamation of 1757, said that the townships had neglected the Acadians and that many of them were in distress. He implied that the failure to reimburse the townships for aid to these people had caused the neglect, and recommended that funds be transferred to townships from the sum granted for the king's use.[46]

While it was not mandatory upon the overseers of the poor that they offer indentures to these Acadians, or that these be accepted if offered, it was quite within the discretion of the overseers to suggest a practice often resorted to for debtors and unfortunates. As this was a way open to the natives of the colony, so it would seem natural that it should be made available to those thrust into the colony from the outside.[47] The indentured system was long regarded, both in the mother country and in the colonies, as a legitimate means of poor relief. Entick was probably quite correct in saying that temporary servitude was offered to the Acadians in Pennsylvania, but this does not necessarily warrant

---

[44] *Votes of Assembly,* IV, 543; *Statutes at Large,* V, 216-219.

[45] *Votes of Assembly,* IV, 637-638. Further petition from the Acadians, February, 1757. *Ibid.,* 684-686.

[46] *Pennsylvania Gazette,* October 20, 1757.

[47] It was directed in 1757 that those incapable of providing for themselves should be cared for by the overseers of the poor "in like manner as the poor inhabitants of this province." *Statutes at Large,* V, 280.

the imputation of discredit with which the statement was made. This opinion is advanced the more confidently because of several related facts. Within a year after the law for distributing the Acadians was enacted, a supplementary act was passed requiring and enjoining overseers of the poor, within two months, or as soon thereafter as they conveniently could, to bind out such Acadian children as were then unprovided for, boys until twenty-one and girls until eighteen years of age. Such action was to be by and with the consent and approval of one or more justices of the peace. The act further directed that the assignment was to be to kind masters or mistresses on the best terms that could be obtained; it was also ordered as a condition of these indentures that the children should be taught to read and write the English language, and that they should be trained in such "honorable and profitable occupations" as gave promise of preparing them to support themselves when their indentures expired.[48] That the action taken was in the interest of the Acadians themselves, and not to the discredit of Pennsylvania, appears from the willingness to relieve the unfortunates from their indentures. A further act of 1757 provided for freeing of the Acadians from apprenticeship, and gave the government's reward to the master for damages.[49] Both general practice and the dealing with separate cases indicate that some of the unhappy people of Evangeline became Pennsylvania servants under indenture.

The home supply of servants was never large. In the early period when jails were inadequate and before sufficient workhouses and almshouses had been established, a number were reduced to this state. A new country offered less temptation to run away, and less opportunity for further misdemeanor; but as the country became more thickly settled, there were increased dangers from having criminals at large; it was also more difficult to prevent offenders from leaving the employment to which they had been assigned; at the same time, better means were provided to care for the evil doers, the needy, and the ill-disposed, in institutions. Court records and advertisements indicate that the home supply of servants grew relatively less during the progress of the eighteenth century.

---

[48] *Statutes at Large*, V. 278-280.
[49] *Ibid*, 315.

CHAPTER VII

TRANSPORTATION AS A SOURCE OF SUPPLY

The demands for servants, treated in earlier chapters, were complementary to the desire of Europe to dispose of a part of her people. Indentured laborers were secured largely from abroad, the colonies serving as an outlet for the peoples that either were not wanted at home or did not desire to stay there. Political, social, industrial, and religious differences impelled large numbers to seek homes elsewhere; so intent were people on reaching the New World that many who were without other means sold themselves into temporary servitude to secure their passage. England of the seventeenth century has been termed a "storehouse from which as large a supply of servants could be drawn as the plantation possessed the means to secure." [1] Pennsylvania could not well have sustained her industry or maintained her sentiment against the employment of slave labor had there not been other laborers to take the place of slaves. The present chapter and the two following will consider the European supply of white servants, a supply which came almost entirely from Great Britain and Germany.

British subjects who came to the North American colonies as servants were of two classes: transported political offenders, felons or convicts; and freemen who sold themselves for their passage in order that they might better their condition. The second class was much the more numerous, but a sufficient number of the others came to affect relations with the mother country in such ways that notice of the policy of transportation is necessary. The chief interest of this subject in Pennsylvania was in preventive measures against admitting felons; the colony took most positive and uncompromising ground against receiving transported convicts. Great Britain's policy and the experience of other colonies are explaining causes for the determined resistance of Pennsylvania. Convicts sent to the settlements would, it was thought in England, be a double source of gain: the policy

---

[1] Cunningham, *Growth of English Industry and Commerce,* 201; Bruce, *Economic History of Virginia,* I, 587.

would rid the home country of a troublesome population; and it would build up the colonies, from which an indirect advantage was expected. The first was an immediate return from colonizing; the second was a prospective gain from colonies. The objection of England's North American settlements was that no distinction was made between colonizing with convicts and colonizing with free laborers; that felons were sent as though they would satisfy every demand of the new settlements for people.

Temporary exile from the home country of those who for some reason were recorded as undesirables was practiced by the nations of antiquity, more particularly by the Greeks and the Romans. Transportation or deportation of convicts was practiced by various nations of modern Europe; it was said to have been begun by the Portuguese, who sent felons to their settlements in Africa and South America.[2] An English merchant, about the middle of the eighteenth century, speaks of the recruiting of the Portuguese settlements by transportation of felons and vagabonds.[3] Early French attempts at founding settlements with felons, and their failure, are well known. France is reported to have sent over large numbers of her vagrant population to the settlements on the Mississippi and in the West Indies.[4] Religious refugees were also sentenced to transportation from France. After the revocation of the Edict of Nantes, some of the Huguenots who would not accept Catholicism were ordered to serve under the system of peonage which was introduced into the French islands by the buccaneers, and perpetuated by the planters who succeeded in control.[5] German convicts were also received as servants; as late as 1753, Franklin cautioned against the admission of German felons, saying that a practice had been adopted by shipowners of "sweeping the German jails to make up the number of their passengers."[6]

That harm might be done to the colonies by sending felons seems not to have occupied a prominent place in the minds of those who furthered the policy. It was believed that New World

---

[2] Merivale, *Colonization and Colonies*, 349.

[3] Appendix to Gee, *Trade and Navigation* (Glasgow Edition of 1767).

[4] Gee, *Trade and Navigation*, 59, 60 (London Edition of 1729).

[5] Baird, *Huguenot Emigration to America*, I, 217-221.

[6] Franklin, *Works* (Bigelow), II, 299.

conditions would give less opportunity and less temptation to pursue the old life.[7] John Marshall, eminent as a protector of American institutions, after noting the introduction of convicts, passed on to say of the effects of their importation: "The policy which dictated this measure was soon perceived to be not less wise than it was humane. Men who, in Europe, were the pests of the body politic, made an acceptable addition to the stock of labor in the colonies; and in a new world, where the temptations to crime seldom presented themselves, many of them became useful members of society."[8] But the best commentary on the effects of transportation is an account of the attitude of the colonies toward the reception of convicts.

Transportation of what are termed political prisoners preceded transportation of convicts. Insurrections and revolts in various parts of Great Britain during the seventeenth century brought to attention a considerable class of inhabitants whom it

---

[7] An exponent of England's colonial system wrote: "We know the greatest part of the Convicts are bold, daring, debauched People; but many of them, when they are transported into the Colonies, we are assured come to severe Repentance for their past Lives, and become very industrious; if Provision was made to allow each of them, 100 Acres or more of Land free for some Time, and afterwards to pay, by Way of quit-Rent, one hundred weight (being 112 pounds) of well dressed Hemp or Flax, for every 100 Acres so granted them, the Prospect of having Land of their own would induce them to continue their Industry; His Majesty would thereby receive sufficient Supplies of Hemp and Flax for the Royal Navy, a Revenue that would far exceed any Income that the Government receives from any of our Colonies; and being under no Difficulty to subsist, they would marry young, increase and multiply, and supply themselves with every Thing they want from us, but their Food; by which Means those vast Tracts of Land now waste, would be planted, and secured from the Danger we apprehend." Gee, *Trade and Navigation*, 60, 61.

Writing in 1625, Sir Francis Bacon said of the practice of transportation: "It is a shameful and unblessed thing to take the scum of people and wicked condemned men, to be the people with whom you plant; and not only so, but it spoileth the plantation; for they will ever live like rogues, and not fall to work; but be lazy, and do mischief, and spend victuals, and be quickly weary, and then certify over to their country to the discredit of the plantation. The people wherewith you plant ought to be gardeners, ploughmen, laborers, smiths, carpenters, joiners, fishermen, fowlers, with some few apothecaries, surgeons, cooks, and bakers." *Essays*, "Of Plantations."

[8] Marshall, *Colonies*, 55, 56.

was desirable to have out of the way, but whose crimes were not sufficiently grave to warrant their execution; consequently the old custom of banishment or ostracism was practiced. Of those transported in the seventeenth century, political prisoners, or offenders against the government rather than against the law, constituted the larger class, though some felons were sent. A late law of Elizabeth's reign provided that those termed "dangerous rogues, vagabonds, and sturdy beggars" might be banished out of the realm and conveyed to places assigned by the Privy Council, and that if they returned, they were to be regarded as felons.[9]

Four years after the act just mentioned, the famous poor law of Elizabeth was passed. Earlier acts were gathered together in this; it also served as the basis for future legislation for poor relief. The essentials of this law were: aid for those who could not labor; a chance to work for those who could and would labor; and punishment and compulsion for those who could labor, but would not do so. In carrying out this act, the distinction was clearly made between the "impotent poor" and "sturdy beggars."[10] Transportation was one of the ways of dealing with the latter class.

It was an earlier practice for convicts to petition for the right to adjure the realm, and sentences were sometimes commuted on condition that they would do this. In advance of a permanent English settlement, Captain Martin Frobisher was given a license to secure from English prisons recruits for colonies which he might establish.[11]

The reign of James I, which saw the first permanent English settlements in America, also began transportation on a considerable scale. Chief Justice Popham, interested in colonial ventures as well as in the administration of justice, is credited with the suggestion to James. It is probable that he aimed to serve the ends of justice as well as to insure colonial success. James exercised the royal prerogative in the transportation of convicts, and in 1619 peremptorily ordered the Virginia council to receive a parcel of a hundred "dissolute persons" intended for

---

[9] *39 Elizabeth*, ch. 4.
[10] *43 Elizabeth*, ch. 2.
[11] Egerton, *Origin and Growth of English Colonies*, 131, 132.

them.[12] In his essay "Of Plantations," Bacon termed the "wicked condemned men" who were being sent out, "the scum of the people," and he called the sending of them a "shameful and unblessed thing." At the time of Charles II, there were in England some three hundred offenses for which the death punishment could be inflicted; in 1661, it was provided that justices might send to the colonies such as were condemned to death for minor crimes, also single men and women, sturdy beggars, and disorderly persons.[13]

A committee of the Council of Plantations had recommended that the Parliament pass the act that the classes above named be transported and consigned to four years of service if above twenty years of age, or to seven years if they were under twenty. An office of registry for those who were sent was provided on September 7, 1664.[14] The later years of Charles II's reign saw other legislation for relieving England from a possible congestion of criminals,[15] but the years in which he was England's king gave a plentiful supply of political offenders which was larger and certainly more troublesome. After the defeat of Charles I at Worcester, his soldiers, sixteen hundred in number, were seized and sent to America. After Monmouth's rebellion in 1685, a circular was issued to the governors of the English possessions, directing that the rebels exiled be received, and not allowed to return or to redeem themselves by payment of money until the term for which they were sentenced had expired. The later Jacobite insurrections also furnished servants for the colonies.[16] Two shiploads of political prisoners were sent to Maryland as late as 1717, and of these eighty were sold as servants.[17] Maryland seems also to have received some of those who championed the cause of the Young Pretender in 1745.[18] But fewer political

---

[12] Lang, *Transportation and Colonization*, 9, 10.

[13] *Cal. State Papers*, "Colonial Series," 1661-1668, pp. xxvii and 35.

[14] *Ibid.*, 221, 232.

Lists of the convicts sent from Newgate to the plantations are mentioned in *Cal. State Papers*, "Colonial Series," 1661-1668, p. 451.

[15] *18 of Charles II*, ch. 3; 33, ch. 2.

[16] Doyle, *English in America*, Virginia, Maryland, and the Carolinas, 383.

[17] List of these and names of purchasers in Scharf, *History of Maryland*, I, 385-389.

[18] Riley, *Ancient City*, 126.

prisoners were available after 1688, and from that time, at least as compared with felons, their number was insignificant.[19]

Protest and resistance to Great Britain's policy of sending felons came from the beginning, and out of all sections to which convicts were sent. The island of Jamaica early made a complaint, speaking of criminals as undesirable and charging that they were corrupt before they were sent forth.[20] A law was enacted in Virginia in 1671 to prevent the landing of felons, who had already been found troublesome, and though it was enforced with difficulty, we are assured that it was rigorously enforced.[21] An act against importation into Maryland was considered at various times and such an act was actually passed in 1676, but it was disallowed by the home government and for fear of forfeiture of charter was not reënacted.[22] Pennsylvania's policy of resistance

---

[19] Butler (*American Historical Review*, II, 16) thinks that possibly throughout the time of transportation felons outnumbered political offenders, and calls attention to what has been a very obvious tendency to call those received political prisoners rather than criminals before the law.

[20] *Cal. State Papers*, "Colonial Series," 1661-1668, pp. xxix, xxx.

[21] Bruce, *Economic History of Virginia*, I, 605, 606.

[22] Scharf, *History of Maryland*, I, 372, 384.

Maryland sought as best she could to protect herself against convicts. In 1728, a law was passed requiring all captains who brought convicts into the colony to furnish a statement of the offense committed, the place of conviction and the number of years which each person was to serve. A fine of five hundred pounds was fixed upon any captain who refused to declare under oath whether any of his passengers were convicts. For each convict imported without full information of the place and nature of the crime committed, the captain was fined five pounds. McCormac, *White Servitude in Maryland*, 101.

Soon after passage of the law just noted, an article appeared in the *Pennsylvania Gazette* as follows: "An errant cheat detected at Annapolis! A vessel arrived there, bringing sixty-six indentures, signed by the mayor of Dublin, and twenty-two *wigs*, of such a make as if they were intended for no other use than to set out the *convicts* when they should go ashore." The annalist after quoting the preceding, adds: "Thus these convicts were attempted, under fraudulent papers and *decent wigs*, to be set off as decent servants and especially when surmounted with wigs." Watson, *Annals*, II, 267.

A New Jersey act under the title, "Duty on Persons convicted of heinous crimes and to prevent Poor and impotent persons being imported," etc., was disallowed by order in council, April 13, 1732. Board of Trade, *Journals*, Vol. 42, p. 202.

to receiving convicts constituted an important part of the history of the relations of this colony to the mother country.

A new chapter in the history of transportation was opened when early in the reign of George I (1717) a sweeping act was passed, to be strengthened by a supplementary law four years later. This legislation claimed that acts in force had not prevented robbery, and that persons to whom royal clemency had been extended on condition that they transport themselves had failed to fulfill that condition. Moreover, it was said that in America there was great need for servants who would by labor and industry make the settlements of greater value to the nation. It was therefore provided that in case of minor offenses, grand or petit larceny, and other misdemeanors for which benefit of clergy was allowed and upon which whipping and burning in the hand were visited, criminals might be sent to the American colonies for seven years. Similar offenders who were in the workhouses were included, as under certain conditions were those who had violated customs regulations in the exporting of wool.

Further, the same act directed that where persons had been convicted or stood attainted of any offense for which death might be inflicted, under the law, or where they were convicted of any crime for which benefit of clergy was denied them, judges might commute the sentences to transportation for fourteen years in the plantations. Royal clemency was to be extended to these offenders by the judges who might under the great seal allow the benefit of pardon, but on the condition of transportation to America. Persons who received or bought stolen goods, knowing them to be stolen, were also subject to transportation for fourteen years, but might be sent for a shorter term. In every case felons were subject to the court before which convicted, or to any subsequent court with equal jurisdiction, and could be conveyed, transferred, or made over for the use of any persons who would contract for their transference, and to the assigns of any such persons.[23]

---

[23] *4 George I,* ch. ii, sec. 1.

Chalmers (*Colonial Opinions,* 334) states that there were three grades of offenses for which the terms of transportation were respectively seven years, fourteen years, and for life. A counterfeiter who had been sent to the colonies for life was advertised as having run away from Alexander Spotswood. *Pennsylvania Gazette,* June 16, 1738.

Should transported felons return before the expiration of the terms for which they were sentenced, they became "attainted of felony," and the death punishment was made not merely optional but mandatory. Pardon was possible for any transported felon during his term in the colonies, but if granted, his "Owner or proprietor" was to be paid a sum agreed upon as reasonable by two justices of the peace residing in the province in which the felon was held. The completion of the term for which convicts were transported was held to be the same as full pardon to all intents and purposes.[24]

The arrangements earlier than this law, viz., that felons be pardoned on conditions that they secure transportation, had proved ineffectual.[25] Now the whole matter was left in the hands of the court. Judges had power to convey, or to assign for conveyance; the latter power was exercised by the letting of contracts with sufficient security to satisfy the court that the felons would be transported ("effectually") to some colony in America. The court required that the contracting party return a certificate of the landing of those transported, which certificate was to be furnished free of cost by the governor or chief customs official of the place to which they were sent.[26]

Colonial opposition to receiving convicts gave trouble in finding a place to which to send them. It was no doubt expected that the sale of their assignments or indentures on arrival would be adequate to secure the necessary contracts to carry them over. But many colonies refused them, in others they found a slow sale, and captains felt that the safety of vessels was endangered if too many criminals were taken at one time. That insurrections on convict ships were not numerous was due in part to the passengers being unable to handle a vessel.

A combination of causes led to the supplementary act of 1719, the preamble to which said that the laws in force had not

---

[24] *4 George I*, ch. ii, sec. 2.

[25] In 1697, the Board of Trade made a representation setting forth the difficulty of disposing of convicts. The matter was referred for inquiry, to determine where convicts might be sent, and what punishment might be imposed in lieu of transportation. Lang, *Transportation and Colonization*, 12, 13.

[26] *4 George I*, ch. ii, sec. 3.

proved effectual to the suppression of robbery, and to the transporting of felons.   It was in giving better security for getting
felons out of the realm that the amended act differed from the
act preceding.   License was given for taking offenders through
any part of Great Britain to the port from which they were to
be shipped.   Persons rescuing felons or assisting them to make
their escape were to be adjudged deserving of death.   Persons
ordered for transportation and found before the expiration of
their terms within the realm of Great Britain were still held
subject to the death penalty.[27]

Pennsylvania's objection to convicts was first expressed in
1683, when it was proposed that "no felons be brought into this
country." [28]   The danger, however, was not immediate and the
opposition did not take the form of laws until after the parliamentary acts in the fourth and sixth years of the reign of
George I.   Following this legislation there was a new interest in
the subject of receiving convicts in the colonies, because immediately larger numbers of them were sent.   The *American Weekly
Mercury's* London letter, appearing February 7, 1721, but dated
October 29 preceding, stated that ninety-two "malefactors" were
carried from Newgate, others also from the Marshalsea, to go on
board a ship for transportation to America.   Among these was
one famous criminal, William Wrigglesdew, who had formerly
robbed the King's Chapel at Whitehall, and it was said that
Wrigglesdew carried with him a great quantity of cutlers' ware
for purposes of trade.   In the succeeding issue of the *Mercury*
(February 14), the Philadelphia letter gave information that the
malefactors formerly mentioned (describing them) had arrived in
Maryland to the number of above one hundred and eighty.   Their
punishment of hard service, it was said, was cunningly avoided
if they could muster money to pay the merchant for the trouble
of their passage, in which case there was "with them only this
part of their sentence to be answered, that they must not return
to England in so many years."   The people of Philadelphia were
warned against these, as positive advice had been received that

---

[27] 6 *George I*, ch. 22, secs. 1-6.

[28] *Colonial Records*, I, 72.   In the same connection was a proposition
concerning the return of runaway servants which was passed in the affirmative.

some of them would be in the city in a short time. Further on in the same letter in a discussion of the policy of transportation the belief was expressed that "what's bred in the bone will never out of the flesh." Examples were cited of Spain and other kingdoms which had particular islands to which criminals could be banished, where they were "sure of getting no better company than themselves" and where they would not be able to "debauch the honest natures and manners of mankind." It was considered a pity that England had no similar islands or colonies to which to transport felons. Two of the three columns of news matter in this issue of the *Mercury* were devoted to the question of receiving felons. In the week following, the statement was made that several of the convict malefactors previously mentioned passed through the city on their way to New York, from which place it was said to be their plan to go to Boston.

On April 13 following, the *Mercury's* London letter said that sixty felons were transported from Newgate in the preceding May, but that sixteen of these had found means to make their escape. That such did not always evade the law is made plain from a later communication: "On Saturday last the Sessions ended at the Old Bailey, when several received sentence of death for having returned after transportation, and several other convicts are ordered to be transported." [29] Additional information on this subject was called to the attention of Pennsylvanians by the *Mercury* during 1721. A significant London letter read: "We hear, that several of our merchants' ships have declined carrying any more felons to the plantations, notwithstanding they have been very much press'd upon that score, and have had large offers to engage them to it; alledging in excuse, that though they may in the general be serviceable to the planters; yet they are so notoriously guilty in corrupting the people there, that the country are heartily weary of them." [30] A further record of the administration of justice ran: "On Saturday last the Sessions ended at the Old Bailey, where twelve malefactors, seven men and five women received sentence of death, sixteen were ordered for transportation, and five to be whipped.

---

[29] *American Weekly Mercury,* June 11, 1721.
[30] *Ibid.,* September 7, 1721. London letter, dated May 20 preceding.
[31] *Ibid.,* October 12, 1721. London letter of July 22.

Public sentiment on this question had been aroused and the exclusion of convicts was a prominent question before the Pennsylvania legislature in the session of 1721-1722. The first law for exclusion was then passed, fixing a duty of five pounds on every convict brought into the colony, and requiring in addition, before such convict servant could be landed, that the person importing him should with satisfactory security become bound to the amount of fifty pounds for the good behavior of the servant during one year. The better to ascertain who were convicts, it was required that those who brought servants should within twenty-four hours after the arrival of their ships furnish a certified list of those imported. One or more justices of the peace, with power to summon witnesses, could examine further into the importation, and if the persons brought were thought fit to be landed, a certificate of permission was issued in the form of a list containing their names. Violation of the above requirements made a servant free, notwithstanding any private agreement into which he might have entered.[32]

The law of 1722 was the basis for numerous other acts passed from time to time. The Assembly of 1725-1726 ordered the reading of the act of 1722, and the officer appointed under it was directed to be very diligent in the discharge of his duty, as the Assembly had been informed that great numbers of convicts, and some Irish servants of "bad reputation," had already arrived,

---

[32] *Statutes at Large*, III, 265-267.

The motion in Assembly was for a duty "on such Servants as shall be imported into this Province that are Suspected or can be made to appear to be Convicts or transported out of a Prison in Europe." The motion prevailed and a bill was brought in accordingly. *Votes of Assembly*, II, 314, 316. For a record of the bill before the colonial council see *Colonial Records*, III, 163, 166. A duty of £10 was fixed by the legislature on the importation of convict Negroes. *Votes of Assembly*, II, 469.

The reasons for the above law were thus stated: "Whereas many persons trading into this province have, for hire and private gain, imported and sold or disposed of, and daily do import and sell as servants for term of years, divers persons convicted of heinous crimes, who, soon after their coming into this province, do often run away, etc., and commit many heinous felonies," etc., "to the great loss of persons purchasing such servants, and to the great hurt in general to His Majesty's good subjects residing in and trading to and from this province:

Be it therefore enacted," etc. *Statutes at Large*, III, 264.

and many more were expected.[33]   Governor Patrick Gordon in
his opening speech to the Assembly, December 17, 1728, suggested
that attention be given to the measures against convicts.   Said
he: "It may also require our Thought to prevent the Importation
of *Irish Papists* and *Convicts,* of whom some of the most noto-
rious, I am credibly informed, have of late been landed in the
River." [34]   During the session that followed, the Assembly addressed the governor, expressing great concern for their civil
and religious rights, and asked him to call the matter of restricting immigration to the attention of the Assembly of the Lower
Counties.[35]   Later in the same session, a committee was ordered
to draw a bill levying a duty on foreigners, Irish servants, and "persons on redemption."   This was directed primarily against others
than convicts and will be noted in another connection, but coupled
with this was the repeal, by means of a new act, of the convict
exclusion law of 1722.   Reasons for the new act are thus stated
in a preamble: "Whereas, it hath been a practice for masters
of vessels, merchants and others trading in this province, with
intent to avoid complying with the payment of duties, and giving
the security . . . to land their passengers, servants and convicts in some of the adjacent governments, which passengers,
have afterwards been secretly brought into this province."   This
law was passed to prevent such practices in the future.[36]

In the Assembly of 1729-1730, a further elaborate regulation
of convict trade was provided for.   In addition to convicts, restrictions were laid on infants, vagrants, lunatics, and impotent persons, and the master of a vessel bringing any such was to become
surety for their return and to indemnify the colony for any loss

---

[33] *Votes of Assembly,* II, 466.

[34] This speech was printed as a broadside and was probably given
considerable publicity.   Text of speech, Sachse, *Sectarians* (1708-1742),
137.   Photographic reproduction of heading, *ibid.,* 136.

[35] *Votes of Assembly,* III, 66.

[36] *Statutes at Large,* IV, 137.
This is in harmony with the declaration of James Logan who said
that convicts were landed at Burlington to be brought later into Pennsylvania.   Watson, *Annals,* II, 259, 260.
The P.S. to a servant advertisement of the time is significant: after
setting forth the other attractions of this consignment, it was said, "They
are no Convicts."   *American Weekly Mercury,* May 20, 1731.

caused by them.[37] Legislation followed in 1738 and in 1742-1743, but not until the latter year was one of these laws sent to England for approval in accordance with the provision of the charter.

Royal instructions to Governor Gordon in 1731 indicate a knowledge of restrictive measures against felons, and a wish that such measures be withdrawn or not approved. In some of the colonies, it was charged, laws existed fixing a duty on the bringing in of felons; such laws were held to be in direct opposition to the acts of Parliament, and Governor Gordon was admonished not to give his assent to, or to let pass, any act whatsoever for imposing duties on the importation of felons from Great Britain into Pennsylvania.[38] Governor Gordon, however, was committed to the policy of exclusion of felons. The wording of the above instructions of Gordon to his Assembly, with the laws which were passed, show that there was not an absolute refusal to receive convicts, because such a policy would have been revolutionary; instead, convicts and other undesirable persons were kept out by a tax so high that they could not be brought in to advantage, and by making the person bringing them in responsible for their good behavior and their support. These acts, like those attempting to prohibit the importation of slaves, opposed the wishes of Great Britain, but on convict exclusion Pennsylvania was even more determined than on the prohibition of slave importation. The fact that this question was the subject of legislation in 1722, 1729, 1730, 1738, and in 1742, before any act passed was sent to the home government for approval, indicates that the action of Pennsylvania was out of harmony with the plans of the home government, and that the Pennsylvania authorities did not wish to submit their laws on this subject. The issue was more fairly drawn in the unpleasant differences of Governor George Thomas with the Assembly in 1740. Under Thomas' authority, servants while under indenture had been enlisted for the king's army, their enlistment canceling their indentures. Against this the Assembly protested. Governor Thomas informed the Assembly that acts of Parliament were in force in England for transporting felons to the colonies; and further that acts of the Pennsylvania Assembly

---

[37] *Statutes at Large,* IV, 164-171.
[38] *Pennsylvania Archives,* First Series, I, 306; Smith, *History of Delaware County,* 241.

had militated against such acts of the British Parliament, an act of this character being then in force. He argued that, inasmuch as the Assembly had refused to permit the exported felons of Great Britain to come into the colony as servants, it was fair to presume that they had no servants under indenture, and therefore that complaint against his enlistment of their servants was groundless.[39]

The first bill to be passed into a law by the Assembly of 1742-1743 fixed a duty on the bringing in of persons convicted of "heinous crimes," and also of poor and impotent persons. Of the felons the act said, "and not warranted by the laws of Great Britain."[40] Within the required five years this act was submitted, and was disallowed by the king. The Board of Trade recommended the repeal of the above act as well as three former acts that had "never been presented to the Crown for approbation as they ought to have been." All of these were said to render ineffectual the parliamentary statute for transportation.[41] A supplement to the act of 1742-1743 was passed before the act was

---

[39] *Colonial Records,* III, 442.

[40] *Statutes at Large,* IV, 360-370.

[41] *Ibid.,* 501-513, for Board of Trade proceedings. But the act of 1738 was before the Board of Trade in February, 1738-1739. *Ibid.,* 463-468.

The official disallowance of the above act was made by the court of St. James on December 17, 1746. Notice of this was made in a communication as follows:

"Whereas in Pursuance of the Powers granted to the Proprietors of the Province of Pennsylvania by Letters Patent under the Great Seal, the Deputy Governor Council and Assembly of the said Province did in February 1742 pass an Act which hath been transmitted and is instituted as follows—viz:

"An Act imposing a Duty on Persons convicted of heinous Crimes brought into this Province and not warranted by the Laws of Great Britain and to prevent poor and Impotent persons being imported into the same. His Majesty this day took the said Act into His Royal Consideration, and having received the Opinion of the Lords Commissioners for Trade and Plantations, and also of a Committee of the Lords of His Majesty's most Honourable Privy Council thereupon, is hereby pleased to Declare his Disallowance of the said Act, and pursuant to His Majesty's Royal Pleasure thereupon Expressed, the said Act is hereby Repealed Declared Void and of none Effect—Whereof the Deputy Governor Council

disallowed and as this had not been sent, it stood in effect; this provided for a collector of duties on felons, and was sent for approval in 1748, when it in turn was disallowed.[42] But the Assembly was resourceful in evasion. The repeals were said to revive the law of 1729-1730 and in the next year a supplemental act to this was passed, which was not sent to England for approval.[43] Again the subject came up in 1751, when a supplementary act repealed the law of 1738, which earlier had been repealed by legislation of 1742-1743, but the latter law had been disallowed after being properly submitted, and the act of 1738 was held as in force; it was, therefore, repealed and the act of 1729-1730 fixing a duty of five pounds and the supplementary act of 1749 for collecting duties continued, and were administered as the law of Pennsylvania until the state legislation of 1789.[44]

Repeal of the numerous acts connected with excluding felons touched on some of the most troublesome phases of colonial administration. The rule for Pennsylvania of having five years in which the colony might transmit the acts and then allowing but six months in which they could be disallowed was termed unfair by a Board of Trade report in 1709.[45] Nothing came of this, however, and the forty years following only aggravated the differences between the colony and the mother country. Later, the question arose as to what constituted presentation of acts according to the terms of the charter. Here was shown the divided responsibility, and the uncertain authority of the Board of Trade and the Privy Council. The Board submitted to Mr. Fane, its standing counsel, a request to determine the power of the king over

---

and Assembly of the said Province and all others whom it may concern are to take Notice and Govern themselves accordingly."

Certified as
"A true Copy" and
signed "Temple Stanyan."

Board of Trade, *Proprieties,* Vol. 16, V.44.

[42] *Statutes at Large,* IV, 50, 51; *Ibid.,* V. 475; Board of Trade, *Proprieties,* Vol. 18, V.59.

[43] *Statutes at Large,* V, 77-79.

[44] *Ibid.,* 131, 132. Petitions for appointment as collector of the duty on felons, as well as appointments, were recorded in the proceedings of the Assembly. *Votes,* IV, 136, 137, 197, 330.

[45] *American Historical Association Report* (1903), I, 273.

laws already passed, whether he could repeal all acts, whether he had limited powers of repeal, and if so, over what acts.[46]

A memorial presented to the Pennsylvania legislature in 1750 revived the several acts that had been passed for the exclusion of foreigners and felons and expressed what appeared to be an honest doubt as to Pennsylvania's rights. The point was made that some of the acts for the exclusion of felons had been before the Board of Trade and that the latter had taken no cognizance of them; this, the memorial argued, was submitting the acts, and, if they were not disallowed within six months, it was maintained that they had passed into laws. On the other hand, the Board of Trade held that these acts had not been properly presented to the council. Therefore, not having been presented, they could not be disallowed. But this was held as an "extraordinary attempt" of the Board of Trade to force an interpretation not authorized by legal decision. The colony viewed with apprehension the wholesale disallowance of this legislation and said that if an act confirmed in 1722 could be disallowed in 1746, there was no telling how far the crown might go back. The proprietors appealed to the king to disregard the report of the Board of Trade, at least until there could be a decision on the question of the proper method of submitting the acts of the Assembly. The fear of having all legislation that had not been submitted to the council declared illegal or of subjecting it to disallowance led the proprietors to delay the hearing on their petition as they said, "by the most prudent way," and thus "not come to the decision of so mischievous a question." [47]

The Board of Trade, in 1721, pointed out that there were three ways, in any one of which colonial business might be carried on: By direct appeal to the crown through one of the secretaries of state; by appeal to the king's council; or by appeal to the Board of Trade. Thus the colonies developed self-reliance and a feeling of insubordination because of the divided responsibility and the imperfect working of the English colonial administration.[48] The prediction of Malachy Postlethwayt, made nearly

[46] Board of Trade, *Journals,* Vol. 41, p. 165.

[47] *Colonial Records,* V, 499-501.

[48] Kellogg, "American Colonial Charter," *American Historical Association Report* (1903), I, 189, 218, 219, 316.

a generation before the Revolution, was fulfilled: if colonies could not be ruled without constant irritation and contention, they would ultimately demand their freedom. At a time nearer the actual revolt Thomas Pownall saw that the colonial differences grew largely out of the difficulties of administration.

In 1718-1719, Mr. Richard West, in an opinion submitted to the Board of Trade, said that after due examination of the charter of Pennsylvania, he could see nothing to prevent the reënacting by the Colonial Assembly of the substance of any law that had been disallowed by the crown. At the same time he defined the six months in which to consider acts passed in Pennsylvania to be six months from the time that they were laid before the Privy Council; the fact that they had been earlier before the Board of Trade made no difference.[49] In 1719, the Board of Trade, after recommending the disallowance of certain Pennsylvania laws, again urged the setting aside of proprietary charters, and the bringing of all the North American settlements under the direct control of the crown,[50] and it seems quite obvious that the ineffectiveness of the Board of Trade is one explanation of the continuance of the proprietary arrangements.

In 1740, Parliament made an effort to get some control over legislation in the colonies by recommending to the king that instructions be issued to the governors that they should withhold assent to laws that did not have a clause suspending their operation until they had been transmitted to England for consideration. In 1752, the governors were directed to carry out the above plan.[54] In consequence of this policy, we find the second of the charges against the king of Great Britain in the Declaration of Independence to be: "He has forbidden his governors to pass laws of immediate and pressing importance, unless suspended in their operation until his assent could be obtained"; and when so suspended it was charged that the king had "utterly neglected" to give attention to these urgent needs of the colonies.

---

[49] Chalmers, *Colonial Opinions*, 336, 337.

[50] Kellogg, *American Historical Association Report* (1903), I, 311. The Board of Trade had objected to the practices of colonial legislatures as early as 1697.

[51] *Ibid.*, 276, 277.

The Board of Trade was well aware that Pennsylvania was not living up to the intent of its charter in submitting laws. The matter was referred by them to the Privy Council in 1738-1739 and after summoning Pennsylvania's agent, Mr. Paris, who was not able to give a satisfactory account of the nontransference of the act for excluding felons, the Board recommended against this act and complained of the dereliction of the colony founded by Penn.[52]   Later a law was sent to England, which required for its

---

[52] Malachy Postlethwayt found much that was unsatisfactory in the method of passing laws and having them approved, and he particularized on Pennsylvania. Of the contests between governors and legislatures he wrote, "Let Great Britain therefore take effectual measures to prevent these broils and contentions for the future or we may lose every inch of property in America." *Britain's Commercial Interest* (London, 1767), I, 300. Written probably in 1758.

Joshua Gee in his *Trade and Navigation* (Chapter XXXII) considered the laws of the colonies, and the means of passing them, as causes for misunderstanding. He said that laws were passed not to the interest of Great Britain. These, he declared, were often passed for temporary purposes, were enforced for two or three years, and then permitted to lapse, as being no longer necessary.

"And whereas Laws which are made in the Colonies, though never so inconvenient, do subsist till they are sent home and disapproved of; yet this is very often delayed, to the great Prejudice of this Kingdom.

"It is therefore proposed, for remedying those Inconveniences, that no Law shall pass in the Plantations, until a Copy thereof be prepared by the Governor and Assembly of each Province, and sent over here to be examined and approved by the King and Council, as the Laws from Ireland now are: Saving only that if the Laws now in Force do not enable them, upon any sudden Invasion from the Indians, *etc.* to raise Men and Money for their own Security and Defence, they shall be empowered, upon such Emergencies, to raise what Supplies they shall see necessary." Gee, *Trade and Navigation*, 106.

The Board of Trade commented thus on the Pennsylvania practice: "But we think it proper upon this occasion to inform your Lordships that according to the limitations of the patent granted by King Charles the Second to William Penn, Esquire, the proprietary of Pennsylvania is obliged to transmit all laws passed in that province within the space of five years after they shall have been enacted and to lay the same before His Majesty for his royal approbation; but the Crown has reserved to itself only the space of six months for considering of such laws after their transmission, and if no decision is made thereupon by His Majesty during that time, they acquire the same force as if they had been confirmed. The inequality between the time fixed for transmission of these

execution the services of the collector of duties on felons, and though what was implied was pointed out by the Board of Trade, it seems to have been winked at, for the law was promptly approved by the Privy Council.[53]

Transportation caused the most bitter denunciation of the mother country; the feeling against Great Britain was intense, and the sending of convicts rather than trade regulation led to early estrangement, and won for England the epithet, "Undutiful Mother." Regulation of trade might mean the loss of dollars, but this was not to be compared to sending convicts, which meant the endangering of life as well as of property and the lowering of private and public morals. The sacredness of the home and the welfare of society were threatened if England made the colonies a dumping ground for her criminals. One writer compared the action of Great Britain to that of a father who would seek to spread a plague among his children by emptying filth on their tables. Franklin exclaimed: "Their emptying their jails into our settlements, is an insult and contempt, the cruellest, that ever one people offered to another," and declared that this would not be equaled if they emptied their offal on the tables of the colonists.[54]

---

laws and that allowed for their consideration is a visible advantage in favor of the proprietary, and should therefore engage him to be more punctually [sic], at least in such transmission; but it is evident in the present case that the laws of Pennsylvania have not been regularly transmitted, and that they are sometimes prolonged, altered or amended even after the time fixed for the laying them before His Majesty, by which means it may happen that by renewing a law after it has remained four years or longer in force they may perpetuate laws to the detriment of the prerogative and of the interest of Great Britain." *Statutes at Large,* IV, 467, 468. Cited from Board of Trade *Proprieties,* Vol.. 32, f. 115. The same matter was recorded in the Board of Trade, *Journals,* Vol, 48, pp. 10, 11, 14.

[53] Act for prohibiting the importation of too many passengers in one ship. *Votes,* V, 94-97, also 488 and 498.

[54] Franklin, *Works* (Bigelow), IV, 255.

Of crimes and punishments about the middle of the eighteenth century, the annalist Watson says: "About this time, a great deal of hanging occurs. They hang for house-breaking, horse-stealing, and counterfeiting. It seems that imported criminals swell the list, and many evil persons come out as redemptioners. This remark is made, to wit: 'When we see our papers filled so often with accounts of the most audacious robberies, the most cruel murders, and other villanies, perpetrated by convicts from

Franklin was prominent in the opposition and his voice was raised against this policy, both before he went to England as colonial agent and repeatedly while he resided there in that capacity. His newspaper published (1751) part of a letter from Maryland in which the opinion was expressed that every year three or four hundred felons were imported into that colony. If, the writer said, when their times were out many of these did not move to the north, the colony would soon be overrun by them. Most of them, it was said, well deserved hanging at home; also, it was declared, there was no necessity for importing thieves, as they throve in America and the country was likely to have enough of its own growth. Convict servants corrupted other servants and Negroes, and even the children of the masters were influenced by them.

The above account was the occasion for a letter addressed to the printers, and signed "Americanus," [55] a letter which was a most trenchant, sarcastic argument against the importing of convicts. This has been credited to Franklin, and has passed into literature as the rattlesnake illustration. The letter was based on England's "solicitude" for the welfare of the colonies, and her "kindness" in sending convicts to them, a kindness, it was said, which it would not be well to let go unrequited. It was proposed that rattlesnakes, to be found in some parts, and harmless at certain seasons, should be sent in return for the "human serpents" that England had shipped to America. In particular should these be placed in the gardens of the king and of the chief ministers, as they had been most active in serving their American settlements.[56] Later, when British ministers urged the necessity of

---

Europe—what will become of our posterity! In what could Britain injure us more, than emptying her jails on us! What must we think of those merchants, who, for the sake of a little paltry gain, will be concerned in importing and disposing of these abominable cargoes!' It is probable they got premiums abroad for bringing them out here." Watson, *Annals*, I, 309.

[55] *Pennsylvania Gazette*, April 11, 1751.

[56] *Pennsylvania Gazette*, May 9, 1751. Paul Leicester Ford gives a comment on the usual version of this story based on Condorcet's "Eloge" on Franklin, before *Academie des Sciences* (1790), and compares this with the original letter in the *Pennsylvania Gazette*. New York *Nation*, September 1, 1898. The following is a condensation of the original letter:

England's getting rid of criminals, Franklin replied by urging a similar necessity of America's getting rid of her rattlesnakes.[57]

Scotland was excluded from the operation of the act of 1717 [58] and when, during Franklin's term as colonial agent, it was proposed to transport Scotch in addition to English and Irish felons, opposition ran high. While the bill was before Parliament, Franklin submitted a statement and made a request. He urged that felons ought never to have been sent; that they had proved a great grievance; that they continued their evil practices and corrupted other servants and poor people. Many of them escaped from their servitude and ran at large, committing crimes and necessitating expenditure for their apprehension. Franklin urged his mutual interest argument, and said that as easing burdens in one part of the realm to have them felt in another did not increase happiness, it was a mistake to transport convicts. He prayed for Pennsylvania and the other colonies that the House

---

"By a Passage in one of your late Papers, I understand that the Government at home will not suffer our mistaken Assemblies to make any Law for preventing or discouraging the Importation of Convicts from Great Britain, for this kind reason, *that such Laws are against the Publick Utility, as they tend to prevent the Improvement and Well Peopling of the Colonies.*

"Such a tender PARENTAL Concern . . . calls aloud for the highest *Returns* of Gratitude and Duty," etc. This duty was then pointed out. In some sections of the country, it was said, there were numbers of rattlesnakes. "Felons-convict from the Beginning of the World." These, the writer said they put to death, etc., "but this is a sanguinary Law and may seem too cruel; and they may possibly change their Natures, if they were to change the climate; I would humbly propose that this General Sentence of *Death* be changed for *Transportation.*

"In the Spring of the Year . . . they are feeble, heavy, slow and easily taken; and if a small Bounty were allow'd *per* Head, some Thousands might be collected annually, and *transported* to Britain. There I would propose to have them carefully distributed, etc. . . . but particularly in the Gardens of the *Prime Ministers,* the *Lords of Trade* and *Members of Parliament,* for to them we are *most particularly* obliged." The writer then dwells upon the parental regard of the home government and the duty of the colonists to reciprocate. His conclusion is: *"Rattle Snakes* seem the most *suitable Returns* for the *Human Serpents* sent us by our *Mother* Country." *Pennsylvania Gazette,* May 9, 1751. This letter is included in Franklin, *Writings* (Smyth), III, 45-48.

[57] Lang, *Transportation and Colonization,* 12.

[58] *6 George III,* ch. 32, sec. 1.

take these facts into account, and repeal the laws for transportation then in force; if not this, he hoped that at least the proposed
bill extending these laws to Scotland would be rejected; or, if
not that, then the extension, he said, should be carried farther so
as to permit the colonies to send their felons to Scotland.[59]   The
pending bill passed and Franklin looked upon it as a further
grievance against England.[60]   In a paper on "Causes of American
Discontent before 1768," appearing originally in the *London
Chronicle* (January 9, 1768), but later added as postscript to a
pamphlet, *Sentiments of America,* Franklin said that Americans
remembered the act authorizing the sending of convicts and its
late extension to Scotland.[61]

The remonstrances of Franklin and others led to a motion
in the House of Commons (1770) that provision be made for
the transporting of criminals to the west coast of Africa and to
the East Indies.   Opposition to this was threefold: 1. Such
transportation would not be freeing men from a death punishment; it would be consigning them to death, as they could not
survive in the climates of the places proposed. 2. The proposal
was held to be impracticable, as convicts had paid, and were to pay,
their own passage.   This could not be done if they were sent to
Africa or India.   3. If they were sent to the new regions, there
would be greater danger from convicts' inciting the natives to
insurrections.[62]

It was reported in England in 1775 that Maryland had laid
a tax of forty shillings on felons imported.   After reviewing the
subject at some length, Attorney-General Murray reached the
following conclusions: "I am of opinion that no colony can make
such a law, because it seems to me in direct opposition to the
authority of the Parliament of Great Britain; . . . it is a
matter of public concern and derogatory to the Crown and legislature of Great Britain.   By the same reason they might lay a
duty or even prohibit British goods." [63]

---

[59] Franklin, *Works* (Bigelow), X, 120, 121.

[60] *6 George III,* ch. 32, sec. 1.   To go into effect March 31, 1767.   Extended *4 George I,* ch. ii, to Scotland.

[61] Franklin, *Works* (Bigelow), IV, 108.

[62] Lang, *Transportation and Colonization,* 14, 15.

[63] Chalmers, *Colonial Opinions,* 336.

England continued transportation to the North American settlements until the outbreak of the Revolution; during the Revolution her jails were "inordinately filled," and at its close it was felt that the pressure must be removed by finding some outlet. A recent writer on the British Empire says that the question involved was crucial in the extension of the English colonial system (Woodward). After considering various devices England adopted the penal settlement and fastened it upon the Australian colonies.[64]

Jeremy Bentham and others in England about the close of the American Revolution insisted that it was the duty of each nation to care for its own criminals within its borders. A powerful anonymous pamphlet attacking transportation appeared in England in 1787 under the title, *A Short Review of the Political State of Great Britain*. The exile and the removal of convicts, rather than the home employment and punishment of them, were savagely criticized. The forced labor in Russian mines or of the French compulsory military service, was thought better than sending felons to the ends of the earth. Australia was said to be too far away to send felons there because of the danger of escape and the possible great damage.[65] The opposition to England's policy continued, but transportation was practiced well into the nineteenth century.

The argument urged in defense of the transportation of felons was that the heavy, menial toil in the sparsely peopled settlements, such as clearing the land of forests, building roads, digging ditches, and improving harbors, could be done by criminals working under compulsion. Of the effects in Australia, Darwin wrote: "As a plan of punishment, it has failed; as a real system of reform, it has failed, as would any other plan, but as a means of making men outwardly honest, of converting vagabonds most useless in one country into active citizens of another, and thus

---

[64] See Lang, 14, 15; Woodward, *Expansion of the British Empire*, 261-263; Morris, *History of Colonization*, II, 83; and Merivale, *Colonies*, 369.

[65] Pp. 77-83. An answer to this pamphlet appeared in the same year, but there was no mention of the author's treatment of transportation. Both the original pamphlet and the answer are in the Colwell Library at the University of Pennsylvania.

giving birth to a new and splendid country, it has succeeded to a degree perhaps unparalleled in history." [66]

In 1789, Pennsylvania again legislated against receiving felons. Convicts had been brought in, it was said, "under various pretences," and these had been sold and dispersed in the state, to the injury of morals and the endangering of life and property. More stringent measures were provided for keeping convicts out. In the future a fine of fifty pounds was fixed for every convict brought, to which were to be added all costs of prosecution and three months' imprisonment; this act was to be enforced without permitting bail. To make more certain of complaints in case this law were violated, one-half of the fine went to the person prosecuting.[67] Other states passed similar acts, and when first the Federal Congress levied a tax on "The importation of certain persons," this was held to apply to convicts as well as to slaves.[68]

Closely related to the sending of convicts was the shipping of the "indigent poor," "sturdy beggars," and the like, as a means of poor relief. Such people could be taken up by constables in England and held until the next assizes or sessions, when they might be acquitted and assigned to some settled abode and occupation, or be sent to the plantations as servants. In the latter case they were termed "vagrant emigrants"; sometimes they were sent by the people of a parish, but more often they came at the charge of municipal authorities. Indigent poor were less objectionable than were felons; they were unfortunate, but theirs were offenses of omission. In part they came in answer to a demand for people; inhabitants of Philadelphia and Bucks Counties sent petitions to the Assembly during the session 1722-1723, requesting that the importation of poor foreigners be encouraged,[69] but six years later the same body had petitions from the overseers of the poor asking that they be relieved from the difficulties under which they labored because of the "great number of poor from foreign parts." [70] After 1729, legislation against receiving help-

---

[66] Cited in Egerton, *Origin and Growth of English Colonies,* 135, 136.

[67] Bioren, *Laws,* II, 485, 486.

[68] McCormac, *White Servitude in Maryland,* 106.

[69] *Votes of Assembly,* II, 338.

[70] *Ibid.,* III, 73. With foreign poor were also mentioned those from neighboring provinces, and insolvent debtors.

less poor was almost invariably coupled with that against receiving convicts, and while the opposition to having them brought in as servants was not so strong as that against felons, their coming was looked upon with disfavor. Practically all servants were poor, but the poor who had to be transported were properly objects of suspicion.[71]

Convicts in Maryland were called "seven years' passengers," or "King's passengers"; 20,000 of these, it is estimated by a Maryland historian, were imported into that province before the Revolution; from 1750 to 1770, not less than 400 to 500 were annually brought in.[72] About the middle of the eighteenth century reports were common of the arrival of vessels into Maryland with 30, 40, 50, 100, and even 150 convicts.

The large number of runaway servants from Maryland into Pennsylvania was due no doubt to the character of many who were imported and condemned to servitude in Maryland. Of the runaways advertised in the *American Weekly Mercury* in 1720, 19 out of a total of 43 were for Maryland servants. In the same weekly for 1730, 7 of the 33 given were for Maryland servants; for 1740 an examination of the runaway advertisements in the *Pennsylvania Gazette* shows that 13 of a total of 64 were for servants from Maryland, while for 1750 in the same weekly, there were 27 Maryland servants advertised out of a total of 134. Seventy-nine runaways were advertised in the *Pennsylvania Gazette* in 1760, of whom 31 had run away from some part of

---

[71] An English historian of poor relief has the following comment on the transportation of debtors and vagrants: "In the midst of all the abuse heaped upon the vagrant in his own time and in our own, it is interesting to remember that he sometimes did something useful when he got the chance. Even in the days of the Stuarts he and his descendants played a part in developing the British Empire and in founding the settlements which led to the existence of the United States." Leonard, *History of Poor Relief*, 230.

[72] Scharf, *History of Maryland*, I, 371, 372. See also letter from Maryland referred to above. Hall, speaking of taxes and ecclesiastical regulations in Maryland, said that people would remove to escape them and that Maryland would be drained of her people, "notwithstanding the number of convicts daily sent there." *Plantations in America*, 91.

An estimate of the *Maryland Gazette* in 1767 was that six hundred felons had been brought into Maryland annually for the thirty years preceding. McCormac, *White Servitude in Maryland*, 98, 99.

Maryland; in the same journal during 1770, 63 out of a total of 201 runaway advertisements were for Maryland servants. The runaways were largely from the corner county, and "Run away from the subscriber, living in Cecil County, Maryland," was a common heading for advertisements.[73]

Pennsylvania was too alert in opposition to have received many convicts. From the early settlement down to and after independence, public sentiment and legislative enactment were to the same purpose, that convicts should not come in, and those who were brought came by indirection. The inference is warranted from the statements of the acts, and from the recurrence of the subject, that some did come. It is fair to suppose that James Logan, Governor Gordon, and the Colonial Assembly meant what they said, a supposition all the more probable in the light of the repeated restrictive measures.

The effect of the importation of convicts could not but be bad, and the more convicts imported, the worse the effects. Maryland probably suffered most;[74] she was saved from some of the

---

[73] A characteristic Maryland advertisement in the *American Weekly Mercury* is appended: "November 17, 1720, Run away from *James Carroll* in *Maryland*, Three white Servant Men, all being of a *Newgate* Stamp, who have Committed divers roberies and Thieveries at Times before their Departure. *Thomas Barns,* aged about 23 years, middling stature, Brown Hair, thinfaced, down looked, and slow in Speech, a fear-nothing Coat, Cotton Jackett and Breeches, Ozenbrig Shirt, Grey Yarn Stockings, and pair of plain Shoes, and old Hat, an *Oxfordshire* man, being bread to farming, As he pretends but knows nothing of it: He's a thieving Sly Fellow. Edmund Lerner aged about 23 Years, small Stature, freckled with the Small Pox, light colour'd short hair, and very pert and talkative, pretends to be a Carpenter, with a Kersey Coat, Cotton Jacket and Breeches, Ozenbrig Shirt, a Pair of Grey Yarn Stockings, and plain Shooes, an *Oxfordshire* Man: a thieving, drunken ill-natur'd Fellow.

"*Henry Goatly,* aged about Eighteen Years, large of his age, pretty long light-coloured Hair, full-faced and very talkative, with a pretty good Felt Hat, Cotton Jacket and Breeches, Ozenbrig Shirt, Grey Yarn Stockings, and a Pair of plain Shooes: a *Scotch-Irish,* thieving, lying, sawcy Fellow.

"Whosoever brings the above Runaways to *Anapolis* shall have Thirty Shillings *per* Head and reasonable charges, from me,
"James Carroll."

[74] Scharf, *History of Maryland,* I, 384, 385.

In the latter part of the century, a traveler describing conditions in Philadelphia, wrote of the prison of the city, and said that he loved to

evil consequences by passing on what were unquestionably the worst of these "King's passengers" as runaways. These convicts were sometimes employed where they would do the most injury to the future colonial society. Jonathan Boucher, who knew well the conditions in Maryland and Virginia, said that of the very few schoolmasters in those parts, two-thirds were from the indentured servants and convicts. No ship came, he said, that did not advertise teachers as regularly as weavers and those of other trades, but with this difference, that the teachers did not sell for so good a price as did the others. A Philadelphia newspaper in 1740 advertised for a convict schoolmaster who had run away.

In the colonies England was regarded as encouraging crime by making it a passport to the New World, and her action was contrasted with what she might have done by sending the worthy poor instead of felons.[75] By the English, at least during its continuance, transportation to North America was regarded with favor. "So far as it prevailed," says Dr. Lang, "transportation to the American colonies proved highly efficient in securing the great ends of punishment—the prevention of crime and the reformation of criminals."[76] True, some who came as felons, as many who came under indenture, rose above their station and became responsible and respected members of colonial society.[77] Lang attempts to account for what did not take place, viz., the losing of all trace of felons, by the larger emigration of freemen. With his favorable account of transportation to America he set forth what he regarded as the comparative failure of the Australian penal system, the latter settlements not having, it was thought, a sufficient population of free emigrants.[78] The trans-

---

think of the earlier years when no prison was necessary, "But since the English, to deliver themselves from the banditti that have infected their island, have practiced letting them loose upon the colonies," etc., and since a great number of adventurers were spread over the country, a prison was needed. In the same connection the writer says that not one prisoner in ten was a native; nearly all of them were French or Irish. Brissot, *New Travels*, Letter 30, I, 316.

[75] Grahame, *History of the United States*, II, 420, 456.

[76] *Transportation and Colonization*, 41.

[77] See Brock, in Winsor, *Narrative and Critical History*, III, 153.

[78] *Transportation and Colonization*, 42-44.

Transportation continued an unsolved question of the British govern-

portation system succeeded in one particular as applied to the
North American settlements—England was largely freed from
further care for those sent. But Americans and Englishmen
alike will now applaud those determined measures to prevent the
colonies becoming a dumping ground for the mother country's
criminal class.

The British *Quarterly Review* descended to say in jest that
the Adam and Eve of the colonies came out of Newgate; some
Englishmen were too ready to accept this as a statement of fact.
The *Critical Review,* in warning Mr. Fox against Americans,
said: "Beware the complicated cunning of that race whose Adam
and Eve emigrated from Newgate." [79] American opposition to
British policy before the Revolutionary War gave occasion for
uncomplimentary expressions, among others from those who
claimed to have served under English generals in American cam-
paigns. A letter in the *London Chronicle* (1769) said, "The most
substantial men of most of the provinces, are children or grand-
children of those who came here at the King's expense; that is,
thieves, highwaymen and robbers." Following this there appeared
Franklin's *Causes of American Discontent* (noted above), in
which the responsibility for felons being in America was placed
where it belonged. Franklin also relieved Americans of the stigma
of being progeny of convict settlers; he showed that advances
in fortunes of convicts were rare; the convict class disappeared
by destroying itself; the habit of criminals followed them, said

---

ment long after the American Revolution. Numerous punishments termed
"secondary" were retained, among them being imprisonment with or without hard labor, confinement in what were termed "hulks" (vessels which
had been dismantled for navigation, but were kept as prison ships), and
transportation. The discontinuance of transportation was widely discussed both within Parliament and without. In the British discussion the
American experience in retaining felons in penitentiaries was frequently
referred to. See *Edinburgh Review,* January, 1834.

[79] Walsh, *Appeal,* 26, 29.

S. T. Coleridge commented on the difficulty of securing a copy of the
Newgate Calendar, because they had all been bought up by Americans,
though he says he was not informed as to whether it was to suppress
information of their forbears, or to aid in genealogical researches. *Letters, Conversations and Recollections* (London, 1836), 214.

he, and it was common for them to be "advanced to the gallows." [80]

Crimes of convict servants were common and were recorded with such frequency and regularity as to make mention of individual instances unnecessary. Buildings of the masters were burned; horses, books, and other property were taken to aid in the servants' escape, and sometimes the masters were murdered.[81] Convicts of a better class came in small numbers.[82] The relatively limited number of convicts reaching Pennsylvania, and their self-destruction from their vicious habits, minimized the effects of transportation so that no lasting trace of the felon remained.

---

[80] Walsh, *Appeal,* 446-453; Franklin, *Works* (Bigelow), IV, 254. The convict class did not always turn out badly. The following remark of Watson commends itself as being based on his own observation: "In some cases the severity of British laws pushed off young men, of good abilities, for very small offences, who made very capable clerks, storekeepers, etc., among us. I have knowledge of two or three among us, even within my own memory, who rose to riches and credit here, and have left fine families. One great man, before my time, had been sold in Maryland as an offender in Ireland. While serving his master as a common servant, he showed much ability, unexpectedly, in managing for him an important lawsuit, for which he instantly gave him freedom. He then came to Philadelphia, and amassed a great fortune in landed estate, now of great value among his heirs." Watson, *Annals,* II, 267.

[81] See *Pennsylvania Gazette,* June 28, 1750; *ibid.,* April 11, and June 27, 1751.

[82] In one instance a wealthy man was transported as a convict. He died three days after arrival in Williamsburg, Virginia. It was reputed that after his death twenty-five hundred pounds in bank notes and fifty guineas were found on his person. *Pennsylvania Gazette,* April 23, 1772.

CHAPTER VIII

SUPPLY OF INDENTURED SERVANTS FROM GREAT BRITAIN

Pennsylvania's early supply of white servants came almost entirely from Great Britain and consisted of English, Welsh, Irish, and Scotch immigrants. These came largely of their own volition, and mostly in the hope of worldly advantage. Not until about 1730 did the German supply reach such numbers as to make it comparable with the British. Some British indentured servants came for more complete religious freedom; ome came to escape burdens of excessive taxation and to enjoy a larger measure of political privilege; but in the main they were those with whom the world had gone badly, and who sought to mend their fortunes by beginning anew. Adventuresome in disposition, they were willing to proffer their service for a term of years in return for their passage, particularly as this offered almost the only means for gaining admission into this land of promise. Emigrants were all the more ready to enter into this arrangement when it was represented to them that the service upon which they would enter was entirely honorable and also that it was not arduous.

The latter part of the seventeenth century was fruitful in projects for the relief of the poor, and from that time forward emigration was looked upon as one of the promising forms of poor relief. With the progress of the colonial period, knowledge of the New World was made more complete and accurate; at the same time the means of reaching the New World were improved. The earlier restless adventurers were succeeded by substantial and dependable passengers who, even though they came under indentures, came to settle and to establish homes.

Servants from Great Britain and Ireland, who were not transported or kidnaped, were mainly poorer people who were without opportunity at home. Such persons went to the colonies rather than to the wars on the continent, or into a life of crime that led to the gallows. Many ways were devised for helping the unfortunate. Says one merchant, "I must confess the poverty and necessity in which I have seen the poor in several parts of the Kingdom has touched me very sensibly, and I have spent a great deal of time from the service of my family, to find out methods for promoting so public a blessing as turning the employment we give the poor of foreign nations to our own." [1] Manifestly no more promising method of aiding those in distress was offered than to give them the opportunity to aid themselves in English colonies. Yarranton's "how to beat the Dutch without fighting," etc., was to employ the poor at home in manufactures, but this had not solved the problem, and later there arose the necessity for some other disposition of those whom men have always with them. New World colonies were opened up and these same helpless, burdensome people went forth to aid in building a new and a greater Britain. [2]

Free persons were secured to go as servants from Great Britain by use of propaganda in the form of broadsides, letters from the colony, pamphlets, and the like, and by personal solicitation. [3] The Virginia Company circulated broadsides in England to secure settlers, and this practice was common throughout the period of British colonization in America. William Eddis, writing from Maryland (1770), commented thus on the methods employed to induce servants to come to the colonies: "In your

---

[1] Gee, *Trade and Navigation* ("Address to the Reader").

[2] Of such settlement Sir Josiah Child said:

"Virginia and Barbadoes were first peopled by a sort of loose vagrant people, vicious and destitute of means to live at home, being either unfit for labor, or such as could find none to employ themselves about, or had so misbehaved themselves by whoring, thieving, or other debauchery, that none would set them on work, which Merchants and Masters of Ships, by their Agents or Spirits, as they were called, gathered up about the streets of London, and other Places, clothed and transported, to be employed upon Plantations; and these, I say, . . . could probably never have lived at home to do service to their Country, but must have been hanged, or starved, or died untimely of some of those miserable diseases, that proceed from want and vice; or else have sold themselves for soldiers to be knocked on the head, or starved, in the quarrels of our neighbors, as many thousands of brave Englishmen were in the low Countries, as also in the wars of Germany, France, and Sweden, etc., or else if they could, by begging, or otherwise, arrive to the stocks of 2s. and 6d. to waft them over to Holland, become servants to the Dutch, who refuse none." *New Discourse of Trade,* 197, 198.

[3] For example, account of George Alsop, *Character of Mary-land,* and William Penn's solicitations treated in Chapter III.

frequent excursions about the great metropolis," said he, "you cannot but observe numerous Advertisements, offering the most seducing encouragement to adventurers under every possible description"; among others, to such as were "Disgusted with the frowns of fortune of their native land," and to those of "An enterprising disposition." Regular agents termed "crimps" were employed, and it is said they represented the advantages to be obtained in America in colors so alluring that it was impossible to resist them.[4]

In addition to the "free-willers" who went out to the colonies, many were secured to go against their will by being enticed on shipboard. This matter had become so troublesome in 1661 that a committee of the Council of Foreign Plantations was asked to consider how to prevent the stealing of women and children from their masters and parents.[5] The mayor of Bristol, in 1662, petitioned the king for the power to examine the ships at his port to see whether those who went out did so of their own free will, and also to learn whether they were entitled to go. He recited the same conditions as are noted above, saying that there were cases of children who ran away from their apprenticeship, wives from their husbands, husbands from their wives, some who were pursued with "hue and cry" for burglary or robbery, and some who had escaped from prison—all taken on the ships to be carried to the colonies as servants. Some of those on board these ships were called "unwary persons" who had been enticed there by what were termed "men stealers."[6]

---

[4] Eddis, *Letters from America*, 67, 68.

An agent who went through the Scotch towns soliciting servants was sometimes termed "the drum" or "a drum." Drum was used repeatedly in the Williamson trials.

[5] *Cal. State Papers*, "Colonial Series," 1661-1668, p. xxvii.

[6] *Ibid.*, 98.

"Another great swarm, or accession of new inhabitants to the aforesaid Plantations, as also to New-England, Jamaica, and all other his Majesty's Plantations in the West-Indies, ensued upon his Majesty's Restoration, when the former prevailing party being, by a divine hand of providence, brought under, the Army disbanded, many Officers displaced, and all the new Purchasers of publick Titles, dispossed of their pretended Lands, Estates, etc., many became impoverished; and destitute of employment; and therefore such as could find no way of living at home, and some who feared the re-establishment of the ecclesiastical laws, under

The same facts were set forth in a letter from the lord mayor of London and the Court of Aldermen in 1664, those who enticed the unsuspecting here being termed "spirritts." [7]

On September 7, 1664, on the report from the Council of Plantations, an act was passed empowering the Duke of York and other officers of the ports to erect an office for registering all persons who were to be transported to the colonies, and fixing a fine of twenty pounds for violation of this requirement. No children under twelve were to be transported, unless friends or relatives appeared in person and gave permission. [8] Despite the provision made, a further petition was presented against the abuses, and Parliament was compelled to provide better regulation. An act was passed, May 18, 1670, to prevent the stealing and transporting of children and other persons. The penalty to any one convicted of this practice was death as a felon without benefit of clergy. [9]

A further order in Council (1686) was directed against kidnapers and the fraudulent securing of servants, providing, first, for the legal execution of all contracts between servants who

---

which they could not live, were forced to transport themselves, or sell themselves for a few years, to be transported by others to the foreign English Plantations. The constant supply that the said Plantations have since had, has been by such vagrant loose people, as I before mentioned, picked up, especially about the streets and suburbs of London, and West-minister, and by Malefactors condemned for crimes, for which by law they deserved to die; and some of those people called Quakers, banished for meeting on pretence of religious worship." Child, *New Discourse of Trade,* 197-199.

[7] *Cal. of State Papers,* "Colonial Series," 1661-1668, p. 220.

The practice is thus described in the *Colonial Entry Book of New Jersey,* Sec. 5: "The waies of obtayning these servants have beene usually by employing a sorte of men or women who make it theire profession to tempt or gain poore or idle persons to goe to the Plantations and having persuaded or deceived them on Shippboard they receive a reward from the person who employed them." Cited in Diffenderffer, *Redemptioners,* 291.

[8] *Cal. of State Papers,* "Colonial Series," 1661-1668, p. 232.

A memorial of the Privy Council concerning the passes of passengers out of the kingdom into the colonies indicated the difficulty of carrying out the regulations. In mentioning the character of the people who were to go to America as servants, it was stated that they were those who had no habitation, and therefore could bring no certificate of residence. *Cal. of State Papers,* "Colonial Series," 1574-1660, p. 261.

[9] *Ibid.,* pp. xix and 555.

wished to embark and their masters, and, second, that no adult could be transported except with his own consent, and no child, except with the consent of the parent or master; for the transportation of children under fourteen, the consent of the parent as well as the master was made necessary.[10]

In the illustration opposite one sees how the certificate for leaving England was attached to the indenture. An original agreement of 1728, made at Bristol, and approved by the justice as having been sealed and delivered in his presence, recited the facts that the person who signed the agreement was sixteen years of age, that he was single, and that he was not under covenant or contract to serve any person in England. This agreement was also signed by the register of the port.[11] Evidences are not altogether wanting of efforts to enforce the regulations for the protection of those who took indentures. A Dublin news note of 1733 said that a man had been sent to Newgate for illegally shipping persons to the plantations.[12] London magistrates in 1757 tried an agent for improper conduct towards a girl whom he had secured to send to America. The comment of the chronicler was, "Mr. Kidnapper stands a chance of being himself forwarded to America." [13]

Despite regulations and their enforcement, agents for servants illegally plied their trade. The claim is made that even under regulation no less than ten thousand persons were annually "spirited" away. Eddis felt that although the "crimps" might comply with the letter of the law against clandestine transportation, they violated its spirit and secured many persons by fraudulent means.[14] After a full hundred years of this trade under regulation, Raynal makes the extreme statement that the great proportion of those who went out as indentured servants would

---

[10] Doyle, *English in America*, Va., Md., and the Carolinas, 385.

The rather surprising statement occurs in Morris, *History of Colonization* (II, 43), that the trade in indentured servants "became so scandalous that the Privy Council in 1686 eventually prohibited it."

[11] Library of Historical Society of Pennsylvania, *Miscellaneous Papers of City Lots, Philadelphia County, 1671-1738.*

[12] *Pennsylvania Gazette,* August 9, 1733.

[13] *Ibid.,* May 12, 1757.

[14] *Letters from America,* 68, 77.

AN INDENTURE WITH CERTIFICATE FOR LEAVING ENGLAND

never have set foot on ship but for false representations made to them. Passengers were deceived and cheated, and the obligations were handed forward so that those with whom they originally dealt were beyond their reach.[15]

But traders and captains were sometimes victimized; petitions of merchants and masters of ships in 1664 said that they were imposed upon by persons who enlisted for transportation, got clothes, etc., and later claimed that they had been enticed on board ship and kept there against their will, and then demanded to be freed from the arrangements into which they had entered. These merchants also asked for the lawful registry of those who expressed a willingness to go to the colonies.[16]

Kidnaping to send to the colonies was common, and it offered such situations and heights of interest that it was taken up naturally by contemporary authors. Accounts of it have also been perpetuated by later writers. The heroine in Richardson's *Clarissa Harlowe* was advised to come to Pennsylvania to escape the effects of misfortune and disgrace. Goldsmith, in his *Vicar of Wakefield,* endangers one of his characters to kidnapers; Smollett's *Adventures of Roderick Random* (1748) and *The Adventures of Peregrine Pickle* (1751) are thought to have been suggested by the publicity given to the ill fortune of James Annesley; Walter Scott's *Waverley,* and Robert Louis Stevenson's *Kidnapped* are classic illustrations of the use to which the kidnaping incident has been put.[17] David Balfour, of the latter book, comes to claim an estate which is his by right but is held by an unprin-

---

[15] Raynal, *British Settlements,* II, 167.

[16] *Cal. of State Papers,* "Colonial Series," 1661-1668, p. 220. The same conditions are indicated by the third charter given by King James to Virginia. Section 14 of this charter reads as follows: "Whereas, divers persons, having received wages, etc., from the company and agreed to serve the colony, have afterwards refused to go thither; and divers others who have been employed in Virginia by the Company, and having there misbehaved themselves, etc., have come back to England, in some treacherous way or by stealth," etc.

The following section provided for the control of such and for their correction, chastisement, reprimand, and return to Virginia. Brown, *Genesis of the United States,* II, 550, 551.

[17] For correspondence of Henry Bartram in *Guy Mannering* to James Annesley (to be noted below), also for suggestion of the latter to Smollett, see *Gentlemen's Magazine,* July, 1840, 38-42.

cipled uncle. David becomes the victim of a plot. The uncle gives a ship captain twenty pounds to carry him on an outward voyage to the Carolinas, where he is to be sold into servitude, and the captain is to have such an additional sum as he can secure from the sale of the boy. The latter is enticed on shipboard at Queen's Ferry, struck down with a club, and kept a close prisoner until the ship is at sea. Other popular novels have similar plots; two recent widely read stories of our colonial and Revolutionary days, *To Have and To Hold,* and *Janice Meredith,* have this romance of servitude woven into their texture. But of the stories dealing with the subject, the one that follows most closely the fortunes of a redemptioner, and pictures most accurately the system under which he was secured and held, is Charles Reade's *Wandering Heir.*[18]

Best known of the cases of kidnaping is that of James Annesley, son and heir of the Earl of Anglesey, Lord Altham. Both his parents died when James was still a lad; while in Dublin, and at the instigation of an uncle who was next of heir, James was kidnaped and sent to America (probably 1728). He was brought to Philadelphia and sold to service at a place some forty miles outside the city in the direction of Lancaster. His claims of noble lineage were not credited, and an attempt to run away resulted only in capture and prolonged servitude. After some twelve years two men arrived from County Wexford, Ireland, who gave such confirmation of James' story as to lend probability to its truth. He was brought to Philadelphia, where Robert Ellis became interested in his welfare, and recommended him to Admiral Vernon. The latter took him to England by way of the West Indies, and on arrival he found other friends who advanced funds with which he could prosecute the suit for his rights. To increase interest in his claims and win favor, James Annesley published a romance, *Memoirs of an Unfortunate Young Nobleman.* Truth and fiction were so intertwined in the *Memoirs* as to make it impossible to determine what was true and what the creation of the imagination. The *Memoirs* claimed to be "a Story founded on Truth and addressed equally to the Head and Heart." An accidental shooting led to the charge of murder

---

[18] See further, Watson, *Annals,* II, 267, 268.

against James Annesley, but of this he was acquitted and the case against the earl of Anglesey came before the court of exchequer in Dublin in 1743.[19]   The public was so impatient to know the evidence and the proceedings in the case that a summary was made by a spectator and immediately published in London.   The chronicler of the trial said that in preparing his work he was under "the disadvantage of the greatest concourse of people, hurry and confusion in a court of justice, that ever had been known in the memory of man." [20]   The jury chosen was of unusual character, containing only men of great property and strict honor.[21]   The defense in the trial attacked the character of the father of James Annesley, attempting to prove the plaintiff illegitimate.   The conflicting evidence indicated, as the *Gentlemen's Magazine* said, "the grossest perjury on one side or the other."   The charge of illegitimacy could not be sustained, and on the other side proof of the kidnaping in Dublin was established; after some fourteen days of evidence and argument, with the court sitting ten hours a day, the case was given to the jury. In one hour a verdict "in ejectment" was returned against the defendant.[22]   But James Annesley did not get his estate; the case was appealed to Westminister and for many years Annesley was unable to renew his claim from lack of funds.   After interest had again been aroused, and when subscriptions were being advanced for the prosecution, James Annesley died, in 1760, and this "mysterious" case came to an end.[23]

---

[19] *Gentlemen's Magazine,* November, 1743, p. 612.   For review of *Memoirs of an Unfortunate Young Nobleman,* see *Gentlemen's Magazine,* same year, in four numbers, pp. 93, 204, 306, and 332.

[20] *Journal of Proceedings,* 3.

[21] *Ibid.,* 6.   *Gentlemen's Magazine,* June, 1831, said that the jury was worth a full million pounds (503).

[22] *Journal of Proceedings,* 30.   An account of this trial runs through eleven numbers of the *Gentlemen's Magazine* of 1744.   See pp. 25, 87, 141, 205, 255, 316, 373, 431, 489, 537, 599, 605.

[23] Manuscript memorandum in copy of trial from library of John Jordan, Jr. (Library of Historical Society of Pennsylvania).   A different account of the events following the trial is presented in a contributed letter in *Gentlemen's Magazine,* June, 1831 (503).   Here it is stated that the Earl of Anglesey, who dispossessed James, died without issue and that Richard, a younger brother, succeeded to the estate; this letter says that James Annesley returned at twenty, refers to the *Memoirs of an Un-*

The case of Peter Williamson appears neither less romantic nor less probable than that of James Annesley. Williamson was born of reputable parents just outside the city of Aberdeen, Scotland. As a lad he was sent to live with an aunt in Aberdeen, and when playing in the city he was seized by two men belonging to a vessel then lying in the harbor. With others similarly taken, he was kept a close prisoner for about a month, first in an old barn, and later between the decks of the vessel; when the vessel had her cargo and had received her complement of passengers, many of them taken by what was termed the common though "villainous and execrable" practice of kidnaping, she sailed for Philadelphia, where the captain conducted a sale of the passengers. Williamson said that the company was scattered and that he never knew what became of his shipmates. He was sold to a fellow countryman who early in life had himself been kidnaped, but with whom fortune had dealt kindly. This master had no children of his own and he took special interest in his servant boy; Peter attended school in winter, where he was taught the rudiments of an education. When he was seventeen the master died, leaving him his freedom and one hundred and twenty pounds, a horse and all his wearing apparel. Peter Williamson prospered; he set up as a contractor and jobber, made considerable money, and married the daughter of a well-to-do Pennsylvania farmer. Later he secured a tract of land on the frontier and settled in the back country. During the Indian ravages at the outbreak of the

---

fortunate Young Nobleman, gives an account of the trial with the decision in favor of James, but says that he died at twenty-four without issue. This account was disputed in the same magazine in November, 1831, and there is furnished detailed information of the family, titles, etc. The correspondent thought that James Annesley died about 1748, although he wished further information of him after the trial in 1743. (*Gentlemen's Magazine,* November, 1831, 405.) The matter was again in the *Gentlemen's Magazine* in 1840, and in this number it was charged that the father of James Annesley was a profligate character. This seems to have been given credence by F. D. Stone, who held that after the death of the boy's mother the father, "a worthless scamp," conspired with the uncle to get him out of the way. The motive was the raising of funds from his title to the estate, which could be better done if he were without heir. Stone, *Publications of Genealogical Society of Pennsylvania,* I, 122, 123.

The account of the Annesley case has, however, found a place among the books of *Famous Trials,* by Andrew Lang.

French War, Williamson's place was attacked, and he was seized and carried away as a prisoner. After being kept for more than a year, he effected his escape and made his way back to the Pennsylvania settlements, but only to find that his family had been murdered.[24]

Williamson soon returned to Scotland, where he brought out a book giving an account of his life and adventures. This attracted attention, but it did not please the magistrates of Aberdeen, and when Williamson came there to sell his book, they ordered him prosecuted. A counter report was brought out that Williamson had said he was not kidnaped, that somehow or other this had been impressed upon his mind, and that he had made use of it in the story of his adventures. He was fined forty shillings for publishing what was charged to be untrue, and he was ordered to cut the leaves with the objectionable matter from the books in his possession; these leaves were to be burned by the common hangman. Furthermore, Williamson was to sign a "recantation," have it inserted in the newspapers, and then be banished from the town. None of these conditions was complied with; the fine seems not to have been exacted and Williamson published in the newspapers what he termed "the scandal" of the magistrates and inserted the same statement in a second edition of his book. This was annexed as the "author's true statement of the case" between the magistrates of Aberdeen and himself. Serious reflections were made against the conduct of the magistrates, and finally he brought suit against them for damages and expenses.[25]

For a series of years suits were in progress, and in these suits important information was furnished bearing on the supplying of servants to the plantations. First (1761), action was brought against the magistrates of Aberdeen for several irregularities committed by them while in office, and after securing judgment for one hundred pounds and expenses, Williamson con-

---

[24] *Life and Adventures of Peter Williamson*, passim.

[25] *Williamson Papers*, 1-3. For these papers, as for other material on the suits of Williamson, the writer is indebted to the late Samuel W. Pennypacker, who generously loaned his collection of the papers containing the "case books." No trace has been found of any other copy of these books.

tinued his prosecutions, next attacking the ship company by whose agents he had been seized and shipped. The statements of his *Life and Adventures* were introduced as evidence, but evidence was produced more convincing than these, for Williamson reported himself as an author, and acknowledged that he took certain liberties in embellishing the accounts of his adventures.

The prosecution clearly showed that James Smith, of Aberdeen, a saddler by trade, had acted as overseer and manager in the securing of servants. An itemized account was offered in evidence, extending from December 3, 1742, to May 12, 1743, at which time the ship set sail. The account covered a total of twenty-two pages in the Case Book, and seems to have been printed in full; it contained items of indebtedness to Smith and to his agents for fees, for clothing, and for food. In the enumeration Peter Williamson was mentioned four times, once in the words, "To the man who brought Williamson, one shilling, six pence." The total of the account was one hundred sixty pounds, fourteen shillings, five pence, and to it there was appended a receipt for settlement.

The testimony of Robert Thomson, town clerk of Aberdeen, showed that the regulations for registering indentures were not faithfully carried out. He said that he knew that it was a common practice for servants to go from Aberdeen to America about 1743, as it had been as long as he could remember; he had often seen advertisements in newspapers asking people to apply for passage at stated places. He knew little of the matter personally, but had heard a company making merry in the barn at the time Williamson said he was sent out and was told that they were servants awaiting shipment; he also remembered the sailing of the defendant's ship, called the "Planter" and commanded by one Captain Ragg. The clerk did not keep a record of indentures as they were attested by the magistrates, and thought that no such record was kept. Indeed, he thought such record was not really possible, as indentures, after being signed by the servants and acknowledged by the magistrates, were carried away by the owners. Thomson referred to the sale in America as protection against abuses in British ports, saying that he had often been told that indentures not acknowledged before magistrates were "not worth two pence in America."[26]

James Smith, mentioned above, was introduced as witness by the defendants. He swore that he had been spoken to about getting servants, but said that he was not engaged to secure any boy or girl under the lawful age. He further testified that he was likely to lose some of the persons secured after he had clothed them and fed them for as much as six weeks, as they were trying to run away; they were in danger from being decoyed by others who were enlisting persons to go as servants. He declared that he had never received orders for the kidnaping of any persons, and described the method pursued as follows: an agent, termed "the drum," was sent through the town inviting persons who would go as servants to America to apply at a stated place. Their operations also extended to Inverness, from which place recruits were brought to Aberdeen. In consequence of such solicitation, it was averred, Williamson was secured.

Practically every phase of this subject was touched upon in the Williamson trials. Andrew Wilson testified that he was engaged by James Smith to go through the town and take up boys for America, and that he received money when these were brought in. This, the witness knew, was a common practice; other ships carried away passengers about the same time. One Alexander Middleton had been engaged as shipwright on the "Planter," 1743, and had fixed up sleeping berths for the passengers. He remembered having heard the boys cry, and thought that they were dissatisfied with their lot. Peter Kemp, a sailor in Aberdeen, was introduced; he had been engaged by James Smith as agent, had signed an indenture as he supposed for five years, but in America he had been compelled to serve for seven years less one month. William Wilson, a sailor on the "Planter" in 1743, said that the boys and girls who were taken out were brought to the ship under guard, and that they were watched by the ship's crew and owners until they sailed. He declared that the hatches were put down and locked every night, both while the ship was in the harbor at Aberdeen and at sea. It was his opinion that the boys were about fourteen years of age; some seemed older and others not more than twelve.

---

[26] *Case Book,* 11-14.

By Wilson's testimony, also by that of Peter Kemp, it appeared that the voyage of the "Planter" was ill-starred; she went aground in the Delaware River, and the crew and some of the passengers first got off in the longboat, leaving the servants to shift for themselves; but later the boat returned for them, and the whole party camped on an island. Finally they were put on board a sloop and taken to Philadelphia, where the servants were offered for sale. Wilson demanded his wages when they reached Philadelphia, but the captain had to delay payment until the sale of the servants, as the ship and cargo were lost and the servants were the only asset. Wilson waited and saw the servants sold and carried away, as he said, "like a lot of sheep," and finally got his money.[27]

The Williamson prosecution claimed that kidnaping was common about 1743, and introduced testimony covering this point. One William Jamison had lost a son by this means. After failing at his home to get a summons against the merchant who had sent his boy away, Jamison went to Edinburgh, and insisted upon its being issued; but when he got the summons, he could find no messenger who would serve it. At last he reached the Earl of Aberdeen, who seemed to interest himself, and promised to have the merchant give a bond to the amount of fifty pounds that the boy would be returned. The bond was not exacted, however, and the father testified that he had not heard of his son, and did not know whether he was dead or alive. It was, he claimed, the common talk of the country that children were "spirited" away, and he himself had seen many persons searching for those so taken.[28]

The defense in this case acknowledged the ownership of the vessel, the voyage of 1743, and that servants were sent to America on this voyage; but it was claimed that all of these were above the required age ("age of pupilarity"), that they were voluntarily engaged, and regularly indentured. The defendants denied that Peter Williamson had been sent out as set forth, but asserted that if it were so, it was without their knowledge. The counter-allegations of the defense were: First, that it was never the prac-

---

[27] *Case Book,* 43-49.

[28] *Case Book,* 54-56.

tice to kidnap boys in Aberdeen or to take them by force or stealth; instead, it was the practice to take them before a magistrate or justice and have the indenture duly recognized, and, further, in America no indentures were taken that were not properly attested; second, that it was not the practice to take in the manner above described boys under thirteen or fourteen years of age, as young boys would not be received by the planters in America; third, that after boys were indentured they were not confined, unless they showed a disposition to run away, and they were all well treated; fourth, that when Peter Williamson sailed in the "Planter" he was above thirteen years and might easily have passed as being older than he was; fifth, that Williamson came to Aberdeen in 1758 and sold books libelous in character and to the harm of the town; that his confessions were voluntary; and that he did not confine himself to the truth.[29]

The case turned largely on the question of Williamson's age at the time when he was secured and the manner of his having been taken. Testimony was introduced showing that the plaintiff was about eleven to thirteen years of age in 1743, though large for this age, and that he might have been thought older.[30] No satisfactory records were produced to show that he was legally indentured, and the evidence was strong that he was not; the finding of the court was in Williamson's favor and the award was for two hundred pounds and costs.[31]

But the Williamson case did not rest here, for in 1768 another petition in prosecution was filed, reciting the facts as above noted and claiming further damages. The plaintiff now requested one thousand pounds for costs, for having been "fraudulently kidnapped and sold as a slave in the plantations." The answer referred to the earlier trials and to the line of defense there pre-

---

[29] The above allegations were concluded by the following: "The proof of the other Side is almost all hearsay—evidence of poor people from the country, concerning the practice of the merchants of Aberdeen, to steal boys to send them to *America;* which is a sort of evidence that your Lordships will certainly not put in the balance with the positive evidence of the merchants of Aberdeen, who themselves carried on this trade." *Memorial,* 5-7.

[30] In his *Life and Adventures* he said that he was but eight.

[31] For an account of Williamson and the practice of kidnaping in Aberdeen and other Scotch cities, see *Chambers Journal,* June 29, 1839.

sented, and further to the facts that judgments were found against the magistrates of Aberdeen and the present defendants. In this defense Williamson was referred to as one now well known, as a result of the publications of his *Life and Adventures* and of the publicity which his earlier trials had given him.[32]   Peter Williamson was an adventurer, and at the best his testimony must be taken with reservation; the publication of the account of his life involved him so that he had to make a defense for what he had said. That defense was made easy by the looseness of the earlier methods by which servants were secured and carried away, and he was not slow to take advantage of this; his cases at law gave him what he coveted, public attention, and no doubt created a demand for his published *Life and Adventures*.[33]

Many were the strange fortunes of the indentured servants. In 1725, William Moraley was disappointed with his father's will, whereupon he went to London, drank to excess, and soon spent all his money. Then he determined to come to America and repair his fortunes. A ship for the plantations received him, and fed him well while in port, though there was a marked change after she put to sea. He was brought to Philadelphia, where he saw many of his companions sold and was himself disposed of for eleven pounds to Isaac Pearson, of Burlington. His master combined the trades of smith and watchmaker and conducted ironworks at Mount Holly. Moraley lived on good terms with his master and was often permitted to travel about and clean and repair clocks. Something of life in the wilderness may be gathered from Moraley's account of his adventures: sometimes, he said,

---

[32] Pennypacker collection of Williamson papers. *Memorial.*

[33] Williamson continued a character of some note, though there can be found but little definite information about him. A miscellaneous clipping in the Pennypacker papers says: "The little known of Peter's everyday life in Edinburgh for thirty years would be ten times more interesting than his adventures among the Mohawks. He seems to have possessed considerable natural ability, inventiveness, and energy, to have been one of the class whose shifts are numberless, yet only moderately successful. He published the first Edinburgh directory, established a cheap local delivery of letters and parcels—a penny postage in fact, was a soldier, an advocate of coast defenses, a political reformer, innkeeper, printer, stationer, newsmonger, author and editor, and possessed that worst of chronic afflictions, a troublesome wife."

he cleared land; sometimes he was a smith; sometimes he was a cow hunter in the woods; sometimes he worked in water to the waist; and sometimes he got drunk in joy that his work was ended.[34]   Moraley served out his time and later returned to England.

Joshua Brown, of the Philadelphia Yearly Meeting, has left an account of the kidnaping and sale of his mother in Scotland when she was between twelve and fourteen years of age. With several others of about the same age she was carried on shipboard by force and brought to Philadelphia. She became a servant to Caleb Pusey, a pioneer of Chester County, served out her time, was honorably married, and left a worthy family.[35]

Colonial newspapers were utilized in the efforts to find those who had been lost by the indenture system. In 1730, one supposed to have been taken under indenture from Bristol to Pennsylvania was informed that money for his return home could be secured by applying to the printer.[36] A London notice of 1771 informed Biddy Fitzpatrick, who had come to New York in 1765 and later passed on to Philadelphia as a servant, that by the recent death of her father she was the inheritor of a fortune, and she, too, was directed to inquire of the printers.[37]

Joshua Gee, after noting the operation of the laws of his time, recommended further changes so that the securing of servants would be easier; he believed that sending them could be turned to account for the good of the realm as well as for the relief of distress and the prevention of crime:

> "In the year 1716, there was a Paper laid before the Lords of Trade for encouraging the raising of Hemp, making of Iron, Pitch, Tar, and other Things, in our Plantations,—wherein Mention was made of the Difficulty of carrying over Servants that were inclin'd to transport themselves. Soon after there was a Law made, which did mitigate the Penalties of ancient Laws, particularly that of the first of James the First, to prevent the carrying away the Subjects of this Kingdom into the Popish Monasteries; as well as

---

[34] Moraley, "Voyages and Adventures," *Chester Republican.*
[35] *The Friend*, Philadelphia, 1861, Vol. XXXIV, p. 136.
[36] *American Weekly Mercury*, November 3, 1730.
[37] *Pennsylvania Gazette*, May 4, 1772.

several other Laws, which were then turned against the Merchants and Captains of Ships that transported those Persons into our Colonies. (The redressing those Laws in part, hath been of great Convenience to the Traders in our Plantations; but still Part of them remain, which prevents transporting Servants, and therefore great Numbers that happen to be out of Employment, and have no possible Way of recommending themselves to any Service, are forced to starve, or fall into the Practice of picking of Pockets, Thieving, or other wicked Courses to supply their immediate Necessities; and by continuing this Practice, run from one Evil to another, till at last they come under the sentence of Felons, *viz.* transportation or the gallows. Now as there cannot be an Act of greater Charity or Humanity, than to put those People into a Way of getting Bread for themselves); if they were sent into the Colonies, and put upon raising and dressing Hemp and Flax, I am of Opinion, they might not only find a most profitable Employment, but also those that are condemned for petty Larceny, or any other Crime less than the Penalty of Death, being sent thither might be rendered useful." [38]

The earliest transportation of these British servants to Pennsylvania was from England and Wales; next, with the enlargement of the colony's trade, demands were made upon Ireland and Scotland. Early English and Welsh proprietors brought with them servants under indenture. A Welsh agreement of 1697-1698 showed that a company of sixty passengers was transported to Philadelphia, the adults at five pounds each, children at fifty shillings, and infants free.[39] A Welshman, David Evans by name, came to Philadelphia in 1703. Although he was of a good family, and had a fondness for books which his parents satisfied, he was apprenticed for four years in Philadelphia county and spoke of his life as hard work at clearing the land of trees. Evans became dissatisfied with this, later learned the carpenter's trade, then studied the classics, and went to Yale College, from which he

---

[38] Gee, *Trade and Navigation*, 58, 59.

[39] *Pa. Mag. of Hist. and Biog.*, I, 330-332.

graduated. He adopted the ministry as a profession and became a preacher of prominence.[40]

As the servant trade grew, Ireland furnished the largest supply from the English-speaking countries. Economic conditions in Ireland during the eighteenth century, the extreme regulative legislation of England following Ireland's support of the Stuarts, evictions from lands, excessive taxation, and famines consequent upon crop failures, all united to make the Irish wish to leave the land of their nativity. As an instance of these harsh measures, an act of Parliament in Anne's reign (8, ch. 3, sec. 41) banished Irish schoolmasters and forbade them to return on pain of death. Ships engaged in colonial trade were in readiness, and Irish in large numbers came, not to Pennsylvania alone, but to other colonies as well. Those at home aided in these projects. At the time of these hard conditions in Ireland, agents from the colonies and solicitors for ships' companies went through the island circulating stories of great plenty in the New World and offering the means of emigration. Augustus Gun, of Cork, advertised in Philadelphia that he had from the mayor of Dublin a monopoly of the supply of Irish servants from that city.[41]

Conditions in Ireland were especially favorable to emigration about 1725, when Dean Swift wrote that he was not sorry to hear that large numbers were going to America, though he expressed regret for the conditions that led to their going. Swift cited a familiar eighteenth century rule, "People are the riches of a nation," but said that it did not apply to the Ireland of that time, because the country had neither manufactures to employ nor food to supply its people. Large numbers of Irish came in the later twenties, and as there were many Catholics among them, the fear grew that Pennsylvania "might become Papist." This fear was expressed by the governor, by James Logan as guardian of the proprietary interest, and by the Assembly. Patrick Gordon said in 1728: "Only I must make use of this first Opportunity to acquaint you, that I have now positive Orders from Britain to provide by a proper Law against those Crowds of Forreigners,

---

[40] From a manuscript sketch in the library of the late Samuel W. Pennypacker.

[41] Watson, *Annals*, II, 267; Cheyney, *Philadelphia Manufacturer*, April 1, 1891.

who are yearly pour'd in upon us, of which the late Assembly took Notice, in a Message to me of the 18th of *April* last: Nor does this arise, as I conceive, from any Dislike to the People themselves, many of whom we know are peaceable, industrious and well affected, but it seems principally intended to prevent an English Plantation being turned into a Colony of Aliens." [42]

Acting on the governor's suggestion, the Assembly passed an act laying a duty on foreigners and Irish servants imported into Pennsylvania. Every alien to the realm of Great Britain who should be brought in was required to pay forty shillings, while for every Irish passenger or servant "upon redemption" or "brought on condition of paying for his or her passage upon or after arrival in the plantations," there was levied a tax of twenty shillings. [43] Later in the same year, James Logan expressed satisfaction that Parliament was to undertake measures to prevent the too free importation of people into Pennsylvania, for if this were not done, he felt, foreigners would become proprietors. He reported that a hundred Irish had already been landed at Burlington to escape the tax of twenty shillings. [44] The act noted above was repealed the following year, and the regulation was apparently further conducted under the law for preventing the importation of criminals, impotent persons, etc. [45] Irish passengers were less numerous after 1730. The explanation is found in a letter to the effect that grain was again being produced in North Ireland and it was predicted that the people would now stay at home and follow their occupations as usual. [46]

The attending evils of the passenger trade led to the securing of Fisher's (Province) Island at the mouth of the Schuylkill as a site for a hospital and pesthouse, for the retention of those diseased, and the better protection of the health of the city. Maintenance of sick passengers was to be at the expense of the

---

[42] Quoted in Sachse, *German Sectarians* (1708-1742), 136.

[43] *Statutes at Large*, IV, 136 sqq.; *Colonial Records*, III, 359, 360. This would seem a definition of "redemption servant"; it is worthy of note that the term is here applied to Irish servants. The term was used earlier in the Assembly when a committee was ordered to draft a bill. *Votes of Assembly*, III, 83, 87.

[44] Diffenderffer, *Redemptioners*, 233, 234.

[45] *Statutes at Large*, II, 164-171.

[46] *Pennsylvania Gazette*, March 5, 1730.

master of the ship, or the importer, who was subject to imprisonment if he would not become bound for their support.[47] After 1700 it was unlawful for vessels with contagious diseases on board, or sailing from regions in which they raged, to come within a mile of any port of Pennsylvania, but there was no adequate provision for the retention of the sick and many of them were secretly brought into Philadelphia.

Large importation of foreigners led to overcrowding of ships in the passage, which, with bad sanitary provisions, caused contagious diseases. The introduction of disease by this means so endangered the health of the people of the colony that means of protection became necessary. In 1738-1739 there was first the address of Governor Thomas to the Colonial Assembly, followed by the reply stating that great numbers of people were annually imported from Ireland and Germany, that diseases were contracted by these on the sea voyage, and that a "pesthouse" was necessary. Further consideration of the subject resulted in the securing of Province Island as a place to keep the sick (1742-1743).[48]

Discussion of the pesthouse project had two attending results: First, plans were devised for limiting the numbers of passengers who might be imported in one vessel, in order to lessen the probability of disease breaking out while at sea; and, second, the making of better provision for the sick in Philadelphia, which led to the incorporation of the Pennsylvania Hospital in 1751.[49]

The Assembly of 1749-1750 passed the first of the acts prohibiting the importation of too many passengers in one vessel. Though German passenger ships were specified, others were included, and it would seem that diseases were quite prevalent on incoming ships from Ireland. Mortal and contagious diseases, the preamble of the law recited, had been bred from lack of room and of necessary accommodations on shipboard, and this had resulted in the death of great numbers in the passage and the infecting of the survivors, causing the spread of contagion after their arrival.

---

[47] *Statutes at Large,* IV, 382-388.

[48] *Colonial Records,* IV, 315, 507, 508.

[49] See Morton, *History of Pennsylvania Hospital* (Philadelphia: 1897). 5, 6.

To put an end to the evil practice it was directed that no ship coming to the province should bring more people than it could furnish with wholesome food and drink for the entire voyage, and that in no event was a vessel to bring such a number of passengers that each adult did not have a deck space of at least six feet in length and one foot six inches in breadth. Two children under fourteen might be reckoned as one adult in fixing the carrying capacity. For violation of the above regulation the master of the vessel forfeited ten pounds for each passenger; one-half of the fine was to go to the person suing and the balance was to be for the use of the trustees of Fisher's Island. It was made obligatory upon the officer for collecting the duty on felons to inquire into the condition of incoming ships and to report any irregularity to the mayor, recorder, or aldermen of Philadelphia. Should any passenger die in passage, the captain of the vessel was to furnish a true inventory of all the deceased's goods, and after the just demands of the captain were paid, the balance was to be delivered over for the benefit of the rightful heirs. Failure to comply with the latter provision subjected the captain to a forfeiture of one hundred pounds.[50] Governor James Hamilton was in accord with the Assembly, for immediately on receipt of

---

[50] *Statutes at Large,* V, 94-97. Reported by title, Bioren's *Laws,* I, 23.

The following is a description of the operation of this law:

"While tyrannical Sea Captains for many years past kept the poor German immigrants in such a plight, that many of them died, the Government of the Province passed a law that when the newly arrived Germans made complaint hereafter, that they were not allowed the room on shipboard that was contracted for nor the food agreed upon, the Captain should pay a fine of ten pounds. But nevertheless we hear that although the poor people almost died of hunger; when they reached the River Delaware they were informed by the Newlanders that visitors would arrive and would ask them whether they had room enough, and sufficient to eat, then they should all exclaim Yes! yes! but if they complained, they would not be allowed to land under four weeks' time. When the passengers are therefore tired of the sea and ship and of the want of food, all who were able to do so, called out, Yes! yes. If they complained after they landed, concerning a lack of food and space, then there was no help for them. The tyrannical captains would rather spend a hundred pounds among Newlanders and visitors than a thousand pounds in fines." *The Pennsylvania Berichte,* Germantown, December 1, 1752. Cited in Diffenderffer, *Redemptioners,* 211, 212.

this bill he gave it his approval and it became a law.[51]   Although
the law contained the objectionable feature of being enforced by
an officer whom the English government refused to recognize, it
was passed upon favorably in England.[52]

In 1754, an important report was made to the colonial government by two physicians, Thomas Greeme and Thomas Bond,
dealing with contagious diseases on the passenger ships.   It
presented evidence covering some fourteen or fifteen years preceding.   Captain Arthur, who had formerly been a mate of one
Captain Davis, said that in the year 1751 they took in a parcel
of convicts from the Dublin jail as well as other servants from
the city; soon after, the people on board were seized with fever,
so that they were in great distress from the number of sick during
the voyage.   "We have this Year had," said the commissioners,
"the same Kind of Fever amongst Us, long before the arrival
of any Palatine Ships.   Where it arose from, we cannot posi-
tively say, but the following Circumstances make it probable it
was owing to the same cause as that of the Year 1741: Mrs.
Elves, who lived near a Wharf, and kept a Ship Chandler's Shop,
was the first Person seized in the City, and soon after Sundry
other Persons in the Neighborhood living about the Wharfs at
or near the time of Mrs. Elves' Death.   A relation of James
Calder's was ill of this Fever, he had lately arrived from Bristol
in a Vessel that had imported Servants and which had been very
sickly in the Voyage.   Likewise soon after two Persons were
under the same disease who came in a Vessel of Capt Simpson's
that brought Convicts and Servants from Dublin.   Capt Simpson
said they had been very sickly from the time of their leaving
Ireland.   He likewise said that many of the indentured servants
on board were such persons as had been lately discharged from
the jails." [53]

A bill further prohibiting the importation of Germans or
other passengers or servants in too great numbers in any one
ship or vessel, and to prevent the spreading of contagious diseases in the province, was received by the governor, January
1, 1755.   Robert Hunter Morris, then governor, opposed the bill

---

[51] *Colonial Records,* V, 427, 428.
[52] *Statutes at Large,* V, Appendix VIII, pp. 498, 499.
[53] *Colonial Records,* VI, 174.

as presented, on the ground that it amounted to an absolute prohibition of the importation of Germans, which he thought would
neither look well in England nor be to the interests of the province.[54] The objections of Governor Morris and the reply of his
Assembly gave evidence that commerce in Pennsylvania depended
in a measure on the importation of servants. The address of the
Assembly to the governor on January 8 was that they considered
the bill of utmost consequence to the health and lives of the
inhabitants of the province, but that the bill itself was calculated
to lay restraints upon the trade of the importers of passengers,
and in all their dealings with it, they had tried to make it effective
without interfering with other sorts of commerce.[55]

The abuses were by no means confined to the Germans.
Proof of this is found in the report of Greeme and Bond in 1754
(*vide supra*), also from the accounts of travelers and others who
observed the importation. In his *Letters,* Hector Saint-John
Crèvecœur gave a description of the arrival of Scotch emigrants.
Most of them appeared on land pale and emaciated from the
length of the passage and the poor and scanty provisions on which
they had lived.[56] The treatment of emigrants was noted by James
Anderson; the poor emigrants were of small "freight" anyhow,
said he, and the captains tried to make their profit out of the
insufficient and indifferent rations which were furnished in passage. He gave an account of a Scotch vessel which he had observed, the vessel having sailed but put back on account of bad
weather. Anderson questioned whether more than one-quarter
of those on this vessel would have survived the voyage and its
consequent diseases.[57] One of William Priest's letters, dated
from Pennsylvania in 1796, is to the effect that some time before
he left Baltimore, the papers were full of an account of the treatment of a cargo of passengers on board an Irish immigrant ship.
The allowance of water to these passengers was insufficient and
contagion broke out on shipboard. Priest said that on his way
to Philadelphia, he had the annoyance to find that more than
one hundred of these same Irish passengers were on board the

---

[54] *Ibid.,* 225, 226.
[55] *Ibid.,* 243.
[56] *Letters from an American Farmer,* 95.
[57] Anderson, *Interest of Great Britain Considered,* 87, 88.

packet. They informed him that the captain went so far as to sell the ship's water by the pint. Priest learned after arriving in Philadelphia that the Hibernian Society had determined to prosecute this "flesh butcher" for murder.[58]

Of the total number of servants, as well as the relative number of these from Great Britain and Ireland, we are alike uncertain. It is probable that down to 1730 the servants from Germany were not equal in number to those from Great Britain, and also that after this time, when better communication with Holland and Germany was established, the supply from Germany was more numerous. (The following chapter will treat of the German redemption trade.) For example, in 1729, there was received in the colony a total immigration of 6,208, of whom 267 were English and Welsh passengers and servants, 43 were Scotch servants, 1,155 were Irish, 4500, chiefly Irish, were landed at New Castle and 243 were Palatine passengers.[59] In 1750, there were imported 4,317 Germans and but 1,000 British and Irish immigrants.[60] A recently discovered record of emigrants leaving Great Britain furnishes an interesting sidelight on the supply of indentured servants just before the Revolution. Four selected weeks in 1773, 1774, and 1775, show that of a total

---

[58] Priest, *Travels* (1793-1797), 142-148.

The following is an account of the servant traffic furnished by Priest: "As the manner of carrying on this *trade* in human flesh is not generally known in England, I send you a few particulars of what is here emphatically called a *white Guinea man*. There are vessels in the trade of Belfast, Londonderry, Amsterdam, Hamburgh, etc., whose chief *cargoes*, on their return to America, are passengers; a great number of whom, on their arrival, are *sold* for a term of years to pay their passage; during their Servitude, they are liable to be *resold*, at the death or caprice of their *masters*." *Travels*, 144.

[59] Gordon, *History of Pennsylvania*, 208; Holmes, *American Annals*, II, 123.

[60] Douglass, *British Settlements*, II, 326.

Phineas Bond, reporting from Philadelphia, 1788, said: "I have not yet been able to obtain any account of the number of Irish passengers brought hither, for any given series of years before the war—but from my own recollection I know the number was great and I have been told that in one year above 6000 Irish were landed at Philadelphia, Wilmington, and New Castle upon Delaware." *Report of American Historical Association,* 1896, 643.

of 699 passengers registered, 474 were under indenture.[61]   The vessel on which Benjamin Franklin returned from England in 1775 brought its complement of passengers under indenture.[62]

Descriptions of runaways as given in the advertisements indicate somewhat the nationality of servants. In 1720, there were 43 runaways advertised, of whom 6 were English, 1 was Irish, 5 were Scotch, 1 was Scotch-Irish, 2 were Welsh, 2 were Indians, and of 26 the nationality was not given. In 1730, there were 36 runaways advertised, of whom 2 were English, 10 were Irish, 1 was Scotch, 1 was an Indian, 1 was a native, 1 was an East Indian, and for 20 the nationality was not given. For 1740, 64 runaways were advertised, of whom 8 were English, 19 were Irish, 2 were Scotch, 2 were Indians, 3 were natives, 1 was Dutch, and for 29 the nationality was not given. For 1750, the total number of runaway servants advertised was 144, of whom 22 were English, 71 were Irish, 3 were Scotch, 1 was Welsh, 4 were natives, 6 were "Dutch," 1 was "High Dutch," while for 36 the nationality was not given.[63]   For 1760, advertisements showed 79 servants as having run away; of these 3 were said to be native, 9 were "Dutch," 24 were English, 27 were Irish, and for 16 no nationality was given. During 1770, the total number advertised was 201; and of these 14 were native, 2 were Welsh, 4 were Scotch, 6 were classed as German and 6 as Dutch, 40 were English and 91 were Irish, while for 37 of the total no indication of nationality was given.[64]

It would be far from just to say from the foregoing that the Irish made so large a part of all the servants as the proportion of the runaway Irish to all the runaways would indicate. Advertisements of runaway Germans were rare, and yet there is abundant evidence that many Germans were indentured. The fair inference is that the Germans patiently bore the terms of

---

[61] *MS. Transcript,* see Appendix II.

[62] *Pennsylvania Gazette,* May 10, 1775.

[63] In New Jersey 165 runaways were advertised from 1751 to 1755, of whom 60 were Irish; 30 Negroes (slaves); 22 English; 16 Dutch; 5 Scotch; 2 Welsh; 2 French; of the remaining 28, there was no means of determining the nationality. Cited from New Jersey *Archives* in Geiser, *Redemptioners,* 81.

[64] For 1720 and 1730 the *American Weekly Mercury* was examined; for the other years the *Pennsylvania Gazette.*

their service, while many Irish ran away before their terms expired.

Emigration of servants to North America from Great Britain and Ireland was largely increased in the years immediately following the Treaty of Paris. The greater security in the New World and the opening up for settlement of extensive territory made their appeal. In the five years from 1769 to 1774, an average of 8,740 persons left five Irish ports alone. Scotland, it was thought, contributed even a larger number, while England was sending emigrants, but perhaps in fewer numbers.[65] Indications warrant the inference that many of these emigrants were poor, and without doubt they resorted to the then common method of selling their services for a term of years to secure their passage. Philadelphia was one of the chief ports of entry for this passenger trade.

The recently discovered collection of lists of emigrants from England in the years immediately preceding the American Revolution throws much light on the system of emigration then in vogue. An official letter from the British Treasury Department in December, 1773, directed that lists should be made of those leaving England. In compliance with this direction, lists were drawn up until 1776, giving names of those leaving, the reasons for their going, conditions under which they went, and their destination. These lists show that servants went out subject to terms of four, five, or six years, and that, in some cases, redemptioners emigrated subject to a seven-year term. Among the reasons given for these emigrants leaving England were "rents raised," "small farms absorbed into larger ones," and "cannot support their families." [66]

---

[65] Johnson, *Emigration from United Kingdom to North America* (New York and London: 1914), 1, 2.

[66] Andrews, *Guide to the Public Record Office,* II, 224, 225.

CHAPTER IX

SUPPLY OF GERMAN SERVANTS

Germany has been a mother land for the countries of western, eastern, and northern Europe, and for lands more remote; successive waves of migration have gone off, first to the regions round about and latterly to more distant parts of the world. The Germans have been good colonizers, adjusting themselves to conditions in new lands, and becoming quickly prosperous. Thrift and dogged perseverance are German characteristics, and for more than a thousand years emigrants with these traits went out to build German settlements. At times Germany's surplus population emigrated from motives of conquest; again, it went to escape religious persecution or to extend German industry and trade.

Conditions were especially favorable for migration from Germany in the period following the founding of Pennsylvania. During the Thirty Years' War, the German states were ravaged again and again, and when the war closed, Germany was the most unsettled of European countries. First, there was the division of the people into Catholics and Protestants, and in addition the Protestants were divided into "church" and "sect" peoples. Of the former there were the followers of Luther, Melanchthon, Zwingli, and Calvin. The number of sect adherents was large, and they did not wholly escape persecution at the hands of their fellow Protestants, much less from the Catholics. Sect peoples wandered out in little groups and, with a devotion to their religious opinions as intense as was that of the Puritans, braved the dangers of the deep and faced the uncertainties of a home in the wilderness that these opinions might be cherished and nurtured. Nor were these religious enthusiasts disappointed in coming to Pennsylvania, for to this day many of the strange beliefs and almost incomprehensible practices of German sects survive in communities in this commonwealth.[1]

---

[1] "The ethnologist studies the habits of prehistoric races not by the uncertain light of early legends, but by going to the Islands of the South Pacific, where savage life still exists, as it was before the dawn of civiliza-

168

To add to the dissatisfaction with home conditions there was the invasion of the German Palatinate by the forces of Louis XIV of France in 1688.   Rhenish and Swabian frontier provinces were occupied and plundered. Cities were burned, as the French had not sufficient forces to retain them with garrisons, and the entire region was laid waste to prevent its being occupied by the German army.   In this devastation many of the inhabitants were driven away, put to the sword, or carried to France as prisoners. What wonder that this, added to the results of the Thirty Years' War, should lead the German to feel that security and freedom could not be obtained in his own land!   Franz Löher pictures the unfortunate people of this region as looking into each others' faces and saying, "Let us go to America and if we perish, we perish." It was from this upper Palatinate region that in colonial times the largest migration of Germans took place; the lower German districts did not send their peoples until later.[2]

The early German migration was not large, and comparatively few Germans were available as indentured servants in the early years of Pennsylvania's history.[3]   Down to 1709 there was no general movement of the Germans to the New World, and emigration consisted of isolated individuals and a few families at a time.   Good authorities have thought it improbable that more than three thousand German people were in Pennsylvania in 1709. Some of these immigrants were indentured; a few sold themselves as early as 1685 and 1686.[4]   Moreover, the early emigrants could pay their passage, or those who were unable to pay for themselves were helped by their countrymen in the Palatinate or by friends in Holland or America.[5]

---

tion.   The historian, who, pursuing the same methods of investigation, would stand face to face with the Reformation, need only visit the Mennonites of Lancaster County in Pennsylvania, where he can still see rigorously preserved, the thought, the faith, the habits, the ways of living, and even the dress of that important epoch." Pennypacker, *Historical and Biographical Sketches*, 3.

[2] Walterhausen, *Arbeits-Verfassung*, 35, 36.

[3] Rupp, Introduction to *Thirty Thousand German Names*, 1.

[4] Seidensticker, *Geschichte der deutschen Gesellschaft*, 22.

[5] Pennypacker (*Historical and Biographical Sketches*, 181) gives an instance of a meeting of the Quakers which contributed fifty pounds to aid German emigrants.

A combination of circumstances delayed the trade in redemp-tioners to Pennsylvania. The numerous appeals of Penn and his agents had slight immediate response, probably because they were looked upon with suspicion.[6] Claims of other colonies were urged, most notably those of Carolina by one Kocherthal, who went to London and prepared a report on that region; two edi-tions of this appeared in Germany. Pennsylvania was refer-red to as a familiar subject, and it was acknowledged that there were attractions here, but the writer found a superior at-traction in the "eternal summer" of Carolina and all that it meant in such matters as the building of houses, cost of clothing, and care of stock. In Chapter V of this account reference is made to the cost of getting to Carolina, and the means available. The total amount was about seven to eight pounds and it was added that persons too poor to pay would sometimes find proprietors willing to advance the funds, in return for which the emigrant would serve the proprietor for some time after arrival in America. The term of service in times of peace, it was said, was from two to three years, but at other times, when the price of passage was higher, the term was necessarily longer. In an Appendix referring to Pennsylvania, Kocherthal said that emigrants who were going there must be supplied with the ready money to pay their pass-age, which was not necessary for those who were going to Carolina.[7]

A society for furthering emigration was active in Germany; it appointed agents, looked after the interests of those who went out, and made reports of their condition. Henry Melchior Mühlenberg was a distinguished representative of the Halle Emi-gration Society in colonial Pennsylvania, and his letters, with other information received by the society, constitute a valuable collec-tion of papers published as the *Hallische Nachrichten*.[8]

But efforts to secure Germans as colonists were not confined

---

[6] Jacobs, *German Emigration to Pennsylvania to 1740*, 33.

[7] Extended synopsis of Kocherthal's tract in Jacob's *Emigration*, 35-43. Clearly, Kocherthal's anxiety for settlers in Carolina led him to an unfair statement.

[8] Editions of this collection in English, Philadelphia, two volumes (1881 and 1882), and Reading, Pennsylvania, one volume (1882). An account of the connection of Mühlenberg with the society and of his reports occurs in Mann, *Life of Mühlenberg*, 131 sqq.

to colonial proprietors; nor was aid for their transportation limited to that given by the proprietors and the Germans themselves. Kocherthal was in London when he wrote saying that if a sufficient number of emigrants would become enrolled, he would ask the Queen to furnish transportation for them.[9] Later events lead to the conclusion that this was a demand of the English government for aliens as colonists. During the reign of Queen Anne books and papers were distributed through the Palatinate and other German provinces encouraging Germans to come to England for transportation to English colonies in various parts of the world. These books, appearing in letters of gold, are commonly known as "The Golden Books."

The German exodus to England in 1709 has been given careful, detailed study. The causes leading to it were: First, persecutions, though rather the memory of them and the fear of their repetition, than their presence; second, an extremely cold winter in 1709; third, the operation of the land companies, Penn's invitations, and letters from Pennsylvania, booklets, etc.[10] Fully 15,000 Germans are thought to have migrated to London in 1709 for distribution to the colonies. Of these, the majority was sent to North Carolina, New York, Ireland, and some to English settlements in Africa, while some remained in London, and a small number of Catholics was returned to the continent.[11]

---

[9] Jacobs, 39-41.

[10] Diffenderffer, *German Exodus to England,* 1709, 273-293. Menzel says that the English desired the Germans, realizing the worth of their honesty and industry. The promises made were so alluring that Menzel says whole communities came, headed by their pastors. He says that there were 33,000, "evidently an unlooked and unwished-for multitude." *History of Germany,* III, 446.

Fisher, *Making of Pennsylvania,* 98, probably follows him in a statement that there were over 30,000, though Diffenderffer's more careful study of the subject puts the number at 15,000.

[11] Diffenderffer, 321, 322. Estimates of the disposal of these are as follows:

Sent to Ireland, 3,800.
Sent to New York, 3,200.
Sent to North Carolina, 650.
Returned to the continent, 2,000.
Enlisted by Great Britain, 350.
Died while in camp, 1,500.

So considerable was the German movement that the English government became alarmed at the difficulties it presented, and a royal proclamation was issued to discourage the continuance of the exodus.[12] The burgomasters of Rotterdam also had circulars issued against the continuance of the migration through their city, and finally prohibited emigrants from coming.[13] The Germans left in such numbers, and from regions that had already been so depopulated by war and persecution, that the ruling princes of the country became alarmed. Frederick William of Brandenburg devised a colonization scheme as an offset to the English plan, and successive proclamations were put forth to prevent the Germans from continuing to leave; these proclamations also attempted to discredit the Quakers. But it was of no avail. The human stream swelled, and as it grew in proportions, it set toward the river Delaware.

Few Germans came during the first decade of the eighteenth century, yet before the second had passed, the numbers were so great as to alarm the authorities. In 1717, Governor William Keith brought the matter to the attention of the colonial council, saying that great numbers of foreigners from Germany, who were strangers to the language and constitution of the colony, had recently been imported and were being dispersed throughout the province; the governor questioned whether this practice might not be of "dangerous consequence." The council ordered that all masters of ships who had recently imported any of these foreigners appear and give an account of the numbers imported and their character. It was further directed that those who had been landed should be, by proclamation, asked to appear before

---

Balance stayed in London. Diffenderffer, 341, 342.

Fisher says that some of these were sent to Pennsylvania. It is true that some of them eventually reached here, but they were of the number sent to New York as shown in Chapter I.

Some of the children of these Germans who were settled in Ireland came to New York in 1760. The news item that chronicled their arrival explained that they did not have "sufficient scope" in Ireland and so came "to try their fortunes in America." *Pennsylvania Journal,* August 21, 1760.

[12] A copy of this is given, Diffenderffer, 272.

[13] Diffenderffer, *German Exodus,* 274; also Appendix A for resolutions and proceedings of the burgomasters.

the magistrate, or recorder, within a month, and give evidence by oath, or otherwise, that they were "well affected to his Majesty and his Government." It was also ordered that in the future the naval officer of the port should not admit any vessel to entry until the master had given an exact list of his passengers. The captains of three ships which had recently arrived appeared and gave evidence as to the persons they had imported. The numbers reported were, respectively, 164, 91, and 108.[14]

Religious differences in Germany still drove the Protestants away. The *American Weekly Mercury's* foreign correspondents gave ample testimony on this subject. An issue early in 1719 had a letter from Hamburg sent on the fifteenth of October preceding, which quoted a communication of Frederick William, King of Prussia, to the Elector Palatine, reciting what was termed the generous action of Protestants towards Catholics, and urging moderation in the treatment of Protestants within the Palatinate. The elector was requested to revoke the orders concerning the Heidelberg Catechism, and to permit Protestant subjects to use the catechism as heretofore. The Hamburg correspondent added that the elector persisted in his former course, and was entering into arrangements with other Catholic electors and bishops for the suppression of the Protestant religion. Not only this, but the elector was said to look to the bringing in of a foreign army. Thus, it was said, he took a sure method of ruining his country by driving away his Protestant subjects.[15] Other letters confirmed the above, and showed reasons for emigration from the Palatinate. A Heidelberg letter charged that the Pope had dispatched messengers to influence the Elector Palatine, and to prevent the redressing of Protestant grievances.[16] Retaliatory measures were proposed in Protestant states. A foreign letter from The Hague, May 7, 1720, announced that the States-General

---

[14] *Colonial Records,* III, 29; Proud, *History of Pennsylvania,* II, 100; Rupp, Introduction to *Thirty Thousand German Names,* 9.

[15] *American Weekly Mercury,* February 16, 1719.

[16] *Ibid.,* date of March 6, appearing July 7, 1720. Later it was reported from New York that information had been received of the purpose of the elector to restore to the Reformed Church the nave of the Church of the Holy Ghost at Heidelberg. *Ibid.,* May 12, 1720, letter of May 9; same mention in a letter from Frankfort, March 24, appearing June 23, and in one from Ratisbone, March 10, printed June 30.

of Holland had determined to banish all Jesuits as a recourse against the persecution of Protestants in the Palatinate. Catholics were ordered to depart before the first of June following, and if at that time they were still within the territory subject to the States-General, they were to be proceeded against by magistrates.[17] The elector continued in the spirit of his former course, and although twenty-four grievances of the seventy-four presented to him were redressed, they were regarded by the Protestants as of slight consequence.[18]

After 1717 it was usual to require all male foreigners, above sixteen years of age, coming into Pennsylvania, to take the oath of allegiance, swearing or affirming fealty to the British king. This oath was administered as soon after the arrival of the immigrants as possible, the men usually being marched in procession to the courthouse.[19] As the oath was administered, the bell was rung announcing that fact; so common had this practice become by 1732 that to ask questions about it was considered "impertinent." It was also considered impertinent to inquire who the Palatines were, from whence they came, and why so many of them came to Pennsylvania.[20]

A largely increased importation of German redemptioners began about 1727. Immediately following this year the regular supplying of them was established and records of their importation are numerous. On January 27, 1727-1728, the attention of the Pennsylvania Assembly was called to the large number of Germans who were being imported, and the question of their desirability was raised. The record was: "It is reported on good Ground that some thousands of *Palatines* are expected to be imported into this Province next summer." It was moved that the Assembly take means to prevent the evil consequences which might result from this immigration, and a committee was ap-

---

[17] *American Weekly Mercury,* August 25, 1720.

[18] *Ibid.,* June 11, 1721, London Letter of April 11.

[19] A copy of an early form of this oath is given in "Names of Foreigners Who Took the Oath of Allegiance," *Pennsylvania Archives,* Second Series XVII, 3, 4.

[20] This was included in a list of "impertinent questions" to which people did not expect answers, and the asking of which, it was said, illustrated a "sort of misbehavior," etc. *Pennsylvania Gazette,* October 19, 1732.

pointed to make diligent inquiry, and report.[21]   On April 17, 1728, the committee reported that some of the Palatines were of a sober character and not objectionable; there was, however, objection to others.   It was believed by the committee that great numbers might soon be expected.   A motion was passed at this time stating that a large number of the subjects of a foreign prince and of a foreign tongue, introduced into the province, might be hazardous to its welfare.[22]   A statute was enacted laying a duty of forty shillings per head on all aliens introduced.   The duty on Irish servants and passengers, subjects of Great Britain, was fixed at twenty shillings.[23]   The act worked hardship, as was shown by petitions from Germans asking that the Assembly relieve them from paying the duty on the ground that it was unexpected, and that they were unable to pay it.[24]

From 1730 the traffic in German servants was well established and ships crossed regularly from Rotterdam to Philadelphia.   Redemptioners formed the chief cargo of incoming vessels which carried the produce of the colony on their outward voyages. Sometimes these ships made a "middle passage" from Philadelphia to the West Indies and, after an exchange of cargo, returned to Europe.   Colonial ships divided the servant trade with the ships of England and Holland.   It was usual to touch at some

---

[21] *Votes of Assembly,* III, 42.

[22] *Ibid.,* 44, 46.

[23] *Statutes at Large,* IV, 135 sqq.

[24] *Votes,* III, 90, 99.

The repeal of this act, also the one against the importation of felons, passed in 1722, was considered by the colonial legislature on January 14, 15, and 16, 1729-1730, and passed on February 14 following. *Votes of Assembly,* III, 117.

The fear of the colonists on account of the large immigration of Germans was indicated in the correspondence of James Logan, who said that he wished the immigration of Germans into Pennsylvania might be stopped "for fear the colony would be lost to the Crown. . . . The numbers from Germany at this rate will soon produce a German colony here."

It may have been, though it is hardly probable, that the duty of forty shillings per head fixed upon Palatines, and of twenty shillings on Irish passengers and servants, was for the purpose of revenue. It was stated in the act that large numbers were expected, and provision was made for the use of the income to be derived. Gordon, *History of Pennsylvania,* 207; also act itself, *Statutes at Large,* IV, 135.

English port and secure clearance papers which served as licenses to land. As this commerce stocked a colony with people and permitted Great Britain to keep her population at home, and as it did not interfere with the navigation laws, clearance was readily given.[25] Immigration was irregular and records of it are incomplete. The record of arrivals shows that, while for some years the numbers reached the thousands, for others there were none at all. . For particular years we have the testimony of observing travelers who were in Philadelphia. This, and estimates of the total population and the part of it that was German, will give the best indication of the number of German immigrants.[26]

If not a majority, certainly a large proportion of immigrants, both Irish and German, became servants under the indentured system. Repeatedly it was said that the great majority of immi-

---

[25] September 21, 1727, there is a record of the colonial council that a petition of the Palatines was read and approved, the record being that the signers and their families numbered about four hundred persons who had come in one ship. This ship was from Rotterdam, and had touched and cleared from Dover; she had no other license for landing than the clearance. *Colonial Records,* III, 282-283. There is a similar record for September 30, 1727, that three hundred persons had been received from Rotterdam, the ship last clearing from Deal. *Ibid.,* 287. See also *ibid.,* 331 and *ibid.,* IV, 58, 59. "Last from Portsmouth," and "Last from Cowes" are common entries in the record of the "Names of Foreigners Who Took the Oath of Allegiance."

[26] See Diffenderffer, *German Immigration Into Pennsylvania,* 41, 42; Rupp, Note to Rush, *Manners,* 8. The numbers of ships as recorded in the names of foreigners who took the oath are thus summarized by Diffenderffer:

1727.... 5	1740.... 6	1753....19	1766.... 5
1728.... 3	1741.... 9	1754....17	1767.... 7
1729.... 2	1742.... 9	1755.... 2	1768.... 4
1730.... 3	1743.... 9	1756.... 1	1769.... 4
1731.... 4	1744.... 5	1757....none	1770.... 7
1732....11	1745....none	1758....none	1771.... 9
1733.... 7	1746.... 2	1759....none	1772.... 8
1734.... 2	1747.... 5	1760....none	1773....15
1735.... 3	1748.... 8	1761.... 1	1774.... 6
1736.... 3	1749....21	1762....none	1775.... 2
1737.... 7	1750....14	1763.... 4	
1738....16	1751....15	1764....11	
1739.... 8	1752....19	1765.... 5	

German Immigration, 45.

grants who landed in Philadelphia were poor people, and that, as they could not pay their passage from means brought with them, they were compelled to sell themselves into temporary servitude.   Good authorities repeat the statement that the prepayment of the passage in money by German immigrants was the exception, while the discharge of the debt for it by means of subsequent servitude was the rule.[27]   The report on the causes of the increase of the population made by Governor John Penn to Lord Dartmouth in 1775 is in confirmation of this statement. The thirteenth question answered in this report was the number of inhabitants in Pennsylvania, whites and blacks; the fourteenth was whether the inhabitants had increased or decreased in the ten years preceding—how much, and for what reasons.   Governor Penn's answer was comprehensive.   He said that there had been a great increase for three reasons: First, the numerous grants of land in new settlements; second, the annual importation of Irish and German servants and passengers; and third, the natural increase from marriages, which were earlier and more general in the province than in Europe.   As to the amount of increase he declared himself unable to answer.[28]

The period about 1730 had a number of contemporary estimates for the population of Pennsylvania.   In 1730, Governor Patrick Gordon thought it to be about 49,000 souls; however, in 1732 there was another estimate which gave about 30,000.   In the same connection the population of New York was placed as nearly 65,000 and that of Virginia as above 60,000.[29]   The colonial council in 1740 reported that not less than 60,000 people had been imported into Pennsylvania in the twenty years preceding,

---

[27] Kapp, *Immigration*, 9, 10; Seidensticker, *Geschichte der deutschen Gesellschaft;* Kalm, *Travels,* I, 388. Kapp gives the same facts for New York.

Dr. Geiser found that from August 19, 1786, to December 31, 1804, 3,622 redemptioners were registered at Philadelphia; during the same period he thinks but 5,509 foreign immigrants landed, and expresses the belief that the proportion of redemptioners to the total immigration was about two-thirds. *Redemptioners,* 41.

[28] *Pennsylvania Archives,* First Series, IV, 597.

[29] Holmes, *American Annals,* II, 132; Dexter, *Estimates of Population,* 18.

an estimate which it claimed was "moderate." [30]   The larger proportion of this immigration was German.   In 1738, Governor
George Thomas thought that the prosperity of Pennsylvania was
due to the character of the Germans who had been secured as
settlers, and pointed out that the industry of the inhabitants of
a country was as important to its welfare as was the fertility of
its soil.[31]

An unusually large immigration of Germans took place in
the later forties and in the early fifties of the eighteenth century,
and at this period the redemption system was at its height.   Rev.
Henry Melchior Muehlenberg said that in the autumn of 1749,
twenty-five German ships came to Philadelphia with 7,049 passengers alive, and that several thousand had perished at sea.   Mittelberger said that while he was in Pennsylvania (1750-1754)
twenty-two to twenty-four passenger ships had arrived each
autumn.   It was such immigration as this that led Burke to say:
"In some years, more people have transported themselves into
Pennsylvania, than into all the other settlements together." [32]
This immigration of Germans led to the belief, as expressed by
Mühlenberg, that soon after the middle of the eighteenth century,
one-half of the population of Pennsylvania was German.[33]   This
large incoming of a people strange to English institutions, and
to the English language, was a just cause for alarm.   It was felt

---

[30] *Colonial Records,* IV, 469.

[31] *Ibid.,* 315.

Governor Thomas later, in a letter to the Bishop of Exeter, wrote,
"The Germans in that Province (Pennsylvania) are, I believe, three-fifths
of all the people, and by their industry and frugality have been the principal
instruments of raising it to its present flourishing condition."   Quoted,
Seidensticker, *German-American Events,* 8.

[32] *European Settlements,* II, 205.

[33] Mann, *Life of Mühlenberg,* 377.

"Six ships with Irish servants have arrived at Philadelphia, and two
ships with German Newcomers, Some say 18 more are on their way here;
others say 24, and still others 10,000 persons." *Pennsylvania Berichte,*
August 16, 1750.   Cited from Diffenderffer, *Redemptioners,* 209.

"Capt. Hasselwood has arrived from Holland with the latest ship that
brought Germans.   It is the fourteenth that has come laden with Germans
this year.   4,317 have registered in the Court House.   Besides these, 1,000
servants and passengers arrived from Ireland and England." *Ibid., in loc.
cit.*

that if the importation were not regulated these aliens would "out the *British* people from the Colony," as it was put, and endanger adjacent settlements, and this subject was recommended to the attention of the Assembly or the Parliament.[34] Mittelberger esti-

----

[34] Douglass, *British Settlements,* II, 326. By the importation of foreigners in great numbers, said Douglass, Pennsylvania grew prodigiously; by their labor and penurious manner of life, he said, they grew rich where others starved. It was at this time that Franklin termed the Palatines "boors," and accused them of herding together and keeping their language and manners to the exclusion of the English. In short, he feared that they would "Germanize" the colony, rather than the colony "Anglify" them. *Works* (Bigelow), II, 233, 234. Also Ford, *Many-Sided Franklin,* 426. In a letter of Franklin to Peter Collinson in 1753, he spoke of the German immigration and its results as follows:

"Those who come hither are generally the most stupid of their own nation, and, as ignorance is often attended with great credulity, when knavery would mislead it, and with suspicion, when honesty would set it right; and, as few of the English understand the German language and so cannot address them, either from the press or pulpit, it is almost impossible to remove any prejudice they may entertain. Their clergy have very little influence on the people, who seem to take pleasure in abusing and discharging the minister on every trivial occasion. Not being used to liberty, they know not how to make modest use of it. They are under no restraint from ecclesiastical government; they behave, however, submissively enough at present to the civil government, which I wish they may continue to do, for I remember when they modestly declined intermeddling with our elections; but now they come in droves and carry all before them, except in one or two counties.

" . . . Few of their children in the country know English. They import many books from Germany, and of the six printing houses in the province, two are entirely German; two half German half English, and but two are entirely English. They have one German Newspaper, and onehalf of the German advertisements intended to be general are now printed in Dutch and English. The signs in our streets have inscriptions in both languages, and in some places only in German. They begin of late to make all their bonds and other legal instruments in their own language, which (though I think it ought not to be) are allowed in our courts, where the German business so increases that there is continued need of interpreters, and, I suppose, in a few years, they will also be necessary in the Assembly, to tell one-half of our Legislators what the other half says. In short, unless the stream of importation could be turned from this to other colonies, as you very judiciously propose, they will soon outnumber us, so that all the advantages we will have will, in my opinion, not be able to preserve our language, and even our government will become precarious." (University of Pennsylvania, *Alumni Register,* December, 1901, p.

mated the people of Pennsylvania at 200,000 (about 1750). In addition to immigration, he accounted for the rapid increase by early marriages, the fertility of the women, and the prolonging of life in the colony.[35]

In 1757, Burke said that there were 250,000 persons in Pennsylvania, one-half of whom were thought to be Germans, Swedes, and Dutch. This estimate was probably too high. In 1766, Franklin, in his examination before the British House of Commons, estimated that in 1760 there were 160,000 persons in Pennsylvania alone. Proud estimated, for 1770, 250,000 in Pennsylvania, while in the lower counties there were, it was thought, 20,000 to 30,000. In 1775, Governor John Penn made the estimate of 300,000 whites and 2,000 blacks in Pennsylvania and its dependencies.[36] It is within reason to say that within ninety years after the establishment of Penn's colony it had a population of some 250,000. Already Philadelphia claimed to be the metropolis of the continent. One would be within bounds also to say that more than one-third of the total population in Pennsylvania was German, though it would probably be too high a claim to say that one-half of the people were of this nationality.

The anxiety resulting from so large an influx of Germans was natural, both for the colony and for England. Pennsylvania was repeatedly referred to as dangerous to the interests of the mother country.[37] The English policy, begun in earnest by Queen

---

132.)   Franklin, however, was too wise not to recognize the worth of the Germans, and under the same date he says, "Yet I am not for refusing to admit them entirely." He recognized in the German practice his cardinal virtues of industry and frugality, and frankly said that these farmers were excellent husbandmen who had contributed largely to the development of the country. Franklin's recommendations were for a more general distribution of the Germans, the mixing of them with the English, and the establishment of English schools. Franklin, *Works* (Bigelow), II, 298, 299.

Burke recognized the same facts as above, but was not so pessimistic. He urged a better regulation of German affairs within the colony, and the naturalization of Germans in fact as well as in name. *European Settlements*, II, 201.

[35] Mittelberger, *Journey*, Translation, 107, 108.

[36] *Pennsylvania Archives*, First Series, IV, 597.

[37] See reference to Postlethwayt in Chapter I, correspondence of James Logan, and record of action of Assembly and colonial council in present chapter.

Anne, was to keep the subjects at home and to colonize America with Germans, but the policy had led to so large a migration of Germans that the English feared the consequences.[38]   Burke, Franklin, and others held it to be good policy for the mother country to encourage the importation of foreigners.   Speaking of their importation to Pennsylvania, Burke said: "By this we are great gainers without any diminution of the inhabitants of Great Britain."

Pennsylvania was a mother colony for the Germans who settled in other parts of North America.   As it was to this colony that the Germans chiefly came, so from here they went out.   To the south and west, Pennsylvania sent her peoples, Irish as well as German.   John Fiske termed the movement of these different peoples as the partial union of the Ulster stream and the Palatinate stream; the "sturdy population, distilled through the Pennsylvania alembic," said he, "had formed the main strength of American democracy, and its influence upon American life has been manifold." [39]   When Mühlenberg reported on a pastor who had been dismissed by a Pennsylvania congregation for improper conduct, he added that this man might, if he chose, continue preaching or teaching school in other regions where he was not known, for, said he, "the German people have spread themselves from north to south in America, over more than a thousand miles." [40]   Pastor Brunnholtz, of the Lutheran Church in Philadelphia, reported in 1746 that while the congregation over which he presided was one of the largest it was also of the poorest; its membership was of those who were temporary residents, paying off the debt of their passage, and when this was paid they moved inland to secure property for themselves.[41]   The overflow from the Pennsylvania German settlement early swept to the southwest down the valleys, reaching as far as the Caro-

---

[38] Watson, *Annals,* II, 255.

[39] Fiske, *Dutch and Quaker Colonies,* II, 331, 351, 354, 355. Some of the Irish when they were supplanted in Pennsylvania by the more industrious Germans, moved to the South and occupied the highlands and mountainous districts of Virginia. Burke, *European Settlements,* II, 216. Pennsylvania and New York are considered by Fiske the chief centers in the distribution of the non-English-speaking peoples.

[40] *Halle Reports,* 200.

[41] *Ibid.,* 158, 159.

linas and Georgia. Sect peoples of Pennsylvania settled in the "back counties" of North Carolina; said one in that colony in 1766, "Africk never more abounded with new masters than Pennsylvania with new sects, who are continually sending their emissaries around." [42]   But the contiguity of Maryland, with easy

[42] Basset, "Regulators of North Carolina," *Report American Historical Association,* 1894, 144, 145.

"The society of pioneers, English, Scotch-Irish, Germans, and other nationalities which formed in the beginning of the eighteenth century in the great valley of Pennsylvania and its lateral extensions was the nursery of the American backwoodsmen. Between about 1730 and the Revolution, successive tides of pioneers ascended the Shenandoah, occupied the Piedmont, or up-country of Virginia and the Carolinas, and received recruits from similar peoples who came by eastward advances from the coast toward this old west.

"Thus by the middle of the eighteenth century a new section had been created in America, a kind of peninsula thrust down from Pennsylvania between the falls of the rivers of the South Atlantic colonies on the one side and the Alleghany mountains on the other. Its population showed a mixture of nationalities and religions. Less English than the colonial coast, it was built on a basis of religious feeling different from that of Puritan New England, and still different from the conservative Anglicans of the southern seaboard. The Scotch-Irish Presbyterians with the glow of the covenanters,—German sectaries with serious-minded devotion to one or another of a multiplicity of sects, but withal deeply responsive to the call of the religious spirit, and the English Quakers all furnish a foundation of emotional responsiveness to religion and a readiness to find a new heaven and a new earth in politics as well as in religion. In spite of the influence of the backwoods in hampering religious organization, this upland society was a fertile field for tillage by such democratic and emotional sects as the Baptists, Methodists and the later Campbellites, as well as by Presbyterians." Frederick J. Turner, *The History Teacher's Magazine,* March, 1911.

Wayland, *The German Element of the Shenandoah Valley* (Charlottesville, Va., 1907), gives an account of the German immigration into the Shenandoah region, and finds that Pennsylvania was the chief distributing center for the German population considered. Chapter III, *passim.*

The practice indicated by the following item was probably an exception: "A letter has been received in Germantown, written in the beginning of August, 1749, in Virginia, in which two potters say they sailed from Rotterdam for Philadelphia. Their company contracted with the Captain of the ship to pay ten doubloons for their passage, but he deceived them and carried them all to Virginia and sold them for five years. They ask whether there is any help for them, as they never entered into such a contract. It appears the ship belonged to the Captain and was not con-

communication, gave it the largest branch of this southern stream. Considerable numbers of Germans passed into Maryland about the middle of the eighteenth century.[43] Uncertain boundaries in the back country, with the natural opening down the Susquehanna, turned the attention of Pennsylvanians to Maryland. Later in the colonial period a road was built down the valley to Baltimore, and Philadelphia ships often touched at the Maryland port because it gave more easy and direct communication with the "back parts."[44] Next after Pennsylvania the redemption system was practiced most extensively in Maryland; there it continued well through the second decade of the nineteenth century, and there in its later history it was subject to the same abuses which characterized it in Pennsylvania.

The Pennsylvania Colonial Records and Archives, the Statutes at Large, the investigations of the Pennsylvania German Society, reports from travelers, and the newspaper letters furnish a wealth of material for studying the means by which German servants were secured and the manner of their transportation. After the slave trade was taken from the Dutch they gave themselves to the servant traffic, though it was not limited to them. The manner of the trade was simple. A cargo of servants was brought over and disposed of, and a return cargo of the produce of the colony secured. The treatment of German passengers was cruel to a degree; and travelers and those unused to such sights were shocked at what they saw on incoming ships, though there seemed little concern in the colony. The accounts of the passage which were preserved are revolting; reports which can be accepted as trustworthy make many of the redemption ships little better than Guinea slavers on the middle passage.

A German traveler in Pennsylvania from 1750 to 1754 has left a somewhat detailed account of the passage of these emigrants down the Rhine, the sea voyage, the arrival of their vessels, the sale of the passengers, and the nature of their service.[45] Per-

---

signed to any agent in Philadelphia." *Pennsylvania Berichte,* cited in Diffenderffer, *Redemptioners,* 208.

[43] Scharf, *History of Maryland,* I, 373.

[44] Priest, *Travels,* 196.

[45] Mittelberger, *Journey to Pennsylvania.* The two latter phases of his account will be considered in the succeeding chapter.

sons who left their homes in the Palatinate were, at every stage
of their advance, fleeced by agents, customs, duties, and other
exactions, so that, although many left home with what might be
considered ample resources to pay for their passage to Pennsylvania, they found their means entirely exhausted before they
embarked at Rotterdam. Those who left the Palatinate were
compelled to pass a total of thirty-six customs in the several prin-
cipalities and cities before they reached Rotterdam. At these
customs there were delays, and consequent use of provisions, and
expenditure of the means brought from home; it was often four,
five, or six weeks before the emigrants reached Rotterdam. After
their arrival, there were further delays, the ship sometimes not
sailing for weeks, and many of the passengers left Holland in
debt.[46] The ship company often paid debts in Rotterdam, but
charged the amount paid and an additional item for interest so
that the emigrant got deeper into debt.[47]

Regular agents of captains and ship companies were sta-
tioned in Rotterdam and Amsterdam to secure redemptioners and
to aid the emigration to Pennsylvania. But not satisfied with
this, the agents sometimes went into the German states and plied
their trade, urging upon the people that they take what means
they had and start for the new land of promise. Schemes proposed were more misleading and seductive than were emigration
inducements of ship companies of later times.[48] The agents were
usually unprincipled Germans who had come as immigrants to
Pennsylvania, and adopted this business as an easy get-rich-quick
scheme. Free passage was furnished them back to Holland, they
were given a regular fee for every emigrant secured, and they had
in addition such sums as could be defrauded from their trusting
countrymen. *Neuländer,* the Germans termed these agents; the
Dutch called them *Zeilverkoopers;* but they were given more
significant names by those who better understood their business:
Menschen-Diebe and *Seelen-Verkäufer* said Mittelberger, while
Christopher Sauer named them *Seelen-Händler.* They went to

---

[46] *Ibid.,* 18.

[47] See below for an account of the ship "Britannia."

[48] See Kapp, *Immigration,* Appendix III, p. 200, for "booking of passengers in Europe." Agents of the companies were termed "emigrant
runners."

Germany, and with show and pretense of wealth, with fine clothes, wigs, ruffles, and jewelry, they represented the New World as a place of certain riches, and offered themselves as illustrations of the ease with which prosperity could be realized. What wonder that Germans dissatisfied with their lot saw in these representations the bow of promise, and converting their little store of worldly effects into movables set forth for the new land of opportunity.[49]

The eagerness of agents is easily accounted for; each emigrant above ten years of age brought them seven to nine dollars from the ship company, and in addition they had such sums as they secured from the emigrants themselves. Passengers were often put on shipboard without their effects, and it was reported that these would follow on another ship. The effects were then broken open and whatever of value they contained was appropriated. Sometimes, too, emigrants intrusted money to these agents, and although they had promised to sail on the same ship, the latter remained in Holland and kept the money.[50] One advertisement only was found indicating that baggage had come to Philadelphia on a ship later than that which brought its owners, but in this was the information that there were back charges which had been incurred in Holland, and these the owners were expected to pay.[51]

Those who reached Pennsylvania after having the experiences above described wrote letters home giving warning to their friends and acquaintances not to come; but the letters were forwarded through the agents in Holland, and were opened. If letters contained complaints, or truthful accounts of the bad treatment, they were either thrown away or falsely copied. It was reported that certain persons in Holland made a business of imitating handwriting for the purpose of giving false information.[52] Mittelberger himself was almost persuaded by these agents, when he reached Rotterdam on his return, that his wife,

---

[49] See Mittelberger, *Journey;* Seidensticker, *Geschichte der deutschen Gesellschaft,* 21-28; Diffenderffer, *German Immigration Into Pennsylvania,* 189; Sachse, *Sectarians* (1742-1800), 27, 28.

[50] Mittelberger, *Journey,* 40.

[51] *Pennsylvania Gazette,* November 21, 1771.

[52] Mittelberger, *Journey,* 42.

child, and sister-in-law had sailed shortly before for Pennsylvania. The agents gave a description of these persons and the name of the ship on which they were said to have sailed. So straightforward was their bearing, and so circumstantial the information which they furnished, that Mittelberger was at one time on the point of returning to Pennsylvania instead of going home. The obvious purpose of the agents in this case was to keep from Germany the information which Mittelberger would carry back of the passage to Pennsylvania and the real conditions in the colony.

Merchants or captains received in the early period from six to ten pounds for each adult carried to America. Children of a certain age, usually from four or five to from ten to fourteen, were carried for half fare, while those below four were carried free. About 1760 to 1770 the prices were advanced to from fourteen to seventeen pounds, and later the amount was raised to twenty pounds and above. To add to the amount which was charged, the captains later resorted to selling the bare necessities to those on board. Instances are recorded in which even the water was sold by the pint. A fee entitled "head charges" was established and passengers were required to pay for places in which to sleep. The preservation of an account book of the captain of a Philadelphia ship, in the redemption trade, gives an insight into the practice as it existed in 1773. In this record, termed a "munstering (mustering) book," was kept an account with each of two hundred and twenty-nine passengers. In the charges, the "freight" was sixteen pounds, to which was added toll or "head money" from one pound to three pounds (generally one pound), "proportion in bed places" from one pound to three pounds (also generally one pound), and in some cases "baggage" and money advanced, and interest. These extra charges seem to have been suited to the ability of the persons to pay. It was evident that dead persons could not dispute charges, and one marked "dead" had against him £97 8s., a sum which was collected. In one case the entry for "money advanced" was twenty-one pounds eleven shillings. The indebtedness was acknowledged by signature, and on the opposite page was recorded the manner of its discharge. "Paid by his brother," "Paid by his children," and "Received from Heirs," were sometimes recorded, but the record

Christiaan Schütts
One freight £16:10
Head money
his proportion of ye bed places . . . /5 —
money advanced . . . . . . /10 —
                                    /11
                      Interest . 2:4 —
                              13:4 . . 2:4 —
      Philadelphia Currency £ 19:14

Christiaan Schütts

Adam Renninger
One freight . . . . £16:10 —
Head money   1 —
his proportion of ye bed places . . . /5 —
money advanced . . . . . /12:12 —
Baggage . . . . /6"1
                              /19·13
               Interest /. 3·18
                      23·11 . . 3·18
      Philadelphia Currency . . £ 21"8

Adam Renninger

PAGE OF BRITANNICA ACCOUNT BOOK
[Original Historical Society of Pennsylvania]

of payment in money was the exception. On the page opposite to that recording charges was usually recorded the name of the person to whom the passenger was sold and the amount received.[53]

The summary by the captain of the "Britannia" shows that on this inward voyage the ship paid her owners a total of £4,660 14s. 6d, made up of "freight" £3,442 11s. 6d.; "head money." £210; advanced in Holland, £426 14s.; and other charges, £581 6s.

In the later practice of the system, the price for which passengers could be sold was about twenty-one pounds, ten shillings, and in some manner, regardless of agreements, the captains would bring the amount against each person up to this total.[54] In case of the death of the emigrant at sea, the members of his family were to pay, if more than one-half of the voyage had been made · if less than one-half of the voyage had been made, there was to be no charge.[55] Captains were accused of actually wishing the death of those who were parents, after the middle of the passage, thus reducing their expenses and making their gain greater. Children were held for the passage money of parents if these had died, or for the balance due on account of charges against parents if the latter could not be sold for the amount of their indebtedness. Children and young people were in larger demand, because they could be purchased for a longer time, and they would bring more than the amount of charges against them, while those more advanced in years found slower sale. Thus it was that parents were said to sell their children to get themselves clear of the captains.

Worst of the captains was one Steadman, who was said to

---

[53] Ship "Britannia," James Peter from Rotterdam, last from Cowes. Passengers qualified September 18, 1773. List of 118 in Registry. *Pennsylvania Archives,* Second Series, XVII, 508, 509. A later record (manuscript in Library of the Historical Society of Pennsylvania) gives list of 53 persons who were landed, with charges and expenses. Dated December 2, 1773.

[54] So common was that amount that Professor McMaster is led to the statement that the price was universally at £20 1s. 6d. *History of the United States,* II, 558.

[55] Mittelberger, *Journey,* 28; also letters of Christopher Sauer to Governor Morris in Seidensticker, *Geschichte der deutschen Gesellschaft,* 32, 33; Lohr, *Geschichte und Zustande,* Chapter XX.

enjoy the right of being first served at Rotterdam; no other trader was to take passengers until he had been supplied. Ships were so overcrowded that there was not sufficient room below, and this, with the extra charge for sleeping places, kept passengers continually on deck. Two contemporary writers said that passengers were packed like herring in a box.[56] Ships bore toward the south into a region of higher temperature; bad sanitary conditions, with insufficient food and water, made the ships disease breeders, and it was necessary that the Assembly propose stringent rules for better regulation of the trade. But the regulations were ineffectual in preventing either the danger from contagious diseases or the robbery and illtreatment in transit. Indeed, in the progress of the German trade, abuses seem to have increased rather than diminished, and the last state of the traffic was worse than the first.[57]

In consequence of conditions as above described, the loss of emigrants while at sea was large. Many of the passengers were buried at sea, but large numbers died at the end of the voyage and were buried in Philadelphia. The colonial council,

---

[56] Diffenderffer computes that for a series of years vessels averaging less than 200 tons' burden, carried an average of about three hundred passengers. *German Immigration Into Pennsylvania,* 51.

"Perhaps no stronger proof can be offered of the wretched situation of these unhappy people than the lists of the different importations would afford. In the list of German passengers which I have carefully perused I observe several instances of upwards of 500 passengers imported in one vessel, this list as I have already remarked was confined prior to the war to *male* passengers of full age who were required to take the oath of allegiance—so that allowing an additional third for women and children, there have been several instances of between 7 and 800 German passengers crowded in one vessel, and I should presume few of the vessels employed in this trade exceeded 250 or 300 tons burden: The Irish vessels were exceedingly crowded before the War but lately the numbers in each vessel have been less, *only* because fewer passengers have offered." Phineas Bond, British Consul at Philadelphia, Letter of 1789. *Report of American Historical Association,* 1896, p. 644.

[57] Brunnholtz, Report (1750), *Hallische Nachrichten,* No. 2, 412-414; Seidensticker, *German-American Events,* 8; Rupp, Note to Rush's *Manners of the Pennsylvania Germans,* 6, 7; *Pennsylvania Archives,* First Series, IV, 472, 473; Gordon, *History of Pennsylvania,* 300; Christopher Sauer, *Letters to the Governor of Pennsylvania* (1755), quoted by Seidensticker, *Geschichte der deutschen Gesellschaft,* 32, 33.

November 14, 1757, ordered Jacob Shoemaker, who was in charge of the "strangers' burying ground," to give under oath the number of Palatines buried there. Shoemaker gave a total of two hundred and fifty-three buried within three months, which number, he said, was not the total. These had been buried for five different captains. With regard to the wholesale death which took place in the passage, it was reported by Mittelberger that one ship containing three hundred and forty-one people had tossed about for months on the sea, and that out of this number only twenty-one were landed.[58]

---

[58] Diffenderffer, *German Immigration Into the Port of Philadelphia.* The following cited by Diffenderffer certainly surpassed anything given by Mittelberger. The ship "Love and Unity" sailed from Rotterdam to Philadelphia in 1731, carrying over one hundred and fifty Palatines. A year later thirty-four of the total number reached Philadelphia. Some of these addressed to a German Reformed pastor the following account of their sufferings:

"Captain Lobb, a wicked murderer of souls, thought to starve us, not having provided provisions enough, according to agreement; and thus got possession of our goods; for during the voyage of the last eight weeks, five persons were only allowed one pint of coarse meal per day, and a quart of water to each person. We were twenty-four weeks coming from Rotterdam to Martha's Vineyard. There were at first more than one hundred and fifty persons—more than one hundred perished . . . To keep from starving we had to eat rats and mice. We paid from eight pence to two shillings for a mouse; four pence for a quart of water . . . In one night several persons miserably perished and were thrown naked overboard; no sand was allowed to be used to sink the bodies but they floated. We paid for a loaf of Indian corn eight shillings. Our misery was so great that we often begged the captain to put us on land that we might buy provisions. He put us off from day to day for eight weeks, until at last it pleased Almighty God, to send us a sloop, which brought us to Home's Hole, Martha's Vineyard . . . Had he detained four days longer every one of us would have famished; for none had it in his power to hand another a drop of water . . . All our chests were broken open. . . . The captain constrained us to *pay the whole freight of the dead and living,* as if he had landed us at Philadelphia, and we agreed in writing to do so, not understanding what we signed; but we are not able to comply, for if we are to pay for the *dead,* we should have taken the *goods of the dead;* but in discharging the vessel, we found that most of *their chests* were broken open and plundered.

"The captain, however, has determined that we shall pay him in three weeks; we, therefore, desire you instantly to assist us as much as is in your power. For if we have to pay, the wicked captain will make us all

The condition of the servant survivors who reached port was indeed sorry. Gottlieb Mittelberger has been charged with over-drawing the facts, that he might discourage emigration, but the worst pictures of the unhappy state of survivors are from Christopher Sauer and Pastors Brunnholtz and Mühlenberg. Sauer turned his house into a hospital where he nursed and supported the sick, and aided them until they were able to help themselves.[59] Brunnholtz confessed that he was utterly unable to lend aid; these people brought letters from their pastors in Germany, but he said they came in such numbers and were in such a state—sick and dying—that he could not minister to them. When they found things other than as had been represented to them, the immigrants pronounced anathemas against the agents who had deceived them, but this was to no effect, and then, said Brunnholtz, they would "whine and cry." He described them as in debt for their passage, corrupted like cattle, half deprived of their reason, so that they could "scarcely perceive anything of the parson's consolation." Brunnholtz was of the opinion that these people had better have stayed where they were, that the province was already full of people, and that living was continually growing more expensive; he favored having inserted in papers both in Pennsylvania and in various parts of Germany such information as would give a true account of the sufferings in the passage and the conditions in the colony, but he questioned whether this would do any good, because of the desire of the people to come and the misrepresentations of the *Neuländer*.[60]

The same sad plight is pictured in the petition presented to the governor of Pennsylvania in 1754 by a number of Germans who asked that he would have regard for their unhappy condition; they claimed that they were not able to pay their passage, nor were they physically in condition to be bound out as servants. Later there was another address to the same effect.[61] Mittelberger

---

beggars. . . . We would have sent two or three men with this letter, but none of us is yet able to stir, for we are weak and feeble; but as soon as there shall be two or three of us able to travel they will follow." Diffen-derffer, *The Redemptioners*, 62, 63. Cited from *Gentlemen's Magazine*, II, April, 1732, 727.

[59] Diffenderffer, *The Redemptioners*, 257 sqq.

[60] *Hallische Nachrichten*, No. 2, 412 sqq.

[61] *Pennsylvania Archives*, First Series, II, 217, 225.

had information in a letter received September, 1755, that twenty-two thousand people had arrived in Philadelphia the previous fall, so poor and sick that most of them had to sell their children.[62] The seeming inhumanity of parents in selling their children was in part accounted for by the barbarous treatment to which they had been subjected and the sorry condition in which they found themselves.

Individual aid to these emigrants was not sufficient, and in 1764 benevolent Germans organized the Pennsylvania German Society. This society was designed as a charitable institution, but gave itself also to enforcement of the laws governing immigration and the treatment of newcomers brought into the colony.[63]

These efforts did not prevent abuse. German immigrants spoke a foreign language; they were unused to the laws of the colony, and, moreover, public sentiment did not demand the enforcement of the laws. The evils of the business were regarded much as were those of the slave trade, and for the same reason—they were condoned because they were thought to be necessary for the continuance of the traffic. If a company of passengers took matters into their own hands, as they might, they only got themselves into additional trouble; for them the easiest way seemed the best way, and this was to make the best of their bad treatment.[64]

---

[62] *Journey to Pennsylvania,* Translation, 37.

[63] Seidensticker, *Geschichte der deutschen Gesellschaft, passim.* An interesting broadside advertising a lottery, the returns from which were to go to the society, has been preserved. This broadside gave an account of the society's origin and work. (No. 23 in collection of Broadsides at the Ridgeway Branch of the Library Company of Philadelphia.) The German Society of Maryland had its origin in the efforts to aid helpless German immigrants who were there illtreated. Hennighausen, *Redemptioners and the German Society of Maryland.* The attention of the Hibernian Society, as indicated above (Chapter VIII), was toward correcting abuses of Irish immigrants.

[64] "Sunday last arrived here Capt. Tymberton, in seventeen weeks from Rotterdam with 220 Palatines, 44 died in the Passage. About 3 Weeks ago, the Passengers dissatisfied with the length of the Voyage, were so impudent as to make a Mutiny and being the stronger Party have ever since had the Government of the Vessel, giving Orders . . . to the Captain and Sailors . .· . having Sight of Land, they carried the Vessel twice backwards & forwards between our Capes and Virginia." Later they

After the German Society had been nearly ten years in existence, and had back of it a record of full thirty years' discussion on the evils of the redemption trade, a distinguished German, one of the founders of the society and later its president, memorialized the governor of Pennsylvania, stating that the irregularities continued. His charges can be best given in his own words: "Passengers having Goods of any value on board of the same ship in which they transported themselves hardly ever take Bills of Lading for such Goods, the Merchants, Captains, or their Subordinates persuading them that it could do them no Good but rather involve them into Difficulties at their arrival. If they leave any Goods in the Stores . . . they will now and then take a little Note, that the Merchant has such Chests, Casks, Bales, &c., and undertakes to send it by next Vessel free of Freight, &c., to the person who deposited such Goods with him. The Passenger puts the note in his Pocket-Book, he has also the Invoice of his Goods, and his Money he has sowed up in his old Rags or in a Belt about his Waist. But in the voyage he or his wife or some of his Family, or all of them grow sick. Then the plunder upon the sick or dead begin and if the old ones recover or small Children survive, the Goods are gone, and the proofs that they have had any are lost. The Captains never reported to any public officer how many passengers he took in at the Port from whence he sailed, how many died on the voyage, never any manifest of the Goods belonging to passengers is produced. But in short hardly any Vessel with Palatine Passengers has arrived in the Port of Philadelphia but there has been Clamours or Complaints heard of Stealing & pilfering the Goods of the Sick & of the dead. And if your Honour will be pleased to enquire of the Register General, whether within the space of twenty-five years or since the passing of the Act 23, Geo. 2, intitled 'An Act for the prohibiting of German & other Passengers in too great Numbers in any one Vessel,' any considerable Number of Inventories of Goods & Effects of Persons who died in their Passage hither or soon after have been exhibited into that office, you will find that the practice is otherwise than the law.

---

came up the river when those concerned in taking command of the ship were committed to prison. *Pennsylvania Gazette* (October 19, 1732). Letter of same date.

"Upon the whole your Memorialist humbly apprehends that if sick Passengers shall by Virtue of the Bill now before your Honour be landed & nursed at the Province Island and their Chests and other Goods go up to Philadelphia, it will require a particular provision of what shall be done for the preservation of their goods on board." [65]

Showing to what extremes the traders in redemptioners would go to realize gain on their shipments, Priest relates the following which was corroborated by others. When the yellow fever plague was raging in Philadelphia in 1793, few vessels would approach nearer to the city than Fort Mifflin, but a redemption ship captain arriving in the Delaware and learning of the conditions in the city, thought it a favorable time to dispose of his passengers. He sailed boldly up to the city and advertised "a few *healthy* servants, generally between seventeen and twenty-one years of age; their times will be disposed of by applying on board the Brig." [66]

Cases of inhuman treatment did not escape the attention of the German Society; an account of the sufferings on the passenger ship "General Wayne" was furnished to it in 1805. Andreas Geyer, Jr., who made the report, said that the passengers on his ship were reduced to such straits that they secured bones, pounded, and ate them; that children, as well as adults, died from starvation; and that the dying at times crawled before the captain and prayed for food, but to no purpose.[67] Equally bad treatment was shown the passengers of the "Ceres" late in the operation of the system (1816). The passengers of this ship united in a letter to the German Society and the society after investigation found the representations to be true. Then the matter was taken to law to secure the release from contract of those who had not paid

---

[65] Lewis Weiss to Governor John Penn, January, 1774, *Pennsylvania Archives*, First Series, IV, 473.

[66] Priest, *Travels* (1796), 147. Professor Seidensticker gives the same incident, taking for authority an English traveler, Isaac Wald (Weld), who was in the United States in 1795 to 1797 (*Geschichte der deutschen Gesellschaft*, 34, 35), quoting from a German translation of his *Travels* published in Berlin in 1800. [Incident in Weld, I, 121, 122.] The account in Weld is said to be on the authority of one who had the original advertisement in his possession.

[67] Kapp, *Immigration*, report cited, 183.

their passage, on the ground that the contract had been violated, but the courts offered no redress. With a case seemingly clearly in their favor the German Society was defeated. So the unsatisfactory conditions continued until the disappearance of redemption labor in Pennsylvania.

PART IV. THE INDENTURED AND REDEMPTION LABOR SYSTEM IN OPERATION

CHAPTER X

SALE AND DISTRIBUTION OF SERVANTS

When ships with their human freight arrived at Philadelphia, the captains or merchants usually inserted in the newspapers advertisements which gave descriptions of the passengers for sale, their nationality, age, sex, and the service for which they were said to be fitted. Sometimes, though not always, the terms for which they were under indenture were also given. The servants were kept on shipboard where, the advertisements said, they could be seen; usually they were not allowed to leave the ship until their indentures had been purchased by some one who would advance the price of their passage, or until they had obtained responsible persons as references and security.[1]

Indentures and methods of sale differed considerably at different times and with British and German immigrants. With those from Great Britain there was usually a definite contract made at the place from which the servant shipped; in this the time and sometimes the terms of the service were clearly stated, and before servants could be legally taken from Great Britain their indentures were to be witnessed before magistrates. In the Peter Williamson trial, witnesses testified repeatedly that indentures which had not been acknowledged before passengers were taken on shipboard were of no value in America. The regulations for signing the indentures were offered as suitable protection of emigrants by the parties in the defense against Peter Williamson;

---

[1] Fearon, when in Philadelphia (1817), saw the following advertisement in a newspaper: "The passengers on board the brig Bubona from Amsterdam, and who are willing to engage themselves for a limited time to defray the expenses of their passage, consist of persons of the following occupations, besides women and children, viz., 13 farmers, 2 bakers, 2 butchers, 8 weavers, 3 tailors, 3 cabinet makers, etc. Apply on board, opposite Callowhill Street, in Delaware, or to W. Odlin & Co., No. 38 South Wharves." *Sketches of America,* 148, 149.

195

later, Thomas Jefferson thought this the proper method of controlling the trade in redemptioners.[2]   On the other hand, the
Germans signed vague agreements promising to pay a certain sum
or sums on arrival in America, or within a reasonable time thereafter. If they had money, they might pay it in discharge of the
debt; if they had friends, these might advance the money for
them; but if they were poor and friendless, they were subject
to sale.

With the English servants the time was fixed by the indenture
and the captains were anxious to make a ready sale at the highest
price; the price and readiness of sale might be matters of indifference to the servants. German servants, on the other hand,
were anxious to secure purchasers promptly, for this lessened
charges against them; moreover, they sought to secure a certain
sum—the amount of their indebtedness—by serving the shortest
possible length of time. In one case the term was fixed, and the
captain was most concerned in the sale for a price that was uncertain; in the other, the captain demanded a fixed sum and it
was the servant's lookout to get as short a term as he could to
satisfy the captain's demands. The maximum legal term for
which persons sixteen years old and above could be sold for misdemeanor within the colony was seven years. Adult immigrants
under indenture were usually sold at from four to five years;
sometimes younger members of families were disposed of for a
longer term to relieve their parents from the burden of debt.[3] It
was this fear of additional debt that made the passengers implore
visitors to purchase them and take them away. When the English traveler, Fearon, visited a ship in 1817, he asked if there

---

[2] Indentures were sometimes issued anew for British servants on
arrival. Illustration opposite.

[3] "The *English* and the *Irish* commonly sell themselves for four years,
but the *Germans* frequently agreed with the Captain before they set out, to
pay him a certain sum of money for a certain number of persons; as soon
as they arrive in *America,* they go about and try to get a man who will pay
the passage for them. In return they give according to the circumstances
one, or several of their children to serve a certain number of years, at last
they make their bargain with the highest bidder." Kalm, *Travels,* I, 390.
This is what Professor McMaster means when he says that redemptioners
were sold for twenty pounds, one shilling, sixpence, regardless of their
terms. *History of United States,* II, 558.

AN INDENTURE ENTERED INTO BEFORE THE MAYOR OF
PHILADELPHIA

Ft. 196

were any shoemakers on board, at which the captain, whose eye was said to flash with "Algerine cruelty," called out, and one who thought to be relieved came running with what was termed unspeakable delight.[4]

Many emigrants signed agreements which they could not read, and still others did not understand the indenture or agreement even though they could read it. In a strange country and unacquainted with both the customs and the laws such new arrivals were often in a pitiable state. Lord Sheffield recited with righteous indignation the reports made to him of German and Irish servants who had emigrated to the New World on representations that they had only to take possession of vacated and confiscated estates, but on reaching their destination they found only exacting servile toil for a term of years. Sheffield told of two Irish youths who found as a master a Negro fruit vendor, black Sam, who employed them in hawking fruit about the streets and in other like occupations. Sheffield added: "Irishmen just emancipated in Europe, go to America to become slaves to a Negro!"[5]

Assignments of servants in any part of Pennsylvania outside of Philadelphia were required at first to be made before at least two (later one) justices of the peace. In Philadelphia the sales or assignments were before the mayor or, in his absence or neglect, before the recorder. (Indenture shown opposite p. 196 was witnessed before the mayor.) Offenders under this act were subject to a fine of ten pounds. The mayor and recorder were enjoined to keep a register of names of servants and the dates of assignment. On going out of office the mayor was directed to deliver this register to his successor. This record was to be carefully kept and made available to those who were concerned.[6] The American Philosophical Society possesses a rare manuscript volume of these records from 1771 to 1773. This volume indicates how extensive the system was. Quite two thousand names are included, the list being made up of incoming Germans and other passengers and of those selling themselves in the colony. Transfers of indentures were also recorded, as were

---

[4] *Sketches of America,* 149-151.
[5] *Observations on American Commerce,* 243, 244.
[6] *Duke's Book of Laws,* 152; *Statutes at Large,* IV, 170, 171.

discharges of indentures by payment for the unexpired terms. The record before the mayor was made until the change of government at the time of the Revolution, when there was a slight break. March 15, 1777, the offices of mayor and recorder were abolished, from which time the indentures were temporarily witnessed in Philadelphia before justices of the peace.[7]

By act of 1785, the register of German passengers was established and indentures were acknowledged before and registered by him until the disappearance of the system. Three manuscript volumes of records were made from 1785 to 1831, known as Books A, B, and C, respectively. Two of these are preserved and furnish a wealth of material for the later period of white servitude in Pennsylvania.[8] In the later period violation of proper method of sale was made subject to a fine of seventy-five pounds.[9]

In the earlier periods the time allowed to passengers in which to secure a sale was fixed by custom. It differed at intervals, and with different captains, mayors, and registers. Some captains gave little free time after arrival. One of the charges made against the trade was that passengers who may have had friends were hurriedly sold to lessen expenses and make sure of returns for passage. Persons who did not pay for their passage were dealt with as debtors, and could be handled by the laws of debt of that time. Formal notices, of which the following is an example, were served on those who did not pay: "Debtors notified. Those Palatines who have hitherto neglected to pay for their passage in the Ship, James Godwill, are to take Notice; that if they do not pay to me on board the said Ship, or to Charles Read of Philadelphia, the Sum from them respectively due, they will be proceeded against according to Law, by David Crockatt."[10]

---

[7] Bioren, *Laws,* II, 328, 329.

[8] Geiser (*Redemptioners and Indentured Servants in Pennsylvania,* 69), refers to these volumes as the most important source of information on this subject, but says that the record is complete in two volumes (1785-1831), *in loc. cit.,* also 114 and 124. Book B of the register has been lost.

[9] Act of 1788, Bioren, *Laws,* II, 444.

[10] *American Weekly Mercury,* November 7, 1728. Time given for payment to the twentieth of November. Cited in Dotterer, *Perkiomen Region.* See below, Chapter XIII, for the abolition of imprisonment for debt and the disappearance of the redemption system.

Passengers were in some instances allowed considerable free-dom to secure purchasers. On one occasion a whole party under indenture was permitted to go towards New York with the agree-ment that if they did not find relatives or others to advance the money for this passage within a month they would return and submit to be sold. When they did not return or give an account of themselves, their creditor advertised that if they did not return within twenty days, they would be prosecuted as runaways.[11] In 1727, public notice was given to the Palatines who had recently arrived in the ship "Molly" that if they did not present them-selves at once at the ship or pay their passage money, they would be dealt with as runaways;[12] and in 1729, a reward was offered for apprehending recently arrived immigrants who had been ab-sent seven weeks to escape the payment of their passage. A little later the names of similar offenders were published and notice given that unless they immediately paid, or gave security for future payment, they would be dealt with according to law.[13] By an advertisement of 1754 it is shown that a German who had come under indenture with his wife was permitted to go among his countrymen in the hope of securing money, after which he was to return and claim his wife. When nothing had been heard of this man for four months, he was advertised for as a run-away.[14]

Servant ships usually arrived in larger numbers in the autumn. The summer was looked upon as the most favorable time for the sea voyage, generally of six weeks. Moreover, in the fall season the people of Pennsylvania had produce to sell, or to exchange for servants, and the ships could be profitably supplied with a return cargo. After the ships arrived, persons from Philadelphia and from the country for many miles around came to purchase or barter for servants that were suited for their work. The bargaining on shipboard was sometimes suggestive of scenes on an African slaver.[15]

---

[11] *American Weekly Mercury,* April 18, 1723.

[12] *Ibid.,* November 21, 1727.

[13] *Pennsylvania Gazette,* March 15, 1732.

[14] *Ibid.,* Decemer 26, 1754.

[15] Mittelberger, *Journey,* 26.

For servants who came under individual indenture (the majority of the British servants came thus), the term was stated in the agreement. From indentures examined for different periods and information furnished by contemporary writers, it has been ascertained that the signed indentures averaged about four years, though sometimes the term was for more, and not infrequently for less, than this time. During the earlier period, if servants came without an indenture, the term for which they could be bound was limited to five years for those seventeen years of age and above, while for those less than seventeen, the term might be until they were twenty-two years of age.[16] Maximum terms for misdemeanor were later fixed by law and judicial procedure at six and seven years.[17] Terms for children were not to be beyond twenty-two years of age, and for adults not to exceed seven years.

The term of service is shown most conclusively by the registry before the Philadelphia mayors. Two years have been taken as typical, the first from October 2, 1745, to October 2, 1746, and the second from January 1, 1772, to January 1, 1773. In the first-named year, out of 769 indentures recorded, 423 were for four years. In the same year, 84 servants were indentured for five years, 72 for three years, 50 for seven years, 39 for six years, 38 for two years, 15 for one year, 11 for eight years, and the others for varying periods up to eighteen years. Of one for whom the term was eighteen years, the statement was added:

---

[16] *Duke's Book of Laws,* 153. Given by Geiser (no authority cited) as four years for all above seventeen. *Redemptioners,* p. 73. The term of those assigned to servitude within the colony was frequently limited to seven years. The terms of indenture are specifically mentioned as four, five, and six years in the manuscript shipping lists of the English ports. (Appendix II for four years.) Servants were frequently bound for five, six, and seven years before the mayor in Philadelphia. (*Manuscript Registry.*) After the Revolution, Irish servants were offered in the *Pennsylvania Packet* for terms of seven years. The Bucks County record tells of a boy who came at three years of age and was to serve until he was twenty-two. Cox, *Transcript of Registry of Arrivals in Bucks County* (1677-1687), MS. in Library of Historical Society of Pennsylvania, p. 58.

[17] Cheyney, *Philadelphia Manufacturer,* March 16, 1891; *Statutes at Large,* III, 331, 332.

"With the consent of his mother, . . . to be taught to read and write and to have customary dues." [18]

In 1772, the larger number of indentures was still for four years, but the proportion for four years was considerably less than in the earlier year. Of the 1,135 registrations before the Philadelphia mayor in 1772, 284 were for four years, 266 for two years, 145 for three years, 127 for five years, 88 for six years, 61 for one year, 48 for seven years, 33 for eight years, 23 for nine years, 21 for ten years, 12 for eleven years, and so on up to those indentured for nineteen years of service. One servant from Rotterdam was indentured for fourteen years and one from Philadelphia for nineteen years. One who was indentured for eighteen years had no indication as to origin.[19]

In addition to the protection as to the manner of sale and the time for which sold, servants were also secure as to the place to which they could be sold. On pain of £10 fine, no servant brought into Pennsylvania under indenture, or bound to service in Pennsylvania, could be sold out of the province without his own consent and that of two justices of the peace in the place where he lived or should be sold.[20]

The first record of consideration for a servant in Pennsylvania was found for 1683, when a petition came before the provincial council setting forth that a servant had changed masters for £6 sterling and six hundredweight of beef, "with the hide and tallow." [21] The price for which redemptioners were sold was gradually advanced during the eighteenth century. In 1722, the Palatine servants were disposed of at £10 each for a term

---

[18] "Register Before James Hamilton, Mayor," *Pa. Mag. Hist. and Biog.,* XXXII, 358.

[19] "Record of Indentures Before Mayors," *Pubs. Pa. Germ. Society,* Lancaster, 1907.

[20] Bioren, *Laws,* I, 10.

In 1803, there were bound to George Taylor of Philadelphia, termed "Gentleman," four men with their families and three single servants, all to go to the state of Georgia. The record added, "To serve with their own consent." They were to have "the customary freedom suits" and each man a deed to fifty acres of land at the expiration of his term of service. *Registry of Redemptioners,* Book A, p. 334.

[21] *Colonial Records,* I, 7.

of five years.[22] A slightly advanced price prevailed about the middle of the century when redemptioners sold at £3 to £4 a year, or at a total of £14 for four years' service.[23] It will be noted that if a redemptioner were fairly treated as to charges, he might sell himself for the legal time for a sum sufficient to satisfy demands against him for his passage, and have a slight surplus.[24] Peter Williamson reported that adults sold at about £16 (1743).[25] As prices at which servants could be sold increased, charges of passage were increased.[26] The difference between the legitimate price of passage and the amount for which a servant could be sold became considerable, and this tempted the captains to increase their demands by adding charges for specials and extras. When servants could be sold for only £14, the traders brought in bills for that amount, but later when servants could be sold for £22 to £23, charges were made to bring the total up to this amount. Captain Peters' account book of the "Britannia" shows charges of five shillings less than the amount for which the sale was effected. In addition to the usual "freight," "head money," and charges for "a part in the bed places," there were sometimes added charges "for advance money," "interest," and "baggage." Extras were omitted when the maximum price for which one could probably be sold was made up otherwise. One George Martin Eberhart of the above-mentioned ship had his total of £23 11s. made up of his own passage (£17 13s.) and one-third of that of his mother (£5 18s.)[27] Washington, who had investigated the matter in Philadelphia (1793), reported to the commissioners of the federal district that the usual price of passage was 11 guineas, and that there should be advanced to the agent 1 guinea per head for each person secured. Part of this fee, he felt, should be paid by the persons who employed the agent and part by the traders who

---

[22] Watson, *Annals,* II, 266.

[23] Mittelberger, *Journey,* 26; Watson, III, 469; Kalm, *Travels,* I, 389.

[24] Smith, *History of Delaware County,* 260. Around 1750, Kalm places passage as low as six to eight pounds, *Travels,* I, 388.

[25] *Life and Adventures,* 3, 4.

[26] Seidensticker, *Geschichte der deutschen Gesellschaft,* 21.

[27] Set over to Richard Wister for £23 16s. *Munstering Book of Britannia,* MS. in Library of Historical Society of Pennsylvania, Passenger No. 39.

brought the passengers.[28]   Under the same terms, and with practically identical conditions, women brought about two-thirds to
three-fourths as much as could be secured for men, though if
they were of good character they usually found a readier sale.
In 1770, it was advertised that the purchase price of an English
servant woman's time for four years was fourteen pounds.[29]

In the later period the amount given for a servant was recognized more and more as wages.   The registry of redemptioners
often specified "consideration" for a certain amount, usually from
sixty to a hundred dollars, though it was sometimes higher.
Samuel Breck admirably described the later method of purchase
and furnished information on the amounts paid and the terms
for which servants were secured.   Having been dissatisfied for a
long time with his servants, he went on board a ship which had
recently arrived from Amsterdam bringing four hundred passengers.   "I saw," he said, "the remains of a very fine cargo, con-
sisting of healthy, good-looking men, women and children.   I
purchased two French Swiss servants who came from Lausanne
in Switzerland, having descended the Rhine in April.   I gave
for the woman seventy-six dollars, which is her passage money,
with a promise of twenty dollars at the end of three years if she
serves me faithfully; clothing and maintenance of course.   The
boy had paid twenty-six guilders toward his passage-money, which
I agreed to give him at the end of three years; in addition to
which I paid fifty-three dollars and sixty cents for his passage,
and for two years he is to have six weeks' schooling each year." [30]

The comparison of prices for indentured servants with those
for free white servants and Negro slaves offers one means of
determining the relative values that were placed on the various
forms of labor.   About 1750, when a four years' indenture was

---

[28] Here he was speaking of German servants, but he recommended that
Scotch laborers be similarly secured.   This price appears low for the
period.   It might have been lower, because Washington had planned for an
advance contract with the traders.   Washington's *Writings* (Sparks), XII,
306.

[29] *Pennsylvania Gazette,* January 11, 1770.

[30] Breck, *Recollections,* 296, 297, under date of August 1, 1817.   Contemporaneous with this was the report of Fearon that men sold for eighty
dollars; women for seventy dollars; boys for sixty dollars. *Sketches of
America,* 150.

worth approximately £14, free laborers commanded from £15 to £20 per year. Food and lodging were included in both cases, but free servants found their own clothes, while indentured servants were clothed by their masters. Moreover, at the conclusion of indentures masters were required to give to the indentured servants a considerable value in what were known as "freedom dues." But the great differences in prices could not be accounted for by these facts alone; free labor must have been more efficient than that of "white slaves"; but, be it also remembered in this connection, that at the time mentioned there were few free servants available. Full-grown Negroes about 1750 were sold at from £40 to £100, though the latter price was exceptional. Negro children of from two to three years of age brought £8 to £14 each.[31]

The estimated value put upon white servants and slaves was indicated in the ratings of property made by the Colonial Assembly in 1763. At that time "bought white servants" from fifteen to fifty years of age were rated at 30s. per head. Negro and mulatto slaves from twelve to fifty years of age were rated at £4 per head. In the same connection, horses above three years of age were rated at 13s. 4d. per head, and cattle at 6s. 8d., while the significant statement is included that ferries, saw mills, grist mills and the like were to be rated at three-fifths of the amount for which they would rent.[32] Similarly, comparison by Peter Williamson fixed the daily wages of free laborers at 3s. in summer and 2s. in winter, and the yearly return at £20 and upwards per year "according to goodness." In either case subsistence of the laborers was included. Williamson found that work horses and fat oxen sold at from £5 to £10 each, cows at from £3 to £6, and sheep at from 6s. to 15s.[33]

By the patriarchal law a brother Hebrew who had served for six years should go out free in the seventh year, but the law provided that he could not be sent away without his reward; the master was charged to provide liberally for his former servant

---

[31] Kalm, *Travels*, I, 391-393; Smith, *History of Delaware County*, 261. The same facts as to the prices of Negroes will be found in Williamson, *Travels*, 100.

[32] *Votes of Assembly*, II, 308; *Statutes at Large*, VI, 358.

[33] Williamson, *Travels*, 99, 103.

when the allotted time had been completed.[34]   White servitude
followed this old custom.   As part of the consideration for an
indentured servant was the freedom dues that the master was
required to pay when the term of the indenture expired.   Those
who served their allotted time could not be sent "empty away";
it was required that they be given "fitting equipage."   The Duke
of York's laws made this as a general declaration, while Penn's
laws said that the amount paid at time of freedom should accord
with the custom of the country.[35]   Legislation varied in specify-
ing what should be included; custom also varied greatly at different periods.   The first Assembly after Penn's arrival enacted
that the master should become bound to pay at the expiration of
the term of five years one new suit of clothes, ten bushels of
wheat or fourteen bushels of Indian corn, and two hoes, one
broad and the other narrow.[36]   Cases at law noted earlier in this
study recognized the servant's right to freedom dues at the
conclusion of his term of service.[37]   In 1693, a Chester County
court sustained the petition of a former servant who desired his
freedom dues, and the master was directed to pay; another decision in the same county specified that the dues were to be one
new suit of clothes, ten bushels of wheat or fourteen bushels of
corn, two hoes, and one ax.[38]   By a law of 1700, servants of four
years' time were to have as a minimum at the expiration of their
terms two complete suits of clothing, one of which must be new,
also one new ax, one weeding hoe, and one grubbing hoe.[39]   Freedom dues were usually enumerated in the indentures and to the
enumeration was added a phrase "according to custom," or something similar.   Customary dues at times took the place of those

---

[34] *Deuteronomy,* 15: 12-14.

[35] *Duke's Book of Laws,* 38, 102.

[36] *Ibid.,* 153.

[37] See above, Chapter II.

[38] Martin, *History of Chester,* 76.

[39] Bioren, *Laws,* I, 10.   That a special contract with regard to clothing
was sometimes entered into appears from the following: "John Nicholas
of his own free will and accord, bound himself Servant to John Maull of
the City of Philadelphia, Sail Maker, for Five Years, wearing apparel of
Servant to be suitable for working in, only; and to teach or cause to be
taught the Said Servant the art and trade of a Sail Maker." *Registry of
Redemptioners,* Book C, p. 129.

required by legal enactment. About 1750, an observing foreigner found the customary freedom dues a horse and a suit of clothes for a manservant who had reached the age of twenty-one, and, similarly, a cow and a new dress for a woman servant.[40]

The custom of freedom dues makes more clear the statement, that the demand for indentured labor was a demand for settlers; the term of labor under indenture was an apprenticeship, and the dues were a form of capital equipment for one to set up on his own account. The ax and the grubbing hoe were for clearing land, corn and wheat were seed grain, and the weeding hoe was for tillage. Two complete suits of apparel, one of which at least should be new, meant that for the immediate future the former servant was provided for; when land was plentiful, he could thus get his start in life. As soon as land became a little scarce, and was cleared for a distance back, the custom began to change. This change found expression in a law of 1771 which took from the freedom dues the ax, the grubbing hoe, and the weeding hoe, as on becoming free it was no longer expected that the servant would go out to clear land. By this act it also appeared that servants got their freedom dues with difficulty and that many were entirely deprived of what was justly theirs. The new act sought to remedy the earlier irregularities, but provided that if a servant made complaint against a master without just cause he should pay all costs.[41]

A summary of the indentures recorded before the Philadelphia mayor in 1772 indicated that the vast majority of freedom dues were according to the established custom. Of the 1,139 agreements registered for that year, 534 bore the statement that servants were to have all necessaries during the terms of their service, and were to have at the conclusion two complete suits of apparel, one of which was to be new. Two hundred and eighty of these indentures had no indication as to freedom dues, meaning clearly that the legal regulation was to operate; of 274

---

[40] Mittelberger, *Journey*. The practice of granting freedom dues varied greatly. In some of the colonies a *gun*, to be worth at least twenty shillings, was included for a man. In the South the fifty acres of land given at the expiration of the indenture were regarded as freedom dues. Walterhausen, *Arbeits-Verfassung*, 37, 186.

[41] Bioren, *Laws*, I, 320, 321. For the legal complications which made this act necessary, see *ibid.*, p. 11, note g.

other indentures the statement was made that the servants were to be paid all necessaries and to have at conclusion freedom dues or two complete suits of apparel. Forty-seven of the indentures recorded before the Philadelphia mayor in 1772, included the provision that the servants were to be paid all necessaries during the term of their indentures and to have at the expiration one new suit of apparel.[42]

Varying plans for meeting the obligation of the master at the expiration of the indenture began to be common about 1770. There was a growing custom of stating an amount over and above the freedom dues which would be paid the servant at the expiration of his indenture.

In 1771, a servant was bound out in Philadelphia with the agreement that he was to have £10 Pennsylvania currency in lieu of freedom dues.[43]   In 1772, a servant, whose former place of residence was not indicated, was sold for a term of five years for a consideration of £11 7s. 2d., but with the further provision that he should have at the expiration of his indenture £5 lawful money of Pennsylvania, over and above his freedom dues.[44]   A woman servant was sold in 1772 before the mayor of Philadelphia for a term of two years, the consideration being 10s., but it was further provided that she should receive immediately a new outfit of clothing.[45]   A German servant and his wife came from Rotterdam in 1772 and were sold to West New Jersey, each for a term of five years.   In addition to the standing agreement that they were to be furnished all necessaries during their term of service and to have at its expiration the usual freedom dues, the master further covenanted to allow them each £10 additional and to the woman a spinning wheel and a chest.[46]   A German servant last from Rotterdam was sold in 1773 to a resident of Kings County, New York, for a period of five years, the consideration being £24 15s. 6d., the servant to have all necessaries and, at the expiration of his indenture, two complete suits of apparel, one of which should be new, and to receive in addition

[42] "Record of Indentures," *Pa. Germ. Soc. Pubs.,* XVI.

[43] *Ibid.,* 17.

[44] *Ibid.,* 110, 111.

[45] *Ibid.,* 102, 103.

[46] *Ibid.,* 136, 137

$16 in money, provided he behaved himself "faithfully in every respect."[47]   In 1773, John Gibson, mayor of Philadelphia, witnessed an agreement between a Rotterdam redemptioner and his purchaser by which it was provided that for £22 paid for his passage the servant would serve his master for five years, and that at the expiration of his term of service the servant should choose whether he should receive the customary freedom dues or £9 in cash.[48]

On May 14, 1773, a servant said to be under "an indenture of redemption" for his passage from Bristol was transferred before the mayor of Philadelphia to serve for three years and to have during his term 1s. per week and, at the conclusion of his service, the option of two suits of apparel, one of which was to be new, or £10 in the lawful money of Pennsylvania.[49]   A Rotterdam woman servant was sold in 1772 for a period of five years, the consideration being £28 1s.   At the expiration of her service the terms provided that she should receive the usual freedom dues and 1 guinea.[50]   In 1772, one Peter Smith, listed as having come from Rotterdam, was sold to a resident of Philadelphia for a term of five years, on the payment of £19, but with the further provision that the servant was to have all necessaries during his term and the usual freedom dues at its expiration, and further that in the event of the servant's behaving himself and serving faithfully, he should have £10 in money at the expiration of his indenture and also lawful interest on this £10, the interest to be paid annually.[51]   A curious agreement was entered into in 1773 by which a servant obligated himself for one year and six months, the amount paid by the master being £9. It was agreed that the servant should be found all necessaries except apparel and, in the event of the master's supplying the servant with any clothing, it should be paid for by the servant at the expiration of his term.   In the same year another servant covenanted for one year's service, the master paying £8, with the further agreement that the servant was to be supplied all neces-

---

[47] *Ibid.*, 194, 195.
[48] Original indenture in Library of Bucks County Hist. Soc.
[49] *Pa. Germ. Soc. Pubs.*, XVI, 224, 225.
[50] *Ibid.*, 144, 145.
[51] *Ibid.*, 143, 144.

saries except clothes and to have at the conclusion of his indenture £20.[52]

With the continuance of the servant system, varying special agreements were entered into and seem to have been recognized under the law. One, as recorded in the list of indentures before the mayor of Philadelphia in 1772, was that the servant should not have freedom dues at the expiration of his indenture, but that neither party to the agreement should be subject to the penalty imposed by the act of assembly for servants absenting themselves from their master's service.[53] In 1773, a London servant was sold with the statement that a part of the purchase money paid for him was to go toward the passage of another person for whom he voluntarily agreed to serve. The same statement was entered against another servant, and in each case there was a provision that in the event of some one's else paying for the passage of the person named, the term of the servant in question should be reduced by one year.[54]

The question of family relationship, and women bearing children, affected the terms of indentures. In 1772, an English manservant and his wife were sold in Philadelphia for a term of four years each, with the special provision that they were to have at the expiration of their term the regular freedom dues and £10 in cash, but that in the event of their having children during their term they were each to serve six months longer, the master providing the necessary care for the children should any be born.[55] An Irish servant agreed in 1772 that he would serve three months over the term stated in the contract for every child his wife should bear during the term of three years, eleven months, and thirteen days. At the same time the wife similarly agreed by separate indenture to serve for a corresponding period in the case of like condition. The consideration paid for each of these servants was £8 10s.[56]

Toward the Revolution it also became increasingly common to have included in the indenture a provision that if the servant

---

[52] Ibid., 278, 279.
[53] Ibid., 48, 49.
[54] Ibid., 216, 217.
[55] Ibid., 66, 67.
[56] Ibid., 88, 89.

should make return to the master of the amount stated in the terms of the indenture, or in some cases slightly more, within a specified time, the indenture should then become void. An Irish servant was sold in Philadelphia in 1772 for a term of one year, eight months, the consideration being £8. It was agreed in the indenture, and recorded, that if the servant should pay or cause to be paid the sum of £8 within the space of two months the indenture would become void.[57]   Another Irish servant was sold in 1772 for a period of two years with the provision that if he should pay his master £11 10s., within one month from the date named, the indenture should be void. This was all the more peculiar from the fact that the record showed that the master had paid £7 10s. for the servant.[58]

Some of the provisions of the indentures were exceedingly quaint; others are difficult of explanation.

An agreement was entered into in 1772 by an Irish immigrant servant who agreed to serve his master for a period of two years, the master having paid £11 for his indenture, and it was provided that at the expiration of the term of service the servant should pay the master £3.[59]   An Irish servant was purchased in 1772 by a resident of Southwark, the term of the service being one year, payment £12, but with the provision that the servant should immediately be given a decent suit of clothes worth £5, which clothes were to be worn on Sundays only.[60]   In 1773, a London servant was sold in Philadelphia with the provision that he should be allowed meat, drink, washing, lodging, six working shirts, three fine shirts, and shoes.[61]   A servant was sold in Philadelphia in 1773 with the provision that he be allowed six hours every week for himself, to be employed in the smith's business.[62]

From time to time it was made a part of the indentures that servants should be taught to read, write, and cipher. Not infrequently was it made a provision in the indenture of German servants that they were to be taught during their terms of service

---

[57] *Ibid.,* 94, 95.
[58] *Ibid.,* 126, 127.
[59] *Ibid.,* 66, 67.
[60] *Ibid.,* 184, 185.
[61] *Ibid.,* 222, 223.
[62] *Ibid.,* 238, 239

to read in the English language. Sometimes it was specifically stated that they were to read the Bible in the English tongue, and again the statement was made that they were to write "a legible hand," and to cipher as far as through the rule of three.[63]

As the arrangements of the terms of indentures came to be more and more a matter of wages, so likewise the freedom dues were regarded as a money return. The rendering of the value of suits of apparel in money became common after the Revolution.[64] In 1803, one Seller was bound to a Lancaster carpenter and was to have at the expiration of the indenture the customary freedom suits or £10, at his option.[65] But the terms "freedom dues" and "the customary freedom suits" continued to be mentioned in the indentures until the disappearance of the system.

Evidently servants secured their rights with some difficulty. A petition to the Chester County court in 1747-1748 recited that a master would not give the servant his indenture which was already served out, or any part of his freedom dues. The master presented himself in court and agreed to dismiss the servant according to law in two or three weeks' time.[66] A similar petition was presented in 1748, but when the case came up the servant failed to appear and the petition was set aside.[67] In 1776,

---

[63] See *Ibid.*, 48, 49. Professor McMasters asserts that it was optional whether the master should furnish the new suit or pay £10 in currency. This was probably a fair money value for the new freedom suit, which was to be a complete suit of apparel.

[64] McMaster, *History of United States,* II, 558.

[65] *Registry of Redemptioners,* Book A, p. 315.

The following record of an indenture shows the money value set upon the clothes which a servant received:

"October 23rd, 1819.

Catharina Rillinger to John Warner of Spring Garden, Penn. township Phila. county, victuler. for three Years, to have at the end of the term, Two complete suits of Clothes, one to be new. Cor. 50 Dollars." *Registry of Redemptioners.* Book C, p. 114.

The above indenture was released by the following:

"By mutual consent of the parties in the Indenture, between John Warner and Catharina Rillinger, recorded page 114, also claims contained therein, are relinquished and the Indenture made null and void. 22 June, 1822." Original MS. Preserved in *Registry of Redemptioners,* Book C.

[66] *Cope Manuscripts,* "Court Papers of Chester County."

[67] *Ibid.*

a servant who had served two and one-half years according to his agreement, and was entitled to his freedom dues, appealed to the court to get his rights. The master was summoned and agreed to pay £4 15s., in lieu of freedom dues.

According to the custom of the time, children under five years of age were obliged to serve until they were twenty-one years old for their raising; those who were from five to ten years of age, and who had been brought over at half fare (pass-age), generally commanded a price large enough for their time until they were twenty-one to pay for their passage, while for children who were above ten years of age, a sum sufficiently large was offered so that the children might assume part of their parents' obligation for passage. Upon arrival a husband must take the place of his wife if she were sick, or the wife must take the husband's place if he were sick. The responsibility of the members of a family for each other, and the power of a father over his children might well suggest to Abbé Raynal "an image of the old patriarchal manners of the East." [68] Sometimes a family found sale together, though one of the worst evils of the system was the breaking up of families. Even if a whole family were indentured to one man at the outset, there was no assurance that he would not later sell the indentures so as to cause separation. In any event the indentures were usually for unequal terms, so that freedom came at different times. In 1785, a Philadelphia butcher secured indentures for a father and mother with their two children, the parents being bound for five years and the children for ten years and ten months and fourteen years and eight months, respectively.[69]

A number of unusual indentures was entered into in December, 1771, before the mayor of Philadelphia. Mark Bird, of Union Township, in Berks County, purchased five families which had recently arrived from Rotterdam. Two of these families consisted of a husband, a wife, and two children each; two, of a husband, a wife, and one child each; and one of a husband and wife without a child. The term in each case was for service of

---

[68] Raynal, *British Settlements*, I, 166.

[69] *Registry of Redemptioners*, Book A, p. 1. This breaking up of families will be further noted in the last chapter, on the results of the system.

seven years, and the conditions imposed were that the servants should be furnished log houses in which to live and gardens, all free of rental, and that they were to be employed in cutting cordwood for which they were to be allowed 22d. per cord. When they had paid the total amount which the master had advanced for their passage, which varied from £22 15s. to £49 3s., they were to be freed from their indentures. It was further stipulated in the record that in the event of these men being employed at any other occupation than the cutting of cordwood, they should be paid at the rate of 22d. per day.[70]

As Pennsylvania spread territorially and the redemption trade increased, it was necessary to take servants back into the country to dispose of them. There grew up a class of men termed "soul drivers," or "soul sellers," not unlike the *Neuländer* who were on the other side of the ocean.[71] Sometimes the two functions were united in one person, and the agent went to Europe and gathered his emigrants, negotiated for their passage, and then peddled them out after their arrival. It was the usual practice of these drivers, however, to buy a parcel of servants at the port and take them back through the country, selling them off as they had opportunity. Droves of redemptioners, sometimes as many as fifty together, were thus taken into what are now Montgomery, Berks, Lancaster, Chester, and Delaware Counties. Peter Williamson described the servants as being taken in tens or twenties and driven through the country "like cattle to a Smithfield market and exposed to sale in public fairs as so many brute beasts." Frequently those for sale were described as "choice" or "well-disposed" and women sometimes as "handsome."

The usual route of the soul seller was a circular swing through the country, and then back to Philadelphia, selling servants as the party progressed.[72] The distribution of servants is

---

[70] "Record of Indentures," *Pa. Germ. Soc. Publications*, XVI, 42, 43.
[71] Mentioned above Chapter IX.
[72] It is reported that on one of these trips a famous "soul driver" named McCullough had disposed of all his company except one fellow, an Irishman, who managed to evade sale, probably by bad behavior. One morning the servant was early astir at an inn where he had spent the night with his master. He then assumed the rôle of master, and sold his master to the innkeeper for a sum of money which he pocketed, and took his departure, but not until he explained that the man whom he had sold

indicated by the registry before the Philadelphia mayors. Out of a total of 769 indentures recorded for the year from October 2, 1745, to October 2, 1746, 600 were to reside in Pennsylvania, 71 in New Jersey, 20 in Maryland, and 5 each in Delaware and Virginia. Of those sold to reside in Pennsylvania, 360 were credited to Philadelphia County, 112 to Chester, 96 to Lancaster and 32 to Bucks Counties, respectively. Those going to New Jersey were assigned most largely to Burlington and Gloucester Counties. Of the 20 going to Maryland, 14 had no local designation. Sixty-six servants in 1745-1746 had their indentures recorded with no indication as to the places of residence of their masters.[73]

In the year 1772, the proportion of those registered to reside in Pennsylvania was much larger. Out of a total of 1,139 recorded, 1,010 were credited to the home colony; 17 were given as going to reside in New Jersey, 13 in Maryland, and 10 each in Delaware and Virginia. In the last-named year the number for whom no future place of residence was given had fallen to 15. The record for 1772 indicated the spread of the Pennsylvania settlement. The six leading counties to which servants were assigned from Philadelphia with the numbers were as follows: Philadelphia, 647; Lancaster, 131; Chester, 85; Bucks, 51; Cumberland, 38, and Berks, 35.[74]

Sale of a servant was to the purchaser and his heirs or assigns. The servant might, therefore, repeatedly change masters; he might be put on sale at the death of the master, or at his reverse of fortune, his change in mode of life, or his caprice or whim. The indenture shown as a frontispiece had on the back the signature of John Dickey and the further endorsement: "By a power invested in me by Mr. John Dickey, I do assign over the within Indenture of Alex. Beard to Thos. Rislie, Esq. his heirs and assigns. Philadelphia, 26th day of March 1785 five." This was signed by Edw. Jones. When the servant was resold, a new

---

was tolerably clever, but was not to be trusted or believed, especially since he sometimes tried to pass himself off as the master. Martin, *History of Chester*, 190. Seemingly on authority of Lewis, *History of Chester County;* newspaper cuttings (Library of Historical Society of Pennsylvania), p. 88.

[73] "Record Before James Hamilton, Mayor," *Pa. Mag. Hist. and Biog.* Vols. 30, 31 and 32.

[74] "Record of Indentures," *Pa. Germ. Soc. Pubs.,* XVI.

entry was made in the registry of redemptioners, but with a reference back to the earlier indenture as recorded.

The original indenture of one Richard Orcle, of the Parish of Siddenton, England,[75] will illustrate the devious path which lay before an indentured servant. In 1773, Orcle agreed with a Philadelphia ship captain to serve in Pennsylvania or West Jersey for a period of five years following his arrival in America. After having had this agreement duly certificated by the proper official at the port of Bristol, Orcle was brought to Philadelphia, and when a purchaser had been found, he was taken before the mayor on May 8, 1773, and according to the record on the indenture was assigned to Joseph Sackett. On May 16, 1776, Joseph Sackett sold the balance of the time of Richard Orcle to Captain Nathaniel Vansout for seven pounds ten shillings, having the transaction registered on the original document and the assignment duly approved by the proper official.

A motive for selling some servants was their inclination to leave the master with whom they were engaged; if they showed a disposition to run away, there was a chance of their being better suited with a new master; if so, it was more satisfactory to all concerned that they should be sold. Some of these redemptioners fancied that their toil might be lightened by change of masters. Sales followed recapture of runaways, and repeated attempts to run away were likely to be followed by sale. Evidence is clear that a runaway might be sold again and again; in 1743, a transported servant came from London under a seven years' term and was purchased by a baker, from whom he promptly ran away; when captured, he was sold to row in a ferry on the Susquehanna; here he stayed until the death of his master, but left the widow whose property he had become. He was again recaptured and disposed of to one Michael Webster, but ran away from that service only to be taken a third time, and again sold; his new master kept this fellow for about two years, when the latter appropriated some of the master's goods and ran away once again.[76]

---

[75] Original indenture preserved in the Library of Historical Society of Bucks County.

[76] *Pennsylvania Gazette,* March 6, 1750. Advertisement for the runaway.

The sale and distribution of servants under indenture presented the least attractive features of white servitude. Similarly, the domestic slave trade was the most objectionable feature of slavery. The local traders and distributors of white servants under indenture inherited the evils of the importation arrangements. They also had the onus of pressing for the sale of servants, and were in a middle position between the new masters and those whom they purchased. If the purchase of a servant did not turn out satisfactorily, the local trader was blamed. The complaints against the evils of redemption and indentured labor could not be readily directed against the agents in Europe or against the ship companies which introduced the servants, but these complaints could be made to reach the local trader who negotiated the sale. Such complaints were frequently lodged.

The enforcement of the regulation for the sale and distribution of servants led necessarily to conditions governing the migration from the home countries, and to agreements for transportation. Laws for the regulation of the servant trade were difficult to secure, and they were even more difficult to enforce.

The Acc: of the Expence that Jeromiah Collet was at to get
his Servant William Pallet when he run away

1729
Aug.t 15   To 1 Day run away
            To a Day riding after for 1 man & horse ——— £o . 4 . 6
            To a Day for a footman - - - - - - £o . 2 . 6
            To Expences - - - - - - - £o . 3 . 0

Sept.t 10 - - To 1 Day run away
            To 2 Men & 2 horses 1 Day - - - - - £o . 9 . 0
            To Expences - - - - - - £o . 5 . 0

            To 2 Days run away at two Sundry times
Sept.r —   To 2 Days run away, then took a way Seth & Shade to } £o . 9 . 0
            Mow in New Castle County & Cost - - - - -
1730   To 1 man & horse two Days after him - - - £o . 9 . 0
            To his Expence - - - - - - £o . 4 . 0

Sept.r —   To 2 Days run away
            To a man & horse one Day - - - - - £o . 4 . 6
1731   To Expences - - - - - - £o . 2 . —

June - - - To 2 Days run away & Lost a pair of New Shoes & } £o . 11 . —
            Stocking in Chester Creek - - - - - -
            To 2 men a Day & horses - - - - - £o . 9 . —
            To Expences - - - - - - £o . 2 . —

Aug.t   To 2 Days run away
26 - -   To a man a foot one Day - - - - - £o . 2 . 6
            To a man & horse one Day - - - - - £o . 4 . 6
            To Expences - - - - - - £o . 2 . —
                                            £ 4 . 5 . 6

£   12 Days Run Away in the whole

to Save 60 days for running times
a gasy of many a broke y month
  febr: 5 f ˢ

ACCOUNT AGAINST A RUNAWAY SERVANT

CHAPTER XI

RUNAWAY SERVANTS

Adventuresome, restless, and discontented men would not submit to sustained servile toil without attempting to be free. Colonial newspapers contained each week an array of advertisements of servants who had run away. Statutes were repeatedly passed imposing disability for running away and providing for the apprehending and returning of runaways. Fines were laid for harboring absconding servants, and for dereliction of duty on the part of justices and sheriffs in the seizing of them and in the giving notice of their capture.

A new era of colonial development opened in Pennsylvania with the eighteenth century and in this era new laws were passed to regulate the servant system.[1] It was now provided that for each day's absence without leave the servant should give five days' extra service, and that he should also make good the costs and damages sustained because of his absence. All runaways, when captured, were to be taken to the sheriff of the county. If the servant were taken up within ten miles of the home of the master, the legal reward to the captor was 10s.; if taken at a distance greater than ten miles, the reward was 20s. Should a servant be concealed, a fine of 20s. was fixed for every twenty-four hours of concealment. If justices did not issue warrants for the arrest of runaways within twenty-four hours after complaint to them, they were subject to £5 fine, and for each day's delay a like amount additional. Sheriffs were liable for 5s. per day for each day's delay in giving notice to the master of the arrest of a servant.[2]

When servants who had run away were secured, the masters submitted to the courts a claim of loss or expense suffered, as well as a statement showing the days of absence. The court then adjudicated, fixing the extra time, or the amount to be paid in

---

[1] Laws obtaining for the earlier period are noted in Chapter II.

[2] Bioren, *Laws*, I, 10, 11. Allowed to become a law in England by lapse of time. *Statutes at Large*, II, 54-56.

217

money, though there was slight prospect of money payment.[3]

In the Chester County decisions, which were usually written on the original petitions, it was common to fix five days' additional time for each day of absence, and to name a sum due the master for costs and damages. In fixing the damages there was also a statement of the length of time additional to be required of the servant if he was not able to pay in money. An examination of quite a number of these decisions given at different times shows that men were required to serve a year additional for damages of from four to six pounds. For damages of an equal amount women were usually remanded to two additional years.[4]

In 1734, a statement was submitted to a Philadelphia court showing that a servant had been absent for four hundred days, and that the master had been to an expense of upwards of £3 to apprehend him.[5] The extra time necessary to satisfy these charges would have exceeded the legal term. About the same time a petitioner set forth his loss because of the absence of his servant. The court's decision in this case is appended to the original petition; it was that the servant should be bound to his master or his assigns for six months' additional time.[6] Similar records show that in Chester County a runaway servant boy was ordered to continue for two hundred and forty days extra time, while a woman was remanded to an extra year for loss of time and damages.

In a court petition of Chester County in 1768 it was certified that a servant had run away three times in the preceding three years, and that the master had been under the heavy expense of £29 for charges and rewards. The servant was in this case ordered to serve forty weeks beyond the time of his original indenture for the time he was absent, and to pay the £29 in money, or serve four years additional.[7] An earlier runaway was said to have four years of his original indenture yet to serve and already to have against him £25 in costs from his running away.[8]

---

[3] Illustration opposite.

[4] *Cope Manuscripts.*

[5] Cheyney, *Philadelphia Manufacturer*, March 16, 1891.

[6] *Manuscript Court Record* (1732-1744). Petition of John Coleman. Library of Historical Society of Pennsylvania.

[7] *Cope Manuscripts.*

[8] *Pennsylvania Gazette,* January 29, 1756.

An Account of the Loss of time and —
Charges with other Disappointments which
John Coleman Sustained by his Servant
Fransis Owen are as followeth (viz.t)
He the said Fransis left the City of Philada. and
went away with his sd. Masters fflatt the 10th
day of January 1738/9 and was not found till the
28 day of ffebruary being 7 weeks And One
days Absence Senc which in the whole Amounts
to fifty days Absence &c

To Charges paid for taking up & prison   }
    fees at New Castle as ⅌ Acc.t . . . . } 1 · 12 · 0
To the fflatt hire during these Seven   }
    weeks at 9ʃ ⅌ week . . . . } 3 · 3 · 0
To Damages done to the fflatt by his Neglect   1 · 4 · 0
To his Masters loss of time & Expences in }
    Searching for & finding his sd. Servant } 2 · 0 · 0
                                                _____
                                             £ 7 · 19 · 0

PETITION AGAINST A RUNAWAY

To his Majesties Justices of the Court of Quarter Sessions held at Chester this twenty
sixth day of Augt 1747

The Petition of Willm Montgomery Humbly
Sheweth

That your Petitioner having a Servant
Commited to the Workhouse for Refusing to
Serve his ~~Petitioner~~ his sd Master Acordin
to his Jadenture your Petitioner therefore
Humbly prays that your Honours will be
Pleased to Admit us to a hearing of the
Difference between us that he may be dealt
with as you in your Wisdom shall think
proper and your Petitioner as in Duty
bound shall Ever Pray

William Montgomery

PETITION AGAINST A SERVANT WHO REFUSED TO WORK

[Original in *Cope Manuscripts*, Historical Society of Pennsylvania]

Ft. 219

It will readily be seen that a servant's time might be almost perpetual as a result of attempts to escape and of recapture. In 1773, a runaway was advertised for with the statement that because of running away his servitude had already extended over ten years.[9]

In a Chester County decision an alternative sentence was resorted to in a case where a servant charged with running away and other misdemeanors was given eight months additional time if he behaved well, otherwise ten months.[10] If a runaway would not comply with the decision of the court for extra time, he was bound to the workhouse, and brought to terms, as is shown by petitions and the manner of dealing with them.[11] A servant who refused to work was committed to the workhouse to be kept and punished until he was willing to return to his service. In the workhouse calendar for April 19, 1789, were listed three servants who had been committed on February 4, March 2, and April 19, respectively, all on the charge of being disorderly.[12] The conditions of the workhouses at the time would in all probability promptly bring refractory servants to terms.[13]

To prevent runaways from making their escape, suspicious characters and persons who could not give satisfactory accounts of themselves were committed to jail and held temporarily. On July 4, 1739, a man who had been taken up and confined for six months petitioned for his release or a "speedy trial"; the court proceedings record that no prosecutor appeared and the man was discharged.[14] It was the custom of servants as well as of slaves who were abroad on legitimate business to carry passes, and a stranger who was without a pass and could not give proper

---

[9] *Ibid.,* March 10, 1773.

[10] Martin, *History of Chester,* 76.

[11] *Manuscript Court Record,* Philadelphia County (1732-1744). Petition not dated.

[12] *MS. Record of Indictments,* Historical Society of Pennsylvania.

[13] For condition of jails and prisons considerably later than this see McMaster, *History of United States,* I, 98-101.

[14] *Manuscript Court Record* (1732-1744). Library of Historical Society of Pennsylvania.

explanation of his business was liable to be lodged in the work-house. A servant's indenture was accepted in lieu of a pass.[15]

When a suspicious person was taken up, the sheriff adver-tised him; if he were a runaway, the master came and paid fees and charges, took the servant, and could have recourse against him by having his term lengthened. If no master appeared, the suspected person was required to prove that he was a freeman, and to satisfy the charges that had accumulated against him. Inability to do the latter might remand him to servitude, and certainly the practice reversed the common law principle that a man is innocent until he is proved guilty. As might be expected, these harsh regulations led to fraud, and forged passes later became common.

The weekly newspaper was the principal medium of com-munication between the authorities and the masters whose servants had left. At times a notice such as the following appeared: "Taken up and committed to Lancaster goal, one Henry Reig-durff, lately advertised for running away from one John Chamber, of Birmingham Township, Chester County: These are to require said John Chamber, or others whom it may concern, to come and take him out and pay the charges to the goaler." [16]   At other times the sheriff or jailer merely advertised suspected persons as taken up. In 1751, the sheriff of New Castle advertised three persons at one time as seized on suspicion of being runaway servants.[17]

---

[15] Passes were altered, and one person sometimes assumed the name of another to whom a pass had been issued. Geiser, *Redemptioners,* 81.

The following indicates one way of RELEASING FROM AN IN-DENTURE:

"Philada., March 15th, 1817.

This is to certify that I am disposed to give John Leanhart, and Mary his wife their freedom, and quit all claims on them whatever, provided they give me a certificate that their inden-tures are legally cancelled in the docket where they are on record.

S. Wiatt."

(Original *MS.* in Historical Society of Pennsylvania.)

(Preserved in *Registry of Redemptioners,* Book A.)

[16] *Pennsylvania Gazette,* December 18, 1760.

[17] *Ibid.,* July 12, 1750. A record of three runaways who broke jail at Lancaster is furnished, *ibid.,* August 30, 1750.

To the Honourable Justices of ye County Court of Common pleas.
held & kept at Chester this 23^d day of febuary A.D 1768
The Petition of Patrick Hambleton

Humbly Sheweth

That Whereas your petitioner was taken Up and
Committed to y^r Goail on suspition of Being
A Runaway servant and since hath Been
Advertised in the Publick gazette By the goaler
& no Master hath Ever appeared against him
and as he looks on himself to be a free
Man therefore Humbly begs that your
Honours May Be Pleased to take it Under
your Consideration & order that Your
Petitioner May be set at liberty on his paying
his fees and your petitioner Shall as in
Duty Bound Ever Pray &c

Patrick Hambleton

Borough of Chester
febuary ye 23^d day A.D 1768

Ð And your poor petitioner hath Been Detained in your
Goal three months past

PETITION OF MAN ARRESTED ON SUSPICION OF BEING
A RUNAWAY SERVANT

[Original in *Cope Manuscripts*, Historical Society of Pennsylvania]

Ft. 220

Masters received bills from jailers or sheriffs, which they paid, and in turn presented to the courts. These receipted jailers' bills, preserved in the original court records, are most interesting. Under date of 1732, Mrs. Parris was made debtor to "prison charges of her man" for his allowance during one hundred and twenty-four days at the rate of 2d. per day, and for other items including turnkey fees and constable charges, in all aggregating £1 11s. 2d.[18] The records show that some servants must have been familiar characters at the Philadelphia workhouse. From 1725 to 1734, James Portude was charged with fees and expenses on account of a mulatto, Ben, termed his servant, under more than forty different entries, making a total of upwards of £5 charges. At the same time a statement was filed showing that this man had been absent over four hundred days.[19]

Of the sixty-four inmates of the county jail in Philadelphia, July 2, 1751, two only were servants, both classed as "criminals." On October 29 following, the number of inmates was reduced to forty-eight, and both servants were gone.[20]

After the Revolution new acts were passed in Pennsylvania, indicating the necessity for a better regulation of apprentice and indentured labor. Provisions were made for runaway servants in 1803 in an act concerning the completion of the prison in Philadelphia; it was ordered that persons already confined in the jails were to be removed to the prison; the enumeration of those to be removed included "runaway or disorderly servants." [21] Earlier rules for the jail of the city indicate that runaway servants were inmates.[22]

---

[18] *Manuscript Book of Indictments* (1715-1790), Historical Society of Pennsylvania.

[19] *Manuscript Court Records* (1697-1732), Historical Society of Pennsylvania.

[20] *Manuscript Book of Indictments* (1715-1790).

[21] Bioren, *Laws,* III, 385, 386, and IV, 87, 88.

[22] *Rules and Regulations,* for the jail of the City and County of Philadelphia, which were approved on February 26, 1792.

No. VI.

"The convicts, prisoners for trial, servants, runaways and vagrants, shall be separately fed, lodged and employed."

. . . .

Meddlesome and malicious neighbors at times suggested running away and aided servants in making their escape.[23]   Again masters were imposed upon, as appears from the following, which was appended to an offer of "Seven Dollars Reward":

"Whereas a certain Henry Bear by trade a miller, came to my house in December last, and hired my servant boy, named William Smith, and was to return him in three months after or pay me for the remainder of his time; and whereas the said Henry Bear has, from other circumstances, proved

---

No. XXIII.

"Runaways or disorderly apprentices and servants shall be separately fed, lodged and employed, and the keeper shall give notice to their masters or mistresses, at the time of their commitment of the charge that will accrue for their daily maintenance, who may, at their option agree to pay the same, or provide the necessary food themselves." Bradford, *Punishment by Death,* etc., Appendix 102, 104.

In April, 1790, the return of all prisoners confined in the jail at Philadelphia was as follows:

Debtors,	6
Criminals,	30
Convicts,	87

This was approved by the jailer and was for the inspection of the chief justice of the commonwealth and his associates. On the back of this was the list of prisoners sentenced to labor, 87 in number. *Original Manuscript of Indictments* (1715-1799).

[23] Merivale, *Colonies,* 375.

The summary and conclusion of an interesting case among the Quakers is shown in the following letter submitted to the Monthly Meeting of the Friends at New Garden, 1725-1726:

"Dear friends whereas Some time Ago, there was a Difference happened between my Master John Smith & My Self about what time I was to be free from his Servitude, & I hearkening to Much to ye Affirmations & presentations of others, though Contrary to ye Credible Accounts yt came from friends, as taken out of ye register book for births belonging to ye Grange Meeting in Ireland ye place of my birth did put my Sd Master & other friends to great Exercise & trouble as also yt I refused to stand to ye friends Judgment yt was Appointed by ye Meeting to Determine yt Difference for all which I do hereby Acknowledge my Self to blame and desire this Meeting to Accept thereof promising by ye Lord's Assistance to be So carefull for ye time to come as no More to give friends any Occasion against me for I desire to live ye rest of my dayes in unity wt friends."

(Signed)   William Lowden."

Myers, *Immigration of the Irish Quakers into Pennsylvania,* 231.

to be a rogue, I have great reason to expect he never will
return, and that he has decoyed the boy away with him; I
do hereby offer the above reward for both or either of them,
if brought from without this State, or Four Dollars if brought
from within it, and lodged in any jail within the same, together
with reasonable charges—to be paid by Matthew Conrad, at
the Sign of the Plough, in Third-Street, near Market-Street,
Philadelphia, or by me the subscriber, living near Hockley's
mill, in New Britain township, Bucks county." [24]

At times servants went in a company, though when they did
so there might be question as to whether they had a better chance
of escape. Arrayed in the cast-off garments of erstwhile masters,
beaver hats, silk waistcoats, and decorated leather breeches, who
could be likened to one of these. When several journeyed together,
they could add confusion to the printed descriptions by changing
clothes.[25]

---

[24] *United States Gazette,* June 9, 1790. Readvertised June 16, and 23.

Servants might return to their masters voluntarily. The *Maryland
Gazette* published the following in 1745:

"Run away from the subscriber living at Annapolis, on the 27th of this
instant August, 1745, a servant man named John Powell, alias Charles
Lucas, a Londoner born, by trade a clock and watch maker; he is a short,
well set fellow, has full goggle eyes, and wears a wig: He had on when
he went away an Osnabrigs shirt, a pair of buckskin breeches, a pair of
short wide trousers, two pair of white hose and a well-worn broad-cloth
coat with metal buttons.

"Whoever secures the said runaway so that he can be had again, shall
have 3 pounds reward, besides what the law allows; and if brought home,
reasonable charges."

A week later appeared this notice: "Whereas John Powell was advertised last week in this paper as a runaway; but being only gone into the
country a cyder-drinking, and being returned again to his Master's Service;
these are therefore to acquaint all gentlemen and others, who have any
watches, or clocks, to repair, that they may have them done in the best
manner at reasonable rates." Riley, *The Ancient City,* 125.

[25] RUN AWAY LAST NIGHT, FROM THEIR MASTERS,

the three following Irish Servants, viz.:

From George Rice Jones, of this City, Butcher, one named Terrence
Tvole, a Butcher by Trade, a short thick set fellow, of a brown Complexion: Had on when he went away, a red great Coat, a brown Jacket, a
pair of leather Breeches, with brass Buttons, and strings at the Knees,
good grey yarn Stockings, one speckled Shirt, and a white one, a thick

Runaways would play the part of servants to each other; men and women assumed the relations of husband and wife in order to aid in their escape. Evidences are not wanting of women attiring themselves in men's clothes the better to hide their identity. The women runaways appear to have been a particularly hard lot, and not infrequently were they advertised for as having run away without serving their masters the additional time due him as damages for bearing illegitimate children.[26] Women who were at large and could not give a satisfactory account of themselves were thrown into jail. A young woman was advertised by the sheriff of Lancaster County as having been taken up on suspicion and it was announced that if no one claimed her she would be sold for the jail charges.[27] In 1776, a Maryland woman

blue gray Jacket, good Shoes, and a good Hat with Spots of Paint on it; also a light crown Wig, a worsted Cap, and a red Silk Handkerchief.

From Samuel Hastings, of this City, Shipwright, one named Thomas Wildeer, of middle stature, red Complexion, down look, about 25 Years of Age: Had on when he went away, a great Coat of an ordinary dark brown Ratteen, with the Cuff of the right sleeve off, a green Grogram Vest, patch'd under one Arm, and bound down the Button holes with green Bays, with two rows of Button-holes, black Mohair Buttons and no lining, a new ozenbrigs Shirt, red Plush Breeches, the Breeches good but the Plush ordinary, a new silk Handkerchief, an old Beaver Hat, light grey yarn stockings, new shoes, and wears a Wig.

From Thomas Sugar, of this City, Carpenter, one named Michael Berry, by Trade a Carpenter, a lusty well-set Fellow, full fac'd, no Hair, but wears a white Cap or Wig: Had on when he went away, a full trimmed blue cloth Coat, a short homespun linsey woollsey Waistcoat, one Garlix and one Ozenbrigs Shirt, leather Breeches half worn, light grey yarn stockins, old Shoes with Steel Buckles in them, and a good fine Hat; took with him a new Handsaw of White's Stamped on the Handle in several Places with T.S.

Whoever takes up and secures the said Servants, so that their Masters may have them again, Shall have Six Pounds Reward, or Forty Shillings for each, and reasonable Charges, paid by

(Signed)   George Rice Jones,
Samuel Hastings,
Thomas Sugar.

Philad. Feb. 4, 1739-1740.

N.B. They are supposed to be all gone together, and perhaps may change Apparel." *Pennsylvania Gazette,* February 7, 1740.

[26] *Pennsylvania Gazette,* September 1, 1773.

[27] *Ibid.,* April 10, 1755.

came to Philadelphia and, when questioned, declared that she had served out her indenture. She was put under duress and, as no one appeared against her, was sold ·for the jail fees and taken to Chester County; but, as might have been expected, she promptly ran away.[28] The keeper of the workhouse in Chester County once indicated in an advertisement the embarrassment that might be caused through the arrest of persons against whom no one appeared. After keeping a girl who had been arrested on suspicion for a considerable time and repeatedly advertising her, the keeper added that if the girl were not claimed and taken away, he would be ruined by the expense of keeping her.[29]

It was not unusual for runaways to appropriate property for their comfort, or to aid them in their escape. Horses were taken at times, as were also boats.[30] With the system of rewards, and the fines and the restrictions upon tenders of ferries, it must have been difficult for servants to get clear from their masters, though many of them did so.

The efforts at recapture were not limited to the time immediately following a servant's departure. After the servant might think himself free of suspicion, he had to face such notices as the following:

"Run away about Two Years ago from Cecil County in Maryland, Nicholas Collings, small Statue, bushy Hair almost Grey: A Shoemaker by Trade. Whoever secures him, and gives Notice thereof to Mr. Abel van Burkeloo of the said County, shall have Ten Shillings Reward." [31]

Close scrutiny was given to those who were at large, and Franklin wrote that as a runaway apprentice he came in for his share of suspicion. Said he of his appearance at Burlington on the journey to Philadelphia, "I made so miserable a figure that I was suspected of being some runaway indentured servant, and was in danger of being taken up on that suspicion." Again after his arrival in Philadelphia he was questioned in the matter of being a runaway.[32]

---

[28] *Ibid.*, June 26, 1776.
[29] *Ibid.*, December 16, 1756.
[30] See *American Weekly Mercury*, July 21, 1720.
[31] *American Weekly Mercury*, December 13, 1720.
[32] Franklin, *Autobiography*, in Bigelow, *Life of Franklin*, I, 123, 127.

Contemporary accounts of travelers and other observers, and the records of the courts, indicate that servants were badly treated and that there was much warrant for their running away. Servants, William Mcraley found, were not supplied with the necessaries of life as specified in their indentures and, morever, in case of complaint the word of the master would be taken against that of the servant, "ten to one," and the servant would likely get his "licks for his pains." The same writer told of the regulation with regard to passes, the rewards offered, the means of communication through the newspapers and by notices posted on the trees and in public places. Moraley saw small chance of escape by running away, and related his own experience to show the vigilance of the authorities. After the expiration of his indenture he returned to Burlington where he was arrested and held until his master appeared to testify that his indentures were discharged.[33]

Gottlieb Mittelberger saw in running away no hope of servants escaping from what he called the bondage of white servitude, for this, he said, would lead to capture and prolonged terms. According to his account each day of absence led to a week of extra time, and a month, to one-half a year.[34] Eddis described similar conditions in Maryland. "For real or imaginary causes," he said, speaking of servants, "these frequently attempt to escape, but very few are successful; the country being intersected with rivers and the utmost vigilance observed in detecting persons under suspicious circumstances, who, when apprehended, are committed to close confinement, advertised, and delivered to their respective masters; the party who detects the vagrant being entitled to a reward. Other incidental charges arise. The unhappy culprit is doomed to a severe chastisement; and a prolongation of servitude is decreed in full proportion to expenses incurred, and supposed inconveniences resulting from a desertion of duty." [35]

Runaway servants were seemingly more numerous in Mary-

---

[33] William Moraley, "Adventures and Voyages," *Chester Republican.*

[34] Mittelberger, *Journey,* 29.

[35] *Letters from America,* 70, 71. The authority does not seem adequate for the statement of Martin (*History of Chester,* 190) that the redemption trade was broken up by the number of servants who ran away.

land than in any other colony. The large number of convicts brought there is one explanation for this. As has been earlier shown, a considerable proportion of advertisements for fugitives in the Philadelphia newspapers were for Maryland servants.[36] In general the movement of runaways was to the north. During the period of Dutch control in New Netherlands there was a supply of absconding servants from the South.[37] In the more populous North, with relatively a larger number of freemen, the fugitive had a better chance of escape. Moreover, in the North there was more opportunity for employment as a free laborer and eventually of setting up as a small proprietor. Just after the middle of the eighteenth century the attorney-general of Pennsylvania petitioned the Assembly for a grant of salary above the usual fees, on the ground of the increase of the business of his office, resulting among other things, it was claimed, from the coming of fugitive servants from other colonies.[38]

Continued insertions of the same advertisements from week to week in the colonial papers, until they had appeared four, five, and six times within two months, indicate that the capturing of servants was slow; certainly in many cases they were not captured at all. Sympathetic friends could hide and aid the fugitives and the wonder is that the whole system did not early break down completely from the inability of masters to keep their servants.

The newspaper advertisements aimed at exactness of description of servants, and are a unique source of information on the personal appearance, dress, character and habits of the runaways.

---

[36] See above p. 137 for runaways from Maryland. These runaways often came in companies. For examples: "Run away from Doctor William Lock, of Annarundel County, in the Province of Maryland, five Servant Men, viz.,

"William Fox a Little Man, he wears a White Wigg and has a New Suit of Cloathes, a Smith by trade.

"William Gaugh somewhat bigger than the other, well clothed wears a brown Wigg and is by Trade a Joyner.

"John Ashwood a pretty Lusty tall Man, with black Hair and is a Cooper.

"Benjamin Cormele of a Middle Statue by Occupation a Gardener.

"Thomas Fiez Likwise of a Middle size. Each of them well Clothed." *American Weekly Mercury*, August 15, 1720.

[37] *Court Minutes of New Amsterdam*, I, 330, and VI, 279.

[38] *Votes of Assembly*, IV, 234.

Incidentally, too, they are often a commentary on the master, and on the social standards of the times. One somewhat out of the usual follows, having appeared under the caption, "Forty Shillings Reward":

"Last Wednesday noon, at break of day
From *Philadelphia* ran away
An Irishman named John McKeoghn,
To fraud and imposition prone;
About five feet five inches high,
Can curse and swear as well as lie;
......................[Description].
He stole and from my house convey'd
A man's blue coat of bear-skin stuff,
(Nor had the villain yet enough);
....
He oft in conversation chatters
Of scripture and religious matters,
And fain would to the world impart
That virtue lodges in his heart;
But take the rogue from stem to stern,
The hypocrite you'll soon discern—
....
Whoe'er secures said John McKeoghn,
(Provided I should get my own),
Shall have from me in cash paid down,
Five dollar bills, and half a crown." [39]

Rewards for the apprehending and return of runaways were generally stated at 40s. and the usual charges. Sometimes they were for less, though more frequently a larger amount was offered. The lowest legal reward of 20s. was offered in some cases, and again the amount was £3, £4, or £5. Special conditions were not frequently stated, as that those who would aid in the capture of an Indian woman servant "would be rewarded to their content." [40]   Ten shillings reward for capture within twenty miles, and 20s. if beyond twenty miles, was often regarded as too small, and a week later the reward offered would be doubled, the conditions of the capture remaining the same. [41]   Places where serv-

---

[39] Signed, Mary Nelson, Water Street, January 10, 1769. Cited from *Maryland Gazette* of March 16, Scharf, *History of Maryland*, II, 17. Another advertisement in verse in Scharf & Westcott, *History of Philadelphia*, II, 884, 885.

[40] *American Weekly Mercury*, March 24, 1720.

[41] *Ibid.*, July 7 and 14, 1720.

ants were delivered also affected the amount offered; if they were taken to the jail, less was offered than if the fugitives were delivered to their masters.[42]

Worthless servants were subject to having the seal of worthlessness set upon them by their former masters. When runaways were described and the rewards offered for their return were fixed at "six cents and no charges," it meant that the master was glad to be rid of the servants and did not wish to be troubled further with them on account of arrest or jail fees. Such offers became quite common in the later period. Once at least a master expressed his joy in verse for a loss which he felt might be his gain:

> "This present instant on the fourteenth day,
> My apprentice boy did run away;
> Thomas Stillenger he is called by name,
> His indenture further testifies the same;
> He has always been a vexatious lad,
> One reason why he is so meanly clad;
>   [Some description of apparel]
> To describe the rest I am not inclined,
> Cloth for a jacket he left behind;
> Of apple pies he took with him but five,
> For to preserve himself alive;
> Three quarter dollars are missed of late,
> Which perhaps he took to pay his freight;
> Believe him not if you be wise,
> He is very artful in telling lies;
>   [Recites thievery]
> For which I whipt him, I thought severe,
> But did not make him shed one tear.
> Whoever doth him safely secure
> Of a reward they may be sure,
> Six-pence at least I do propose
> To give for him with all his clothes;
> Or clear me of him forever and mine.
> And his indentures away I will sign;
> Now to inform you further still,
> I keep a saw and fulling mill;
> In East-Fallowfield township
> and Chester County is the place of my abode,
> I subscribe my name unto the same, and that is
>   William Moode." [43]

---

[42] See *ibid.,* August 4, 1720.
[43] *Pennsylvania Gazette,* March 6, 1776.

Reasons for running away varied, as did the character of masters and the temperament of servants. Servants of spirit, who felt that they had been deceived and decoyed, resented the whole arrangement, and recognized neither the justice of their indentures nor the legal regulations of the system as binding them. If a servant had been intoxicated and led to sign an indenture without knowing what he signed, he could hardly be blamed for breaking it.

Men took chances in withdrawing from the arrangements by which they were bound. The runaways were principally servants from Great Britain, largely Irish, who came with elaborate specific agreements. The dull round of toil was monotonous, and adventure at least came from attempting to escape. Then, too, there were chances of being successful; and even if captured and returned, it only made a bad job slightly worse. Among the Germans, on the other hand, several facts reduced the runaways. The servants themselves were less impulsive and adventuresome, and they better endured the demands of exacting toil. Besides this they were not familiar with the country, the laws, or the language, and were less likely to escape if they attempted to do so. So it was that there were many runaway Irish and but few Germans.[44] The indentured system succeeded best with those foreign immigrants who were ignorant of both the language and the ways of the country.[45]

Some servants were said to have been forced to run away by illtreatment. When the time of the indenture had nearly expired, if the servant could be goaded into leaving, it was to the advantage of the master either way. If the servant were caught, he was subject to five additional days for every day of

---

[44] The nationality of runaways is given above at the close of Chapter VIII.

Benjamin Peter Hunt summarized the advertisements for runaway servants in one hundred and fifty-two numbers of the *Pennsylvania Gazette,* extending from 1752 to 1756. The total number of advertisements was 809; the number of new advertisements 444; the number of persons advertised for 551. Of the total last given, 221 were Irish, 119 were English, 100 were "Dutch," 9 were native, 9 were Welsh, 8 were Scotch, 7 were Negro, 3 were French, and the remainder of 75 had no indications as to nationality. Hunt, *Manuscripts,* I, 221, 227.

[45] Egerton, *Origin and Growth of English Colonies,* 132.

To the Worshipful the Mayor Recorder &
Aldermen now sitting in Court—
The humble Petition of William Smith

Sheweth

That your petitioner's Servant Richard Tilly has
several times during his Servitude Runaway from
your petitioner whereby he has been Oblig'd to Expend
divers Sums of Money in Apprehending him as will appear
by the Accot Annext That the sd Servants time being
near Expired humbly Prays you worship will be
pleased to Order the sd Servant to serve him such term as you shall
think reasonable in Satisfaction for the Money so Expended
And your petitioner shall pray &c—

Wm Smith

Order'd that the servt do serve his Master in his
Office seven Months beyond the time he is now Contracted
for or pay to his Master the sum of seven pounds ten
shillings in Satisfaction for the Moneys Expended

PETITION AGAINST A SERVANT WITH THE DECISION
INDORSED

[Original Historical Society of Pennsylvania. Court Papers]

Ft. 230

absence, and, moreover, had to make return for damages and expenses resulting from his leave-taking. In case the servant made good his escape, the master was gainer, for he was then freed from supplying the customary freedom dues required when the indenture was discharged.[46] Masters were self-convicted by their advertisements: servants were often insufficiently clothed and poorly cared for. The advertisements for the runaways are a sad commentary on the redemption labor system.

As slavery had its worst features in the cruel treatment accorded those who sought to escape its effects, so the indenture system shows at its worst in the study of runaways. From Alexandria, Virginia, came a news item just after the Revolution that runaway servants who had been captured were sentenced to have their hair and eyebrows shaved off and this was to be continued during the term of their service, or until they by proper behavior evidenced that they had come to a sense of their duty as servants.[47] Naturally, such disfiguring of a servant would make his capture easier if he ran away again. Runaway servants who had been returned to their masters in Pennsylvania were sometimes made to wear iron collars. Advertisements indicate that in some cases these collars had the initials of the master engraved upon them, thus treating men as dogs are treated in later days.[48] The collars were advertised as heavy and sometimes they were mentioned as having as many as four iron rivets.[49] At times the masters advertised for servants wearing iron collars as having run away, but more often the notice was of one wearing a collar having been arrested and thrown into jail.[50] Such practices as are recorded by the runaway advertisements could not but be injurious to master, servant, and community. The spirit of the early acts

---

[46] At the time of the Spanish War controversy (1740) Governor Thomas charged masters with encouraging the enlistment of servants into the king's army, when their terms had nearly expired; thus masters would not be held for the customary freedom dues. Thomas also implied that complaints for damages were made on account of the enlistments of these same servants. *Colonial Records*, IV, 441.

[47] *New York Journal*, February 16, 1786.

[48] *Ibid.*, July 31, 1776.

[49] *Ibid.*, September 21, 1773.

[50] See *New York Journal*, January 8, 1754; June 6, 1755; June 23, 1773, and May 31, 1775.

dealing with the capture, punishment, and return of runaway servants was suggestive of the spirit of the fugitive slave laws of one hundred and fifty years later. The inability of the master effectively to enforce the servant agreement because of servants absconding was one of the explanations for the disappearance of the indentured servant system.

CHAPTER XII

ENLISTMENT OF SERVANTS FOR COLONIAL WARS

White servants were subjects of the British sovereign, and when their services were needed in defense of the realm, a question arose as to how far the rights of the sovereign could override the property interests of the masters. Fighting men were required to defend the frontiers against Indian outbreaks, and to protect England's interests in the contest for colonial and commercial supremacy in the New World. It is a picture of Arcadian simplicity which Walterhausen gives of master and servant fighting side by side in the Indian and border wars, and at their conclusion going back to assume the old relation of master and servant.[1] But this picture does not correctly represent the facts for Pennsylvania. In this colony, masters were largely opposed to the wars on principle, or else they found neither interest nor inclination leading them to enlist. In a colony chiefly Quaker and German, enlistments of freemen were slow, and the recruiting officers opened their regiments to the indentured servants. Thus it was that regiments were filled up in Pennsylvania, to the surprise of those who thought of it as a colony dominated by the peace principles of the Quakers. Try as they would to have no part in war, the Quakers could not avoid it; one of their historians has termed their "holy experiment" an "oasis of peace in a desert of war;" in the eighteenth century war was so ever present and pressing a fact that it was forced upon the Quakers, and they could not avoid becoming involved. The millennium had not come. Pennsylvania was requested to furnish both men and supplies; delinquency in providing the former led to enlistment of servants, and this against the will of their masters, and, it was said, to the injury of the colony. The colonial legislature then refused the requisitions of money and supplies. The continued hostility of Quaker Assemblies was based in part on motives other than

---

[1] *Arbeits-Verfassung,* 74. Walterhausen also represents the phase of the subject in which the masters were unwilling to have servants enlist.

opposition to carnal warfare; the official proceedings of these Assemblies clearly show that they resented also the treatment accorded them in the method of carrying on the wars.

Recognition of the rights of masters as violated by the enlistment of servants appears as early as 1711, when an act was passed reciting the "great inequality and hardship which appears to fall upon such masters" as "lose their servants and yet pay proportionably their rates." This was in the act levying supplies for the queen's government. On proof of enlistment of a servant within a specified time, there was to be set aside from the sum to be raised for the queen's use an amount in satisfaction for the time and service of the servant so enlisting. A computation was to be made of what the unexpired term of service would amount to at ten shillings per month, but in no case was the total sum to be paid to exceed twenty pounds. On payment, however, the master was required to assign all interest in the indenture to the governor or to such person or persons as the governor should direct or appoint.[2] But in case an enlisted servant was returned to his master on or before the eleventh of December next following (the act was passed August 10), and also if the master was under no expense for the return and the servant was in good condition, then no payment was to be made. To make the act effective, the treasurer was empowered to retain until the first of December such money and valuables as would be sufficient to satisfy the demands likely to arise under it.[3]

The grievance of the masters by which the above act was called forth seems to have been satisfied, and in the supplementary act providing for the collection of the supplies specified by the act of 1711, no mention was made of servants.

The status of servants next came into question in 1740, when England was recruiting and equipping regiments for her war with Spain. Masters considered servants as their property, not to be taken without their permission; the recruiting officers and Governor George Thomas regarded them as the king's subjects,

---

[2] *Statutes at Large*, II, 398, 399. The preamble said that these servants had "enlisted themselves in the Queen's service in the Province of New Jersey."

[3] *Ibid.*, 399. A supplementary act of 1712-1713 makes it appear that the taxes as provided above were not collected. *Ibid.*, III, 5.

privileged to enlist for the defense of his realm if they so wished. The Pennsylvania Assembly of 1740 was controlled by the Quakers, who were not in sympathy with the war, and they were delinquent in meeting the demands placed upon them. Governor Thomas sought to comply with the requisitions for men and supplies, and this led to an open rupture between the popular Assembly and the proprietary. The quarrel began early in 1740 and continued with great bitterness for about two years, after which the feeling subsided in the four additional years that Thomas continued as governor. It was charged that the motives of the controlling party in the Assembly were "selfish and narrow"; worst of all was the hiding behind Quaker scruples to escape taxation. Neither can it be denied that Governor Thomas was injudicious; in his zeal to comply with the request of the crown he lacked diplomacy.[4]

The issue was drawn when the Assembly charged the governor with having caused the enlistment of servants; he had issued a proclamation on April 14, it was said, in which he told servants that they "were freed from their former masters, and were obliged to serve none but the King."[5] This was in a personal report to servants who had applied to the governor and expressed a desire to enlist, but Governor Thomas' official proclamation, though it did not mention servants, was entirely conclusive on the point of his wishing them to join the king's troops. The recruiting officers were "strictly enjoined" not to reveal the name of any person who should desire to have it withheld. It was announced that His Majesty would supply the troops raised with arms and clothing and they were promised pay; in addition, the king "engaged his Royal word to send all persons back to their respective habitations when the service shall be over"— adding with much meaning, "unless they shall desire to settle themselves elsewhere.[6]

Governor Thomas defended himself on the grounds that his

---

[4] For an account of this period see Gordon, *History of Pennsylvania*, 231 sqq.

[5] *Colonial Records*, IV, 453.

[6] Printed in *Pennsylvania Gazette*, April 24, 1740; cited in Geiser, *Redemptioners*, 95. The proclamation of the governor is printed also in the *American Weekly Mercury*, April 17, 1740.

directions to the recruiting officers were general, and that he did not know of the enlistment of servants; he had been informed, however, that certain men were met on their way to New York and had enlisted; these might have been servants, but if so they had already left their masters. The Assembly made much of this acknowledgment of the governor, charging that these were runaways, and that they ought to have been returned.[7]

The proclamation of Governor Thomas bore immediate results in securing men; in May petitions began to come in from Philadelphia and Chester Counties, reciting that servants had been enlisted without the permission of their masters. These petitions were taken under consideration, and a resolution passed the Assembly declaring that "the King's General Invitation" for men to enlist ought not to be understood to give power to enlist any servants who did not have the consent of their masters.[8] Advertisements for runaways early began to imply that they might have enlisted. Desertions from the king's regiments also were common, and deserters were advertised with descriptions and rewards as in the case of runaway servants.[9]

The governor redoubled his efforts to get men; on May 1 a notice appeared in the *Mercury* by the "Governor's command," directing "all such as shall be willing to enlist in the important Expedition now on foot for attacking and plundering the most valuable part of the *Spanish West Indies*," to report to various gentlemen named, and there to await the call for a general rendezvous which was to be in Philadelphia. This notice was continued on May 8 and 15; at the latter date, a letter was added urging enlistment in the following terms: "Would you make your *Names Famous!* Would you throw off your Home spun and shine in *Silver* and *Gold Lace* and *Embroidery!* Would you grow Rich at once! Would you leave Great Estates to your *posterity? Go Volunteer in this Expedition, and take the Island of Cuba.*"

The likelihood of enlistment of servants immediately affected

---

[7] *Colonial Records,* IV, 455.
[8] *Votes of Assembly,* III, 388; *Colonial Records,* IV, 453.
[9] *Pennsylvania Gazette,* July 24, 1740. Reward of forty shillings; nine men were advertised for at one time. One of these advertisements appeared as early as May 22.

sale for them, and an importer added to the other attractions of a consignment of Irish passengers that in case they should go off in the king's service, the money paid would be returned to the purchaser.[10]

For about two years the chief business of the Pennsylvania Assembly was directed to securing what were termed the rights of the inhabitants against having their property taken without their consent. Governor Thomas did not ignore the royal instructions as Patrick Gordon had done.[11] Interests and wishes of the proprietary and the popular parties were squarely at issue; then the conflict between the supremacy of an appointed governor and the will of the people, represented in their Assembly, was most intense; but to understand this conflict one must keep in mind the fact that it had been going on from the early days of the colony, and that it continued until the proprietary was abolished. President Sharpless termed the Quakers "competent politicians"; but astute as they were, they never manipulated practical politics more to their advantage than in the long struggle by which they brought Governor Thomas to terms; enlistment of servants was an incident which led to one of the most significant chapters of Quaker history.[12]

Early in the controversy Governor Thomas suggested that a bounty be given for the enlistment of freemen, but of this the Assembly at first took no notice, though when it was later called to their attention they pleaded inability to provide funds. Before these differences had arisen in Pennsylvania (i. e., April 3, 1740), a bounty of two guineas had been offered in a proclamation from the council chamber of Virginia.[13] Notice of this action must have destroyed the effect of quoting from a later declaration of Virginia's governor in council that no person making enlistments should enlist servants under any pretense whatever.[14] Governor Thomas kept to the declaration that if freemen would come for-

---

[10] *American Weekly Mercury,* July 24, 1740. Advertisement repeated in several successive issues of the paper.

[11] See above, Chapter IV.

[12] *Quaker Experiment,* 105.

[13] Letter from Williamsburg, Virginia. *Pennsylvania Gazette,* May 8, 1740.

[14] Reprinted from *Virginia Gazette* in *Pennsylvania Gazette,* May 26, 1740.

ward for enlistment, there would be no cause for complaint
against enlistment of servants; he reminded the Assembly that
when it wished for an additional amount of paper money, Pennsylvania was represented as prosperous and her trade as great,
but now, when called upon for men and supplies, the people
pretended that both their numbers and their property were inconsiderable.[15]

This is the period of all others when the Quakers "reveled
in the possession of the Assembly"; though numbering but one-
third of the population, they had and kept the majority of its
members and, what is more to the point, they made use of the
control to accomplish their own ends.[16]   That a minority of one-
third could carry elections, and retain control through years of
heated political controversy, is evidence of shrewd political management.   This might be called, as it was by George Thomas, the
"Union" among the Quakers; Governor Thomas felt sure that the
Quaker Yearly Meeting took into consideration the political
affairs of the government.[17]

Did the Quaker represent popular rights, or did an alien
population without affection for or interest in the realm of Great
Britain find Quaker scruples a convenient cloak with which to
cover their indifference?   Those who professed Quaker opposition to war as a way to escape the burdens of taxation earned
condemnation.   Such there must have been.[18]

John Wright, a Quaker member of Assembly and magis-

---

[15] *Colonial Records,* IV, 441.

[16] Governor Thomas (*Colonial Records,* IV, 442) ; Benjamin **Franklin**
described the population, by "rule of thumb," one-third Quaker, one-third
German, and one-third mixed.

President Sharpless took Dr. Shepherd to task for what he declared
to be a misstatement of the facts with regard to the "political intrigues"
of the Quakers, but after all it seems only a matter of terminology.   See
Sharpless, *Quaker Experiment,* 75, 76, for strictures on Shepherd, *Proprietary Government in Pennsylvania.*

[17] "Your Lordships may be apt to conclude, that the *Quakers,* from
their great Weight in Elections, are a Majority of the People in the
Province; but they are not one Third by the best computations I can get;
yet, from their Union, they have a much greater Influence on all publick
Affairs here than the other Societies."   Governor **Thomas'** *Letter to the
Lords of Trade,* p. 3.

[18] Egerton, *Short History of British Colonial Policy,* 171.

trate of Lancaster County, was made to suffer for his hostility to the policy of Governor Thomas. When a new commission was issued for magistrates, his name was omitted; he had news of this before the new commissions arrived and made a stirring valedictory address to the grand jury, dwelling at length on the rights of Englishmen. His closing was: "For the cause of *English liberty,* for standing in the civil defense of right and property are we dismissed; and I rejoice and am heartily glad, that I am one of those who have been thought worthy of displeasure." [19]

John Wright was continued, however, as a representative in the Assembly, and in the following June (1741) was appointed as the first member of a committee to consider a petition signed by eighty-five men, reported as "gentlemen, merchants and others," and all inhabitants of Philadelphia. These petitioners opposed the action of the Assembly, saying that there were daily reports of that most dreaded of all calamities of the time, "Spanish Privateers off the Capes"; they declared the war to be just, and credited Pennsylvania with a willing people and a treasury sufficient to provide adequate defense. Trade, they said, was already suffering and worse dangers were threatened. It was hoped that the Assembly would take these facts into account and do something that would afford relief.[20] The Assembly's disposal of this petition was summary. On June 4 it was referred, on June 5 the committee reported, and on June 6 the following resolution was passed regarding it: "That the Representation itself is extraordinary; that it insinuates facts which are in themselves untrue; . . . that it is a high insult and menace of the Assembly, a breach of their privileges, and has a Tendency destructive of their freedom and constitution; and that the same be rejected." [21] Both the wording of this resolution and the manner of its passage are indicative of the temper of the Assembly.

Beginning early in August, 1740, the Assembly at intervals stated its side in the controversy. It declared that the governor had misrepresented the condition of the treasury and Pennsyl-

---

[19] Speech printed and circulated at the time as a statement of popular rights. Given in full in Proud, *History of Pennsylvania,* II, 221-226.

[20] *Votes of Assembly,* III, 433.

[21] *Ibid.,* 435.

vania's ability to pay; the Assembly denied that Pennsylvania was rich, and said that by going no further than New York double the wealth could be found that was in Pennsylvania. The Assembly therefore refused the bounty for the enlistment of freemen. Again and again the governor was reminded that a majority of the Assembly's members were "principled against the bearing of arms, or applying money to any such purpose." However, they said they had resolved upon a sum of money "for the support of the Crown," but difficulties in collection had made it impossible to pay this. In the meantime they had noticed the enlistment of "great numbers of bought servants" to the loss and injury of the public; this it was thought "called loudly for redress"; while these considerations occupied their time, their harvest became full ripe, and even then their servants were being enlisted. Laborers, it was declared, were scarce and, except for these bought servants, difficult to be obtained.[22] The Assembly made a formal declaration of grievance and resolved to send a petition and remonstrance to the king.[23] So great was the grievance felt to be that the members said that they would be untrue to duty to appropriate money without first seeking redress.[24] Unity of interest of crown and subject, it was urged, had been violated; members of Assembly could not sit to transact its business, as they were compelled to go and take the places of the servants who had been enlisted.[25]

Governor Thomas' replies to these complaints were considered unsatisfactory. He referred to the nature of the instructions to recruiting officers, said that he was assured by the officers

---

[22] *Colonial Records,* IV, 435-438.

[23] *"Resolved,* That the Taking and Detaining of great Numbers of bought Servants from their masters, within this Province, under Pretence of enlisting them in the King's Service, is an unjust invasion on the Properties of their Masters; a Discouragement to the Trade of Importing White Servants; and a great Hurt and grievance to the Inhabitants of said Province.

"Resolved, That an humble Petition and Remonstrance be drawn up, in order to be represented to the King, praying Redress of the said Grievance." *Pennsylvania Gazette,* August 14, 1740. Extract from *Votes of Assembly.*

[24] *Colonial Records,* IV, 438.

[25] *Ibid.,* 451.

that no more servants would be enlisted if they were known to be such, and that if the servants already enlisted could be persuaded to return to their masters they would be permitted to do so—but only after freemen had come to take their places.[26] Again the governor said that he had directed officers to discharge the servants of those who had applied to him, "if they can be persuaded to return to their masters, and if it can be done consistent with the service."

Two things are to be observed throughout the whole quarrel: the Assembly claimed that industry in the colony was largely dependent on the labor of indentured servants, and the governor did not deny the claim. The following address of the Assembly is illustrative of the general contention of the colonial representatives:

"It must afford but a very melancholy Prospect to discover the Farmer and Tradesman, whose Subsistence and the Subsistence of their Families very much depend on the Labor of their Servants, purchased, perhaps, at the Expence of most they are worth, deprived of that Assistance and put under the greatest difficulties—the former to secure what he has already sown, and to cultivate and to sow what is absolutely necessary to subsist on another Year, and the latter to carry on his Trade and Business—all owing to the Caprice of the Servant and Will of an Officer, under Pretence of serving the Crown, when hardly any greater Disservice could be done it."[27]

Instead of appropriating money for the conduct of the war and attending to its usual affairs, the Assembly gave itself to ascertaining how many servants had been enlisted and to offering some sort of relief to their masters. Notice was given to all masters of servants in Philadelphia, Bucks, Chester, and Lancaster Counties that they should report any cases of grievances to the constables of their respective townships; these in turn were to report them to a committee on grievances of the Assemby.[28]

One result of the lists as above requested was to furnish

---

[26] *Ibid.,* IV, 440, 449.
[27] *Ibid.,* 437, 438.
[28] *Pennsylvania Gazette,* August 14, 1740.

information on the number of servants enlisted.   Governor
Thomas' officers reported that the numbers had been greatly exaggerated, that many men were called servants who denied this
absolutely.[29]   On the other hand, the Assembly declared that in
the seven companies raised in Pennsylvania there were several
hundred servants under indenture;[30] this claim is tolerably well
borne out by an examination of the Assembly's summary of
enlisted servants which make a total of 276.[31]   Thus out of the
goodly number of 800 men which the zeal of Governor Thomas
mustered for the king's service, approximately 300 were bond
servants.[32]

When the Assembly went into the business of making good
the losses sustained by enlistment of servants, it received promptly
numerous petitions and statements; one of these was from Anna
Nutt and Company, owners of ironworks at Coventry and Warwick.   These petitioners recited that no fewer than ten servants
had been taken from them, and that among these were the firemen
who had been instructed in their business at a considerable expense, and on whom they were dependent for supplying the
furnace with fuel when in blast.   It was affirmed that the loss
in consequence of putting a stop to the works was several hundred pounds, and the petitioners prayed for relief.[33]

These various petitions found such favor with the Assembly
that the masters were compensated to the amount of £2,588.[34]
On June 3, 1741, for example, Chester County was given upwards
of £500 for the loss of 58 enlisted servants, the form of payment
being orders on trustees of the loan office.   There was a later
additional sum of £84 11s. and, subsequent to this, two men were
given £7 10s. and £3 13s. 7d., respectively, for losses of one

---

[29] *Colonial Records*, IV, 467.

[30] *Ibid.*, 436, 437.

[31] Proud, *History of Pennsylvania*, II, 220, 221.

[32] Cheyney, *Philadelphia Manufacturer*, March 16, 1891.

George Chalmers (*Revolt of the American Colonies*, II, 205) says of
Governor Thomas's experience, "He easily raised eight hundred men in a
province into which the emigrants of Germany, of Ireland, and of Great
Britain had long run with the fullness and the rapidity of an American
river."

[33] *Votes of Assembly*, III, 432.

[34] Proud, *History of Pennsylvania*, II, 221.

servant each.[35] This method of compensating the masters was recognized as just by all the parties to the controversy; indeed, it seems to have been suggested by Governor Thomas and his council as a means of avoiding the evils incident to the enlistment of servants, for in August of 1740 the council declared its opinion that the loss suffered by the masters could be easily repaired out of the public funds, which, it was said, were sufficient to meet that expense, and to make the other provision expected by the king.[36]

This controversy blocked the usual procedure of the colonial government and no legislation was effected from 1739 to 1742. In a proposed appropriation for the civil needs of His Majesty's government there was involved the payment to the masters for servants enlisted, as in 1711; this was disapproved by Governor Thomas.[37] In the governor's report to the Board of Trade he recited his difficulties, saying that they were greater than those of any other governor in America. A whole year had been spent in fruitless disputes characterized by "an acrimony not at all agreeable to the professions of meekness and humility generally made by this people."[38] By 1742, the governor had got much

---

[35] Futhey and Cope, *History of Chester County,* 49.

[36] *Colonial Records,* IV, 469.

[37] Mentioned above.

[38] Governor George Thomas to Board of Trade.

"Your Lordships will observe, that the Assembly insinuate, that the Trade of Servants is advantageous to *Britain,* and insist upon Masters having a Property in those Servants. If that be a Property against the King, then his Majesty has, by their Entring into Indentures, lost the Service of some Thousands of his Subjects in this Province, in a War either offensive or defensive. I am sensible there is an Act of Parliament permitting Persons to transport themselves to the Plantations, by entring into Indentures with Merchants and others; but these are supposed to be Vagabonds and idle Persons: The Case is quite different with the Generality of those brought here; for Merchants and Masters of Vessels, by deluding Promises of mighty Advantages, persuade a great Number of Tradesmen to enter into Indentures with them; and, when brought here, sell them for their own Benefit, the Tradesmen not receiving *One Shilling* Wages during the whole time of a very hard Servitude; and by this Means the Inhabitants here are enabled to carry on, at a very cheap Rate, Manufactures of several Sortz, directly interfering with those of *Great Britain;* and it may be plainly seen from the Advertisements in the weekly News-Papers here, of the Sale of Servants, that they are principally Tradesmen, and not Labourers for the

the worst of the trial of strength; the Assembly held a whip hand by withholding appropriations, even for the governor's salary, declaring that they could not appropriate funds for salary until the other matters of government had received attention. The matter became personal at last and in 1742 the governor felt called upon to defend himself against "attacks," "slanders," etc., before he could attend to the public business which was laid before him.[39]

A new situation was evidenced by a news item of 1742. Servants had enlisted to go to Jamaica, but the captain of the ship on which they were to sail ordered them ashore; when they refused to go, a warrant was issued and the servants were lodged in jail. The comment on this incident is significant; enlistment, it was said, was looked upon as a great hardship on all hands, and it was a pleasure to see that the action of the recruiting officer was not approved by the government.[40]

When Governor Thomas became conciliatory, the Assembly voted him fifteen hundred pounds for salary in arrears. Necessity for further enlistments had ceased, claims of masters had been satisfied, and now the conflicting factors of colonial government began to work in harmony. The balance of Thomas's administration was fairly popular and he parted with his Assembly in 1747 on terms of good feeling.[41]

In 1752, an address was issued to the inhabitants of Pennsylvania and the adjacent provinces, and it was also particularly addressed to masters of vessels lying in the ports, asking for vigilance in taking up suspicious persons and holding them on the charge of being runaways. It was claimed that the roads were too free to those who were not known, on the plea that they were soldiers or were returning privateersmen. The excuse of war, the address said, had now passed and stragglers were to be dealt with according to the law.[42]   Three years later the threatened

---

Raising of Hemp, Flax, or manufacturing of Pot-ash, which would be of real advantage to Great Britain, and at the same time furnish the Inhabitants here with a commodity to purchase the Manufactures of their Mother Country." *Letter* dated October 20, 1740, pp. 5, 6.

[39] *Votes of Assembly*, III, 471.

[40] *Pennsylvania Gazette*, April 22, 1742.

[41] Proud, *History of Pennsylvania*, II, 230.

[42] *Pennsylvania Gazette*, July 9, 1752.

French and Indian War was referred to as an encouragement to servants to run away.

When Great Britain resolved on determined resistance to French aggression in the New World, she required from Pennsylvania three thousand recruits with necessary subsistence and transportation. The attempts to get men soon precipitated the old controversy about enlistment of servants. In September of 1755, eight months before war was formally declared, General Shirley, then in command of the British armies in America, cautioned Colonel Thomas Dunbar, recruiting regiments in Pennsylvania, against enlisting either apprentices or indentured servants. Shirley said that he had received advice on this matter and felt that the enlistment of servants would be burdensome to the people, and might prove injurious to the king's interests; he added also that he himself had observed the precaution of not enlisting servants. The letter of Shirley, with a favorable comment of Governor Robert Hunter Morris, was sent to the Assembly.[43]

In January following, however, in the absence of Governor Morris, the provincial council dispatched a letter to General Shirley, reminding him of his former orders against the enlistment of servants and saying that his officers who were recruiting in the province, and General Braddock as well, had avoided enlisting servants until about three days previously, when the sergeants had invited servants to enlist, saying that they had instructions to do so. Contentions immediately arose among the officers and the masters of the enlisted servants, and the council could not undertake to say where the affair would have ended had not the magistrates interfered and secured a promise that no new enlistments would take place until the pleasure of General Shirley could be made known. The council reminded the governor of what they said he already knew, that every kind of business, of

---

[43] *Colonial Records*, VII, 39, 40. At this time servants who tried to enlist found it difficult to do so, as appears from the *Pennsylvania Berichte*, September 16, 1755: "Many Redemptioners have joined the army in Philadelphia, they will again be delivered to their former masters. They are sharply questioned whether they are servants, but when they declare they are not, when they really are, they are whipped." Cited in Diffenderffer, *Redemptioners*, 212.

tradesman and mechanic, of planter and farmer, was chiefly carried on and supported by the labor of indentured servants, and the council hoped that the general would give an order against the enlistment of other servants and for the return of those already enlisted.[44]

The Assembly soon addressed a statement to Governor Morris, reciting all the old grievances of the Spanish War period and adding that as the province had so few slaves, it was obliged to depend principally upon servants to assist in the tilling of lands. If servants were to be taken away at the pleasure of recruiting officers, it was felt that this would be to the great harm of the colony: "Thus the growth of the country by the increase of the white inhabitants will be prevented, the Province weakened rather than strengthened (as every slave may be reckoned a domestic enemy), one great and constant source of recruits be in great measure cut off, and Pennsylvania soon be able to afford no more men for the King's service than the slave colonies now do." It was further urged that the policy of enlistment had a bad effect on servants who continued at service; the masters had to humor their servants in everything for fear they would enlist. This was daily threatened in case servants were displeased; servants were said to grow idle, neglectful, and mutinous, and to occasion many disorders in the families to which they belonged; "besides, while this practice continues," said the Assembly, "many leave their masters on pretense of going to enlist, and not being pursued, they often go off without enlisting, so the master is injured and no service arises to the King." It was felt that the practice of importing servants in the years preceding had given a sufficient number of freemen fit for service without taking the servants legally bound.

Governor Morris did not antagonize the Assembly; he merely acknowledged its claim and regretted that the conditions had arisen; he called attention to the old dispute still unsettled, and said that he would not attempt to speak on the law involved in the case.[45] The governor wrote in a different strain to General Shirley, however, and with his letter sent the address of the Assembly.

---

[44] *Colonial Records*, VI, 777, 778.
[45] *Ibid.*, VII, 37-40. "Address of Assembly," February 13, 1756.

Shirley has been termed a "worn-out barrister"[46]; he evidently knew more of law than he did of war. The Assembly's address gave him his opportunity, and he proceeded to give the arguments for the legal right of enlistment of servants. He explained the reversal of his former policy of having no indentured servants enlisted from the necessity for men and the slowness with which volunteers were forthcoming. General Shirley acknowledged the inconveniences that might arise from enlistments of servants and announced himself as ready to offer any relief consistent with His Majesty's service, but he said that when a country was in danger of being lost, it was not time to go into critical dissertations on what would be the probable effects of the enlistment of servants upon future servant importation.[47]

So far as Pennsylvania was concerned, Governor Morris dissented from the decision of General Shirley. He did not deny the legal right to take into the king's service any subject that presented himself, but he did question the expediency of taking indentured servants in Pennsylvania. More white servants, he said, were held in this colony than in any other, so the burden of their enlistment would be greater here than elsewhere. When General Shirley's argument for the legality of the action of the recruiting officers was placed before the Assembly, and it was clear that the course entered on would be followed through, the Assembly bolted and adjourned at a critical time for a whole week without giving any reason. The main features of the differences in the French and Indian War only repeat the earlier story of 1740-1742, but with this difference: the contest was with the king's officers directly, and not with the governor.

Governor Morris attempted to serve as pacificator, but on the whole he seemed rather favorable to the course of the Assembly;[48] he profited by the experience of Governor Thomas, and while he did not make himself obnoxious to the British government, neither did he antagonize the Assembly; but his task

---

[46] Bancroft, *History of the United States,* II, 443, 444.

[47] *Pennsylvania Archives,* First Series, II, 587-592.

[48] In his message of June 29, 1756, Morris did recommend the enlisting of servants, and the reimbursing of their masters, but said that he did so by order of the English government. *Colonial Records,* VII, 178; *Pennsylvania Gazette,* July 15, 1756.

was a thankless one and he retired in disappointment late in 1756.

General Shirley offered relief that was not acceptable. He said that all enlisted servants should return to their masters, if they so desired, and if their places were taken by other efficient men. He also added that it rested with the Assembly to relieve any distress arising from the enlistment of servants.[49]

The upshot of the whole matter was expressed in Governor Morris' letter saying he feared that the Assembly would be in "such temper" that it would prevent Pennsylvania from taking any part in the concerted measures for safety.[50] Pennsylvania's lack of interest in the French and Indian War, and her half-hearted support of it have long been familiar;[51] the usual explanation, generally thought adequate, has been the pronounced peace policy of the Quakers, but to this should be added the dissatisfaction consequent upon the taking away of the laborers who were regarded as property and the disregarding of the industrial and economic needs of the colony.

When General Shirley's letter of instructions against enlisting servants was received in 1755, the Assembly seemed to have clear sailing, and in November passed an act for regulating enlistments; one of the provisions of the act was that no minor, redemptioner, or indentured apprentice should be permitted to enroll in the regiments without the written consent of parents or masters.[52] This act was promptly sent to England and as promptly disallowed; in the disapproval it was directed that the governor, the Assembly, and others who might be concerned should "take notice and govern themselves accordingly."[53] Within the two years next following, the Assembly three times attempted to regulate the enlistment of servants.[54]

To prevent any colonial interference, to make enlistments more likely, and to provide return for the property interests of

---

[49] *Pennsylvania Archives,* First Series, II, 592.

[50] *Ibid.,* 576.

[51] "The Quaker legislature of Pennsylvania earned the reproaches of posterity and the execrations of its contemporaries by refusing to vote a dollar or a man for the public defense."

[52] *Statutes at Large,* V, 197-201.

[53] *Ibid.,* 532.

[54] *Ibid.,* 268, 282, and 336.

masters, Parliament in 1756 enacted that officers in the king's armies in the colonies might, as they wished, enlist any indentured servant, and were not to be bound by any colonial law, custom, or usage. The property rights of the masters were recognized in a proviso that if the former owner objected within six months, the servant was to be released, or the master recompensed as two justices of the peace should decide.[55] The provision about making return was not mandatory upon the recruiting officers; however, servants were enlisted as before, and the masters had no satisfactory recourse against the British government. As before, however, Pennsylvania undertook to take care of her own people; and in November of 1756 the clerk of the Assembly published a notice requesting a statement of losses due to enlistment of servants.[56]

In 1757, Franklin, who seemed omnipresent in this war, was sent to New York to lay before Lord Loudoun the grievance over enlistments. He reported in May that he had succeeded in getting a number of conferences with Loudoun, but could accomplish nothing. The objections Franklin said were four: (1) The larger number of servants were enlisted in the recruiting of Shirley and Braddock; (2) before the passage of the act of Parliament providing for reward, the king was entitled to the services of the redemptioners without reward to their masters; (3) proofs of men being servants were insufficient; and (4) it was not thought necessary to pay in Pennsylvania, as it was understood that the Assembly would provide for the reimbursing of masters whose servants were enlisted. Franklin did not regard these excuses as given in good faith, and attributed the failure of the British to pay to their lack of available funds.[57]

The Pennsylvania Assembly considered the cases of those whose servants were taken into the army, and passed acts affording relief. An act looking to this was passed as late as April, 1763.[58] England's failure to make return for servants taken was treasured against her, affording another cause of dissatisfaction in Pennsylvania. When Robert Walsh "appealed" from "the

[55] *29 George II,* ch. 35, secs. 1, 2.
[56] *Pennsylvania Gazette,* November 11, 1756.
[57] *Works* (Bigelow), II, 512, 513.
[58] *Colonial Records,* IX, 17, 24; Bioren, *Laws,* I, p. xxx.

judgments of Great Britain" (1819), he dismissed England's conduct and her criticism of America's dealings with Negro slavery as follows: "The act which dissolved the indentures of servants . . . is the only one in the records of the British parliament, that looked to the 'tearing of manacles' here."[59]

Much bad feeling was engendered by the Pennsylvania controversies of the Spanish War and the French and Indian War. During the latter, Dr. William Smith became an active participant and produced two powerful political tracts. In the first, which was entitled, *A Brief State of Pennsylvania,* there were set forth the "political machinations" of the Quakers and their "deals" with the Germans, by which they were enabled to keep control of the Assembly (with less than two-fifths of the population), against the wishes of both crown and proprietors.[60] *A Brief State* was published anonymously in London in 1755, and was followed a year later by a sequel entitled *A Brief View of the Conduct of Pennsylvania for the year 1755.* In the latter, Smith spoke of the effects of the first pamphlet as of a "clap of thunder"; the Quakers, he said, "were not accustomed to such plain dealing." [61] As might be expected, these pamphlets called forth letters in the newspapers and counter pamphlets; *Brief State* and *Brief View* were also attacked in the Assembly and termed libels. But in 1756 the Quakers retired from the Assembly and from this time exercised less and less influence in the government.

Other colonies were involved in England's policy of enlisting servants. Protests against General Shirley's recruiting a regiment with servants in Kent County, Maryland, extended to insolence and bloodshed.[62] In 1756, George Washington wrote to the governor of Virginia, referring to the act of Parliament which

---

[59] Walsh, *Appeal,* 319.

[60] Original edition, pp. 12, 13, 28, 29, 36, 37. See also from German side in Rupp, *History of Northampton, Lehigh and Other Counties,* 10. See also Douglass, *British Settlements,* in which Quakers were put down as one-fourth of the population, and were said "artfully" to persuade the Germans to join with them by making them believe that other people would impose the militia law upon them and get them into war. Vol. II, p. 326. By these measures the Quakers were said to keep about three-fourths of the Assembly.

[61] *Brief View,* 7.

[62] *Pennsylvania Gazette,* February 26, 1756.

gave compensation to masters whose servants had gone into the royal service. Washington mentioned the authority to Lord Loudoun, and urged the enlistment of servants in the Virginia volunteers; these servants, it was said, *would* enlist, and if no provision was made for their enlistment in the volunteers, they would run off and enlist in the regulars. Should the permission required be granted, Washington felt that he could soon complete the regiment. Later, Washington wrote again, saying that he had already enlisted more than fifty servants, and he asked how the masters were to be paid, as he was daily appealed to for the payment. Dinwiddie answered Washington that the masters were to be paid for the time which the servants had yet to serve, basing the computation on their purchase price. He also cautioned against the enlistment of convicts, as these were "factious" and would have a bad influence on the other men.[63]

At the opening of the Revolutionary War, Dunmore, the royal governor of Virginia, raised the British flag and declared freedom to all, including "indentured servants, negroes and others appertaining to rebels," on condition of their joining to reduce the colony "to a proper sense of its duty."[64] This attempt to hold the colonies to the king's cause proved abortive, though Washington looked upon it as dangerous. "That man," said he, speaking of Dunmore, "will be the most formidable enemy of America if some expedient cannot be hit upon to convince the servants and slaves of the impotency of his designs."[65] Washington spoke after an experience in enlisting servants in the French War.

In less than a month after the battle of Lexington, the Pennsylvania Board of War adopted a minute in which they made reference to a recommendation of the Congress that the different state legislatures authorize the enlistment of apprentices and serv-

---

[63] Washington's *Writings* (Sparks), II, 169, 199.

[64] Bancroft, *History of the United States,* IV, 317, 318.

Minute of the Pennsylvania Council of Safety, December 14, 1775. "David Owen, a Person Suspected of enlisting Negroes, was brought before this Committee, and not giving proper and Satisfactory answers to the questions put to him, *Resolved,* that he be committed to the Work House of this city 'till further orders." *Colonial Records,* X, 427.

[65] Cited by Geiser, *Redemptioners,* 100, 101.

ants for completing the regiments then being raised. The Pennsylvania legislature was not then in session, but the Supreme Executive Council and the Board of War were entirely agreed on the propriety and necessity of the proposal for enlistments, and further resolved that they did "esteem it their duty to use their influence (if necessary), with the Legislature, as soon as convened, to pass a law to make full compensation to such Masters of apprentices and servants, as have or may suffer by this necessary measure being carried into execution." [66]

With the foregoing resolution was embodied a recommendation that for the future no apprentices be enlisted if they were under sixteen years of age. In January of the following year, a Philadelphia blacksmith complained that an apprentice, for whom he had "paid a consideration," had been taken into the Continental service without his permission; after inquiry the Council of Safety ordered that the apprentice should be discharged.[67] The Board of War, in April, 1777, directed that an enlisted apprentice should be dismissed from the army. The recommendations of the Congress, and the state committees of government, had regard for property rights in servants. The Council of Safety, on September 19, 1776, passed a resolution as follows: "That indentured servants and apprentices ought not to be enlisted for the Flying Camp of this State, without Consent of their Masters in writing, and that all who have been enlisted heretofore, shall be discharged on the application of their Masters for that Purpose." [68]

Even these precautions and provisions did not pass unchallenged. A committee of Cumberland County met at Shippensburg in May, 1777, and memorialized on servants as property, dwelling on the rights of mankind and the violation of the constitution and laws of the state by enlistments of servants. The Shippensburg committee asked for the confirmation of the resolutions of the Congress by the Assembly. In addition, they asked for the return of apprentices and indentured servants who had already enlisted.[69] The Assembly took the matter into considera-

[66] *Pennsylvania Archives,* Second Series, I, 42.

[67] *Colonial Records,* X, 470.

[68] *Ibid.,* 723, 724.

[69] *Pennsylvania Archives,* First Series, V, 340.

tion and, on March 12, 1778, passed an act giving compensation to all masters whose servants had enlisted.[70] This act concluded the official dealings with enlistments of servants in Pennsylvania.

[70] Bioren, *Laws,* I, p. xlvii.

PART V. CONCLUSION

CHAPTER XIII

LATER HISTORY AND DISAPPEARANCE OF REDEMPTION LABOR

The American Revolution and the years immediately following are in contrast with the earlier periods of Pennsylvania's history—a contrast expressed alike in industrial, social, and political affairs. Attendant upon the separation from England and the discussion by which this was brought about, there was a new sentiment on the rights of man which was shown first in the voluntary manumission of slaves in the early stage of the Revolution and later in acts for the gradual abolition of slavery. In the same period the Pennsylvania Abolition Society was organized, and finally an attempt was made for the better regulation of the servant system. The separation from England was followed also by an era of unusual industrial activity.

During the Revolution, importation of servants was so largely interfered with that by 1783 the redemption system might almost be said to have disappeared; the exception to this was in the children who had been indentured for long terms at the outbreak of the war. No sooner was the war closed, however, than efforts were redoubled for the establishment anew of the redemption trade, and again the efforts were directed principally to Ireland and Germany. English ships were employed in this importation until Parliament enacted that no English ship should carry persons for servitude.[1] By 1785, a new chapter had been opened both in the British relations to North American trade, and in the regulation of trade by the United States.

An illuminating comment on this new situation occurs in

---

[1] 26 of George III, ch. 67. Walterhausen (*Arbeits-Verfassung,* 66) says that the motive that prompted this law was not humanitarian, and he implies that England's purpose was to weaken, cripple, and punish her former colonies and, if possible, to win by competition the trade which she had lost by a stupid colonial policy and the arbitrament of arms.

254

AN INDENTURE MADE BEFORE THE REGISTER OF
GERMAN PASSENGERS

the letters of the British Consul, Phineas Bond, written from Philadelphia from 1787 to 1794.[2] These letters have an increased historical value from the fact that the writer was born and reared a Philadelphian, and spoke with an intimate knowledge of the practices preceding the Revolution. Bond first referred to this subject in 1788, expressing pleasure that steps had been taken to check the seducing of emigrants, and said that he was sure that strict attention to the means by which passengers were secured would show that very improper schemes were practiced. Unwary natives were decoyed from Britain, only to find that "the door of competence and comfort was shut against them forever."[3] The difficulties in regulating the trade were recognized by Bond: he said that the English Constitution would not permit direct restraints upon the right of British subjects to remove if they chose so to do. But restraints, he felt, were possible in requiring better provision for the comfort of those who came, thus lessening the profits from the trade and discouraging its continuance. Reference was made to the "wise and humane provisions" for the regulation of the slave trade, and it was thought only just that these be extended "to relax the rigor of Egyptian taskmasters towards their white slaves."[4]

Pennsylvania's later provisions for regulating the redemption system were first expressed in the act of 1785. An office of registry was established for all German passengers. Records were kept of the indentures by which they bound themselves for their transportation, and of the transference of these indentures; moreover, the duties of register were to be performed by an officer familiar with both the English and the German languages. The indentures were to be certified to, as well as recorded, and all persons who were concerned in them were entitled to a copy or abstract of the register.[5] (An agreement under this act is shown opposite.)

---

[2] *Annual Reports of American Historical Association,* 1896 and 1897.

[3] *American Historical Association Report,* 1896, 586.

[4] *Ibid.,* 586, 587.

[5] Bioren, *Laws,* II, 328, 329, 522.

The register by which German servants were bound was kept from 1785 to 1831. (Two manuscript volumes of the original three are in the Library of the Historical Society of Pennsylvania.)

The law went promptly into operation. Lewis Weiss petitioned to be chosen first register, but the appointment was postponed to permit "the German Society to make a recommendation
of a suitable person." Lewis Farmer was later appointed.[6] The
register of German passengers worked in conjunction with the
health officer, but the abuses of the old trade continued. Bond
reported that the condition and treatment of passengers were the
consequences of great encouragement given to emigration from
Europe. He felt that regulation could not be left to Pennsylvania, for, although salutary laws were passed, these were evaded;
vessels were crowded and food was inadequate.[7] Later (1790)
Bond forwarded a paper which afforded, he said, "a sad speci-
men of the brutal treatment of indentured servants," and which
he thought, if it were widely distributed, would serve to discourage a "wretched race of people from leaving their homes." [8]

Migrations from Ireland were a source of grave concern
to both Phineas Bond and the government which he represented.
In 1788 and 1789, the numbers of Irish who came are reported
to have been greater than those from all other ports of Europe
combined, though it was thought at this time that the numbers
were decreasing.[9] Bond kept close watch on Pennsylvania's different movements to get immigrants and reported promptly such
efforts as were made. He sent word in January, 1790, that he
was sure attempts would be made the following summer to draw
a large number of people from Ireland, and he presumed that
these would succeed if obstacles were not at once put in the way.
In the same connection assertion was made that New Castle,
Wilmington, and Philadelphia were chief of the ports into which
servant passengers were brought; "there are," said he, "no other
ports of the United States now engaged in this traffic." [10] On
the first of November following, Bond reported, "The number
of passengers imported this summer into the Delaware from
Ireland I am happy to find falls very short of the general ex-

---

[6] *Colonial Records*, XIV, 445, 447.

[7] *American Historical Association Report*, 1896, 643.

[8] *Ibid.*, 1897, 455. The reference was to the condition of immigrants
after arrival.

[9] *Ibid.*, 1896, 586, 643.

[10] *Ibid.*, 1897, 455.

pectation." "However," said he, "the number is important; many hundreds of useful inhabitants have landed here and the trade is eagerly pursued." Of the preceding summer's traffic he wrote, "Some complaints of ill-treatment on the passage having been made by the passengers in one vessel, a society of persons established here for the encouragement of Irish emigrants have interposed and have prosecuted the master of the vessel under the old law of Pennsylvania regulating the passenger trade." [11]

The gain to the United States through reception of emigrants and the loss to Great Britain from their departure were thus set forth by Bond in 1791: "The passenger trade from Gt. Britain and Ireland is a constant source of population and advantage to this country, manufactures are frequently introduced thro' this channel; besides we suffer a severe depopulation and America derives vast benefit from it:—already upwards of 4,500 passengers have arrived this season in the Delaware from Ireland alone; —more are expected here, and other vessels with passengers are destined for Maryland and South Carolina." [12] The price of passage at this time had become very low and the profits of a voyage were precarious. Favorable weather and a short passage would bring a return, but a tedious passage might result in little or no gain. Bond again recommended that obstacles in the nature of regulations of the passage be imposed, urging that this would serve the double purpose of correcting abuses for those who came, and of limiting the number secured by making the gains precarious.[13] Toward the close of 1791, this faithful servant, ever zealous for the interests of Great Britain, sent to his government a list of the vessels which had arrived that year on the Delaware, and, so far as he could ascertain, in the other ports of the United States. The accompanying letter referred almost apologetically to his numerous former reports and recommendations: "The number of passengers is sufficient to confirm the anxiety I have always expressed upon this important subject; the rage for migration which now prevails excites well-grounded fears that some of the northern counties of Ireland will be depopulated unless a seasonable interposition be made to correct this alarming evil; and, my

---

[11] *Ibid.*, 464, 465.
[12] *Ibid.*, 488.
[13] *Ibid., in loc. cit.*

Lord, I conceive with great humility the plan of reform I submitted to the Government in 1788 might under some modifications prove salutary." [14]

Phineas Bond attempted to frighten his government with the specter of American competition; in nearly every direction, he said, the United States was aiming to compete in matters which affected Great Britain's best interests. The United States, "tho' but an infant rival," was nevertheless already regarded as "the avowed rival" of Great Britain; the rivalry was shown first in the attempt to secure population at the expense of the mother country. After dwelling on the evils of losing skilled workmen, Bond continued: "The penalties which are imposed upon persons contracting with or seducing artificers might be increased and extended to all handicraftmen and labourers as well as to individuals of every description. . . . The spirit of migration has gone forth, it is encouraged not only by shipowners and shipmasters engaged in the passenger trade but by societies formed here to encourage emigrants, at the head of which are extensive landholders who by this adventitious increase of the population secure rapid and enormous fortunes." [15]

The Irish immigration was later noted by a traveler who visited Philadelphia in 1796. Report was that in that year the immigration had been large; the traveler said that he had left a vessel full of passengers from Ireland at Baltimore; he found three other vessels at New Castle and one at Philadelphia. It was claimed that there could not have been fewer than two hundred and fifty passengers to each vessel, and all of these had arrived within six weeks.[16]

The account thus far has been from the side of the demand for Irish immigrants. In this connection some notice should be taken of conditions in Ireland. Arthur Young, in his *Tour in Ireland,* dwelt on the heavy emigration from Ulster and County Antrim, emigration which was at its height, he said, in 1772-1773. Some of those who went had money, but most were poor people and some were characterized as "dissolute and idle" and of such

[14] *Ibid.,* 493.

[15] *Ibid.,* 566, 567.

[16] Priest, *Travels,* 146.

a sort as would not be missed at home.[17]   The desire for emigration continued; in 1782, Reuben Harvey wrote from Cork to Benjamin Franklin, then in France, to the effect that about one hundred poor tradesmen and husbandmen had offered themselves under indenture for passage to America, but the uncertainty of the policy of the United States deterred the captain of a ship about to sail from taking them.[18]

The way began to open, however, in the next year.   Notice of the arrival of three hundred and fifty Irish was followed by this statement: "We also learn that the inhabitants of the Isle of Great Britain and Ireland are panting earnestly after the milk and honey of this promised land, and that nothing but the want of means prevents them from emigrating in tens of thousands." [19] A little over a year later, a letter from Ireland commented on the desire for emigration, saying that not one-half of those who wanted to go could be carried.[20]   A Dublin letter saw in the "vast emigration" from North Ireland an "alarming tendency." [21]

The "dangerous spirit of emigration" was declared to have been revived in Ireland in 1789, and the London correspondent of the *Packet* said that the call was loud for some form of Parliamentary interference.[22]   In 1793, a Philadelphian received the information that the government was stopping the emigration from Ireland of servants under indenture; only those were permitted to come who could pay the passage.[23]   Later, American vessels were actually detained in Irish ports and ordered not to take tradesmen, seamen, and other able bodied men for the New World.[24]

The Scotch emigration, though not so extensive as the Irish, was carried on at the same time and in much the same way.   A Scotch emigrant from Aberdeen reappeared in that city after an absence of two years, well dressed and in evident good circumstances.   His improved worldly estate was a source of surprise,

---

[17] Young, *Tour in Ireland,* London Edition: 1780, Part I, p. 139.
[18] Franklin, *Writings* (Smyth), I, 204, 205.
[19] *Pennsylvania Packet,* August 7, 1783.
[20] *Ibid.,* November 19, 1784.
[21] *Ibid.,* June 27, 1786.
[22] *Ibid.,* October 6, 1789.
[23] *American Daily Advertiser,* May 22, 1793.
[24] *Ibid.,* June 29, 1795.

but he immediately showed commissions which he had brought from merchants and planters in the New World to secure artisans, manufacturers, and laborers. A poor girl had shipped as a servant from Aberdeen, had married well, and later returned to her native city and lived with such a show of wealth that others wished to go to the new land of opportunity. These and like incidents were of marked effect in stimulating emigration from the region of Aberdeen.[25]

The large emigration of passengers under indenture continued down to the time of the disturbed trade relations caused by the Embargo of 1807. West Scotland and North Ireland were the sections that supplied the largest shipments. Thirty thousand a year are believed to have come; fourteen thousand is the record of the Philadelphia ships alone in 1807. Comments were frequent at this time concerning the overcrowding of ships, and the evils practiced could be compared with the evils of the slave trade.[26]

The trade in German servants following the Revolution was in direct contrast with the Irish and Scotch passenger trade. For the earlier years after the war the number of Irish passengers was much larger than was the number of Germans, though a small proportion of Germans arrived in Philadelphia and were able to redeem themselves on arrival. Bond reported in 1788 that there was almost a total cessation of German immigration, due to restrictive measures in the Palatinate and other German states, and to difficulties in securing passage. The few who came, it was said, left their states by stealth, and secured passage in Holland.[27]

Reasons are obvious why Bond wished to make the British immigration appear large and the German small. There are numerous indications that his report on the German servant sys-

---

[25] *Pennsylvania Packet,* November 18, 1784.

[26] *American Advertiser,* April 30, 1808.

[27] *American Historical Association Report, 1896,* p. 643. From the close of the war, Bond gave the total of redemptioners and servants as 25,716, and of these 1,893 were given as German. In 1788, to the time of his writing, the total was 2,176, of whom 114 were given as German.

tem did not properly represent its proportions.[28]   An Amsterdam letter of 1791 showed the German servant trade to be large. Companies of three or four hundred came down at one time to get passage, and the belief was expressed that the shipments would be larger than ever, for, it was said, the German princes, fearing the dire results of a revolution, had granted their subjects more liberty, which liberty was used in many cases for leaving the country altogether.[29]

President Washington, in 1792, commented favorably on securing German servants for public work in a letter to the commissioners for building the Federal City.   An earlier letter of the commissioners detailed the failures of attempts to import laborers from Scotland and Ireland. Washington expressed himself as apprehensive for the future; if the next work in the city were not pushed with vigor, he said, enemies of the project would give it its deathblow, or a wound from which it would not easily recover.   Greater economy and the certainty of having labor for a term of years made it expedient, Washington felt, to import workmen.   He said that upon inquiry he found that neither in Philadelphia nor in Holland would merchants enter into a contract to bring redemptioners from Germany, and he recommended that an agent—a German who was acquainted with the country— be secured to engage the number and sort of laborers desired. Merchants in the ship trade to Holland would bring these over, but the difficulty was to get them to the seaports.[30]   Nothing came of this suggestion, as nothing came of Washington's earlier request for Palatines to settle his lands on the Ohio River.

---

[28] Menzel (*History of Germany,* III, 447) goes to the other extreme in a statement that from 1770 to 1791 there landed at Philadelphia, on an average, twenty-four German emigrant ships annually.   The same statement is made by Geiser (*Redemptioners,* 39, 40) on authority of Franz Löher, *Geschichte und Zustände.*

Hunt's summaries of servant vessels advertised in the *Pennsylvania Packet* and the *Daily American Advertiser* are as follows: 1782, none; 1783, 3—one from London, one from Great Britain and one place of shipment not indicated; 1785, 6—four from Amsterdam and two from Hamburg; 1787, 4—one each from Cork, Hamburg, Amsterdam, and Rotterdam; 1788, none; 1789, 2—one each from Londonderry and Amsterdam. *Manuscripts,* Vol. V, pp. 75, 101, 111, 135.

[29] *Pennsylvania Packet,* April to June, 1791.

[30] Washington, *Writings* (Sparks), XII, 305-308.

The industrial activity of Pennsylvania had been exceptional for forty years preceding the Revolution (see Chapter IV), but in the time immediately following the war it was even more remarkable. It was said that from 1790 to 1793 more money was expended in Pennsylvania for the improvement of roads and rivers and the cutting of canals than had been devoted to this purpose in the entire period from 1681 to 1790.[31] The trade of Pennsylvania for the latter part of the century assumed unusual proportions. For the year ending September 30, 1793, the amount of Pennsylvania's exports was near to $7,000,000, or more than one-fourth of the amount of the total exports of the country.[32] Coxe's account of the produce of the state gave a most impressive list of articles; their variety had grown with the growth of colony and commonwealth. This was not without influence upon immigration. Coxe said that the purpose of his *Summary View* was "to exhibit to the inhabitants of the populated districts of other states, and to foreigners, the real advantages to be realized by trade and manufactures in Pennsylvania." [33]

Labor conditions in Pennsylvania in the latter part of the eighteenth century were noted and described by various European travelers, as well as by Coxe. Cooper, who was in the state in 1793, wrote that land was then cheap and labor dear. He said that masters had only a slight command over their hired servants, as these had the alternative of becoming farmers on their own account. Cooper described the industry of Pennsylvania as largely agricultural, the staple commodities being the immediate products of the soil.[34] Exceptions, however, were made in the manufacture of stockings, paper, and certain heavy kinds of iron.[35]

---

[31] Coxe, *View*, 60, note.

[32] *Ibid.*, 76, 478.

[33] Heading of Chapter IV of Coxe's *View*, 57. See Coxe, 57 to 74, for an account of the productions.

[34] Cooper, *America*, 1, 2.

[35] *Ibid.*, 59, 60. In his description of the agricultural conditions in the country, Cooper seems to have recognized the economic law of diminishing returns in agriculture. He pointed out that in America there was less grain produced per acre than in England, but far more was produced per man, and he contrasted the carelessness of the American agriculturist with the accuracy and carefulness of the English cultivator. *America*, 114.

The rights of education for children under indenture were recognized in a law passed early in 1810. Masters were required to give six weeks of schooling for every year of service. It was made the duty of the register to insert this provision in the indentures.[36] This law, however, only gave legal sanction to a custom that had been practiced for many years. Schooling for redemption children began to be mentioned in the indentures as early as 1785, and before 1810 had become common. Among the Lutherans, the custom went further than the law; their indentures provided that children be taught the catechism and confimed in the Church.

The final provision for the regulation of importation of German servants was in 1818. By this it was ordered that a bill of lading be given to passengers for all goods transported with them, under pain of one hundred dollars for neglect. The passengers, on the arrival of their ship, were to be set on shore with their goods, when they had paid the price upon which they had agreed in Europe, and there was to be no extra charge for landing; the fine for violation of this provision was fifty dollars. All indentures were to be acknowledged before the mayor of Philadelphia, except in the case of German passengers, for whom they were to be acknowledged before the register. An indenture separating a husband and wife without their mutual consent was void.[37] Persons bound to serve in the state were not to be sold out of it against their will, on penalty of a hundred dollars' fine. The captains of ships were to give proper food and drink to their passengers and to provide care for them for thirty days after arrival. Sick passengers were to be removed from the ship and cared for, if they were able to be moved; if not, they were to be cared for on shipboard. The penalty for the violation of the latter provision was five hundred dollars. The captains were compelled by law to report upon all passengers whom they shipped; an accounting was required for those who died on the voyage and on shipboard after arrival, and, if such accounting were not made within fifteen days, a penalty of three hundred dollars was fixed. In case of the death of a passenger in transit, a just accounting of his goods was to be rendered by the ship captain to the register of

---

[36] Bioren, *Laws*, V, 113.
[37] *Ibid.*, VII, 29-31.

wills for the benefit of the heirs, or creditors, of the deceased; a penalty for violation of this provision was five hundred dollars. That no uncertainty should arise in enforcing the above, the register of German passengers was empowered to collect the penalties. In conclusion, it was directed by the Pennsylvania legislature that the governor of Pennsylvania transmit a copy of the act above described to the governor of Delaware, with a request that he lay the same before his legislature and invite coöperation to make the legislation more effective.[38]

In the later period, the register of German passengers received from the health officer a license stating what persons were in physical condition to be landed. They were then received and record was made of their indentures. The register in turn reported to the secretary of the commonwealth.[39]

---

[38] *Ibid.*, 31-34. The next year a law was passed by the federal government limiting the shipment to two passengers for every five tons burden of a ship. See *American Daily Advertiser,* December 19, 1818, and March 18, 1819.

[39] *The Pennsylvania Journal* for January 3, 1784, had a statement signed by Benjamin Rush, and one other man, saying that with the health officer they had often been on immigrant ships from Great Britain, Ireland, and other parts of the world.

The quotations below indicate the way certificates were issued:

"Health Office, October 5, 1815.
"Sir,

I do hereby certify that Captain Benjamin X. Hamson, of the Ship Baloon, has entered Twenty Five passengers from Amsterdam, the whole of them in perfect hearty condition.

James Ph. Puglian,
Health Officer.

"Andw. Latineau, Esquire,
Register of German Passengers."
From original MS. in Library of Historical Society of Pennsylvania.
Preserved in *Registry of Redemptioners,* Book C.

"Health Office, Philadelphia, March 10, 1824.
"To J(acob) F. H(oeckley),
Register of German Passengers,

I do hereby report, that I have received all the above named passengers (25 in number) on board of Ship JANE

The redemption system declined early in the nineteenth century. There were changed conditions in Europe. At the conclusion of the Napoleonic wars large numbers of men were discharged and sought new homes. The introduction of the factory system found those who were unable, or unwilling, to adjust themselves to the new methods of production, and many of these emigrated to America. These emigrations gave freemen in larger numbers for the supply of the labor demand of Pennsylvania. It was found by the employers of labor that it was cheaper to hire when laborers were needed than it was to keep servants the year around. Increased population within the state also aided, but the principal reason for the disappearance of the redemption labor system was that a better class of laborers was introduced from Europe. The same law held here as had earlier held between white servants and slaves: the most efficient labor was the cheapest.

A new intelligence office was advertised in Philadelphia in 1813 and those who wished to dispose of indentured servants were requested to call and have them registered so that information could be given to purchasers. The invitation was also made to free laborers to become registered for employment.[40]

The indentured system continued much later than is generally supposed. Indeed, it did not disappear until near the close of the first third of the nineteenth century. Dr. Hiram Corson, formerly of Montgomery County, stated late in the nineteenth century, at a meeting of the Historical Society of Pennsylvania, that he could vividly recall the passage of droves of redemptioners past the Plymouth Meeting House near Norristown. The records which are preserved in the registry of redemptioners close in

---

John Smith, arrived this day at the Port of Philadelphia from Amsterdam, and that none of them are superannuated
, or otherwise likely to become chargeable to the Public, but all of them are sound, without any defects in mind and body.

William Mandr
Health Officer."

MS. in Library of Historical Society of Pennsylvania.
Preserved in *Registry of Redemptioners*, Book C.

[40] *American Daily Advertiser*, August 19, 1813.

1831.[41] But many of the indentures for the later years of the system show the apprentice as well as the redemption feature.

It is worthy of note that legislation dealing with redemptioners was never directed avowedly to restricting their importation. Measures were humanitarian, regulative, corrective, but were not calculated to exclude these laborers. When the system disappeared, it was not directly legislated out of existence as was slavery. This form of labor declined rapidly after the act for the abolition of imprisonment for debt. The latter act has been termed the "legal deathblow" to redemption labor, for there was no longer the means of compelling absconding servants to fulfill their contracts.[42] Moreover, indentured immigrants were not required to supply the economic demand for labor.[43]

---

[41] The entries had grown fewer and fewer. At times the system seemed to have stopped, and yet it had further recurrence. For illustration, there is no record from September 10, 1827, to October 15, 1828, and nothing from 1829 to 1831. Frederick Kapp, in his study, *Immigration* (p. 12) states that we do not hear of the sale of indentured servants after 1819.

[42] Geiser, *Redemptioners*, 42.

[43] The later history of the redemption system in Maryland is similar to the account of it in Pennsylvania. In regard to legislation for and sentiment toward redemptioners Maryland seems to have adopted the policy of control that was exercised in Pennsylvania. The time for which the redemptioner could be bound was reduced, registration was required, and general supervision given. The last act of the German Society of Maryland for aiding redemptioners was in 1819. Hennighausen says that the system died out there about 1820, giving as a reason that public sentiment was against it. (*Redemptioners and the German Society of Maryland.*) Two other factors might be added: public sentiment in Maryland was not averse to employing slave labor, and the labor market there was in part supplied by freemen.

CLOSING RECORD IN REGISTRY OF REDEMPTIONERS

[From Original *Registry,* Historical Society of Pennsylvania]

CHAPTER XIV

RESULTS OF WHITE SERVITUDE IN PENNSYLVANIA

Different points of view could but furnish varying opinions on what have been variously termed the iniquities and the blessings of indentured and redemption labor. Blessings such labor sometimes brought, but it also brought temporary, and often continued, misery. That it was less iniquitous than was Negro slavery can be readily granted; that it was not seemingly necessary, or that Pennsylvania could have been so quickly and satisfactorily developed without it, is not so evident. It was neither an unmixed good nor an unmixed evil.

Some who have touched on this subject have taken the pleasant view that there was no discredit attending indentured service. Forbears of well-known and highly respected Pennsylvania families were of those who by service redeemed themselves from the debt for their passage. Lists of what have been termed "the noble names of redemptioners" furnish personages from Pennsylvania no less notable than Charles Thomson, clerk of the Continental Congress during the Revolution, and George Taylor, one of the signers of the Declaration of Independence.[1]

George Taylor was an Irish lad whose father wished him to study medicine, but he disliked school and ran away with but a shilling in his pocket. The boy found passage on a servant ship to Philadelphia, and after arrival was sold to the proprietor of the Durham furnace located below Easton. Here he was put at shoveling charcoal and ore into the furnace, but his master soon took pity on him and asked him if he could handle a pen better than a shovel. Taylor's education and pleasing manners made him popular and he continued for some years with his master. After the master's death he was retained and later mar-

---

[1] According to Harley, the Thomson children were separated at New Castle, 1739, and the author adds, "It was quite possible that they were bound to serve as redemptioners." *Life of Charles Thomson* (Philadelphia, 1900), 20.

ried the widow of his former employer and became the proprietor.
Taylor amassed a considerable fortune and bought a large estate
in Northampton County.   He was elected to the Pennsylvania
Assembly in 1764, and was active in the affairs of the colony
from 1764 to 1770.   For five years he withdrew from public life
and gave himself to the introduction of the iron industry into the
back country.   In 1775, the issues of the Revolution called Taylor
from retirement, and he was again elected to the Assembly, and
by the Assembly was sent to the Continental Congress, where he
was one of the "Signers." [2]

Even more spectacular than the preceding was the career of
another Irish lad, Matthew Lyon by name.   Lyon's boyhood home
was in Dublin, where, as a boy, he read Burke's *European Settlements* and other descriptions of the New World.   In contrast
with the opportunities set forth in these books, he saw the eviction
of tenants in Ireland, and the hardship and misgovernment of
the Irish.   Lyon met a sea captain who was to sail for New York
and entered into an agreement to work his way over as a cabin
boy.   He gave this captain a guinea for safe-keeping until they
should reach their destination.   The captain appropriated Matthew
Lyon's guinea, and when they reached New York held the boy
for sale as a redemptioner.[3]

Lyon reached New York at the time of the Stamp Act ex-
citement and was soon sold to a Connecticut merchant, who in
turn transferred his indenture to a native of Vermont, receiving
a pair of stags valued at twelve pounds.   Lyon worked out a
part of his time and bought the balance.   He continued his studies
and rose rapidly.   He married a niece of Ethan Allan, became an
ardent patriot, and fought in the Continental Army during the
Revolution.   Following the Revolution, Matthew Lyon continued
his interest in public life and was chosen a member of Congress,
where his hot temper made him a "mark" in the political controversies of the time.   Lyon's favorite oath was "By the bulls

---

[2] Sanderson, *Signers of the Declaration of Independence* (revised and
edited by Robert T. Conrad, Philadelphia, 1846) ; Hazleton (*Declaration
of Independence and its History,* 305) points out that George Taylor was
not in the Continental Congress on July 4, 1776, and that he was not elected
to that body until July 20, though his name is appended to the Declaration.

[3] McLaughlin, *Matthew Lyon* (New York, 1900), 36-40.

that redeemed me." Federal rhymesters sneered at him as an Irish adventurer who had been "bought for a pair of stags," and the matter came to a personal encounter with one Griswold on the floor of the House in 1798, known as the "first fight in Congress." Lyon showed that he was able to take his own part. In the Adams administration his conduct was peculiarly objectionable. In 1798, he published a paper entitled "The Scourge of Aristocracy," and John Adams was said to have secured the passage of the Sedition Law to protect himself from the fierce attacks of Lyon and those like him. Lyon was tried, convicted, sentenced to imprisonment, and placed under a fine of one thousand dollars. He was reelected to Congress while still in prison, and was popularly known as "the Hampden of Congress."

Of settlers in the early period, those who took indentures often fared much better than did those who bought land at once. The indentured servants were trained to industry, familiarized themselves with the ways of the country, and many of them became rich, while some of those who came with money and purchased estates immediately were not able to adjust themselves to the new conditions and lost their means.[4] Jefferson, writing of the system in 1786, said that it was common for those who had sufficient funds to pay their passage and buy a farm, to enter into indentures "to learn the husbandry of the country."[5] By such a course immigrants obtained a training for colonial industry, learned values, as well as ways and customs, and in the end were safer in their investments.

Jonathan Dickinson, writing about 1720, said that many redemptioners turned out to be frugal and industrious citizens, and that many persons of means originally saw service under inden-

---

[4] Smith, *History of New Jersey* (Edition of 1890), 103; see also Kalm, *Travels*, I, 389.

Hugh Mill, in a work on *New Lands: Their Resources and Prospective Advantages* (Griffin & Co., London, 1902), gives this advice to prospective settlers: "No newcomer in any country should invest money or start any new enterprise on his own account until he has resided some little time in the place and has become familiar with the peculiarities of the climate and resources and with the mode of life which the experience of earlier comers has proved to be the best." Cited in *Bulletin* of the Bureau of American Republics, April, 1902, pp. 559, 560.

[5] Jefferson, *Writings* (Ford), IV, 159.

ture.[6]   Women who came as servants were enabled to advance
their station, and sometimes canceled their indentures by marrying
into the families of their masters.   Observation on advances in
station led a Quaker traveler early in the nineteenth century to
say, "I noticed many families, particularly in Pennsylvania, of
great respectability both in our Society and amongst others, who
had themselves come over to this country as redemptioners, or
were the children of such." [7]

The success of those who had been redemptioners was so
marked that one feels like finding in this a justification for their
privation and toil.   The redemptioners' school of experience was
severe, but it fitted him for the exacting demands of claiming a wilderness, and if health were not broken, those who completed indentures were well prepared to carve out fortunes in the New World.
Thousands of redemptioners achieved success.   If a servant were
a deserving man he lost no caste by reason of his service.   Many
of those around him were working as hard as he was to repay
their borrowed money, or to pay for the lands or other valuables
which they had purchased.   The servant's situation was not different; he was only paying a debt which had voluntarily been
incurred.

Indentures offered the means of passage to many who otherwise could not have reached the New World; they were also one
way of beginning for those who had arrived without capital or
with limited capital.   Indentures thus were a means of overcom-
ing the difficulties of getting started.   As practiced at special
times, in certain localities and by particular individuals, redemption labor was mild, and accounts of it could be but favorable.
From the American side, Thomas Jefferson saw nothing to complain of in the practices.   The evils of which he knew were those
of the agents and importers, and he felt that they should be cor-
rected by the European governments which were responsible for
their continuance.   Jefferson went on to say that the servants
under contract in America were satisfied with their contracts and

---

[6] "Many who came over under covenants for four years are now the
masters of great estates."   Dickinson, cited in Watson, *Annals*, II, 266;
Smith, *History of Delaware County*, 260.

[7] Robert Sutcliffe, *Travels*, 32-34.

did not wish to withdraw from them.[8] Peter Kemp, in the trial of Peter Williamson, testified that he was well used during his term of service in Pennsylvania, and that he had seen others of his fellow passengers after they had been sold, from none of whom had there been any complaint of illtreatment.[9]

The story of the redemptioners is made less forbidding by the high order of skill and intelligence to which it extended. White servitude was not confined to manual toil. Many redemptioners were artisans of considerable efficiency, and could have been retained and employed to advantage only by fair treatment. The records show that masters gained control of trained minds as well as of trained hands.

Not infrequently were persons of some education offered under indenture as schoolmasters, and families, groups of families, and schools purchased the indentures of such and retained them as teachers. This was an earlier custom in the South, but it was afterwards practiced in the middle colonies. Jonathan Boucher, a Maryland rector who was a tutor to Washington's stepson, wrote that a ship never arrived, either with redemptioners or convicts, without schoolmasters being as regularly advertised for sale as were weavers, tailors, and others, but with the difference that the schoolmasters did not find so ready a sale or bring such good prices as the others. Boucher said that two-thirds of the Maryland schoolmasters were convicts, and added of Washington that his education was limited to reading, writing, and accounts, which had been taught to him by a convict servant.[10]

A Bristol servant advertised himself for sale as a schoolmaster in Pennsylvania, stating that his indenture might be taken by a group of families for a period not to exceed seven years.[11] A servant who could teach reading, writing, and arithmetic was

---

[8] *Writings* (Ford), IV, 159, 160.

[9] *Williamson Evidence,* 45, 46. Kemp's statement is not altogether convincing, from the fact that he testified also that he had never heard of the kidnaping of any passengers (p. 46). The testimony of several other witnesses showed that he must have heard of this.

[10] Boucher, *American Revolution,* 183, 184; Heston, *Slavery and Servitude in New Jersey,* 28, 29. Washington was given the rudiments of his education by one Hobby who was sexton of the parish, and who possibly had come over under indenture.

[11] *Pennsylvania Gazette,* May 6, 1762.

earlier requested.[12] A servant schoolmaster owned by a number of families at Freehold, New Jersey, was advertised for as having run away.[13]

Incoming servants were frequently mentioned as knowing Latin, and sometimes French and other languages, also as writing a good hand and being able to teach reading and accounts. Mention of these and the occasional notices of schoolmasters who had run away, broken jail, and forged passes, show that servant schoolmasters were common.

As teaching required a high order of intelligence, so special favors were often extended to servant schoolmasters. We read concerning one master that the arrangements made by a given teacher to supply a substitute for his services had not proved satisfactory, and he was therefore requested to come back and teach the school, or otherwise to make satisfaction. Should neither of the alternatives be complied with, the master gave notice that he would advertise for the servant as a runaway, offering a reward sufficient to bring him back.[14] A Maryland teacher of 1745 was advertised for as having run away.[15] Less than a month later he replied from New Jersey, saying that he was sick, had had no idea of running away, and that it was to his advantage to return to Maryland.[16]

About the middle of the eighteenth century, a Lutheran congregation at York, Pennsylvania, purchased and held under indenture one who ministered to them as their pastor—a relation that must surely have kept alive the early notion of a minister as one who served. An advertisement gave notice that the congregation would prevent another congregation from taking away the minister without first getting the permission of the people among whom he labored.[17]

It would be difficult to find a relation of life, or an occupation, to which indentures were not made applicable. An advertiser in 1750 offered an Irish servant for four years with the

---

[12] *Ibid.,* February 4, 1735.
[13] *Ibid.,* April 27, 1738.
[14] *Ibid.,* August 23, 1775.
[15] *Maryland Gazette,* August 15, 1745.
[16] *Ibid.,* September 5.
[17] Seidensticker, *German-American Events,* 9.

attractions that he understood all kinds of laboring work, also arithmetic, and possessed the desirable requisite of being a good penman.[18] Some months later a fellow countryman of the preceding was offered as a baker, with the added accomplishments of understanding bleeding, shaving, and dressing wigs.[19]

When Franklin returned to Philadelphia from London in 1726, he was engaged by his former employer, Keimer, to take charge of the printing office and instruct others in the business. Franklin felt that he was paid good wages in order that he might train Keimer's servants, after which he would be promptly discharged. In service at Keimer's he found John ————, "a wild Irishman," and George Webb, "an Oxford scholar," whose indentures had been purchased for four years from a ship's captain. These servants illustrated the lottery of the purchase of redemptioners. The Irishman was incapable of being trained and soon ran away. Webb, on the other hand, was a fellow of unusual parts. Franklin remarked upon it as an odd thing to find an Oxford scholar working as a "bought servant." He was thought to be not more than eighteen years of age and of his life Franklin ascertained that he was a native of Gloucester, had attended the grammar school of his home town, and was distinguished for scholarship. He had written both prose and verse for the Gloucester papers. Later he went to Oxford and remained about a year, but became dissatisfied and wanted to see London. When he received his quarterly allowance of fifteen guineas, he left Oxford without paying his outstanding bills, hid his scholar's gown, and walked to London. Here he fell in with bad company, squandered his money, and even pawned some of his clothing. Soon he suffered from lack of food. While walking in want through the streets a "crimp's bill" was given him; this offered immediate relief to those who would sign to come to America. Webb signed, after which he was put on shipboard and brought to Philadelphia.[20]

Importers tried to supply the demand in the colony by adver-

---

[18] *Pennsylvania Gazette,* May 3, 10, and 24, 1750.

[19] *Ibid.,* October 25, November 15 and 29, December 11, 18, and 25, 1750.

[20] Franklin, *Works* (Bigelow), I, 131-133.

tising servants of a wide range of occupations, and such announce-
ments as the following were common:

"GERMANS—We are now offering fifty Germans just
arrived, . . . to be seen at the Golden Swan, kept by
the Widow Kreider. The lot includes schoolmasters, artisans,
peasants, boys and girls of various ages, all to serve for payment of passage." [21]

Records of the satisfactory results of redemption labor are
not uncommon; its application to callings other than manual toil
freed it from some of the depressing influences of Negro slavery;
but the fact remains that much was said in condemnation of the
holding of bought servants. Indentured labor could be justified
only from its seeming necessity—necessity to the emigrants and
necessity to the colony which wrought the brain, skill, and brawn
of these newcomers into the texture of its political, social, and
economic life. But exactly the same plea has been made for
Negro slavery.[22] Wherever white servitude was tried, it resulted
in unsatisfactory social and moral conditions. Students of white
servitude in the southern colonies place the servant under indenture on the same plane as the slave. Indeed, it has sometimes
been felt, in comparing the two systems, that Negro slavery was
less objectionable.[23] In cases where white servants and Negro
slaves were owned side by side, it not infrequently happened that
the Negroes were better treated. Negroes were property for life;
for them larger sums were paid than were necessary to secure
servants for a term of years; in case of death of a slave the
master's loss was greater than in the death of a servant; it was
even worse in case of sickness, since with the servant the responsibility of the master passed with the expiration of the indenture,
while with a slave the master was responsible until death; hence
the master's interest would make him more careful to protect the
health of his slave than that of his servant. Especially does this
seem true when one remembers that the servant was held but for
a brief time, and it was to the interest of the master to get all

---

[21] *Pennsylvania Messenger*, January 18, 1774. Cited by Groff, in article,
"White Slavery," *West Chester Village Record*, August 22, 1894.

[22] For a review of the moral, political, and economic effects of slavery
see DuBois, *Suppression of the Slave Trade*, 196-199.

[23] Bruce, *Economic History of Virginia*, II, 60.

Thee Humble Petiton of Edmond magonen
to thee Honnurable Bench now Siting in Chester
that your petroner Beeing an Endented Saruent to
Joseph wharton John wharton & John pennale —
in Companey and was to be Suftain'd with meate
Drink washing and Lodging with fiue pounds
pr year for other Suftainance and now Beeing
willing and Redey to Serue my Empleyrs
an Likely to Starne for want of Suportement
youre Humble petroner hopes that the Honour able
Bench will other order your petroner a —
Suftarnance or other ways alow him to
go Elce where to Earn his bread for his
wife and famely
                          June ye 16th 1747

                    Edward magoaen

A Servant's Petition for Better Treatment

[Original in *Cope Manuscripts,* Historical Society of Pennsylvania]

Ft. 275

he could by way of labor in this period, and to give the least possible by way of food and clothing. A servant might be over-worked for the years of his indenture, and be broken in health, after which he could be turned away without redress. Not so a slave—the master had him for life and it was to the master's interests to prolong his life and keep him strong and well. Over white servants, says William Eddis, there was exercised an "in-flexible severity," and in the colony to which felons were most freely introduced, there was little to distinguish the freewill servant and the felon. We are told that the condition of the "free-willer" was generally even worse than that of the convict, though for what reason does not appear unless it were that the convict served for a longer term.[24]

Probably the most striking arraignment of the evils of the redemption system was by Gottlieb Mittelberger, written about the middle of the eighteenth century, to furnish a complete ac-count of what he termed the sad condition of most of the Germans who had come over as servants.[25] Their state was de-scribed as pitiable and the action of the captains and merchants who brought them, as irresponsible and merciless. Mittelberger said that many of the Germans in Pennsylvania, when they learned that he was to return to Germany, besought him to make known there their condition and sufferings so that no more of their innocent countrymen would be enticed into what was termed slavery.[26] Mittelberger said that these Germans were far better off at home. Many of them had left good homes, had been robbed and illtreated in the passage, and finally had been sold into what was real slavery. For these men his comment was that the edict, "in the sweat of thy face," had been well fulfilled.[27]

Indentured servitude was set forth by numerous other writers as little better than actual slavery, the master having full con-

---

[24] Eddis, *Letters*, 69-71. See also Hennighausen, *Redemptioners and the German Society of Maryland*, 2-4.

[25] *Journey to Pennsylvnaia*, Title-page.

[26] *Ibid.*, 16.

[27] *Ibid.*, 29, 30. "But the most important part of this publication will no doubt be found in the account of the fate of most of the unfortunate people who leave Germany to seek uncertain prosperity in the New World, but find instead, if not death, most certainly oppressive servitude and slavery." (Mittelberger, "Address to the Esteemed Reader.")

trol, and public sentiment permitting the illtreatment of servants. An English traveler in the latter part of the eighteenth century described the system as he saw it in operation as follows: "The laws respecting the *redemptioners* are very severe; they were formed for the English convicts before the Revolution." To mitigate these, he said, the Irish and German Societies "did all in their power to render their countrymen, during their servitude, as comfortable as possible." [28]   A little later another traveler, who had seen the sale of redemptioners and the labor of those sold, declared that the system as practiced could not but arouse the indignation of Englishmen. [29]

The colonial newspapers frequently give evidence of the cruelty of masters. A runaway of 1746 was described by the cuts on his back and arms from the whipping he had received for attempting to run away the night before. [30] The death of a New Jersey servant was attributed by a physician, who had made an examination, to his master's violence in chastising the servant,

---

[28] Priest, *Travels,* 145.

[29] Wakefield, *Excursions, 23.* The treatment of redemptioners in Maryland for the corresponding period, is thus described by Hennighausen: "He [the redemption servant] was in many respects treated like the black slave. He could not purchase nor sell anything without the permission of the master. If caught ten miles away from home without a written permission of his master, he was liable to be taken up as a runaway, and severely punished. The person who harbored a runaway was fined five hundred pounds of tobacco for each twenty-four hours, and to be whipped if unable to pay the fine. There was a standing reward of two hundred pounds of tobacco for capturing runaways, and the Indians received for every captured runaway they turned in a 'match coat.' For every day's absence from work, ten days were added to his term of servitude.

"The master had a right to whip his Redemptioner for any real or imaginary offense, provided he gave him no more than ten lashes for each offense, which must have been a very difficult matter to determine, for offenses may be multiplied. The laws also provided for his protection. For excessively cruel punishment the master should be fined and the Redemptioner set free. I presume in most cases this was only effective when the Redemptioner had influential friends who would take up his case."

Redemptioners and the German Society of Maryland, 37, 38.

[30] *Pennsylvania Gazette,* August 14, 1746.

A SERVANT'S PETITION TO SECURE HIS RIGHTS, (1741)

[Original Historical Society of Pennsylvania. Court Papers]

and the master was arrested and placed in jail to await trial.[31] A runaway from Maryland was described as having been whipped at the October court of 1772; he had also been earlier whipped in Trenton, and was said to be familiar with the whipping post in Philadelphia.[32]

No one can go far into this subject without being convinced that purchasers were sometimes deceived, and found themselves in possession of servants who were worthless, or worse than worthless. Samuel Breck compared the purchase of a servant to buying chances in a lottery, or taking a leap in the dark.[33] Advertisements descriptive of runaways abounded in such phrases as "down-looked," "has something of a condemned look," and "cannot look you in the face." Enumeration of physical defects were also common, such as "has sore eyes," "is blind in one eye," "is bandy-legged," "is lame," and "is stoop-shouldered." Runaways were so frequently described as "pock-marked" that one wonders how this could have been a distinguishing characteristic.

In one way or another servants were frequently before the courts. An examination of bills of indictment from 1715 to 1790 [34] shows that they were sometimes petitioners to be protected against illtreatment, to have indentures dissolved, or to secure the customary freedom dues to which they were entitled. (See illustration opposite.) But more frequently servants were arraigned for running away, or on charges of felony, assault, bigamy, bastardy, fornication, drunkenness, congregating in disorderly houses, and other offenses. The advertisements for runaways and the court records indicate that a large number of servants were scapegraces and the masters who purchased these and took them into their homes must have been entitled to sympathy. Petitions to the courts frequently were made to restrain persons from keeping disorderly houses for the congregating of servants. Sometimes the petitioners instanced these disorders as happening on Sunday, and again late at night.[35]

---

[31] *Ibid.,* January 21, 1755.

[32] *Ibid.,* December 8, 1773.

[33] *Recollections,* 296, 297.

[34] *Manuscript Record* at Library of Historical Society of Pennsylvania.

[35] In 1722, a true bill of indictment was found against Richard Scott and wife, of Philadelphia, for receiving and harboring "sundry Negro

The introduction of European servants instead of African slaves was favorably regarded by political writers as tending to democracy rather than aristocracy. Jefferson expressed himself on this subject, and his feeling was shared by both Washington and Franklin. But indentured servants supplied the most troublesome elements in the democracies of the North American colonies. With the expiration of their indentures the Germans settled down, chiefly to agriculture. Not so the Irish; they were of adventuresome and roving dispositions, and became traders, especially on the frontier. The worst evils of the Indian trade, selling whisky and cheating Indians of their furs, are chargeable to former servants. With such men in the trade, attempts to regulate the Indian traffic in Pennsylvania were unavailing, for the traders would regard neither law nor right.[36]

Servants had a degree of protection, for example, in not being sold out of Pennsylvania without their own consent, against secret sale, and against personal violence. If a charge were made against the master which could not be substantiated, the servant was subject to additional servitude for costs. If the servant established his charge of harsh treatment, the court might admonish the master, and if a well-founded charge of cruelty came up a second time, the servant was likely to be freed. Servants also were exempted from the usual toil on Sunday.

There were no hard and fast rules of procedure: justices exercised discretion. In 1684, a servant woman complained to the court that her master beat and ill-used her. After going into the case, the court ordered that two persons who were named should find for the woman a new master who would pay down the seven pounds necessary to free her from the one against whom complaint was made.[37] Servants, however, did not find it easy to get their rights. Discharge of an indenture for cruelty

---

Slaves and Christian Servants belonging to sundry persons living in Philadelphia," to the disgust of all the people living in the neighborhood. *Manuscript Court Papers.* Similar records were frequent, e.g., indictments, January 1, 1736, October 30, 1738, January 1, 1739; also manuscript record for 1741.

[36] Thomson, *Enquiry into Causes of Indian Alienation,* 76, 77; Walton, *Conrad Weiser,* 271.

[37] Martin, *History of Chester,* 76.

was unusual. Generally a charge of harsh treatment was not followed up and the indictment was set aside.

On the other hand, the master was well protected against servants marrying, running away, disposing of his goods, or refusing to work according to the custom of the time. A servant who, without his master's consent, married during his term of service was subject to serve one year additional after his indenture had expired. Free persons who married servants were required to pay damages to the amount of twelve pounds, if the servant were a man, or six pounds, if a woman, or such persons were to give one year's additional service.[38] Mittelberger's observation on the working of the law was that if servants wished to marry, they had to pay five or six pounds for every additional year that was still required by their indentures.[39] A woman servant who bore a bastard child during the term of her indenture was subject to such additional service as the justice of the peace thought fit, but the time for which such a servant could be reassigned was not more than two years or less than one.[40] Both court procedure and the testimony of travelers show that women servants were frequently remanded for extra time because of loss from their bearing children. The indenture system as it applied to women tended to social immorality. A woman sold from the Philadelphia jail for her fees in 1757 was later found to be with child, and she charged that she had been seduced while in jail.[41]

Masters who suffered loss because of servant women bearing children during their terms petitioned the courts for extra service. The extra term in such cases was sometimes one year, more often a year and a half, and not infrequently two years. In 1737, the

---

[38] Bioren, *Laws,* I, 21, 22. In 1786, Thomas Jefferson said that in some states servants had a right to marry without the master's consent. He supposed this to be so in all the states. *Writings,* IV, 159.

[39] *Journey,* 29.

[40] Bioren, *Laws,* I, 28. This law was disallowed by the queen in council, 1705-1706. *Statutes at Large,* II, 6, 7. With slight modification the same law was passed in 1705-1706 and this continued in force until the disappearance of the servant system. *Ibid.,* 182. In 1722-1723 the Assembly was petitioned for new legislation regarding servant women bearing bastard children, but after consideration it was decided that the law then existing was sufficient. *Votes of Assembly,* II, 344, 355.

[41] *Cope Manuscripts.*

Chester county court, on the representation that a master had been under expenses amounting to five pounds from the bearing of a child by his woman servant, adjudged the woman to one year and a half beyond the expiration of her indenture.[42]   A different sort of case came before the court of the same county in 1754.   A woman servant bore a child of which a manservant was the father.   These two were later married and, the terms of their service having elapsed, the master petitioned for an extension of time for both of them.   The court, after taking the case into consideration, gave the man one year extra and the woman two years.[43]   In 1788, a Chester County servant woman was sentenced to two years' extra time for bearing a bastard child, and in 1791 the same sentence was imposed upon a white woman who had given birth to a mulatto child.[44]

A woman with child was less desirable as a servant, a fact at times clearly recognized in the advertisements.   The printers of the *Pennsylvania Gazette* were advertised to give information of a pregnant servant woman with three years yet to serve, who was offered at a low price because of her condition.[45]

Not all servants were vicious.   Some who came to Philadelphia under indenture brought certificates of good character, either from individuals or from Friends' Meetings in Great Britain. Certain of these credentials were recorded on the books of Friends' Meetings in the colony, and they were no doubt otherwise used to give standing to the new arrivals.[46]

The history of one Daniel Kent was romantic.   When twenty years of age, Kent, who was a cutler by trade, went from Limerick to Cork.   There trade was dull and he could not find work, so he started for Dublin, but while on the way he turned aside to Waterford, where he found a vessel making up a list of passengers for the New World.   Kent signed indentures to serve for three years from the time the vessel cast anchor.   On arrival at the Delaware, Kent's vessel lay for four weeks in the harbor, after which the mate took about twenty passengers into the back country to be

---

[42] *Ibid.*
[43] *Ibid.*
[44] *Ibid.*
[45] *Ibid.*, July 26, 1764.
[46] Browning, *Welsh Settlement of Pennsylvania*, 261.

We whose names are hereunto subscribed do assure all Persons whom it shall or may concern to know, That Daniel Trent, who is now an Indented Servant to Mr Joseph Mawby of West Bradford County of Chester Pensilvania in America, as by his Letter appeart, is the Son of William Trent of this City Butler; and has been decently and honestly Reared by his said Father & Mother in the Love & fear of God & in the Protestant Religion, That being bred to his said Fathers Trade by his said Father & thinking himself too much restrained from the Liberties that the folly of Youth is subject to or howsoever led by some foolish infatuation departed from his father without cause or compulsion in state of Innocence and free from Vice & Blemish in the Month of March last & we testify that from his behaviour while in his Fathers Care and from the Religious & pious honesty of his Parents the said Daniel Trent is worthy to be Noticed. Given under Our hands in the City of Limerick & Kingdom of Ireland this 24 day of January 1706

I know the above named

Daniel Trent to be a very honest and
Industrious Man as he served his
time in 98 Parish of St Marys.

Jaques Ingram ...... that
Trine Trent
of St Marys.

Maxwell Blunett Jr

David Hallaghan th D

Joseph Gibbins

Garbett

Byrn

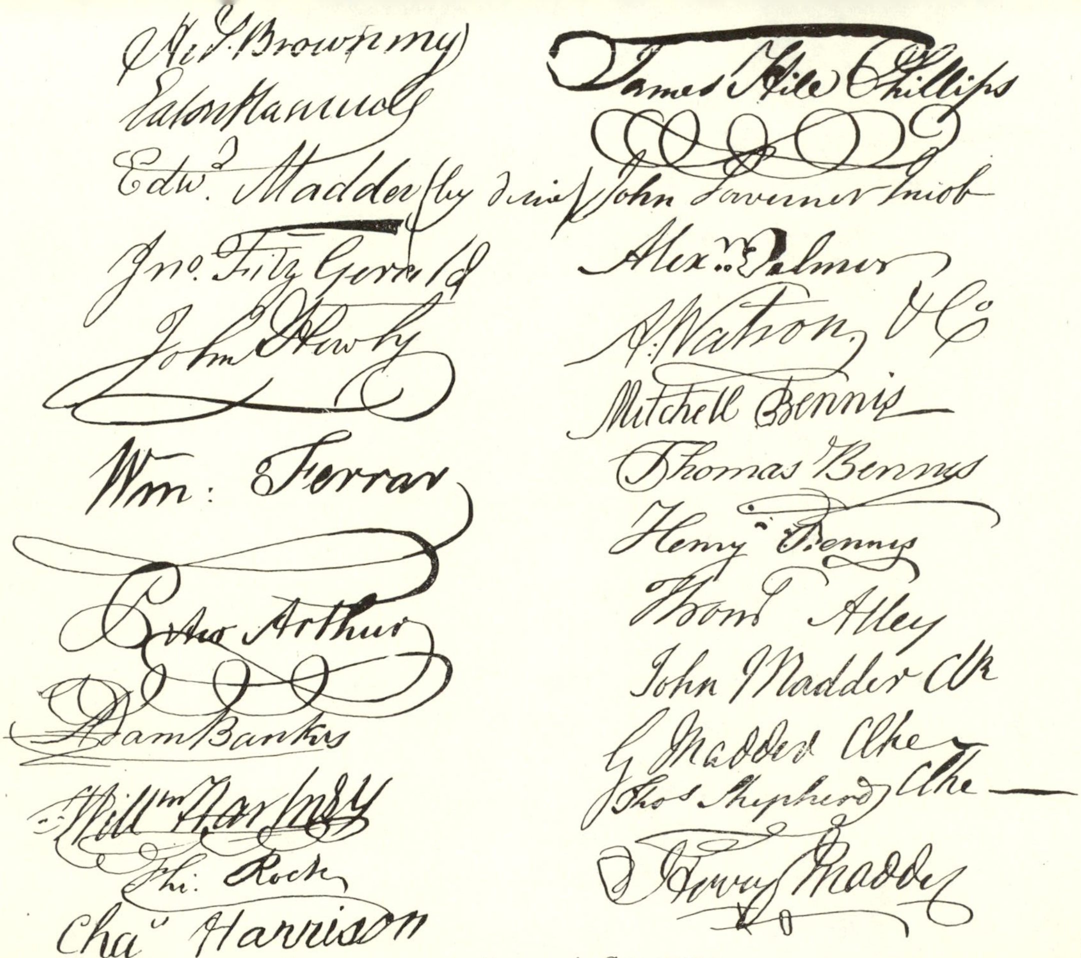

Certificate of a Servant's Character

sold. The parents of Kent secured an endorsement of his character and sent it to be of service in a strange land. (Illustration opposite.) Kent joined the Quakers, married the daughter of his former master, and established a large family, which has been of influence in Pennsylvania.[47]

It was true, however, that reckless adventurers were most likely to reach the New World under indenture, and these were the classes most prompt to break away from temporary servitude. The administration of the law was affected and often embarrassed by the servant relationships. A petition to the Common Council of Philadelphia in March, 1730, set forth that a servant had been convicted of rape and long confined in jail, to the loss of his master, and prayer was made for the remission of the fine. The action of the Council was that the fine would be remitted to twenty pounds; that on the payment of this and costs by the master, and the master's becoming further bound to the amount of thirty pounds for the future good behavior of his servant, the latter would be released to his master, but that if the master refused to pay, the servant's bond would be taken for the whole fine, and on payment of cost the servant would be sent out of the province.[48]

In 1734, the Common Council of Philadelphia remitted the fine of a servant whose master did not pay for the servant's burglary, and on petition of the servant he was returned to the master.[49] Fines against servants were remitted repeatedly on condition that the offender be sent out of the colony. Sometimes the master was made responsible for the payment of costs and a bond guaranteeing the future good behavior of the servant released.

Recourse against masters was by canceling or shortening indentures, while against servants it was by extending the term. One of the evils of the system was this extension of time—the master often bringing charges against his servants sufficient to keep them sometimes almost indefinitely. Servants seem to have secured their rights with difficulty. As late as the nineteenth

---

[47] *Daniel Kent, Emigrant,* 16, 17.

[48] "Minutes of Common Council," p. 310, cited from Hunt, *Manuscripts,* II, 227, 228.

[49] "Minutes of Common Council," cited in Hunt, IV, 229.

century, the Pennsylvania German Society had reported to it the case of a man who had been held under indenture for seventeen years. The Society took the case to court, but was defeated and, moreover, was compelled to pay the costs incurred in the proceeding. According to the historian of the Society, no explanation was given for this high-handed action of the court.[50]   In 1732, the court in Philadelphia had a complaint from one who had signed an indenture in Dublin for a term of four years, which, he said, he had honestly and faithfully worked out more than three months before. The record recited the facts of the case, which were as the servant had stated, and gave the finding of the court for the dismissal of the indenture, but no mention was made of the overtime to which the servant had already been subjected.[51]

Descriptions of runaways are proof that servants were not properly clothed. The advertisements often offer ample evidence to justify servants for having left their masters. Christopher Sauer, the Germantown printer, accepted advertisements describing servants as insufficiently clad, and with them published the statement that if masters would treat their servants decently, and properly clothe them, it would not then be necessary to pay for advertisements to capture them, as they would not run away.

On no other consideration does white servitude deserve such strong condemnation as from that which resulted in the separation of families. A large number of those who came, especially among the Germans, came as families, and sale for whole families or for several members of one family to one master was not readily found. Parents and children, brothers and sisters, even husbands and wives, were often widely separated, to be reunited only after years, or possibly never reunited. Sometimes small children were taken into the families of those who purchased them and given the family name, so that their true name and family were forgotten or ignored. The most advanced legislation for controlling the sale of servants was that husband and wife could not be separated, except with their own consent.[52]

---

[50] Seidensticker, *Geschichte der deutschen Gesellschaft,* 99, 100.

[51] *Manuscript Court Papers* (1732-1744), November 8, 1732. Collection in Library of Historical Society of Pennsylvania.

[52] 1818. See above in Chapter XIII.

Emigrants who shipped expecting that friends or relatives would redeem them on arrival were sometimes disappointed. In other cases, the captains hurried the passengers from the ship and sold them before their friends could have notice of their arrival.[53] Divisions of families were common, and in after years efforts were made to secure information of the lost members. Sometimes children were estranged from their parents by sale and chose rather to continue with the families of their masters than to return to their parents who might have sold them to lighten their own burdens. Five times over the following appeared in a Philadelphia paper in 1750:

"Whereas Anna Weis, a servant girl, was sold to Richard Parks for four years some time in September, 1749: If any person will inform her father, Johannis Weis, at Lancaster, where she, or the above-said Parks lives, he or she shall have a reasonable reward, paid by
Johannis Weis." [54]

At the same time the following was running:

"Whereas Maria Fisher, a servant girl, was sold to one John Smith, on the 23d of September, 1743, for 7 years: If any person will inform Daniel Stonemat, in Second-Street, Philadelphia, or her father, Melchior Fisher, living near Neshaminy ferry, where she, or the aforesaid John Smith lives, he or she shall have a reasonable reward, paid by
Melchior Fisher." [55]

Records of sales of redemptioners were not sufficient to trace members of a family who had been lost, and the newspapers offered the most promising means of securing the desired information. A Swiss family was broken up in Holland by the necessary return of the father to the home country. On arrival in the New World, his children were sent to Nova Scotia, and after a long delay, he came to Pennsylvania. Twenty years had

---

[53] Bond, "Letters from Philadelphia," *American Historical Association Report,* 1896, 643, 644.

[54] *Pennsylvania Gazette,* October 11, 25; November 8, 22, and December 6, 1750.

[55] *Ibid.,* November 1, 8, and 22.

elapsed when there was a determined, though probably fruitless, effort to reunite the members of this family.[56]

Much that is revolting and objectionable is brought to light by a study of redemption labor. On the part of ships' captains and taskmasters, the trade in servants fostered cruelty towards fellow men; profit depended upon a violation of the rights of brother Caucasians, even of the same nation, and rights were overridden for gain. Not the least of the unfortunate results was the spirit engendered in many who bought and sold, fed and worked redemptioners as though they were cattle. For many who came as servants, the future held only gloom and disappointment; their sanguine hopes of ready sale and easy service were far from realized; the New World required of them excessive toil for long periods; in addition, servants were not infrequently separated from friends and family, and drank the cup of bitterness to its dregs.

On the other hand, the good effects of white servitude are not to be dismissed as of slight consequence. This system of labor gave to thousands of sturdy pioneers a home in the wilderness, and an opportunity to build both for themselves and for the commonwealth. If there was sometimes broken health and despair for the future, let it be remembered that there was more frequently buoyant hope and future prosperity. What, after all, would have been the future of these servants had they continued under the Old World conditions? And what would have been the history of the colony and commonwealth of Pennsylvania if they had not come? The findings on such questions would determine the answer to another, viz., what were the ultimate results of redemption labor?

Redemption emigrants as a class, and in the long run, probably enjoyed a larger measure of comfort and happiness in the New World than would have been theirs in the Old. Here was more of religious privilege, political enfranchisement, material prosperity, and social equality. As the blessings were greater to the first generations, so they increased incalculably to those that followed.

White servitude had a determining effect on the development

---

[56] *Pennsylvania Gazette,* June 9, 1775.

of Pennsylvania. In her sentiment against Negro slavery, and in her labor history, Pennsylvania occupied a peculiar position, a position not to be easily explained without considering white servitude. The opposition of Pennsylvania to slavery as an institution was more than sentiment; the interest of the colony was in the direction of the use of this other form of labor. In all the antislavery discussion in America, Mason and Dixon's Line was a mark of separation of free from slave states, but Mason and Dixon's Line was the southern boundary of Pennsylvania. That the line of division between slavery and freedom was drawn south of Pennsylvania was due in no small measure to the substitute form of servile labor which was available in this state. Pennsylvania's industrial development, and her social and political history, can be fully comprehended only from a study of white servitude. Indentured and redemption labor influenced Pennsylvania more largely than this form of labor influenced any other state. As colony and commonwealth, Pennsylvania's history was largely affected by white servitude.

APPENDIX I

LAWS AFFECTING WHITE SERVITUDE IN PENNSYLVANIA

One hundred and fifty years of legislative enactment reflecting the changes in an institution, afford an outline of its evolution. The legislation on white servitude has a twofold significance: First, new laws, or amendments to those already existing, indicated changed conditions and the necessity for new machinery of administration; legislation is generally in answer to demands expressed in petitions, appeals through the press and in other ways, and back of legislative enactment is a public sentiment favorable to the legislation. Second, laws supplied the machinery under which the indentured and redemption system operated. Under these laws servants were imported, they were bought and sold, they were held in servitude, and finally they secured their freedom. A summary of the legislation on white servitude is almost necessary to see the system in its entirety.

LAWS OBTAINING PRIOR TO 1682

Bond Slavery Permitted

"No Christian shall be kept in Bondslavery, villenage or Captivity, Except Such who shall be Judged thereunto by Authority, or such as willingly have sould, or shall sell themselves, In which Case a Record of such Servitude shall be entered in the Court of Sessions held for that Jurisdiction where Such Matters shall Inhabit, provided that nothing in the Law Contained shall be to the prejudice of Master or Dame who have or shall by any Indenture or Covenant take Apprentices for Terme of Years or other Servants for Term of years or Life."[1]

Children and Servants

"The Constable and Overseers are strictly required frequently to Admonish the Inhabitants of Instructing their Children and Servants in Matters of Religion, and the Lawes of the Country."[2]

If "Children or Servants become rude, Stuborne, etc., the Constable and Overseers (or Justice of the Peace) have power upon the Complaint . . . to call such an offender and to Inflict such Corporall punishment

---

[1] *Duke of York's Laws*, 12.
[2] *Ibid.*, 19, 20.

as the merit of their fact in their Judgment shall deserve, not excepting [exceeding] ten Stripes," providing the offender be sixteen years of age.[3]

Runaways

Such "shall be Adjudged by the Court to double the time of such their absence by future Service over and above other Damage and Cost."

Any aiding the runaway "Shall forfeit twenty pounds to the Master . . . and be fined five pounds to the Court . . ."

Any harboring or concealing a runaway shall forfeit "ten shillings for every Day's entertainment or Concealment."[4]

Marriage of Servants

Such without the consent of the Masters to be void, "shall be proceeded against as for Adultery or fornication," and Children to be "reputed as Bastards."[5]

Servants Not to Sell Goods

"No Servant . . . shall either give sell or Truck any Commodity . . . , under the penalty of fine or Corporal punishment, . . . And whatsoever Person shall either Buy, receive or Truck with any such Servant . . . shall be compelled to restore the said Commodityes . . . and forfeit the double value thereof to the poor of the Parish . . ."[6]

Work by Servants

"All Labourers and Servants shall work in their Callings, being thereunto required, the whole day, the Master or Dame allowing them convenient time for food and rest."[7]

Runaway Servants to Be Brought Back

"If any servant shall run away . . . (officials) Have power to

---

[3] *Ibid.*, 20.

"Lawes digested into one volume for the publicke use of the Territoryes in America. . . .

"Collected out of the Severall Laws now in force in his Majesties American Colonyes and Plantations."

Published March 1st, 1664, on Long Island. *Duke of York's Laws*, 3.

These laws were introduced on the Delaware by ordinance of Governor Andross, passed September 25th, 1676. Nead, "Historical Notes" to *Book of Laws*, 455, 456.

Vide: Pennsylvania Archives, Second Series, VII, 783-785, for ordinance passed. Date of ordinance there given is September 22. Armstrong's Introduction to *Upland Court Record*, p. 26, makes it appear as tho' introduced May, 1672. Elting, *Dutch Village Communities on the Hudson River*, says that the *Duke's Laws* were not introduced on the Hudson until September 22, 1676, though given in 1664. J. H. U. Studies, Fourth Series, No. 1, p. 34.

[4] *Duke of York's Laws*, 28.

[5] *Ibid.*, 37.

[6] *Ibid.*, 37.

[7] *Ibid.*, 37.

press Men, Horses, Boats, or Pinnaces, at the Publique Charge, to pursue such Persons . . . and to bring them back by force of Armes. . . ." [8]

Abuse of Servants

Redress was by complaint of servant to Constable and Overseer. First complaint, "Admonishing the Master" . . ., on "Second Complaint" the servant was taken from the master and kept until "the ensueing Sessions."

In the case the Master by cruelty and tyranny "shall smite out the Eye or Tooth of any such man or maid servant, or shall otherwise Maime or disfigure them such Servants, after due proof made shall be sett free from their Service, And have a further allowance and recompence as the Court of Sessions shall judge meet." [9]

Causeless Complaint Against Abuse

In case a servant "causelessly Complain . . . If they cannot make proofe of a just occation for such Complaints . . ." Servants were "enjoyned to serve three Months time extraordinary (Gratis) for every such vndue Complaint." [10]

Assignment of Servants

"No Servant, except such are duly so for life, shall be Assigned over to other Masters or Dames by themselves, their Executors or Administrators for above the Space of one year, unless for good reasons offered; the Court of Sessions shall otherwise think fitt to order, In such case the Assignment shall stand good Otherwise to be void in Law." [11]

Dues of Servants and Neglect of Servants

"All servants who have served Diligently; and faithfully . . . five or Seaven yeares, shall not be Sent away empty, and if any have proved unfaithful or negligent in their Service . . . They shall not be dismist, till they have made satisfaction according to the Judgment of the Constable and Overseers of the Parish where they dwell." [12]

Hues and Cryes to Secure Runaway Servants

(An Amendment to the *Duke of York's Laws.* Passed in New

York, October 2 to 7, 1672)

"Whereas great Abuse hath been practized in the Government by private persons pursuing their Servants with Hue and Cryes at the Publick Charge, the Gayne whereof redounds only to themselves, It is

---

[8] *Ibid.*, 38.
[9] *Ibid.*, 38.
[10] *Ibid.*, 38.
[11] *Ibid.*, 38.
[12] *Ibid.*, 38.

from henceforth Ordered that the Chaeges of all Hue & Cryes shall bee
borne by the respective persons concerned; . . . unless in Cases of
Criminalls, or upon capitall Crimes." [13]

Strangers to Carry Passes in Traveling

. . . frequent Complaints have been made of Servants who runn
away from their Masters . . . if hereafter any Stranger . . . without a Pass port or Certificate from whence hee came and whither he is
bound, shall bee lyable to bee Seized upon . . . to bee Secured untill
hee can Cleare himselfe to bee a free Man, and shall defray the Charges
of his Detention," (by labor if he was not able otherwise to do so satisfactorily). [14]

LAWS OBTAINING FROM 1682 TO 1700

Indentured labor was recognized by the Laws of William Penn Agreed
Upon in England.

"Twenty-fourth. That all lands and goods of felons shall be liable to
make satisfaction to the party wronged twice the value; and for want of
lands or goods, the felons shall be bond-men to work in the common
prison or work-house, or otherwise, till the party injured be satisfied." [15]

"Twenty-ninth. That servants be not longer kept than their time, and
such as are careful, be both justly and kindly used in their service, and
put in fitting equipage at the expiration thereof, according to custom." [16]

LAWS PASSED AT AN ASSEMBLY AT CHESTER

(Dec. 7, 1682)

Thieves and Felons Subject to Service

Chapter XVIII. Thieves and felons as above (Twenty-fourth, of
"Laws Agreed Upon in England"), but with the difference, that the repara-
tion to the party wronged should be four-fold the amount of wrong. [17]

Master Protected From Violence of Servants

Chapter XXIII . . . "if any Servant Assault or Menace his or
her Master or Mistress, and be Convicted thereof, hee or shee shall be
punisht at the Discretion of two Justices of the peace, so it be sutable to
the nature of the offence." [18]

Pass for Traveling and Runaways

Chapter CXXXIV. "Unknown persons shall not presume to travell
or go without the limits of the country wherein they reside, without a pass
or Certificate under the seal of that country, . . .; And that every

---

[13] *Ibid.*, 72.
[14] *Ibid.*, 72.
[15] *Ibid.*, 101.
[16] *Ibid.*, 102.
[17] *Ibid.*, 112.
[18] *Ibid.*, 113.

person offending herein, shall be lyable to be apprehended . . ., at his
or her proper Costs and Charges, . . . That every person that comes
out of anie other province, without the pass of the province, . . .,
shall be apprehended and secured in the house of correction, . . . till
notice can be given to the master or mistress of the said Servants; . . .
And what Chairges such servant shall Occasion, more that his or her work
will Defray shall be made good by the master or mistress of such servants,
And such master or mistress shall over and above give . . ., twenty
shillings for their reward." [19]

Sale of Servants Out of the Province

Chapter CXXXIV (cont'd). No servant could be sold "into any other
province, . . . when bound to serve . . . in the province of Pennsilvania, . . ., Under the penalty, That every person so offending, shall
for every such Servant so sold, forfeit ten pounds, . . ." [20]

Assignment of Servants

Chapter CXXXV . . . "if any person within this province . .
shall Assign or Turn over any servant to anie person . . ., without the
knowledge of an consent of two Justices of the peace, such persons shall
forfeit ten pounds." [21]

Servants Not Attachable for Debt

Chapter CXXXII . . . no Servant white or black, within this
Province, . . . shall be Attached . . . for his Master or Mistress
debt or debts, To the end that the means of Livelyhood may not be taken
away from the said Master or Mistress. [22]

Harboring a Servant

Chapter CXXXVII. No person was to "Conceal, Entertain, or harbour
any Servant . . . for the space of twenty-four hours and not make
the same known to one of the Justices of the peace, on penalty of "five
shillings for every day that such servant shall be concealed, entertained or
harboured, . . ." [23]

Dealing With Servants

Chapter CXXXVIII. The above forbidden, penalty, "to pay to the
owner of such Servant, Double the value thereof, And Return the said
goods to the owner again or the value thereof." [24]

---

[19] *Ibid.*, 151, 152.
[20] *Ibid.*, 152.
[21] *Ibid.*, 152.
[22] *Ibid.*, 152.
[23] *Ibid.*, 152-153.
[24] *Ibid.*, 153.

Time of Service—Length of, How Determined and Dues at Expiration of Service

Chapter CXXXIX. Servants brought in "without Indenture or Covenant for the time of their service, Every such Servant being seventeen years of age or upwards, shall serve five years; And all those who shall be under seventeen years, of age, shall serve till they Come to the age of twenty-two; . . . And every Master or Mistress shall be bound to bring such Servant or Servants within three months time after their arrival before the said Courts to be adjudged."

Chapter CXXXIX. Master or Mistress "shall then and there (before the Court as above) oblige themselves to pay unto every Servant, at the Expiration of their time One new Sute of Apparell, ten bushels of Wheat or fourteen bushels of Indian-corn, one Ax, two howes one broad and another narrow, and a Discharge from their Service." [25]

Punishment for Runaway Servants

Chapter CLIII. Laws made at Philadelphia, Oct., 1683.

"To prevent the Running Away of Servants . . ." penalty "five days for every days absence, after the expiration of . . . Servitude"; further, make "Satisfaction for the Damages, costs, and chairges," to be determined by the County Courts.[26]

LAWS MADE AT NEW CASTLE, MAY 10, 1684

(Inter State Comity)

Chapter CLX. "For the increase of Union and good Understanding between the Government of Pennsilvania, and territories, and that of West Jersey, . . . all hyes and Cryes and Warrants granted by any of the Magistrates of West Jersey, against any offender for Treason, Felony, Run-away servants," etc. "shall be of the same force to all the respective Officers of this Province and Territories as if they were granted by any Magistrate in this Province . . ."

"*Provided always,* that that Government do within Two Months after the passing hereof enact a Law to empower the Magistrates and Officers of this Province and territories to the like purpose"; i.e., to issue warrants, etc., valid in West Jersey.[27]

Registry of Servants

Chapter CLXIII. That "there be a Registry kept of all freemen, as well as servants that already are, or from time to time shall come into this Province . . ." [28]

---

[25] *Ibid.,* 153.
[26] *Ibid.,* 166.
[27] *Ibid.,* 168, 169.
[28] *Ibid.,* 170.

Reward for Apprehending a Runaway Servant

Chapter CLXXX. Reward twenty shillings to be paid by the owner, the owner to pay also "the chairges the Sheriff shall be att, above the advantage of Such Runaway's labor, . . ." [29]

Menacing Masters or Mistresses

In the amended laws, Chapter 17.
Re-enacts Chapter XXIII, as above. [30]

Servitude for Debt

New Laws, Chapter 28.
"But if no estate can be found, the debtor shall satisfy the debt by Servitude, as the County Court shall order, if desired by the creditor." [31] (Might be in prison.)

Selling Servants Out of the Province

New Law, 64, Re-enactment of part of Law, Chapter CXXXIV, as above. [32]

Attaching Servants for Debt

New Law, 65, Re-enactment of Law, Chapter CXXXVI, as above. [33]

---

[29] *Ibid.*, 177.

Abrogation of all laws in Pennsylvania by the King and Queen, October 21, 1692; the government of Pennsylvania was taken out of the hands of William Penn and Benjamin Fletcher was made Governor.

After the above changes, the Pennsylvania Assembly sent to Governor Fletcher a "Petition of Rights" in the name of "the freemen of said Province and Country," asking for "the administration of justice within this government to be agreeable with these following laws which are now in force. . . ." In the enumeration were the following:

The 23rd law, against menacing Masters or Mistresses.
The 134th, About Passes.
The 135th, Against selling servants out of the Province.
The 136th law, Against attaching Servants.
The 137th law, About entertaining Servants.
The 138th law, About Trucking with Servants.
The 153rd and 180th law, About Runaway Servants.

> *Duke's Laws,* 188-191.
> Bioren, *Laws of Pennsylvania,* I, iv-vi.
> *Votes of Assembly,* I, 99-101.

The Petition of Rights was amended and embodied in 86 laws; Governor Fletcher gave order June 1st, 1693, that these laws be carried into execution. New laws were enacted, but all old ones not in the Petition of Rights lost their validity.

> Nead, "Historical Notes" to *Duke's Book of Laws,* 551.

[30] *Duke of York Laws,* 197.

[31] *Ibid.,* 200.

[32] *Ibid.,* 212.

[33] *Ibid.,* 212.

Against Harboring Servants

New Law, 66, Re-enactment of Law, Chapter CXXXVII, as above.[34]

Dealing With Servants Refused

Law, 67, Re-enacted Law, Chapter CXXXVIII, as above.[35]

Runaway Servants: Punishment, Apprehending

Law, 68, Re-enactment of Laws (pp. 8, 9), CLIII & CLX, as above.[36]

LAWS OBTAINING AFTER 1700

"An Act for the better regulation of Servants in this Province and Territories." [37]

(Laws XLIX passed 1700 allowed to become a law by lapse of time.)

Selling Servants Out of the Province

Section I. No servant bound to serve in the province was to be sold out of it, without his consent and the consent of two justices of the peace where he lived or should be sold. Fine for violation £10.

Assignment of Servants

Section II. No servant was to be assigned over to another in the province, but in the presence of one justice of the peace. Penalty for violation, £10.

Freedom Dues

Section III. ". . . Every servant that shall faithfully serve four years, or more, shall, at the expiration of their servitude, have a discharge, and shall be duly clothed with two complete suits of apparel, whereof one shall be new, and shall also be furnished with one new axe, one grubbing-hoe, and one weeding-hoe, at the charge of their master or mistress." Amended 1771.

---

[34] *Ibid.*, 212, 213.

[35] *Ibid.*, 213.

[36] *Ibid.*, 213.

In the Session of the Pennsylvania Assembly from May 15th to June 1st, 1693 (Benjamin Fletcher, Governor), a Bill was passed for the support of the Government, entitled, "An act for granting . . . one penny per pound . . . upon Reall, Capital of and personal estates, & six shillings per head, upon such as are not otherwise Rated by this act." One of the provisions of this Act was, "That all freemen . . . as have been out of their servitude by the space of six months, and shall not be otherwise rated by this act, . . . shall pay . . . the sum of six shillings per head."

Proud, *History of Pennsylvania*, I, 391.
Duke's Laws, 221-224.

[37] *Statutes at Large*, II, 54-56.

Punishment for Runaway Servants

Section IV. Five days extra for each day's absence and further satisfaction for damages sustained, to be determined and ordered by the County Court.[38]

Apprehending a Runaway Servant

Section V. Reward for bringing the runaway to the Sheriff of the County, 10 shillings if the servant was taken within 10 miles of the abode of the master, 20 shillings if he were taken at a distance greater than 10 miles.[39]

Retaining Servants

Section VI. (a) HARBORING A SERVANT, 20 shillings for each day's concealment.

(b) NEGLECT OF DUTY BY JUSTICE. If warrant was not issued within 24 hours after complaint, £5 forfeit.

(c) SHERIFF'S NEGLECT. Forfeiture of 5 shillings for each day's delay in giving notice to the master of the seizure of a servant.

Dealing With Servants Without Consent of Masters

Section VII. Persons so dealing forfeited to the owner treble the value of the goods involved. In addition, the servant was to make satisfaction . . . by servitude, after the expiration of his or her time, to double the value of the goods; (if the servant were black, he or she was to be severely whipped in the most public place of the township where the offence was committed.[40]

Servitude for Debt

In cases of debt, if no estate could be found, the debtor should satisfy the debt by servitude as the county Court ordered.[41]
creditor.[41]

(Law XCIV, Section 2, passed November 27th, 1700. Disallowed in Council, 1705-6)

Usual Toil on Sunday

Servants freed therefrom. Fine upon the Master for compelling servants to labor as above, 20 shillings.[42]

---

[38] Bioren, I, 10.

[39] *Ibid.*, 10, 11.

[40] *Ibid.*, 11.

[41] *Statutes at Large*, II, 129, 130; Bioren, *Laws*, I, lvii.

[42] *Statutes at Large*, II, 4. Disallowed in Council, 1705-6. No record of the above or its repeal in Bioren, *Laws*.

Marriage of Servants

Law CIX. "For the preventing of clandestine marriages." Servants marrying without the consent of their respective masters were each held for "one whole year, after the time of their servitude by indenture or engagement is expired."

"And if any person, being free, shall marry with a servant as afore-said, he or she so marrying shall pay the Master or Mistress of the serv-ants, if a man, twelve pounds, and if a woman, six pounds, or one year's service; and the servant so being married shall abide with . . . master . . . according to indenture . . . and one year after . . ."[43]

Servant Woman Bearing a Bastard Child

Law vs. Adultery and Fornication, passed 1705. If a child was born to a single woman during her indenture "She shall serve such further time . . . as the Justices of the Peace . . . shall think fit, . . .; *Provided* it be not more than two years, nor less than one."[44]

Orphans to Indentures

"An Act for establishing Orphans' Courts."

Executors, administrators, etc., could, under the authority of the Orphans' Court, and observing certain conditions, apprentice orphans. Passed March 27th, 1713.[45]

PARLIAMENTARY LEGISLATION FOR TRANSPORT-ING FELONS, ETC.

For the Punishment of Rogues, Vagabonds and Sturdy Beggars

Dangerous rogues might be committed to jail and banished out of the Realm, and conveyed to Places assigned by the Privy Council; and return-ing were to be Felons without the benefit of Clergy.

"Provided, always . . . If any of the said Rogues shall appeare to be dangerous to the inferior sorte of People where they shall be taken, or otherwyse be such as will not be reformed of their rogish kind of lyfe by the former Pvisions of this Acte, That in every such case it shall and may be lauful to the said Justice of the Lymitte where such Rogue shall be taken, or any two of them, whereof one be of the Quoz, to Commit that Rogue to the House of Correccon, or otherwyse to the Gaole of that County, there to remaine untill their next Quarter Sessions to be holden in that County, and then such of the same Rogues so comitted, as by the Justice of the Peace then and there psente or the most parte of them shalbe thought fitt not to be delivered, shall and may be lawfully by the

---

[43] Bioren, *Laws*, I, 21, 22.

[44] *Ibid.*, I, 28. A law similar to above passed in 1700, in which the extra service is stated as "one whole year," given in *Statutes at Large*, II, 6, 7. Disallowed by Queen in 1705-6.

[45] Bioren, *Laws*, I, 33-43; *Votes of Assembly*, II, 135.

same Justice or the most part of them be banyshed out of this Realme and all other the Domynions thereof, and at the Charge of that County shall be conveied unto such parte beyond the Seas as shal be at any tyme hereafter for the purpose assigned by the Privie Counsell unto her Majesty her Heires or Successors, or by any six or more of them, whereof the Lord Chancellor or Lord Keepr of the Great Seale, or the Lord Treasourer for the Tyme being to be one, or otherwyse be judged ppetually to the Gallyes of this Realme, as by the same justice or the most part of them it shal be thought fitt and expedynt; And if any such Rogue so banyshed as aforesaid shall returne agayne unto any Parte of this Realme or Domynion of Wales without lawful Lycense or Warrant so to do, that in every such case such offence shal be Felony, and the Party offending therein suffer Death as in Case of Felony; The said Felony to be heard and determyined in that County of this Realme or Wales in which the offender shal be apphended.[46]

An Act to Prevent Rapine and Theft on the Northern Borders of England

"It shall and may be lawful to and for the Justices of Assize and Commissers of Oyer and Terminer or Gaole delivery before whom such Offenders shall be convicted within the said Countyes or either of them to transport or cause to be transported the said Offenders and every of them into any of His Majestyes Dominions in America there to remaine and not to returne. Any former Law, Statue or Usage to the contrary in any wise notwithstanding." [47]

(Provided alwayes, That nothing in this Act shall extend to give benefit to any person who shall by Contract in Writing agree with any Merchant or Owner of any Plantation or other person whatsoever to be transported to any parts beyond Seas and receive earnest upon such Agreement although that afterwards such person shall renounce such Contract.[48]

Provided alwayes and be it enacted That if any person or persons lawfully convicted of Felony shall in open court pray to be transported beyond the Seas and the Court shall thinke fitt to leave him or them in Prison for that purpose such person or persons may be transported into any parts beyond the Seas This Act or anything therein contained to the contrary notwithstanding.[49]

To Prevent Robbery, Etc., And for the More Effectual Transportation of Felons, Etc.

Reasons for Act and Provisions for Operation.

"*Whereas* it is found by Experience, That the Punishments inflicted by

---

[46] *39 Elizabeth,* ch. 4.
[47] *18 Charles II,* ch. 3.
[48] Annexed to the original Act in a separate Schedule.
[49] *31 Charles II,* ch. 2.

the Laws now in Force against the Offences of Robbery, Larceny and other felonious Taking and Stealing of Money and Goods, have not proved effectual to deter wicked and evil-disposed Persons from being guilty of the said Crimes: And whereas many Offenders to whom Royal Mercy hath been extended, upon Condition of transporting themselves to the *West-Indies,* have often neglected to perform the said Condition, but returned to their former wickedness, and been at last for new crimes brought to a shameful and ignominious death; and whereas in many of His Majesty's colonies and plantations in *America,* there is great Want of Servants, who by their Labour and Industry might be the means of improving and making the said Colonies and Plantations more useful to this Nation:

"Be it enacted by the King's most excellent Majesty, . . . (by and with the advice and Consent of Parliament) That where any Person or Persons have been convicted of any Offence within the Benefit of Clergy, before the Twentieth Day of *January* one thousand seven hundred and seventeen, are liable to be whipt or burnt in the hand, or have been ordered to any Workhouse, and who shall be therein on the said Twentieth Day of January; as also where any Person or Persons shall be hereafter convicted of Grand or Petit Larceny or any felonious Stealing of taking of Money or Goods and Chattels, either from the Person, or House of any Other, or in any other Manner, and who by the law shall be entitled to the Benefit of Clergy, and liable only to the Penalties of Burning in the hand or Whippung (except Persons convicted for receiving or buying stolen Goods, knowing them to be stolen) it shall and may be lawful for the Court before whom they were convicted, or any Court held at the same Place with the like Authority, if they think fit, instead of ordering any sich Felons to be burnt in the Hand or Whipt, to order and direct, That such Offenders, as also such Offenders in any Workhouse, as aforesaid, they shall be sent as soon as conveniently may be to some of his Majesty's Colonies and Plantations in *America* for the Space of seven Years; and that Court before whom they were convicted, or any subsequent Court held at the same Place, with like Authority as the former, shall have power to convey, transfer and make over such Offenders, by Order of Court, to the Use of any Person or Persons who shall contract for the Performance of such Transportation, to him or them, and his and their Assigns, for such Term of seven Years, and where any Persons have been convicted, or do now stand attainted of any Offences whatsoever, for which Death by Law ought to be inflicted, or where any Offender shall hereafter be convicted of any Crimes whatsoever, for which they are by law to be excluded the Benefit of Clergy, and his Majesty, his Heirs or Successors, shall be graciously pleased to extend Royal Mercy to any such Offenders, upon the Condition of Transportation to any Part of *America,* and such Intention of Mercy be signified by one of his Majesty's Principal Secretaries of State. It shall and may be lawful to and for any Court having proper Authority, to allow such Offenders the Benefit of a Pardon under the Great Seal, and to order and direct the like Transfer and Conveyance to any Person or

Persons (who will contract for the Performance of such Transportation), and to his and their Assigns, of any such before mentioned Offenders, as also of any Person or Persons convicted of receiving or buying stolen Goods, knowing them to be stolen, for the Term of fourteen Years, in case such Condition of Transportation be general or else for such other Term or Terms as shall be made part of such Condition, if any particular Time be specified by his Majesty, his Heirs and Successors, as aforesaid; and such Person or Persons so contracting as aforesaid, his or their Assigns by Virtue of such Order of Transfer as aforesaid, shall have a Property and Interest in the Service of such Offenders for such Terms of Years.[50]

Return of Felons

And be it further enacted by the Authority aforesaid, That if any Offender or Offenders, so ordered by any such Court to be transported for any Term of seven Years or fourteen Years, or other Term or Terms as aforesaid, shall return into any Part of *Great Britain* or *Ireland* before the end of his or their said Term, he or they so returning, shall be liable to be punished as any Person attainted of Felony without the Benefit of Clergy, and Execution may and shal be awarded against such Offender or Offenders: Provided nevertheless that his Majesty, his Heirs and Successors may at any Time pardon and dispense with any such Transportation, and allow of the Return of any such Offender or Offenders from *America,* he or they paying their owner or Proprietor, at the Time of such Pardon, Dispensation or Allowance, such sum of Money as shall be adjudged reasonable by any two Justices of the Peace residing within the Province where such owner dwells; and where any such Offenders shall be transported, and shall have served their respective Terms, such Services shall have the Effect of a Pardon to all Intents and Purposes.[51]

Contract for Transportation

"And be it further enacted, That every such Person or Persons to any such Court shall order any such Offenders to be transported, he (or they) shall contract and agree with Such Person or Persons as shall be ordered and appointed by such Court, as aforesaid, and sufficient Security to the Satisfaction of such Court, that he or they will transport or cause to be transported, effectually, such Offenders so conveyed to him or them, to some of his Majesty's Colonies and Plantations in *America,* as shall be ordered by the said Court, and procure an authentick certificate from the Governor or the Chief Custom House Officer of the Place (which Certificate they are hereby required to give forthwith, without Fee or Reward, as soon as conveniently may be) of the Landing of such Offenders so transferred, in the Place whereto they shall be ordered, (Death and Casualties of the Sea excepted) and that none of the said Offenders shall be

---

[50] *4 George I,* ch. 11, sec. 1 (1717)

[51] *Ibid.,* sec. 2.

suffered to return from the said Place to any Part of *Great Britain* or *Ireland* by the wilful default of such Person or Persons so contracting.[52]

Those Aiding Felons Subject to Transportation

"And whereas there are several Persons who have secret acquaintance with Felons, and who make it their Business to help Persons to their stolen Goods and by that means gain Money from them, which is divided between them and the Felons, whereby they greatly encourage such Offenders, Be it enacted by the Authority aforesaid, That wherever any Person taketh Money or Reward, . . . as aforesaid, (unless such Person doth apprehend or cause to be apprehended, such Felon who stole the same, and cause such Felon to be brought to his trial for the same, and give evidence against him) shall be guilty of Felony, and suffer the Pains and Penalties of Felony, according to the Nature of the Felony committed in stealing such Goods, and in such and the same Manner as if such Offender had himself stole such goods and Chattles, in the Manner, and with such circumstances as the same were stolen." [53]

Conditions Under Which Exporters of Wool Subject to Transportation

"And be it further enacted by the Authority aforesaid, that from and after the said twentieth Day of *January,* one thousand seven hundred and seventeen, if any Person or Persons shall be in Prison for want of sufficient Bail, for unlawful Exportation of Wooll or Woolsells, and shall refuse to appear or plead to a Declaration or Information to be delivered to such Person or Persons, or to the Gaoler, Keeper or Turnkey of the Prison, at the said Prison, for the said Offence, by the Space of one Term, Judgment shall be entered against him by Default, and in case Judgment shall be obtained against any such Person or Persons by Default, Verdict or otherwise, and such Person or Persons shall not pay the Sum recovered against him or them for the said Offence, within the Space of three Months after entring up of such Judgment, the Court before whom such judgment shall be obtained shall cause such offender, or Offenders to be transported, in the same Manner as Felons aforesaid, for the Term of seven years; and if such Offender or Offenders shall return into Great Britain or Ireland before the Expiration of the said Term, he or they shall suffer as Felons, and have Execution awarded against them, as Persons attainted of Felony, without Benefit of Clergy." [54]

Felons from Scotland not Included

"Provided always, That nothing in this Act contained shall extend or be construed to extend to such Persons as shall be convicted or attainted in that Part of *Great Britain* called Scotland." [55]

---

[52] *Ibid.,* sec. 3.

[53] *Ibid.,* sec. 4.

[54] *Ibid.,* sec. 6.

[55] *Ibid.,* sec. 8.   This was made applicable to Scotland in 1765.   *6 George III,* ch. 32, sec. 1.

Transportation Made More Certain

"Whereas the Laws in being have not proved effectual to the Suppressing of Robbery, Burglary, and other Felonies, and to the Transporting of Felons, and some of the said Laws wanting to be amended and enforced: Be it enacted by the King's most Excellent Majesty, by and with the Advice and Consent of the Lords Temporal and Spiritual and Commons, That all the Powers and Authorities which are in and by an act made in the fourth Year of the Reign of his present Majesty, intituled, *An Act for the further Preventing, Robbery, Burglary and other Felonies, and for the more Effectual Transportation of Felons, and unlawful Exporters of Wool, and for declaring the Law upon some Points relating to Pirates,* given to any Court before whom Felons and Offenders, tried for and convicted of any Offences for which they may be sent or transported to any of his Majesty's Colonies or Plantations in America, shall and may be observed and executed by any other subsequent Court with like Authority, held for the same County, Riding, Division or Liberty where such Offenders or Felons were or shall be tried and convicted, notwithstanding such other subsequent Court shall happen to be held at or in any other Town or Place than that wherein such Trials or Convictions were or shall be." [56]

Sections 2 and 3 of the above act regulated payment of charges, method of letting contracts, etc., for transportation of felons.

Securities for Transportation

"And it is further enacted by the Authority aforesaid, That all Securities for Transportation hereafter to be taken, pursuant to this or the said former Act, shall be by Bond, in the name of the respective Clerks of the Peace of the County, Riding Division or Place, and their Successors shall, from Time to Time, prosecute such Bonds in their own names, to which Purpose they shall be deemed and taken to be a Body Corporate, and be paid all such Costs, Charges and Expenses, as they or any of them shall sustain or expend in any such Suit, as the said Justices of the Peace, shall at their General Quarter Sessions of the Peace direct, for the Penalty of such Bond, or otherwise howsoever by Reason thereof, out of the public Stock, and by the respective Treasurers, as aforesaid; and that all monies recovered on any sich Security or Bond entred into, as aforesaid, shall be to and for the Use of the respective county, riding division and place. [57]

And it is further enacted . . . that the Person or Persons so contracting and to whom any such Felons or Offenders shall be delivered in order to be transported as aforesaid, or any Person or Persons directed by the said Justices (impowered to contract as aforesaid) or their Assigns, may, in such Manner as they shall think fit, carry and secure the said Felons and Offenders in and through any County and Counties of *Great Britain* whatsoever, toward the Sea Port, from which they are to be trans-

[56] *6 George I,* ch. 23, sec. 1.
[57] *Ibid.,* sec. 4.

ported, and That if any Person or Persons shall rescue such Felons or Offenders, or any of them, he, she, and they so rescuing, or aiding or assisting them, in making their escape from such Person or Persons as shall have them in their Custody, shall be deemed and adjudged guilty of Felony, and shall suffer Death as in Case of Felony, without Benefit of Clergy." [58]

Section 6 of above act provided that persons ordered for transportation were found within the realm of Great Britain without some just cause, should suffer death, "without Benefit of Clergy."

Shipment of Others Than Felons to the Plantations Regulated

"And whereas there are many idle Persons, who are under the age of one and twenty Years, lurking about in divers parts of *London,* and elsewhere, who want employment, and may be tempted to become Thieves, if not provided for; And whereas they may be inclined to be transported and to enter into Services in some of his Majesty's Colonies and Plantations in *America,* but as they have no power to contract for themselves, and therefore that it is not safe for Merchants to transport them, or take them into such Services: Be it enacted . . . That where any Person of the Age of fifteen Years or more, and under the Age of twenty-one, shall be willing to be transported, and to enter into any Service in any of his Majesty's Colonies or Plantations in *America,* it shall and may be lawful for any Merchant, or other, to contract with any such Person for any such Service, not exceeding the Term of eight Years; providing such Person so binding him—or herself do come before the Lord Mayor of *London,* or some other Justice of the Peace of the City, if such contract be made within the same, or the Liberties thereof, or before some other two Justices of the Peace of the Place where such Contract shall be made, if made elsewhere, and before such Magistrate or Magistrates acknowledge such Consent, and do sign such Contract in his or their Presence, and with his or their Approbation; and that then it shall be lawful any such Merchant or other, to transport such Person binding him—or herself, and to keep him or her within any of the said Plantations or Colonies, according to the Tenor of such Contract, as aforesaid, any law or Statute to the Contrary in any wise notwithstanding; which said Contract, and Approbation of such Magistrate or Magistrates, with the Tenor of such Contract, shall be certified by such Magistrate or Magistrates, to the next general Quarter Sessions of the Peace, held for that County where such Magistrate or Magistrates shall reside, to be registered by the Clerk of the peace without fee or reward." [59]

LATER PENNSYLVANIA LEGISLATION

Importing Felons

"An Act for imposing a duty on persons convicted of heinous crimes and imported into this Province as Servants, or otherwise."

[58] *Ibid.,* sec. 4.
[59] *4 George I,* ch. 11, sec. 5.

Section I, Duty of £5 on each convict, before landed, and the master or merchant importing such, to be bound to the treasurer of the province (with "good and sufficient security") to the amount of £50 for the good behavior of such convict for one year.

Section II, And for the better ascertaining of who were convicts, the master of the ship, or the merchant owner was ordered to appear within twenty-four hours after arrival before two or more Justices of the peace and give under oath, names of persons or passengers brought and their former condition. The Justice could summon other witnesses and make an examination, after which he might issue a permit giving the names of those entitled to be landed.

Violations of the above provisions on the part of a Master would make a servant free, regardless of any private agreement.[60]

Servitude for Forging, Counterfeiting, Etc.

For the above offences penalty, in the pillory, and both ears cut off, to make good double the amount defrauded, and fined £100. If unable to meet the above, then the offender was to be sold by order of the Court trying the offence, for a term not to exceed seven years.[61]

Duty on Foreigners and Irish Servants Imported in the Province

"An Act for Laying a Duty on Foreigners and Irish Servants Imported into this Province."

Called attention to the Act of May 5th, 1722, and said further provision necessary to discourage great numbers of foreigners and of blind, idle and ill affected persons. Enumerated "Aliens, Irish Servants, or Passengers." [62]

Enforcing Law vs. Importing Criminals

Definitely provided (1729) for the examination of all persons suspected as having come contrary to the law of 1722; the Master or Merchant forfeited £20 for every such person.[63]

Sales or Assignments of Servants in Philadelphia

All sales or assignments of servants were to be before the mayor of the city . . . or before the recorder. Penalty for violation, £10.

---

[60] Passed May 5th, 1722. Reported by title Bioren, *Laws,* I, xvi. Law given in full in *Statutes at Large,* III, 265-267. Account of the Bill in *Votes of Assembly,* II, 318, 319.

[61] Passed 1721-1722, *Statutes at Large,* III, 331, 332; Re-enacted 1723, *Statutes at Large,* IV, 113; (Re-enacted May, 1739), *Statutes at Large,* IV, 359.

[62] Passed May 10th, 1729. Given by Title, Bioren, *Laws,* I, xix. Given in full in *Statutes at Large,* IV, 135-140. See *Colonial Records,* III, 359, 360, for account of this before Provincial Council.

[63] *Statutes at Large,* IV, 138. The above was re-enacted 1729-1730. *Ibid.,* 166; and again in 1742-43, *Ibid.,* 360-370.

Register of Assignments of Servants

The mayor and the recorder were obliged to keep a register of the names of servants by whom and to whom they were assigned, the term of years mentioned in the indenture and the date of the assignment.[64]

Duty on Criminals And to Prevent Importation of Impotent Persons

Repealed act of 1722. Those who were not wanted, in addition to criminals, "Those who by age, impotency or idleness have become a heavy burden and charge upon the inhabitants." Duty, fine and bond for criminals were preserved.

Lunatics, infants, vagrants and impotent persons were enumerated and the Master or Merchant was to become surety for the return of all such and to indemnify the inhabitants for loss incurred because of them.[65]

Supplementary Act to One vs. Importing Criminals

"Duty on persons convicted of heinous crimes, and to prevent poor and impotent persons being imported into this province." [66]

Further Enactment Against Importing Criminals and Impotent Persons

Different from preceding in the idea, "brought into this province, and not warranted by the Laws of Great Britain." Called attention to the practice of bringing in servants that were infirm or afflicted with a secret or loathsome disease. Enacted that if servants were sold who were with child or afflicted with such diseases as should render them incapable of performing the ordinary duties of servants, etc., the seller to make good, with costs and damages.[67]

Supplement to Act Against Importing Criminals

Impotent persons, etc. Supplementary Act passed on August 19th, 1749.[68]

---

[64] Law 314, Section VIII, passed February 14, 1729-30. *Ibid.*, 170, 171.

[65] *Ibid.*, IV, 164-167.

[66] Passed September 2nd, 1738; Repealed 1742-43. Given by title Bioren, *Laws*, I, xxi. Given in full *Statutes at Large*, IV, 320, 321. Record of and manner of passing, *Votes of Assembly*, III, 313.

[67] Passed Feb. 3, 1742-43. Before the Assembly, *Votes*, III, 369. *Statutes at Large*, IV, 360-370. Reported by title, Bioren, I, xxii. Act of 1742-43, disallowed by the King in Council, December 17th, 1746. Bioren, *Laws*, I, xix.

[68] Reported by title, Bioren, I, xxiii. History of, before the Assembly, *Votes*, IV, 110. Final passage, *Ibid.*, 112. Law amending above act passed Aug. 22, 1751. *Votes of Assembly*, IV, 193, 194.

Regulating the Importation

"An Act prohibiting the importation of Germans or other passengers in too great numbers in any vessel." [69]

Compensation for Enlisted Servants

An Act "for the relief of persons, whose apprentices or servants have enlisted in the late King's or his present Majesty's service." [70]

An Act for making Compensation to Those, whose Servants and Apprentices have been Enlisted. [71]

Freedom Dues, Recovery of

Said that no clear and express authority was given, . . . to order and enforce the delivery and payment of freedom dues . . . and that many servants, after having faithfully discharged their duty, and servitude, were discouraged from prosecuting their suits, and thereby deprived of their just dues, which was to be remedied by this act. Servants complaining without just cause were required to pay all costs. [72]

Freedom Dues, Amendment

It was enacted that so much of the former Act, as related to servants having a new grubbing hoe, an axe, and a weeding hoe, at the expiration of their servitude, should be repealed, and made null and void. [73]

Servants Running Away

In cases of absence without leave during the term of service the Justices were directed to compel servants to make a full recompense for the damages and charges adjudged to be sustained by such absence, either by serving five days for every day of absence, or by such other reasonable satisfaction, as to the Justice should seem proper. [74]

Indentured Servants Getting a Residence

"An Act for the relief of the poor."

Section 18 of above act. Indentured servant legally imported, to have settlement where he or she served first for 60 days, and if afterwards service was in any other place for 12 months, legal settlement was to be in that other place. [75]

---

[69] Passed January 27th, 1749-1750. Reported by title, Bioren, I, xxiii. Law Chapter 527, supplementary to Act above was passed May 18th, 1765.

[70] Passed March 4th, 1763. Reported by title, Bioren, *Laws,* I, xxx.

[71] Reported by title, *Ibid.,* xlvii. Supplement to the general Act of 1700. Passed March 12, 1778.

[72] Bioren, *Laws,* I, 320, 321.

[73] *Ibid.,* 321.

For the legal complications that made this Supplementary Act necessary, see Bioren, I, 11, Note G.

[74] Bioren, *Laws,* I, 321.

[75] *Ibid.,* I, 339.

Assignment of Servants Again Before Justices in Philadelphia

"An Act to empower two Justices of the peace for the City of Philadelphia to do and perform certain acts, including the assignment of servants,
formerly directed to be done before the Mayor, recorder and alderman of
said city.[76]

Negro Apprentices, Gradual Abolition of Slavery

No person born after the passing of the Act to be a slave for life.
Negro and Mulatto children of slaves to be servants until 28 years of age.
Section V. Registry ordered of all slaves held, before the 1st of the
succeeding November.
Section X. Only those registered as above should continue in servi-
tude.[77]

Apprehending Runaway Negroes, Etc.

Section IX. The reward for taking up runaway and absconding Negro
and Mulatto slaves and servants, and the penalty for enticing away, dealing with, or harboring, concealing, or employing Negro and Mulatto slaves
and servants, were fixed the same, and to be recovered in like manner, as
in case of "servants bound for four years." [78]

Negroes' Term of Servitude

No Negro or Mulatto was to be held in servitude or apprenticeship
for a longer term than seven years, unless such Negro or Mulatto were
less than twenty-one years old, in which case, he might be held until
twenty-eight years of age, but not longer than that time.[79]

Supplementary Act to Act for Gradual Abolition of Slavery (1780)

Passed "to explain and amend" the earlier act. Slave and "servant
for a term of years" both named in the Act. Slaves or servants for a
term of years were not to be removed out of the State without their own
consent. Penalty for such offence, £75. Slaves or servants for a term of
years, were not to be separated from their parents without the consent of
those concerned, nor were husbands and wives to be separated without
consent.[80]

Register of German Passengers

Establishment of the office of a Register of all German passengers and

---

[76] Passed March 14, 1777. Reported by title in Bioren, *Laws,* I, xliv. By change
in government in Pennsylvania, the offices above in Philadelphia became vacant and
the Act above noted made provision for their duties to be performed by Justices of the
Peace either collectively or any three of them. (*Ibid,* II, 328.)

[77] *Ibid.,* I, 492-497.

[78] *Ibid.,* I, 495.

[79] *Ibid.,* I, 496.

[80] Passed, March 29th, 1788. *Ibid.,* II, 443-446.

of all indentures by which any of them should be bound servants for their passage and of the assignments of such servants in the City of Philadelphia.

Recited the Practice under the former Acts of 1749-50 and 1765. Called attention to the change in practice since Act of 1777 (March 15th), when offices of Mayor and Recorder were vacated and duties performed by Justices of the Peace. Duty of Registration of these German passengers now to be by a special officer who should be familiar with both English and German languages.[81]

Indentures of German Passengers (1785)

". . . all indentures of such German passengers men, women and children, by which they shall be bound to serve, and all assignments of servants made within the said city, shall be made and acknowledged before the said Register, or his lawful deputy, and by him certified, and the full contents thereof entered and registered in the same manner, and to the same effect, as servants' indentures and assignments of servants were heretofore by law made and acknowledge before the Mayor of the City of Philadelphia, and by him registered; and that all persons whom it may concern shall be entitled to have a copy or abstract of such register."[82]

Vs. Importing Convicts

Laws Chapter MCCCCIII represented that a practice prevailed of importing felons and convicts into this state, said felons and convicts sold and dispersed among the people, "whereby much injury hath arisen to the morals of some, and others have been greatly endangered in their lives, and property. . . ."[83]

Penalty for Importing Convicts

For every convict imported three months imprisonment and £50 fine: one-half of the fine to go to the commonwealth and one-half to the person who made complaint.

Imported Convicts to Be Transported Out of the United States

Persons importing convicts to give surety that they be transported again or the importer committed to jail without bail and kept there until transportation was made, or surety given that it would be made.[84]

Provisions for Runaways, Etc.

Ordered that when a prison was completed, the inspectors were to have removed thither persons confined under several denominations, among which were "vagrants, runaway or disorderly servants and apprentices . . ."[85]

---

[81] *Ibid.,* II, 328-330.
[82] Passed April 8, 1785. Bioren, *Laws,* II, 329.
[83] *Ibid.,* II, 485.
[84] Passed March 27, 1789. *Ibid.,* 486.
[85] Passed April 2nd, 1803. *Ibid.,* IV, 87, 88.

Apprenticing Poor Children

Directors of poor in Chester and Lancaster Counties were given power to apprentice such children as came under their care as overseers of the poor. Passed January 30th, 1804.[86]

German Redemptioners, Schooling of

All Masters and Mistresses of German Redemptioners who were minors, were directed to give six weeks' schooling for each year of servitude. It was made the duty of the Register to insert the provision for this in the indentures. Passed, March 19th, 1810.[87]

Regulation of Importation of German And Other Passengers

Laws Chapter 4488. Passed February 7th, 1818.

Bill of Lading

A bill of lading to be given to all passengers for all goods brought and stored in the hold of the vessel. Fine for neglect, One Hundred Dollars.[88]

Landing of Passengers

Persons to be put on shore with their goods without extra charge on payment of the price agreed upon in Europe. Penalty for violation, Fifty Dollars.[89]

German Immigration. Acknowledgment of Indentures. Separation of Husband and Wife

Indentures to be acknowledged before the Mayor of Philadelphia, or in case of Germans, before the Register of the German passengers. Husband and wife were not to be separated except by mutual consent, and unless they agreed to separation indentures separating them were void. Penalty for violation, One Hundred Dollars.[90]

Sale Out of the Commonwealth

Those bound to serve in the Province not to be sold out of it against their will. Fine, One Hundred Dollars.[91]

Provisions for Passengers. Sick Passengers

Captain to give proper food and drink and to care for, during a term of thirty days. Additional time to be at the expense of the passengers.

---

[86] *Ibid.,* IV, 109, 110.
[87] *Ibid.,* V, 113.
[88] *Ibid.,* VII, 29, 30.
[89] *Ibid.,* 30.
[90] *Ibid.,* VII, 30, 31.
[91] *Ibid.,* 31.

Sick persons to be removed and cared for; those that could not be removed to be cared for on shipboard.[92]   Penalty for violation five hundred dollars.

Report of Passengers to Be Made

German passengers who died on the voyage and those who died after arrival, to be reported within fifteen days, under penalty of three hundred dollars.

Goods of a Passenger Who Died

Just account of same to be rendered to the Register of Wills for the benefit of heirs or creditors.   Penalty for violation five hundred dollars.[93]

---

[92] *Ibid.*, 31.

[93] *Ibid.*, 33.

Penalties as above to be collected by the Register of German passengers. *Ibid.*, 34.

February 25th, 1818, the Governor directed to transmit a copy of the above Act to the Governor of Delaware with the request that he would lay it before the legislature of that state and invite their co-operation. *Ibid.*, 34.

It will be observed that from 1749 the legislation is in the direction of a better regulation and administration of the Redemption system. No act was passed looking to its abolition, but the above body of legislation looked to its control. When the indentured labor system passed out of existence, as it did in the first third of the last century, it was not legislated out, as was the system of slave labor. Changed economic conditions, both in the labor supply and the labor demand, doomed indentured labor to give place to that of freemen.

APPENDIX II

EMIGRATION RECORD FROM GREAT BRITAIN

An Account of all Persons who have taken their Passage [at a] Port in England, with a description of their Age, Quality, Occupation... to go, and on what Account & for what purposes they leave this Country

Names		Quality Occupation or Employmt. former residence
		Embarked from the
Thomas Ramsey	18	Gentleman — Edinburgh
John Harlow	30	Do. — London
Willm. Thomas Esqe.		refused to give any Answer.
W. H. Ricketts	19	Gentleman — Southampton
H. Ferguson	20	Do. — Aberdeen
Will. Clark	23	Baker — Surry
Will. Shillingford	18	Gentleman — Hertfordshire
Robt. Hoggart	21	Gentleman — London
Thos. Parsons	33	Gentleman — London
Esther Parsons		Wife to the above Gentleman
W. A. Maxwall	31	Bookkeeper — London
Thos. Houlton	45	Merchant — Do.
Jas. Campbell	26	Attorney — Do.
Will. Thomas	20	Gentleman — Do.
John Hill	18	Baker — Do.
Will. Smith	42	Taylor — Surry
Will. Morgan	31	Husbandman — Dublin
Thos. Weatherley	21	Edge Tool maker — Kent
J. Wetherell	31	Bricklayer — Lincolnshire
Thos. Hanham	21	Plaisterer — London
John Turner	25	Cordwainer — Do.
Edme. Deneau	45	Schoolmaster — Eaton
John Howard	25	Smith — Surry
Aaron Pigeman	29	Bookkeeper — Bucks
John Carry	24	Stone Mason — Fifeshire
Will. Emmins	27	Husbandman — Lincoln
Thos. Sewell	22	Bookkeeper — Westmoreland
Thos. Draper	22	Silk Dyer — London
Saml. Young	21	Cordwainer — Westminster
Wm. Wingfield	30	Husbandman — Berks
Wm. Howard	26	Schoolmaster — Worcester
Robt. Dellemore	22	Brazier — London
Robt. Hoggart	21	

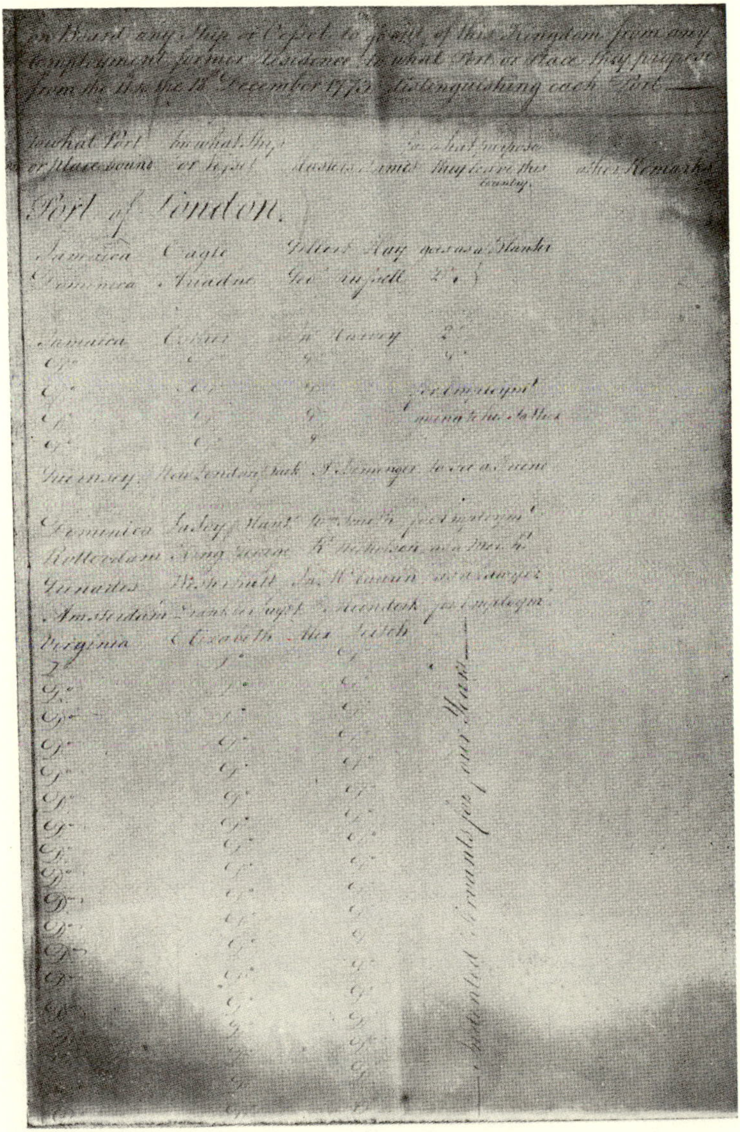

RECORD OFFICE, LONDON

Names		Quality	Occupation	Employment	Former Residence
Willm Allison	18			Labourer	London
Thos Suttle	21			Husbandman	Cambridge
Willm Boyle	26			d^o	Ireland
Jno McCloud	20			Labourer	London
Alex^r Muir	21			Weaver	Scotland
Robt Ogelvie	19			Husbandman	London
John Suder	18			Leather dresser	D^o
John Oakeley	19			Perake maker	D^o
Ja^s Weatherfield	20			Blacksmith	D^o
Jno Seek	17			Whitsmith	Worcester
Jno Onwin	19			Baker	Greenwich
Thos Pemberton	20			Bricklayer	Chester
John Welch	31			Halster	Surry
Thos Wood	23			Schoolmaster	
Jos^h Stevenson	25			Carpent^r & Joyner	Westminster
Benjn Smith	21			Bricklayer	D^o
John Yeates	21			Weaver	D^o
Rich. Obrian	21			Butcher	Dublin
Benjn Parrott	32			Carpenter	London
John Garth	39			Sawyer	D^o
Willm Parker	22			Edge Tool maker	Deptford
Richd Thomas	36			Haberdasher	London
John Dawson	22			Ostler	Surry
Thos Howard	28		Surgeon		London
Elizabeth his Wife	19				D^o
Willm Fogg	23			Blacksmith	Warwickshire
Wm Kilman	23			D^o	Scotland
Richd Harris	35			Gardner	London
Jno Ockershanson	25			Baker	D^o
Ja^s Jameson	21			Husbandman	D^o
Jno Carl Keller	21			Taylor	D^o
Peter Cagaux	26			Cooper	D^o
Alex^r Chesailler	21			Hatter & Painter	D^o
John Young	21			Blacksmith	D^o
George Dame	33			Cabinet Maker	D^o

Ft. 309

2

Continued

In what Port or Place Bound	by what Ship or Vessel	Masters Name	for what purpose they leave this Country	other Remarks

Virginia   Elizabeth   Alexr Fitch

——— Intented Servants for four Years ———

Port of London

Names	Age	Quality	Occupation	Employment	From/Residence
Tho.ˢ Taylor	41			Bricklayer	London
Tho.ˢ Jerman	41			Schoolmaster	Ireland
Lewis Bryant	22			Plaisterer	Bath
Rob.ᵗ Bagwell	23			Schoolmaster	Westminster
Will.ᵐ Rice	26			Husbandman	Essex
John Saunders	41			Peruke maker	London
James Pemsay	21			Husbandman	D.º
John Low	23			Blacksmith	Herts
Tho.ˢ Williams	30			Labourer	London
Geo.º Clark	18			Stocking weav.ʳ	Gloucestersh.
Edw.ᵈ Pemberton	30			Blacksmith	Stafford
Pat.ᵏ Reiley	23			Husbandman	Ireland
James Major	27			Butcher	Ditto
Tho.ˢ Mape	21			Wool comber	Somerset
Isaac How	24			Husbandman	Suffolk
Jn.º Sangster	21			Carpenter	Reading
Jn.º Patterson	22			Gardner	Aberdeen
Jas. Lambert	21			Ditto	Middlesex
John Asher	28			Ditto	Edinbourg
Ja.ˢ Whitehead	27			Cordwainer	Ditto
Tho.ˢ M.ᶜKoin	28			Schoolmaster	London
Will.ᵐ Herssey	23			Husbandman	Bucks
Will.ᵐ Gann	32			D.º	Sunderland
Bar.ᵗ Walker	28			Sawyer	Bucks
Geo.º Lambert	25			Cordwainer	Westminster
Benj.ⁿ Richards	35			Mat Maker	Deptford
John Orpwood	25			Joyner	Oxford
Rich.ᵈ Miller	21			Necklace mak.ʳ	London
Rob.ᵗ Hairjames	21			Bookkeeper	London
Peter Westphal	24			Husbandman	D.º
Terence M.ᶜdonald	30			Painter	
John Thornler	35			Peruke maker	D.º
Cha.ˢ Watson	23			Baker	Surry
Ben.ⁿ Edwards	22			Broad Cloth weav.ʳ	Somersetsh.
...	21			Husbandman	Nottingha...

To what port or place bound	by what Ship or Vessel	Masters Name	for what purpose they leave the country	other remarks
Virginia	Elizabeth	Alexr Fitch		
Do	Do	Do		
Do	Virginia	Henry Eaton		
Do	Do	Do		
Do	Do	Do		
Do	Do	Do		
Do	Do	Do		
Do	Do	Do		
Do	Do	Do		
Do	Do	Do		
Do	Do	Do		
Do	Do	Do		
Do	Do	Do		
Do	Do	Do		Intended servants for Four Years
Do	Do	Do		
Do	Do	Do		
Do	Do	Do		
Do	Do	Do		
Do	Do	Do		
Do	Do	Do		
Do	Do	Do		
Do	Do	Do		
Do	Do	Do		
Do	Do	Do		
Do	Do	Do		
Do	Do	Do		
Do	Do	Do		
Do	Do	Do		

RECORD OFFICE, LONDON

Port of London

Names		Quality	Occupation	Employment	Former residence
Jos.ᵗ Cheauvant 20				Gilder	London
Peter Auber — 26				Dyer	D.º
Peter Challe — 23				Blacksmith	D.º
Cha.ˢ Diaonne — 30				Taylor	D.º
Peter Macquel — 34				Locksmith	D.º
Beale Lowis Dah 21				Masnor	D.º
W.ᵐ Ashburne — 28				Cutler	D.º
Tho.ˢ Hill — 35				Schoolmaster	Essex
Ant.º Chevaillier 21				Brickmaker	Westminster
Will.ᵐ Burgess — 34				Weaver	London
Sarah Harris 21				Sempstress	D.º
Henry Brandes 35				Cordwainer	D.º
Jos. Isaac — 19				Perukemaker	D.º
Anth.º Lawrence 36				Cabinetmaker	D.º
Ja.ˢ Heming — 26				Husbandman	Cornwall

To what port or place bound	by what Ship or Vessel	Masters Name	For what purpose they leave this country	other Remarks
Virginia	Virginia	How⁰ Eaton		
D⁰	D⁰	D⁰		
D⁰	D⁰	D⁰		
D⁰	D⁰	D⁰		
D⁰	D⁰	D⁰		
D⁰	D⁰	D⁰	Indented Servants for Four Years	
D⁰	D⁰	D⁰		
D⁰	D⁰	D⁰		
D⁰	D⁰	D⁰		
D⁰	D⁰	D⁰		
D⁰	D⁰	D⁰		
D⁰	D⁰	D⁰		
D⁰	D⁰	D⁰		

Embark'd from the Port of London.

For different Purposes	10
For Employment	3
Indentured Servants in the Ship Elizabeth	56
Indentured Servants in the Ship Virginia — To Virginia for 4 Years	48
Total Embark'd from the Port of London	117

RECORD OFFICE, LONDON

APPENDIX III

I. PRIMARY SOURCES

ACRELIUS, ISRAEL.

History of New Sweden.
Translated from Swedish by William M. Reynolds.
Memoirs Historical Society of Pennsylvania, XI.
Philadelphia: 1874.

ALSOP, GEORGE.

A Character of the Province of Mary-land.
London: 1666.
Reprinted in Gowans' Bibliotheca Americana No. 5.
Also in Maryland Historical Society Publications, No. 15.
Baltimore: 1880.

ANDERSON, ADAM.

Origin of Commerce (Historical and Chronological).
Treats Colonies, Commerce, Manufactures, etc. Published 1764.
Revised and with an Appendix by William Coombe.
6 volumes, Dublin: 1790, also incorporated into Macpherson, *Annals of Commerce.* London: 1805.

ANDERSON, JAMES.

The Interest of Great Britain with Regard to her American Colonies Considered.
London: 1782.

ANNESLEY, JAMES.

Trial at Bar Between, and Richard, Earl of Anglesey.
At the King's Court, Dublin. 1742 and 1743.
London: 1744.

————.

Authentic Journal of the Proceedings in the Great Case tried at Dublin between J. A., and "a Noble Person Defendant."
With List of Witnesses, Summary of Evidence and Names of Jury, etc.
Third edition, London: 1743.

————.

Memoirs of An Unfortunate Young Nobleman, Returned from a Thirteen Years' Slavery in America, Where He was Sent by the Wicked Contrivances of His Cruel Uncle, etc.
Part II Concludes with a Summary View of the Trial.
2 volumes. London: 1743.

BETTLE, EDWARD.
Notices of Negro Slavery as Connected with Pennsylvania (1681-1770).
Memoirs of Historical Society of Pennsylvania, I, 351-388.
Philadelphia: 1826.

BOARD OF TRADE JOURNALS: 1675-1782.
Transcribed from original MSS. in the British Public Record Office, 93 Vols.
Library of Historical Society of Pennsylvania.

BOARD OF TRADE PAPERS: *Plantations General,* 1689-1780.
Transcribed from original MSS. in Public Record Office, 31 Vols.
Library of Historical Society of Pennsylvania.

———, *Proprieties.*
1697-1776.
Transcribed from original MSS. in Public Record Office, 24 Vols.
Library of Historical Society of Pennsylvania.

BOND, PHINEAS.
(British Consul at Philadelphia.)
Letters from 1787-1794.
Annual Reports American Historical Association, 1896 and 1897.

BRADFORD, WILLIAM.
An Enquiry into how far the Death Punishment is Necessary in Pennsylvania, to which is added a Description of Jail and Penitentiary of Philadelphia by Caleb Lownes.
Philadelphia: 1793. (London Edition: 1795.)

BRECK, SAMUEL.
Recollections of, With Passages from his Note-Books (1771-1862).
Philadelphia: 1877.

BRISSOT, J. P.
New Travels in the United States of America, made in 1788.
Second Edition, London: 1794.

BRITANNIA, Ship.
Munstering (Mustering) *Book* of the (Rotterdam to Philadelphia), 1773.
MS. Library Historical Society of Pennsylvania.

BRITANNIA, Ship from Rotterdam.
Passengers Landed From, with Charges.
Philadelphia, 11th Month, 1773.
MS. Library Historical Society of Pennsylvania.
Broadside of lottery for the Philadelphia German Society. 1764. Ridgeway Branch, Library Co. Philada. Collection of Broadsides, No. 23.

BROWN, ALEXANDER.
> *The Genesis of the United States* (1605-1616).
> Series of Historical Manuscripts collected and edited.
> 2 volumes, Boston: 1890.

BUCKS COUNTY, ARRIVALS IN (1677-1787).
> Registry of all the People in the County of Bucks, Province of Pennsylvania, that have come to Settle the Said County. MS. transcription of the original MS. in the Office of the Recorder of Deeds at Doylestown, Pennsylvania, by J. Bellangle Cox: 1865.
> Library Historical Society of Pennsylvania.

BUCKS COUNTY, MISCELLANEOUS.
> *Manuscripts,* Indentures, records of transfer of indentures, and other papers.
> Library Historical Society Bucks County, Doylestown, Pa.

BURKE, EDMUND.
> *An Account of the European Settlements in America.*
> 2 volumes, Fifth Edition, London: 1770.

BURNABY, ANDREW.
> *Travels through the Middle Settlements in North America* (1759-1760) With Observations on the State of the Colonies.
> Second Edition, London: 1775.

CHALMERS, GEORGE.
> *Opinions of Eminent Lawyers on Various Points of English Jurisprudence,* Chiefly Concerning the Colonies, the Fisheries, and Commerce of Great Britain.
> Burlington: 1854.

CHESTER COUNTY, Miscellaneous Manuscripts of, Collected by Gilbert Cope, West Chester, Pa., including court papers, indentures, and records of transfer of indentures, etc., Historical Society of Pennsylvania.

CHILD, SIR JOSIAH, *A New Discourse of Trade.*
> Fourth London Edition, n. d. First draft published 1668.

COLONIAL POLICY OF GREAT BRITAIN.
> Considered with Relation to North American Provinces.
> Dangerous Tendency of American Competition, etc.
> "By a British Traveller."
> Reprinted; Philadelphia: 1816.

COOPER, THOMAS.
> *Some Information Respecting America.*
> With Letters written from America to a friend in England (1793-1794).
> Second Edition, London: 1795.

COPE MANUSCRIPTS.
See Chester County Miscellaneous MSS.

COXE, TENCH.
View of the United States of America.
Series of Papers written between 1787 and 1794.
Interspersed with Documents.
Philadelphia: 1794.

CRÈVECŒUR, MICHEL, G. J. DE., *Letters from An American Farmer.*
Written by a farmer in Pennsylvania. London: 1782.
Issued under pseud. J. Hector Saint John.

DAY, SHERMAN.
Historical Collections of Pennsylvania.
Philadelphia: 1843.

DOUGLASS, WILLIAM (M. D.).
British Settlements in North America.
Summary,—Historical and Political.
2 volumes, Boston: 1749 and 1753. Reprinted London: 1755.

EDDIS, WILLIAM.
Letters from America,—Historical and Descriptive (1769-1777).
London: 1792.

Emigration Record From the Ports of Great Britain (1773 to 1776).
Persons leaving England, with their ages, occupations, former resi-
dences, reasons for leaving England, destinations, etc. Three bundles
of manuscripts in the Treasury Records, London. These Records
show that many emigrants left England under indenture and they
are invaluable to the student of indentured labor. The author is
indebted to Charles M. Andrews for photographs and transcripts
of four of these weekly records. (See Appendix II for reproduction
of some of these.) See also Andrews, *Guide to Material in Public
Record Office of Great Britain.*. Vol. II, Washington, D. C.: 1914.

FALCKNER, DANIEL.
Curieuse Nachricht from Pennsylvania.
Translation by Julius F. Sachse.
Lancaster, Pa.: 1905.
Series of 103 questions and answers, on all aspects of Pennsylvania
Conditions. Written at close of the seventeenth century. Several
editions printed in Germany.

FEARON, HENRY BRADSHAW.
Sketches of America (1817-1818).
Narrative of a Journey of 5,000 Miles through the Eastern and West-
ern States of America.
Second Edition, London: 1818.

FRANKLIN, BENJAMIN.
The Complete Works of, Including Private, Official and Scientific
Correspondence, etc.
Compiled and Edited by John Bigelow.
New York and London, Putnams: 1887 and 1888.

GEE, JOSHUA.
The Trade and Navigation of Great Britain.
London: 1729.

GORDON, THOMAS F.
History of Pennsylvania (Discovery to 1776).
Philadelphia: 1829.

HALL, F.
The Importance of the British Plantations in America, with State of
their Trade and Methods of Improving It; also Description of the
Several Colonies.
(Author said he had lived in America many years, he had traded to
most of the places of which he gave an account and occasionally
been at many of them.)
Pp. 114. London: 1731.

HALLE REPORTS.
New Edition, With Historical, Literary, and Critical Annotations and
Numerous Documents Copied from the MS. in the Archives of the
Francke Institution at Halle, by Rev. W. J. Mann, Rev. B. M.
Schmucker, and Rev. W. Germann.
Translated from the German by Rev. C. W. Schaeffer.
With Preface by Dr. John Ludwig Schulze, of Halle (1787).
Vol. I. Reading, Pennsylvania: 1882.

HALLISCHE NACHRICHTEN.
Reports on United German Evangelical Lutheran Congregations in
America, Especially in Pennsylvania.
Published in the Orphan House, Halle, 1750.
Translated from the German by Rev. Jonathan Oswald.
2 Vols. Philadelphia: 1880 and 1881.

HAMMOND, JOHN.
Leah and Rachel, or the Two Fruitfull Sisters Virginia, and Maryland: Their present Condition Impartially Stated and Related.
With a Removal of Such Imputations as are Scandalously cast on
those Countries, whereby many deceived Souls, chose rather to Beg,
Steal, or rot in Prison, and come to shameful deaths, than to better
their being by going thither, wherein is plenty of all things necessary for Human Subsistence.
London: 1656. Reprinted in Force's Tracts, vol. III.

HART, ALBERT BUSHNELL, Editor.
American History Told by Contemporaries.
4 Vols. published, New York and London: 1897, 1898, 1901.

HAZARD, SAMUEL.
Annals of Pennsylvania (1609-1682).
Philadelphia: 1850.

HOLM, THOMAS.
Short Description of the Province of New Sweden.
Stockholm: 1702.
Translated from the Swedish by Peter S. DuPonceau.
Memoirs of Historical Society of Pennsylvania.
Philadelphia: 1834.

HOLMES, ABIEL.
American Annals; Chronological History of America.
2 Vols. Cambridge, Massachusetts: 1805.

HUNT, BENJAMIN PETER.
Facts and Notes Relating to the Redemptioners and the Early Emigration of the Poor to America.
8 Vols. Boston Public Library.
Manuscripts, Extracts from books, and newspapers, newspaper cuttings, personal observations and miscellaneous notes. A wealth of material.

JEFFERSON, THOMAS.
Writings of (1760-1826).
Collected and Edited by Paul Leicester Ford.
10 Vols. New York and London, Putnams: 1892-1899.

KALM, PETER.
Travels into North America (1748 and 1749).
Translated from Swedish by John Reinhold Forster.
1st Vol. Warrington: 1770; 2nd and 3rd Vols. London: 1771.

LAWS, DUKE OF YORK'S (1676-1682).
Charter to William Penn and Laws Passed 1682-1700, Preceded by the Laws in force in Pennsylvania from 1676 to 1681. Historical notes. Harrisburg: 1879.

————, *BIOREN, JOHN* (Publisher).
Laws of the Commonwealth of Pennsylvania, 4 Vols. (1700-1810.) Philadelphia: 1810. Supplementary Vols. V, VI, VII, down to 1822.

————, *STATUTES AT LARGE OF PENNSYLVANIA.*
Vols. II-XVIII (1700-1809) appeared.
Harrisburg: 1896-1915.

LINCKLAEN, JOHN.
(Agent of the Holland Land Company.)
Journals of Travels into Pennsylvania, New York and Vermont (1791-1792).
Translated from French by Helen Lincklaen Fairchild.
With biographical sketch and notes.
New York, Putnams: 1897.

LOHER, FRANZ VON.
Geschichte und Zustande der Deutschen in Amerika.
Gottigen: 1855.

MARSHALL, JOHN.
American Colonial History.
(Settlement to the Revolution.)
Philadelphia: 1824.

MELISH, JOHN.
Travels in the United States of America (1806, 1807, 1809, 1810, 1811).
2 Vols. Philadelphia: 1812.

MELLICK, ANDREW D., JR.
The Story of an Old Farm, or Life in New Jersey in the Eighteenth Century.
Somerville, New Jersey: 1889.

MERCURY, THE AMERICAN WEEKLY (1719-1746).
6 Vols. Ridgway Branch, Philadelphia Library.
Philadelphia, Pennsylvania.

MITTELBERGER, GOTTLIEB.
Journey to Pennsylvania.
Translated by Carl Theo. Eben. Philadelphia: 1898.

MORALEY, WILLIAM.
Voyages and Adventures of. Original Edition, New Castle (England), 1743. Later printed in the *Chronicle* of New Castle, and later in Chester (Pa.), *Republican.*

NEW AMSTERDAM RECORDS.
From 1653 to 1674.
Edited by Berthold Fernow.
7 Vols. New York: 1897.

OLDMIXON, J.
British Empire in America.
Account of the Country, Soil, Climate, Product and Trade.
2 Vols. London: 1708.

PENN, WILLIAM.
Plan for Union of the Colonies—1696-97, February 8th.
Memoirs Historical Society of Pennsylvania, VI, 264.

PENNSYLVANIA COLONIAL RECORDS.
Minutes of the Provincial Council, and of the Council of Safety.
Published by the State, superintended by Samuel Hazard.
16 Vols. Harrisburg: 1852.

PENNSYLVANIA ARCHIVES.
First Series.
Published by the State, superintended by Samuel Hazard.
12 Vols. Harrisburg: 1852.

———.

Second Series.
19 Vols. Harrisburg: Imp. 1896, 1895, 1890, and 1893.

———.

Third Series.
30 Vols. Harrisburg: 1894 to 1899.

PENNSYLVANIA GAZETTE, WEEKLY.
From 1728 to 1845.
Philadelphia.

PHILADELPHIA, ARRIVALS AT.
A Portion of the Registry of 1682-1686.
MS. in Library Historical Society of Pennsylvania.

PHILADELPHIA COUNTY, COURT PAPERS.
"Records of Court Proceedings" (1697-1732): "Indictments" (1715-1790).
MS. Volumes in Library Historical Society of Pennsylvania.

POSTLETHWAYT, MALACHY.
The African Trade the Great Pillar and Support of the British Plantation Trade in America. London: 1745.
A rare and valuable tract originally signed "A British Merchant." In the British Museum, also in the John Carter Brown Library at Providence and in the library at Harvard University. In the latter place it was incompletely catalogued and was discovered by accident.

PRIEST, WILLIAM.
Travels in the United States of America (1793-1797).
London: 1802.

PROUD, ROBERT.
History of Pennsylvania (1681-1742).
Also Description of the Province from 1760-1770.
2 Vols. Philadelphia: 1797 and 1798.

RAYNAL, ABBÉ.

Philosophical and Political History of the British Settlements and Trade in North America.

Translated from the French.

(Dependence of Great Britain upon colonies and Discussion of taxation. Colonies held as "Shackled in their Industry and Commerce," etc.)

2 Vols. Edinburgh: 1776.

Record of Indentures, Individuals Bound Out as Apprentices, Servants, etc., and of German and Other Redemptioners in the office of the Mayor of the City of Philadelphia.

October 3, 1771 to October 5, 1773. Before Mayors John Gibson and William Fisher.

MS. Presented to American Phil. Society by Thos. P. Roberts, 1835. Reproduced in publications of Pennsylvania Germany Society, Vol. XVI, Lancaster, Pa., 1907. 321 closely printed pages averaging about twenty-two names to each double page or above 3,500 names recorded; both recently arrived and transfers recorded. Full description of terms, considerations, previous place of residence, etc.

RECORD BEFORE THE MAYOR. (1745.)

James Hamilton, Register. MS. contributed by George W. Neifle, Chester, Pa.

Pa. Mag. Hist. and Biog., Vols. 30, 31 and 32.

REDEMPTIONERS, REGISTRY OF THE

"Book A" Germans, etc. (1785-1804); "Book C" (1817-1831).

MSS. Library Historical Society of Pennsylvania.

RICHARDS, M. H.

"German Emigration from New York Province into Pennsylvania," *Pennsylvania-German Society Proceedings,* Vol. VII

Lancaster: 1899.

RUSH, BENJAMIN.

An Account of the Manners of the German Inhabitants of Pennsylvania (Written, 1789). Notes by I. D. Rupp.

Philadelphia: 1875.

SCHEFFER, J. G. DE HOOP.

"Mennonite Emigration to Pennsylvania."

Translated from the Dutch by Samuel W. Pennypacker.

Pa. Mag. Hist. and Biog., II, 117sqq.

SHEFFIELD, JOHN LORD: *Observations on the Commerce of the American States.* Sixth Edition, London: 1784.

SMITH, SAMUEL.
History of New Jersey (From its settlement to 1721).
Burlington: 1765. Re-printed Trenton: 1877.

SMITH, DR. WILLIAM.
A brief State of the Province of Pennsylvania, etc.
London: 1755. Also Sabin's Reprints No. IV, New York: 1865.

———.
A brief View of the Conduct of Pennsylvania for the Year 1755, being
    a sequel to a brief State, etc.
A Second Letter to a Friend in London.
London: 1756

ST. JOHN, J. HECTOR, Pseud, for Crèvecœur, which see.

STATE PAPERS, CALENDAR OF.
Colonial Series, 20 Vols., 1574-1711.
Edited by W. Noel Sainsbury, J. W. Fortescue and Cecil Headlam.
London: 1860-1924.

SUTCLIFF, ROBERT.
Travels in Some Parts of North America (1804-1805-1806).
York, England: 1811.

THOMAS, GABRIEL.
*Historical and Geographical Account of the Province and Country of
    Pennsylvania and of West Jersey in America.*
London: 1694. Reprint New York: 1848.

THOMAS, GOVERNOR GEORGE.
Letter to Lords of Trade, October 20, 1740. Printed copy in Library
    Historical Society of Pennsylvania.

THOMSON, CHARLES.
*An Enquiry into the Causes of the Alienation of the Indians from the
    British interest.* London: 1759.

UPLAND COURT, RECORD OF THE (1676-1681).
Edited with Introduction by Edward Armstrong.
Memoirs Historical Society of Pennsylvania, VII.
Philadelphia: 1860.

VOTES AND PROCEEDINGS OF ASSEMBLY.
The House of Representatives of the Province of Pennsylvania.
    Vol. I, Two Parts (1662-1707), Philadelphia: 1752; Vol. II
    (1707-1726), Philadelphia: 1753; Vol. III (1726-1744), Philadel-
    phia: 1754; Vol. IV (1744-1758, Philadelphia: 1774.

WAKEFIELD, EDWARD GIBBON.

England and America: A Comparison of the Social and Political
State of Both Nations.
New York: 1834.

WAKEFIELD, PRISCILLA.

Excursions in North America, described in Letters.
Second Edition. London: 1810.

WASHINGTON, GEORGE.

Writings of, With Life by Jared Sparks.
12 Vols. Boston: 1858.

WELD, ISAAC, JR.

Travels through the States of North America, and the Provinces of
Upper and Lower Canada. (1795, 1796, 1797.)
Third Edition, 2 Vols. London: 1800.

WILLIAMSON, PETER.

Papers Relating to,

Memorials, Petitions, Evidence and Arguments in the Trials of Peter
Williamson from 1761 to 1769.
Rare Collection of Papers earlier in private Library of the late Samuel
W. Pennypacker, and generously placed at the disposal of the writer.

———.

State of Process Against Captain William Fordyce, Walter Cochran,
Patrick Barrow & Co., and others.
Evidence in the Case for which Petition of 1767 presented.

———.

Travels among the Indian Tribes of North America.
Edinburgh: 1768.

———.

Life and Adventures of (Memoir).
Liverpool: 1807.

———, *PETITION.*

Addressed to the Right Honourable Lords of Council and Session.
December 23, 1767. (Williamson Papers.)

II. SECONDARY SOURCES

BAIRD, CHARLES W.
History of the Huguenot Emigration to America.
2 Volumes. New York: 1885.

BALLAGH, JAMES CURTIS.
White Servitude in the Colony of Virginia.
A Study of the System of Indentured Labor in the American Colonies,
J. H. U. Studies, XIII, Nos. VI, and VII.
Baltimore: 1895.

BASSETT, JOHN SPENCER.
Slavery and Servitude in North Carolina.
J. H. U. Studies, XIV, Nos. IV, and V.
Baltimore: 1896.

BITTINGER, LUCY FOORNEY.
The Germans in Colonial Times.
Philadelphia and London: 1901.
Treats: "Conditions in Germany Which Led to Emigration"; "Penn's
Visit to Germany"; "The Great Exodus of the Palatines"; and "The
Redemptioners."

BRANTLY, WILLIAM T.
"The English In Maryland" (1632-1691).
Winsor, *Narrative and Critical History,* III, 517-562.

BROWNING, CHARLES H.
Welsh Settlement of Pennsylvania.
Philadelphia: 1912.

BRUCE, PHILIP A.
Economic History of Virginia in the Seventeenth Century.
2 Volumes. New York: 1896.

BUCK, WILLIAM J.
Montgomery County, History of. Philadelphia: 1877.

BUTLER, JAMES DAVIE.
"British Convicts Shipped to American Colonies."
American Historical Review, October, 1896.

COBB, SANFORD H.
The Story of the Palatines.
An Episode in Colonial History.
New York and London: 1897.

COMAN, KATHARINE.
History of Contract Labor in the Hawaiian Islands. Publications of American Economic Association. New York: 1903.

COOLEY, HENRY SCOFIELD.
A Study of Slavery in New Jersey.
J. H. U. Studies, XIV, Nos. IX, and X.
Baltimore: 1896.

DEXTER, FRANKLIN BOWDITCH.
Estimates of Population in the American Colonies.
Paper presented to American Antiquarian Society in 1887.
Worcester, Massachusetts: 1887.

DIFFENDERFFER, FRANK R.
The German Exodus to England in 1709.
Proceedings Pennsylvania-German Society, VII.
Lancaster: 1897. Also separately printed.

————.
German Immigration into Pennsylvania Through The Port of Philadelphia (1700-1775).
Part II—*The Redemptioners.*
Lancaster, Pennsylvania: 1900.

DOTTERER, HENRY S.
Perkiomen Region, Past and Present.
Volume I—Philadelphia: September, 1894, to August, 1895.
Volume II—April 15, 1899, to March 15, 1900.

DuBOIS, W. E. BURGHARDT.
The Suppression of the Slave Trade in the United States. New York, London and Bombay: 1896.

EGERTON, HUGH EDWARD.
Origin and Growth of the English Colonies and of Their System of Government.
Oxford: 1903.

————.
A Short History of British Colonial Policy. London: 1897.

FUTHEY, J. SMITH, and COPE, GILBERT.
History of Chester County with Sketches, Biographical, etc.
Philadelphia: 1881.

GANNETT, R.
Edward Gibbon Wakefield.
Builders of Greater Britain Series. New York: 1898.

GEISER, KARL FREDERICK.
Redemptioners and Indentured Servants in the Colony and Commonwealth of Pennsylvania.
New Haven, Conn. : 1901.

GRAHAME, JAMES.
History of the United States of North America from Plantation of British Colonies to Independence.
4 Vols. Second Edition enlarged.
Philadelphia: 1845.

HARLEY, LEWIS R.
The Redemptioners.
Sketches of Historical Society of Montgomery County for 1895.
Norristown: 1895.

——.

"The Redemptioners."
New England Magazine, October, 1896.

HEFFNER, WILLIAM C.
History of Poor Relief Legislation in Pennsylvania (1682-1913).
Cleona, Pa.: 1913.

HENNIGHAUSEN, LOUIS P.
The Redemptioners and the German Society of Maryland.
An Historical Sketch.
Second Annual Report of the Society for the History of the Germans in Maryland.
Baltimore: 1888.

HESTON, ALFRED M.
Slavery and Servitude in New Jersey.
Camden, N. J.: 1903.

IRELAND, ALLEYNE.
Tropical Colonization. An Introduction to the Subject.
New York and London: 1899.

——.

The Far Eastern Tropics.
Boston and New York: 1905.

JACOBS, HENRY E.
The German Emigration to America. (1709-40).
Proceedings Pennsylvania German Society, Vol. VIII.
Lancaster: 1898.

JERNEGAN, M. W.
"Slavery and the Beginnings of Industrialism in the American Colonies," *American Historical Review,* January, 1920.

KAPP, FRIEDERICH.
Immigration and the Commissioners of Immigration of the State of New York (Kapp one of the Commissioners).
New York: 1870.

LANG, ANDREW.
The Annesley Case. In Famous Trials Series.
Edinburgh and London: 1912.

LANG, JOHN DUNMORE.
Transportation and Colonization, or Causes of Comparative Failure in Transportation System in the Australian Colonies.
London: 1837.

LEONARD, E. M.
The Early History of English Poor Relief.
Cambridge, University Press: 1900.

LORD, ELEANOR LOUISA.
Industrial Experiments in the British Colonies of North America.
Baltimore, J. H. U. Studies, Extra Vol. XVII: 1898.

MacFARLANE, JOHN J.
Manufacturing in Philadelphia (1683-1912).
Philadelphia (Commercial Museum): 1912.

MANN, WILLIAM J.
Life and Times of Henry Melchior Mühlenberg.
Philadelphia: 1887.

MENZEL, WOLFGANG.
History of Germany. From the Earliest Periods to the Present Time.
Translated from the Fourth German Edition by Mrs. George Horrocks.
3 vols. London, Bohn Library: 1853, 1854, 1859.

MERIVALE, HENRY.
Lectures on Colonization and Colonies.
Delivered at University of Oxford 1839, 1840, 1841.
New Edition, London: 1861.

MOMBERT, J. I.
An Authentic History of Lancaster County, Pennsylvania.
Lancaster, Pennsylvania, Barr & Co.: 1869.

MORTON, THOMAS G.
History of the Pennsylvania Hospital.
Philadelphia: 1895 and 1897.

MYERS, ALBERT COOK.
*Immigration of the Irish Quakers into Pennsylvania*s 1682-1750.
Swarthmore: 1907.

PENNYPACKER, SAMUEL W.
Phoenixville and Vicinity, Annals of (Settlement to 1871).
Philadelphia: 1872.

————.
Historical and Biographical Sketches.
Philadelphia: 1883.

————.
Pennsylvania Colonial Cases: The Administration of Law in Pennsylvania prior to A. D. 1700, as shown in the cases decided and in the Court Proceedings. Based on Colonial Records and MSS. Docket of Courts.
Philadelphia: 1892.

————.
Hendrick Pannebecker. Surveyor of Lands for the Penns (1674-1754).
Philadelphia: 1894.

————.
Settlement of Germantown. Pennsylvania and the Beginning of German Emigration to North America.
Philadelphia: 1899. Also Vol. IX, *Pennsylvania German Society Publications.*

PROPER, E.
Colonial Immigration Laws. Study of the Regulations of Immigration by the English Colonies in America.
New York (Columbia University Publications): 1900.

READE, CHARLES.
The Wandering Heir.
London: 1887.

RUPP, I. DANIEL.
Collection of upwards of Thirty Thousand Names of German, Swiss, Dutch, French, and other Emigrants in Pennsylvania (1727-1776). With notes and introduction.
Second Edition, Philadelphia: 1876.

————.
History of Northampton, Lehigh, Monroe, Carbon, and Schuylkill Counties.
Lancaster: 1845.

SABINE, LORENZO.
The American Loyalists of the War of the Revolution. Boston: 1847.

SACHSE, JULIUS F.
The Fatherland (1450-1700).
Pennsylvania German Society Proceedings (Vol. VII). Also published separately.
Philadelphia: 1897.
(Introductory to Series of Pennsylvania German Society on German Influence in New World.)

————.

German Pietests of Provincial Pennsylvania (1694-1708).
Philadelphia, privately published: 1895.

————.

The German Sectarians of Pennsylvania (1708-1742).
A Critical and Legendary History of the Ephrata Cloister and the
Dunkers.
Philadelphia: 1899.

SCHARF, J. THOMAS.

History of Maryland from the earliest Period to the present day.
3 Vols. Baltimore: 1879.

SCHARF, J. THOMAS, and WESCOTT, THOMPSON.

History of Philadelphia (1609-1884). 3 Vols.
Philadelphia: 1884.

SEIDENSTICKER, OSWALD.

Die Erste Deutsche Einwanderung in Amerika, 1683.
Philadelphia: 1883.

————.

Geschichte der Deutschen Gesellschaft von Pennsylvanien.
Von der Zeit der Grundung 1764 bis zum Jahre 1876.
Philadelphia: 1876.

————.

German-American Events, Principally of Pennsylvania up to 1870.
No date.

————.

"William Penn's Travels in Holland and Germany in 1677."
Pennsylvania Magazine of History and Biography, II.

SHARPLESS, ISAAC.

Quaker Experiment in Government.
Philadelphia: 1898.

————.

Quakers in the Revolution.
(Vol. II of History of Quaker Government in Pennsylvania).
Philadelphia: 1899.

SMITH, GEORGE.

History of Delaware County, Pennsylvania.
"By far the best county history of Pennsylvania yet published."
"Thoroughly trustworthy." "Treats fully the settlements of the
county." F. D. Stone in Winsor, *Narrative and Critical History,*
III, 509.
Philadelphia: 1862.

STONE, FREDERICK D.

"The Founding of Pennsylvania."
An account of, with a Critical Essay on the sources of Information in
Winsor, *Narrative and Critical History,* III, 469-517.

THOMPSON, ROBERT ELLIS.
"English Mystics of the Puritan Period."
New Englander, October, 1877.

TILLINGHAST, JOSEPH A.
The Negro in Africa and America. Publications of American Economic Association.
New York: 1902.

TURNER, EDWARD RAYMOND.
The Negro in Pennsylvania.
Slavery—Serfdom—Freedom.
1639-1861. Prize Essay American Historical Association.
Washington, D. C.: 1911.

TYSON, JOB R.
The Social and Intellectual State of the Colony of Pennsylvania, prior to the year 1743.
Read before American Philosophical Society, 1843.
Philadelphia: 1843.

WALTERHAUSEN, von. A. SARTORIUS FREIHERRN.
Die Arbeits-Verfassung der Englishen Colonien in Nordamerika.
Strassburg (Trübner): 1894.

WALTON, JOSEPH S.
Conrad Weiser and the Indian Policy of Colonial Pennsylvania.
Philadelphia: 1900.

WATSON, JOHN F.
Annals of Philadelphia (and Pennsylvania).
Memoirs, Anecdotes and Incidents. 3 Vols.
Philadelphia: 1881.

WEEDEN, WILLIAM B.
Economic and Social History of New England (1620-1789).
2 Vols. Boston: 1890.

WEEKS, STEPHEN W.
Southern Quakers and Slavery.
Baltimore, J. H. U. Publications: 1896.

WRIGHT, RICHARD H., JR.
The Negro in Pennsylvania. A thesis offered in partial fulfilment of the requirement for the degree of Doctor of Philosophy at the University of Pennsylvania.
Philadelphia: n. d.

YOUNG, JOHN RUSSELL (Editor).
Memorial History of the City of Philadelphia.
2 Vols.
New York : 1895 and 1898.

INDEX

Acadians, supply of to Pennsylvania, 109; distribution of, 110-112.

Annesley, James, kidnaping of, 148, 149.

Assembly, control of by Quakers, 235; charges against Gov. Thomas by, 235, 239, 241-243; protection of property of inhabitants by, 237; control of by Quakers, 238; citation from address of, 241; losses of masters through enlistment made good by, 242, 243; reconciliation with Gov. Thomas, 244; statement of to Gov. Morris, 246; passage of act by, giving compensation to masters, 253.

Board of Trade, 59, 61, 64-68; *Proprieties*, cited, 126, 127,n.; plans for Colonial administration, 128; urged that sovereign control the colonies, 129; *Journals*, cited, 130, 131.

Board of War, directed enlisted apprentices be dismissed from army, 252.

Bond, Phineas, cited, 55, 56, 165,n., 188,n.; slave trade situation shown by, 255, 256; migration from Ireland grave concern over, 256, 257; set forth losses to Great Britain through emigration, 257; letter of, to Great Britain, 257, 258.

British, attempted control of Colonial manufacturers, 66, 67.

Burke, Edmund, on *Conciliation with America*, 178, 181.

Capital dependent on labor, 1.

Carolina, inducements for going to, 170.

Child, J., *New Discourse of Trade*, 143,n.; 144, 145,n.

Children bound to service under indenture, 107, 108; education for, 263.

Colonial Wars, servants in, 233; slow enlistment of freemen for, 233; Pennsylvania's attitude toward, 235; inducements for enlistment in, 236; bounty to freeman enlisted in, 237; necessity for enlistments ceased, 244.

Council of Foreign Plantations, preventing of kidnaping, 144-147.

Cunningham, William, cited, 2,n.; *Western Civilization in Its Economic Aspects*, 76,n.

Declaration of Independence, quotation from, 129.

Delaware River, "Clyde of America," 65; effect on Philaadelphia, 66.

Diffenderffer, *Redemptioners*, 145,n., 162,n., 178,n., 245,n.

Douglass, sorts of people, 7,n.

Dutch furnished slaves, 27.

Economic interests, conflict of between colonies and England, 69.

Eddis, William, on kidnaping, 143, 144.

England, "Undutiful Mother," 131; problem with criminal, 135; charged with encouraging crime, 139; great reduction of crime in, 139, 140.

Enlistment of servants for Colonial Wars, 233-253; controversies between England and colonies over, 234, 235; controversies between Assembly and proprietary over, 235; Gov. Thomas's attitude regarding, 234-238; contentions among officers and masters over, 245.

Europe, lack of employment in, 41, 47-49; supply of white servants from, 113, 114.